CHURCH SPACE AND THE CAPITAL IN PREWAR JAPAN

CHURCH SPACE AND THE CAPITAL IN PREWAR JAPAN

Garrett L. Washington

University of Hawaiʻi Press
Honolulu

Paperback edition 2022

Printed in the United States of America

Library of Congress Cataloging-in-Publication Data

Names: Washington, Garrett (Garrett L.), author.
Title: Church space and the capital in prewar Japan / Garrett L. Washington.
Description: Honolulu : University of Hawaiʻi Press, 2022. | Includes bibliographical references and index.
Identifiers: LCCN 2021022885 | ISBN 9780824888862 (hardback) | ISBN 9780824891725 (adobe pdf) | ISBN 9780824891732 (epub) | ISBN 9780824891749 (kindle edition)
Subjects: LCSH: Protestantism—Social aspects—Japan—Tokyo—History—19th century. | Protestantism—Social aspects—Japan—Tokyo—History—20th century. | Religion and civil society—Japan—Tokyo—History—19th century. | Religion and civil society—Japan—Tokyo—History—20th century. | Protestant church buildings—Japan—Tokyo—History—19th century. | Protestant church buildings—Japan—Tokyo—History—20th century. | Tokyo (Japan)—Church history.
Classification: LCC BR1315.T65 W37 2022 | DDC 306.6/8040952135—dc23
LC record available at https://lccn.loc.gov/2021022885

ISBN 9780824891718 (paperback)

University of Hawaiʻi Press books are printed on acid-free paper and meet the guidelines for permanence and durability of the Council on Library Resources.

Cover illustration: Sketch of exterior of Reinanzaka Church by Yuasa Yozō, 1917. From *Nobiyuku kyōkai* (Tokyo: Kyōbunkan, 1941).

Contents

Illustrations

Figures

Color Plates

Color plates follow page 58.

Acknowledgments

This book began long, long ago, in 2005, and I am so grateful for all of the help I have received on this transformative journey. I would like to first and foremost thank my wife, Camille, who has been with me every step of the way. Her patience, proofreading, encouragement, and problem-solving skills have been fundamental to this project. But of perhaps more importance are the many other ways that she has created time and sacrificed herself so that I could complete and share this research. In Japan, in the United States, in Kenya, and in France, you have always been there, even when you weren't, and I am forever grateful. Noah and Théo, you are both with me always too, and I thank you both for your support and your strength. I want to thank my parents, Ellie and Larry, for allowing me to chase my passions and for always making it so clear that you believed in me and my dreams. I have also been so fortunate to have the constant support of Michèle and Jean-Paul, my parents-in-law, for these many years as well, from laptops to beds to babysitting. All of you have made this possible, and that deserves to be said first.

In terms of academics, I am most grateful for the guidance and support of Sally Hastings, who took me on as her graduate student way back then and was the most attentive, challenging, insightful, and helpful adviser I could have asked for. In writing and thinking about Japan, I owe most to her. I am also grateful to Sally for introducing me to Jim Huffman. Jim generously shared his time and knowledge with me at conferences and as I completed my dissertation, so I am immensely grateful to him as well. Through Jim, I made the acquaintance of Yamamoto Nobuto of Keio University, who literally made my field research in Japan possible. I thank Nobuto for hosting me as a visiting researcher at Keio, for writing letters of introduction to religious leaders and scholars in Tokyo and Kyoto who in turn greatly assisted me with my research, and also for making time to welcome me whenever I am in Tokyo. I am forever grateful to pastors Sugawara Tsutomu of Hongō Church, Yokono Asahiko of Banchō Church, Kurahashi Yasuo of Fujimichō Church, and Oshikawa Sachio of Reinanzaka Church for opening their church buildings and records to me. Over the years, I have benefitted from the wisdom, kindness, and connections of Makoto Hara, Motoi Yasuhiro, and Tanaka Tomoko at Dōshisha University as well. I thank you all for helping me to access the abundance of resources at the Jimbunkagaku Kenkyūsho (Institute for the Study of Humanities and Social Science Studies) and for providing me guidance in making my way through materials. Librarians Ochiai Mariko and Azama Shōgo at the Jimbunkagaku Kenkyūsho were extremely helpful, particularly during my early research, and deserve my thanks. Most of my research writing, however, has had to take place in the United States. So I am enormously grateful for the many librarians who made it possible for me to view materials electronically or directly. I have made especially good use of both the Harvard-Yenching Library and Yale University's Sterling Memorial Library, so I would like to thank the staff of those great institutions. Since I arrived at the University of Massachusetts Amherst, our East Asian Studies Librarian Sharon Domier has truly gone above and beyond, always keeping her eyes open for relevant material and proficiently handling my requests for obscure sources. I am enormously grateful to you!

In its early stages and then its (long!) development into a monograph, the project has benefited from the critiques, insights, and helpful ideas of dozens of scholars to whom I am very appreciative. Questions and comments at the Modern Japanese History Workshop, Midwest Conference on Asian Affairs, and Association for Asian Studies have been instrumental as I have written and rewritten this book. Paul Watt provided great insight as discussant for my MCAA panel in 2009. And I recall excellent questions and suggestions made by Lou Perez, Lane Earns, Steven Covell, and Noriko Reider at the Midwest Japan Seminar that were central to my plans to revise the manuscript. Thanks to all of you. I am also grateful to Helen Ballhatchet, A. Hamish Ion, Jordan Sand, and Peter Nosco, who each at one point or another during the past fifteen years responded generously to a narrow, specific inquiry of mine and truly helped me continue moving forward in my research. I would also like to thank Helen Hardacre, a scholar whose work is obviously fundamental to this research, for sharing a brief but encouraging comment with me after my presentation at AAS in 2010. To all of you and the others I've not managed to mention, I want to express my gratitude.

I could not be happier that University of Hawai'i Press is publishing this book and for that I must thank several people as well. Albert Park has been a supportive, inclusive senior colleague, and I was honored to be part of the edited volume that you and David Yoo put together. But I am very thankful as well that you put me in touch with Masako Ikeda. To Masako, I thank you for believing in this project, expressing your enthusiasm about it, and guiding it through the peer review and revision process with such kindness and grace. The book in its current form is greatly indebted to two anonymous readers whose thorough, constructive reports pinpointed areas of weakness and ways to make them stronger. As you will see, your comments have truly informed this work.

Ultimately, this book would have been impossible without the support of several sources of research support for which I am grateful as well. I did the original archival fieldwork for this project at Keio University in Tokyo thanks to a generous ten-month ABD fellowship from the Japan Society for the Promotion of Science, selected by the Social Science Research Council. The following year, I completed the dissertation with the support of a yearlong Bilsland Dissertation Fellowship at Purdue University. The project continued to evolve while I worked as an Andrew W. Mellon Postdoctoral Fellow at Oberlin College and then as an assistant professor at the University of Massachusetts Amherst. In these positions, research trips to Tokyo and Kyoto funded by an H. H. Powers Travel Grant from Oberlin College, an Association for Asian Studies Northeast Asia Council Research Travel Grant, and a UMass College of Humanities and Fine Arts Research Grant allowed me to complete the new research for writing this book. Back at UMass, I was grateful to be awarded a Research-Intensive Semester, during which I finally composed this monograph. I thank my university and department for their support and encouragement as I have moved this project toward publication. Financial support was also provided by the Office of the Vice Chancellor for Research and Engagement at the University of Massachusetts Amherst.

(Re)Introducing Christianity in Modern Japan

In 1908, the famous journalist Tokutomi Sohō (1863–1957) looked out at the audience from the pulpit of Hongō Church, one of Tokyo's largest Protestant congregations. Though not a Christian, he described his close relationship with the institution this way:

> All along, I have never been a member of Hongō Church. But I do have somewhat of a connection with this church. To start with, in this church's ancient history I gave a speech titled "The Time of Commentary, the Time of Application." That was . . . 1888, early summer as I recall. This was my first lecture standing before the public in Tokyo. To put it another way, I received a baptism in speaking at Hongō Church. . . . In the days of the church's second pastor Yokoi Tokio, I gave a lecture on Yoshida Shōin. That was on a spring evening in 1892. That was the origin of my book *Yoshida Shōin*. . . . So then . . . I think that I can say that I have somewhat of a connection.[1]

One can only imagine how exciting the occasion must have been for his listeners. Many young audience members may not have agreed with his increasingly conservative stance on politics. But one of Japan's best-known and most influential voices was speaking fondly about the church in which they were seated and affirming its role in hosting sociopolitical discourse. Tokutomi went to Hongō Church frequently, and those experiences were important in his development as a speaker and writer. Even for the nonmember and non-Christian, then, the church offered something of value.

Tokutomi's testimony encapsulates much of the story this book sets out to tell. Here he provides clues to the kinds of Japanese who attended urban Japanese Protestant churches in imperial Japan (1868–1945), why they did so, and the ways in which their attendance related to their roles in Japanese society more broadly. Like Tokutomi, most attendees belonged to the educated elite, particularly in major urban areas. University students and professors, secondary school teachers, lawyers, judges, reporters, novelists, poets, physicians, politicians, entrepreneurs, and other well-educated professionals of both sexes attended church. Like Tokutomi, attendees were often drawn to the social atmosphere of the church. From stimulating the intellect to expressing moral outrage, the speeches, lectures, sermons, and meetings that occurred in Protestant churches made them lively and attractive places. It was often in these contexts that secular subjects such as Yoshida Shōin—a famous scholar-activist who inspired several leaders of the Meiji Restoration—brought national and international issues into the church. Also, like Tokutomi, many attendees found their church experience had important repercussions well beyond the church. At church they exchanged news and ideas and formed networks that proved instrumental in the development of the country's foremost theory of popular democracy, its first labor union, its first modern magazine for housewives, and its first public kindergarten, among many other contributions.[2] Tokutomi also hints at how urban Protestant churches in particular became sites through which Protestantism achieved social acceptance, prominence, and influence in imperial Japan and contended with competing religious movements.

Urban, Japanese-led Protestant churches were vital in Christianity's transformation from a chiefly foreign, heavily stigmatized religion into a legitimately Japanese religion with connections, relevance, and significant impacts on Japanese society. After more than two centuries of prohibition, Christianity was reintroduced in Japan starting in the late 1850s by Roman Catholic, Protestant, and Greek Orthodox missionaries.[3] From that point on, and even after the new Meiji government decriminalized the religion in 1873, Christianity confronted forbidding obstacles to its spread. Myriad social, cultural, legal, and ideological factors stymied all efforts to build bridges between Japanese society and Christianity. These did not principally originate in an incongruity between an essentialized, authentic Japanese identity and highly Occidentalized forms of Christian ideology. Rather, these deterrents were very much the result of purposefully constructed strategies of identity and difference spanning from the 1580s to the 1890s. Catholicism, with its close association to the same Christianity that had been forbidden and persecuted for more than two centuries and its lack of Japanese clergy and Japanese funding, found these barriers to social relevance on a national scale extremely difficult to overcome.[4] Greek Orthodoxy, despite already boasting eleven Japanese priests by 1883, failed to rise in the public's estimation due to its strong ties to Russia, Meiji Japan's nearest imperialist competitor.[5] So it was Protestantism that finally began to take root among the urban Japanese population. However, a new barrage of challenges materialized during the 1890s that threatened to undo Protestant leaders' efforts to destigmatize and popularize this strand of Christianity as well. Among them were Buddhist opposition and competition, the rise of anti-Western sentiment, the development of ideological orthodoxy around patriotism and loyalty to the state, and new policies limiting the social activism and autonomy of all religions in Japan.

This book argues that the ability of Protestant Christianity to survive in this tumultuous climate and to develop deep, impactful connections to Japanese society depended heavily on urban Japanese Protestant churches. In addition to well-documented missionary and Christian-led schools, these relatively unexamined institutions distinguished Protestantism from its Christian and non-Christian religious rivals, hosted events and networks that linked it with the discursive authority of the West, and facilitated its ability to reach Japanese hearts and minds. Ultimately, prominent Japanese-led urban churches in the Meiji and Taishō eras were wellsprings of social activism. They served as incubators for social reform movements, providing political dissenters, conformists, and those in-between with literal and figurative space to think and speak.

The largest Japanese Protestant churches in Tokyo largely took shape through the institution-building and pastoral efforts of dynamic leaders in the first generation of Japanese pastors. They established new congregations near the nation's highest concentrations of intellectual, political, and economic leaders and commissioned buildings that represented a new type of religious gathering space for Japan. Pastors filled the spaces with a Japanese Protestant Christianity, a "creolized" Western Protestant Christianity whose beliefs and ideals they had adapted to the modern Japanese cultural context.[6] However, they also worked to ensure that the voices of lay speakers like Tokutomi figured prominently at their churches as well. From the 1890s until the early 1920s, churchgoers internalized Protestant social visions and worldviews relevant to Japanese modernity and developed a heightened awareness of major social problems. Thus equipped, they participated in social activities that empowered them to be agents of change beyond the church, hosting the creation of reform-minded networks that operated within the greater Japanese public sphere. Individually as well, women and men drew on their church experiences in the capital to found periodicals, schools, organizations, and other institutions that aimed to improve Japanese society, several of which contributed directly to the social and political development of so-called Taishō Democracy.[7]

An Empty Space within the Japanese Protestant Story

In the early twentieth century, Protestant Christianity's links to Japanese society and empire were visible and undeniable. Despite constituting less than half of the

1 percent of the population that identified as Christians in the country, Japanese Protestants maintained an extremely high profile in imperial Japan.[8] Their leading roles in fields such as journalism, education, law, and politics and the religious movement's associations with social activism, countercultural ideologies, and debates about nationalism and national identity all contributed to this status. Cognizant of the reputation and influence of the religion, the Meiji state eventually took an active interest in fostering collaborations with Christianity. In 1912, the Home Ministry awarded Christianity recognition as one of Japan's three official religions. This they did in exchange for a pledge from Protestant pastors to cooperate with the state, just as Buddhist and sect Shinto clergy did, to improve morality and promote the honor of the emperor.[9] The efforts of Japanese Protestants, and Christian women's organizations in particular, to support Japan's military projects received official endorsements and financial support as well.[10] In addition, the Japanese Government-General of Korea even supported one Japanese Protestant denomination's project to facilitate the cultural assimilation of Japan's colonial subjects through Christianity.[11] These interactions and the contributions mentioned briefly above go a long way toward explaining why such a small religious movement attracted such a large amount of attention in prewar modern Japan, and why it has continued to do so in the postwar period and beyond.

The most widely used modern Japanese history textbook in the United States asserts that Japanese Christians "played a disproportionately large role in Japanese cultural and political life."[12] This conclusion reflects a scholarly consensus among not only religious historians but also political, cultural, social, intellectual, and gender historians and other Japan specialists. Scholars of Japanese Christianity have been highlighting the visibility and impact of social reform-oriented Protestantism in Japanese society since the late 1950s. A considerable body of scholarship has, since then, been preoccupied with the quest for explanations. These scholars have asked *how* this illegal, highly punishable, and thoroughly vilified alien religion developed to have such a significant impact on modern Japan. I would argue that, beyond its significance to the history of Christianity in Japan or of global Christianity, the value of this line of inquiry lies in its implications for the broader history of modern Japan. Explicitly and implicitly, scholarship on Protestant Christianity has helped in reframing knowledge on the development of political ideology, modern educational institutions, government policy on religion, mass print media, voluntary associations, the women's movement, and colonial administration, among other areas.

This well-established narrative begins with the reintroduction of Christianity by Western missionaries and experts in the 1860s and 1870s. It then moves on to the conversion and intellectual development of Japan's first native Protestant pastors between the late 1870s and the early 1910s. Concurrently, the narrative describes the growth of missionary schools and Christian education, the birth of Christian literary and religious periodicals, and their impact on young Japanese women and men during this same period. Next, works on Protestant Christianity and other fields describe the involvement of well-known Japanese Protestants with movements for social change. And last, scholarship has analyzed the growing relationship between Christianity, the Japanese state, and its larger empire. This rich historiography has taken shape largely through the work of long-standing research groups on Christianity at Dōshisha University, Meiji Gakuin University, and Fujimichō Church in Japan and affiliated scholars in Japan, the United States, and Canada. However, despite the literally thousands of pages devoted to the study of this movement in imperial Japan, major questions still remain about Protestant Christianity's survival and influence amid the growing complexity of Japanese sentiments about the West and Westernization and the implementation of new legal and ideological restrictions on religion and gathering in the late Meiji period.

Existing scholarship has repeatedly highlighted the close association between Protestant Christianity and the discursive authority both of the West and of Progressivist movements for social change in Meiji Japan. Works have accurately pointed to Christian periodicals and Christian educational institutions as key contributing factors in the development of this connection. However, as religious historian Yamaguchi Teruomi and, more recently, religion scholar Michel Mohr have revealed, the elaboration of Protestantism's ties to Western discourses of science, civilization, and modernity did not occur uncontested. Instead, Buddhist intellectuals and reformers challenged Christianity's mantle as the religion best suited for importing and interpreting Western ideas and ideals for the Japanese nation.[13] The religion boasted institutions like the Nishi Honganji Futsū kyōkō, a normal school where Western subjects and English were taught in Kyoto, and the Tetsugakkan (Philosophy Academy) of lay Buddhist intellectual and educator Inoue Enryō (1858–1919) in Tokyo. Publications like the monthly *Shin Bukkyō* [New Buddhism] (1900–1915) broadcast the ideas of leading young progressive Buddhist thinkers on religion and its relationship to other forms of specifically modern knowledge.[14] Meanwhile, lay figures like Sōtō Zen social worker Ōuchi Seiran (1845–1918) promoted education for the disabled and worked to raise government support of Buddhism.[15] And Shin (True Pure Land) priests in Tokyo like Kiyozawa Manshi (1863–1903) and his successor Chikazumi Jōkan (1870–1941) strove to reconceptualize Buddhist theology and practice in order to make it capable of responding to the promise and perils of Japan's modernization.[16]

With these elements Buddhism fought to associate itself as well with both the discursive authority of the West and Japanese modern social issues. So, what distinguished Protestant Christianity in this competition and allowed it to eclipse Buddhism as the religion best aligned with Westernization, modernization, and progress? This is a question that scholars working on this religious movement have not sufficiently explored.

Furthermore, recent research on the Meiji government's efforts to separate religion from the state and confine religion within a "subjectified," private realm distinct from the public, social realm has also raised important questions about Protestantism.[17] Between 1890 and the early 1920s, the Japanese government made its greatest efforts to decisively sever the ties between religion and the professedly secular realms of social life. However, it was in this same period that Japan's Protestants developed deep ties to movements for social and political change. Protestant Christianity's relationship with "progress," a term that increasingly referred more to "advances in social reform and policy" than to science and technology, remained strong.[18] It was also in those very decades that the regime so successfully strove to limit the populace's rights to gather, discuss, and undertake grassroots activism. However, Japanese Protestants gathered regularly and openly exchanged ideas on topics that were unarguably social and political. In that context, how did Protestantism not only survive but prosper as a socially relevant and socially focused religion in urban environments like the capital? The existing scholarship offers few concrete, research-based responses to these questions.

Lacking such explanations, the narrative acts something like a well-made key that is missing a tooth. Fuller and replete with such explanations, however, the narrative becomes more capable of unlocking the mystery of Protestantism's ability to reach and impact the educated elite in late nineteenth- and early twentieth-century Japanese society. Furthermore, behind these questions about the development of Protestant Christianity are other significant questions that continue to preoccupy scholars as well. What did the religious movement have to offer the women and men of Japan's new urban middle class, including the many who never actually converted? In Meiji and Taishō Japan, what distinguished Protestant Christianity's sociality from that of its primary religious competitor, Buddhism, and with what consequences? What explains the especially strong association between politically active, socially aware women and Protestant Christianity? To what extent did the pervasive demands of the emperor-centered ideals, symbols, and rites that one scholar aptly terms the "Shinto secular" restrict or facilitate the social visions and mandates of Japanese Protestant leaders and laypersons? And amid accusations of lèse-majesté and "unpatriotism," in what ways did Protestant Christianity assert itself as Japanese? The answers to these and other questions can shed new light on the larger questions of Protestantism's development and social impact in Japan.

We can begin to respond to these lingering questions by opening the literal door of the Japanese-led urban Protestant church. In the substantial literature on Protestant Christianity in imperial Japan, the unit of the urban Protestant church has never been the subject of in-depth scholarly historical analysis. The names of a few well-known urban Japanese Protestant churches have appeared frequently in discussions of Japanese Protestantism before World War II, but always briefly and without analysis. Theological and intellectual biographies of famous pastors or especially prominent attendees often note their churches' names and include short, synoptic descriptions of their membership and social atmosphere.[19] Works on Protestant education and voluntary associations include similarly brief descriptions of churches.[20] This is not to say, however, that scholars have completely ignored the unit of the church.

In his pioneering study of the rural congregation of Annaka Church and its outspoken Pacifist pastor Kashiwagi Gien (1860–1938), sociologist Morioka Kiyomi has illuminated the church founding and development processes at work within Japanese Protestantism.[21] He describes the growth, stagnation, and social connections of this dynamic church and illustrates the need for more church-centered research. In fact, his own work nearly fifty years later continues to focus attention on Annaka Church and its place in local and regional Japanese society.[22] Although the church as a unit is not the primary analytical subject of her study, Emily Anderson has woven brief descriptions of this same rural Annaka Church in rural Gunma Prefecture and the well-known Hongō Church in Tokyo into her work as well. She deftly demonstrates the lines connecting these two churches and the larger Congregationalist denomination with the discourses and implementation of Japan's empire.[23] Anderson's scholarship along with the church-centered work of Morioka highlights the value of considering the individual church in the study of Japanese Protestantism and of modern Japanese history. A logical next step would be an analysis of the urban Protestant church and its relationship to broader Japanese society, but scholars have not yet taken it.

It is clear that for most scholars, the development and impact of the Nonchurch (Mukyōkai) Movement of Uchimura Kanzō (1861–1930) has firmly directed scholarly attention away from Protestant churches. This small movement, which would become "the fountainhead of indigenous Christianity" and inspire other movements, is by far the best-known form of Japanese Christianity.[24] Educated in Japan and then in the US at Amherst College and Hartford Theological Seminary, Uchimura returned to Japan to establish a "churchless

Christianity, calling no man bishop or pastor, save Jesus Christ."[25] Through sermons, lectures, and periodicals, he had a deep impact on some prominent intellectuals who wrote for leading publications and taught at leading institutions in the late Meiji, Taishō (1912–1926), and early Shōwa (1926–1989) periods. And throughout the early twentieth century, Uchimura was one of the most famous Christian voices in Japan. Amazingly, he achieved such fame and such an influence on important figures without a church building or congregation, the attendant social spaces, or organizational structure.

But even the exceptional case of Uchimura's Nonchurch Movement implores us to include churches in studying the nature and influence of Protestantism in prewar Japan. In fact, Uchimura had a private lecture hall constructed in 1907 near his home in today's Shinjuku Ward with seating for eight hundred and space for twenty overnight guests.[26] The Imai Kan served as the principal preaching place for Uchimura, who gave Bible lectures to his disciples there each Sunday.[27] Furthermore, in lecturing and meeting with young Japanese religious seekers in Tokyo in this building, other rented halls, and homes, the intentionally nonordained Uchimura played a patently pastoral role. The Imai Kan and other gathering venues often functioned like church spaces for Uchimura. So if this site, which did not represent the theoretical or concrete focus of his ministry, is worthy of inclusion in the history of Uchimura Kanzō's Nonchurch Movement, how much more worthy of inclusion are the mainline Protestant groups who emphatically proclaimed the importance of their churches?

It has been left to churches themselves to compile their own respective histories, a task that members—some of whom have been professional historians—have taken seriously since the late Meiji period. Revised and expanded over the course of the twentieth century, these works do tell the story of their congregations' development. These histories of individual churches are narrowly focused and circulated, however, and do not aim to engage with or contribute to the larger histories of Christianity, of religion more broadly, or of society in modern Japan. In undertaking these tasks, this book revises the existing narrative so that it better explains and contextualizes Protestantism's emergence and influence. To do so, it mobilizes new sources and perspectives that complement those used in church histories and the wider historiographies of Protestant Christianity and of religions in imperial Japan.

Churches provide an ideal vehicle for pursuing an important line of inquiry that scholars have essentially ignored in their efforts to understand the transformation of Protestant Christianity in Japan and its relationship to Japanese society: that of space. The works of Daniel V. Botsman and Jordan Sand were pivotal in applying the so-called spatial turn to the historical study of Japan in the

United States.[28] Drawing on the space-focused approach and perspectives of innovative historian Michel Foucault, among others, Botsman describes how Japanese administrators and officials borrowed from Western models to create the physical space of the modern Japanese prison so that it instantiated and exercised power over inmates.[29] Likewise, Sand traced the impact of the confluence of architecture, discourse, and identity on and within the space of the home in his seminal *House and Home in Modern Japan*.[30] Scholars of Christianity in Japan have also given questions of space more attention recently. Motoi Yasuhiro, for instance, has analyzed the different buildings that have housed Dōshisha University's School of Theology.[31] In the case of Protestant church edifices, however, space is seldom mentioned, let alone analyzed. Morioka Kiyomi's most recent study of Annaka Church is a rare example of a scholarly work that treats the Protestant church building in Japan as a concrete form of built space.[32] In a few brief sentences within his larger study, Morioka notes the development of Annaka Church from a silk factory into a newly built two-story edifice with glass windows between 1878 and 1883.[33] These few sentences are illustrative in that they shed light on the nature of Annaka Church as a built space and its connections with Japanese clerical and lay leaders as well as attendees. Michel Mohr's monograph on the relationship between Buddhism and the Unitarian Movement in Japan includes another brief, spatially explicit description of church space. He highlights the purposeful location of the 1894 Unity Hall in Shiba, near Keio University, and the varied spaces of the lounge, lecture room, publication storage rooms, and fireproof library that the building included.[34] Using the words of Unitarian missionary Clay MacCauley and other sources, Mohr demonstrates that the space was effectively designed to promote the sharing of knowledge through teaching and publications. Although Morioka and Mohr pay only limited attention to church space in these studies (it is not their central focus), their works point to the possibility and usefulness of studying Japanese Protestant churches as built spaces.

At the same time, Protestant churches were largely defined by their relationship to and emplacement within Japan's larger built environments, and their study must be informed by recent research on those forms of space as well. The history of churches in late Tokugawa and early Meiji Japan begins in Japan's intentionally isolated treaty ports. These were physical and social spaces well encapsulated by literature scholar Mary Louise Pratt's insightful definition of "contact zones." Michael Auslin, Joseph Henning, and James Hoare all explore the contours of these spaces "where disparate cultures meet, clash, and grapple with each other" in Japan and their legal, diplomatic, and cultural repercussions.[35] By the 1890s, however, the country's largest Protestant churches had entwined themselves into the fabric of Japan's largest cities. The location and relocation of Protestant churches intersected with processes of urbanization and urban development. And in the capital, this positioning often embodied aspects of the spatial logic of the metropolis that well-known scholars like architectural historian Jinnai Hidenobu and renowned literary scholar Edward Seidensticker have done so much to decipher.[36] In addition to being buildings, Protestant churches were participants in new local, regional, and national spatial dynamics.

The characteristics of Japanese Protestant churches as architectural and locational spaces were integral to the social spaces that took shape inside them. While it would be easy to draw a sharp distinction between the former two and the latter, they were in fact intrinsically connected. Sociologist Henri Lefebvre captured the essence of this tie when he wrote, "Social relations, which are concrete abstractions, have no real existence save in and through space."[37] Many of the illuminating scholarly works on which this book builds briefly discuss the social atmosphere in churches without identifying or analyzing the relationship between these churches' social spaces and their more tangible urban and architectural spaces. However, this book applies Lefebvre's insights to argue that for these social relations, "their underpinning is spatial."[38] So while the spatiality of urban Protestantism's development in imperial Japan did not create or cause the movement's metamorphosis, it played a hugely important role and one that as yet has been neither explored nor explained. Emphasizing these three interconnected forms of physical and abstract space—locational, architectural, and social—this book presents a story that will contribute to a more complete narrative of the development of Japanese Protestant Christianity. Such a narrative can offer clearer explanations for the religious movement's connections with and influence on Japanese society, its appeal to the new middle class, its singularity in the Japanese religious landscape, its engagement with the emperor-system ideology, and its indigenization.

Spatializing the Reintroduction of Christianity in Japan

The development of urban Japanese Protestant churches as built spaces within the built environment in fact has roots back in the spatial context of Christianity's reintroduction to Japan in the mid-nineteenth century. In 1858, four years after Commodore Matthew Perry (1794–1858) forced Japan to open its doors wider to trade with the West, American merchants and missionaries brought Christianity back to Japan. By that time, however, spatial strategies had served as a critical tool for the consolidating Tokugawa government to contain Western foreigners and their religion for more than two centuries. These policies show that, like the spatial bases of social relations, the efforts to control or even prevent social relations were also dependent on the mobilization of space. From the 1630s, the Tokugawa Shogunate imposed physical boundaries that separated and thereby protected Japanese space from Western, Christian space.[39] This strategy was part of a larger push by the shogunate to suppress Christianity and centralize authority in Japan. Between 1614 and 1639, the shogunate criminalized the practice of Christianity, expelled European Catholic missionaries, and ceased trade with Catholic Europe.[40] The outcome was a violent and highly effective campaign of persecution that all but removed Christianity from Japan. The shogunate then confined the only Christians allowed in Japan—Dutch East India Company merchants, physician-scientists, and chaplains who vowed not to proselytize—to a man-made island called Dejima in Nagasaki's harbor.[41] In doing so, the government created a separate built space for the only legal Westerners in Japan and instituted a spatial separation between them and the Japanese population.

Even after any real menace of Christianity had unarguably subsided, the regime maintained its containment policy and protective isolation, undergirding them with a suite of ideological devices that emphasized Japan's cultural unity and the challenge posed to it by the West. The rhetoric of official edicts and government ideologues vilified Christianity as the epitome of religious and political heterodoxy in Japan—an ideology that could undo the very fabric of the social order.[42] The government also established a temple registration system that mandated adherence to Buddhism, verified the absence of Christian beliefs, and deputized temples as the country's record keepers. Predicated on the ideological and cultural threat of Christianity, this system became a bulwark in the creation of a powerful, centralizing government. It further ensured that throughout Japan, people would be indoctrinated with a combination of Buddhist and Neo-Confucian ideology—cultural elements that represented the polar opposite of Christianity. At the same time, it amplified the role that not only the personnel but also the space of Buddhist temples played in the lives, and deaths, of the Japanese population.[43]

On Perry's arrival, this same combination of spatial strategies and their justifications persisted, and the reopening of the country merely led to variations on the theme. As it had done for more than two centuries, the Tokugawa Shogunate deployed the spatial strategy of separation to protect Japan from Christian Westerners.[44] The Japanese government's signing of the Treaty of Amity and Commerce between Japan and the United States in 1858 opened seven treaty ports to Western powers, guaranteed Americans the right to practice Christianity in Japan, and led to the granting of equivalent rights to other Westerners. This might have signaled a retreat from such mobilizations of space.[45] However, the execution of these provisions demonstrated that the administration, the *bakufu,* still intended to use spatial means to separate and contain Westerners—a policy with clear implications for Christianity. The case of the new treaty port of Yokohama, established in 1859, is particularly illustrative. There a combination of wide canals, a swamp, a cliff, and Kanagawa Bay impeded access from neighboring areas. As a young interpreter for the British consulate in the early 1860s, Ernest Satow (1843–1929) observed that at the approaches to the bridges over those canals, "ingress and egress were controlled by strong guards of [Japanese] soldiers."[46] Subsequently, similar natural and man-made barriers enclosed newly created foreign settlements in Nagasaki's Ōura neighborhood (1860), Osaka's Kawaguchi neighborhood (1868), the Kobe Foreign settlement (1868), and Tokyo's Tsukiji neighborhood (1869).[47] All but the highest-ranking senior officials and foreign experts were forced to live and work within these boundaries during Japan's first decade as a reopened country. Similarly, at the time the practice of Christianity was technically legal in the country only within these boundaries.

Even in this context, however, Christianity was not entirely obedient to the spatial prerogatives of the Tokugawa government or the new Meiji government that replaced it in 1868. From the late 1850s, Japanese exposure to Christianity took place with increasing frequency within and just outside treaty ports. Henry Wood, chaplain of the USS *Powhattan,* taught English to Japanese interpreters in Nagasaki for two months in the fall of 1858 and made sure to incorporate information on Christianity into his lessons.[48] Japanese in Hakodate, Yokohama, and, most famously, Nagasaki broke the law and entered the Roman Catholic churches completed in 1859, 1862, and 1864, respectively, in those foreign settlements.[49] The teaching of French by Paris Foreign Missions Society Roman Catholic priests including Eugène-Emmanuel Mermet-Cachon (1828–1889) in Hakodate and Bernard Petitjean (1829–1884) also exposed Japanese to the religion.[50] The same was true for other Western Protestant evangelists in the early Meiji period, like Dutch Reformed missionary Guido Verbeck (1830–1898). After arriving in Nagasaki in late 1859, he began to teach English to inquiring Japanese using the Bible at his home just outside the foreign concession in Nagasaki. In 1864, Verbeck accepted a position teaching English at the newly created government school for Western studies, the Yōgakusho, and there he relied heavily on the US Constitution, the Declaration of Independence, and the New Testament.[51] So he too transmitted key Christian concepts through his teaching. The roster of future government leaders, including Prime Minister Itō Hirobumi (1841–1909), Prime Minister Ōkuma Shigenobu (1838–1922), Home Minister Ōkubo Toshimichi

(1830–1878), Foreign Minister Soejima Taneomi (1828–1905), Justice Minister Etō Shimpei (1834–1974), and Education Minister Ōki Takatō (1833–1899), among others, who encountered the ideas and ideals of Protestant Christianity and the religion's discursive authority through their classes with him is long and impressive.[52]

Medical treatment and education also afforded Christian missionaries with opportunities to share Christianity with Japanese men and women within and around treaty ports. From the opening of his dispensary in the treaty port of Yokohama in 1862, Presbyterian medical missionary and educator James Hepburn (1815–1911) and his wife Clara (1818–1906) discreetly proselytized. While patients waited in the expansive waiting room, Clara handed out Chinese Bibles and tracts and discussed their contents.[53] By the end of the decade, Dr. Hepburn also operated a teaching clinic on the site. Students such as future prime minister Takahashi Korekiyo (1854–1936) came into contact with new secular as well as Christian knowledge as students there.[54] Similarly, after becoming medical director of the new International Hospital of Kobe in 1870, American Board missionary physician John Berry (1847–1936) connected medicine with evangelism. He cured hundreds of Japanese patients—often in exchange for nothing but their brief attention for Bible readings.[55] So just as Dejima had evolved into the premier destination for Japanese searching for Western scientific, medical, and military knowledge during the Tokugawa period, treaty ports attracted the country's curious and ambitious in the Bakumatsu era. They and their Western interlocutors capitalized on these opportunities to contravene the government-imposed spatial segregation of Western Christianity from Japanese society.

The consequences for Japanese who made their way across the physical and cultural threshold of the new treaty ports in search of spiritual guidance, however, were sometimes grave. Despite prominently posted signboards upholding the prohibition of Christianity, stipulating collective punishment, and offering rewards for informants, Japanese risked attending churches in the foreign settlements where Westerners were free to practice Christianity openly. In 1862 dozens of Japanese ignored the restrictions and attended services administered in Yokohama by Paris Foreign Missions Society priest Prudence Girard (1820–1867). On discovering the transgression, the governor's officers arrested dozens of Japanese and led them away in ropes.[56] Whereas these men and women were released, Japanese spiritual seekers who emerged in Nagasaki's foreign settlement endured significantly harsher penalties. At the opening of a new Catholic church in Ōura in February 1865, fifteen descendants of Japanese "hidden Christians" *(kakure kirishitan)* who had been practicing Christianity in secret on remote islands near Nagasaki appeared. Their proclamations of faith to Paris Foreign Missions Society priest Bernard Petitjean and his efforts to minister to the larger still-hidden groups of *kirishitan* led to intense persecution. In 1870 alone, American and European ships transported 3,300 Japanese Christians away from the Nagasaki area into exile in some of the country's more remote areas.[57] Along the way to or on arrival in exile, those who refused to recant were reportedly subjected to torture, humiliation, imprisonment, starvation, inadequate medical care, and in several cases death.[58] These examples underline the danger Japanese people faced by investigating Christianity—a risk that many were clearly willing to take. They also demonstrate that while Japanese and Westerners crossed the boundary of the foreign settlement with increasing freedom and frequency, Christianity continued to operate in an environment of ambiguity and constraint. When in 1868 the new Meiji government ordered the reposting of the signboards proscribing Christianity, local officials found the message clear: Western Christianity had no legitimate place, or space, in Japanese society.[59]

However, the establishment of the Kaisei Gakkō, the forerunner of Tokyo Imperial University, in 1869 marked a turning point for the spatial limitations of the practice and propagation of Christianity. The religion increasingly escaped the confines of the treaty port system as governments at the local and national level solicited the expertise of Western educators and advisers. Among them were dozens of Christians who traveled outside the limits of Japan's foreign settlements and brought their faith and ideals with them. Protestantism in particular expanded its reach. Hepburn, for instance, left his teaching duties in Nagasaki to accept a professorship at the new Kaisei Gakkō in 1869 in the heart of the capital, not its peripheral foreign settlement.[60] Although he resigned from his mission responsibilities then, he infused his courses on language, law, and science at the institution with a distinctly Protestant Christian perspective. He held that "Christianity was the force of forces in true civilization."[61] Like Verbeck, many of the Christian laymen hired by the new government as educators believed that "all Western learning and civilization was permeated with Christian truth."[62] Several of the Western experts who arrived in 1871 typified this trend as they brought their Protestant convictions to secular education outside of Japan's treaty ports. They ranged from the new headmaster of the Kumamoto Yōgakkō, Captain Leroy Lansing Janes (1838–1909),[63] to the new superintendent of education for Echizen province, William Elliot Griffis (1843–1928), to the first foreign teacher at the government's Gakumonjo (School for Western Studies) in Shizuoka, Edward Warren Clark (1849–1907).[64] In each case, these teachers underlined the important role that Christianity played in Western civilization and the role of God in the workings of the world.[65]

In the early 1870s, the new Meiji government's ability to circumscribe Christianity within foreign concessions and punish transgressions of the boundaries separating it from Japanese society changed quickly and dramatically. Suspicion, disapproval, and occasionally violence continued to hound Western missionaries and Japanese who showed an interest in Christianity, and this legacy of the Tokugawa period never fully disappeared. However, in the early 1870s, amid Japan's integration into intensifying processes of globalization, legal and spatial strategies deployed by the Japanese government against Christianity became anachronistic. Official policies dictating the confinement and persecution of Christianity complicated Japan's aspirations to participate in diplomacy with the West. Although Western governments did not explicitly make legalizing Christianity a necessary condition for the renegotiation of Japan's treaty relationships, legalization's diplomatic utility became undeniable.[66] In 1873, the national government ordered the removal of the boards proscribing Christianity while strategically opting not to pronounce it legal. Again, fear, prejudice, and mistrust of Christianity still persisted after this de facto legalization. Nam-Lin Hur notes that the Meiji government's strategic 1872 ban on "private funerals"—those not conducted by a Shinto or Buddhist priest—remained conveniently in place after this change.[67] But the 1873 decriminalization removed a crucial obstacle between the religion and the Japanese public. Immediately afterward, Christianity began to gain new access to previously forbidden Japanese zones and to Japanese religious seekers.

The increased flow of Christian people and ideas into and out of treaty ports took part in the context of important spatial shifts in the Japanese religious landscape. Tokugawa-era anti-Christian policies of spatial isolation and separation were rooted in an ideological binary, at least discursively speaking. Japan stood in stark opposition to the dangerous West, and Japanese religion was made to signify the antithesis of Christianity. The shogunate claimed to be administering the protection of Japan through the quarantine of both these elements in Dejima and by deputizing Buddhist temples to verify their absence in Japan proper. During the late 1860s, however, Buddhist spaces and institutions came under attack, irreversibly diluting the binary that justified the sequestering of the Western other and nullifying that system's unifying potential. Shinto advocates in the newly formed Meiji government enacted the official separation of Buddhism from Shinto *(Shinbutsu bunri)* in 1868, economically and politically disempowering temples in a very sudden move.[68] In the wake of this edict, Shinto priests and proponents carried out the so-called Haibutsu Kishaku (Abolish and Demolish Buddha) campaign, which destroyed as much as 30 percent of the more than one hundred thousand temples in Japan by 1874.[69] Meanwhile, in early

1872, officials established a new national family registration system that relieved temples of this duty that they had held for more than two centuries. The government's subsequent attempt to shift the responsibility for registration and anti-Christian surveillance to Shinto shrines lasted only a year before it passed directly to the Home Ministry.[70] Yet in revoking Buddhist temples' role in protecting Japan, in dismantling Buddhist authority, and in destroying Buddhist spaces, these processes blurred the once clear and stable state-endorsed binarism of Japan and Christianity. Combined with the momentous decriminalization of Christianity in 1873, these developments weakened the barriers erected to spatially delimit Christianity and the spaces through which the justificatory anti-Christian ideologies were disseminated and maintained.

After 1873, two types of institutions were especially instrumental in carrying Christianity across the threshold and out more widely into Japan in the wake of these changes. First among these were schools. While Roman Catholicism boasted six boys' schools and a girls' school by the end of that year, its institutions for education beyond the primary level were focused on developing priests, sisters, or tradesmen dedicated to church service.[71] By contrast, Protestant missionary schools and secular schools where outspoken Protestants taught were central in instilling Christian beliefs and ideals in secondary and postsecondary students who popularized the religion for the first time among the greater Japanese public. Protestant educators at existing and new secular schools such as the Imperial University (1869), the Dōjinsha (1873), Tokyo Women's Normal School (1875), and Meiji Girls' School (1885) in the capital were now free to more openly marry Western knowledge with Christian theology and moral education.[72] In addition, the same process increasingly took place both beyond the former borders of treaty ports and in the various newly legalized missionary schools that opened in the mid-1870s. Dōshisha English School (1875), established in Kyoto by Japanese Protestant missionary and educator Niijima Jō (1843–1890) as the first Christian higher school in Japan, would became the most famous, but was part of a much larger trend.[73] This was especially true for Protestant mission schools, and, as Kohiyama Rui asserts, "women's education was among the areas in which Christian missionary work had the largest social impact."[74] At institutions such as Kobe College (1873), Aoyama Girls' School (1874), Tokyo Friends Girls' School (1887), and Joshi Gakuin (1890), students found the opportunity to cultivate a new social awareness and set of ambitions.[75] In all of these contexts, Westerners and Japanese Protestant educators demonstrated the social mandate of Protestantism and emphasized Christian social activism at school.[76] By the early 1880s, these students formed the core of an unprecedented surge in the number of Japanese Christians, which continued to grow until the end of the decade, further broadening the geographical area in which Christianity was practiced in Japan.[77] This development caused an increase in Protestant Christianity's visibility and influence in Japanese society.

Playing a connected and equally significant role in bridging the divide between Christianity and Japanese society were churches. Japanese congregations of Roman Catholic, Greek Orthodox, and Protestant Christians formed earliest after 1873 in the foreign settlements of Tokyo, Osaka, Yokohama, Kobe, and Hakodate. There the beliefs, practices, and edifices of foreign Christians had prospered under official protection since the late 1850s. Churches also developed early in peripheral areas, like Urakami and Hirado, with old ties to Catholicism, and rural areas with more recent links to missionaries and Japanese Christians, like Gunma and Okayama Prefectures.[78] However, the establishment of churches squarely within the capital, well outside the foreign settlement at Tsukiji, represented an especially important development for the relevance, accessibility, and impact of Christianity for Japan's population. Japanese Protestants led the way in this expansion from 1875, complementing the proselytization efforts of secular and missionary Christian educators already underway in—and most concentrated at—schools in Tokyo. This type of expansion continued as the real and imaginary boundaries separating the foreign concessions from their adjacent major metropolitan areas came down further in the 1880s and the Japanese-led Protestant churches of Osaka, Kobe, and Kyoto gained larger urban and regional importance. Ultimately, in conjunction with educational institutions, the social spaces created within urban Japanese Protestant churches proved fundamental to the rapprochement between the foreign, stigmatized religion of Christianity and Japanese society.

Urban Japanese-led Protestant churches were in fact instrumental in establishing intellectual and concrete connections between Christianity and the social dilemmas, priorities, and aspirations of Japanese women and men. At school, at work, and in the burgeoning print media, Japan's educated elite constantly encountered and contributed to debates about the meaning of Westernization, modernization, and civilization. This was particularly the case for the so-called new middle class, a group within this category. Although there were many exceptions, ranging from aristocrats to day laborers, the bulk of urban Protestants were part of the middle-class intelligentsia.[79] These women and men from various socioeconomic backgrounds were most definable by their educational accomplishments, social vision and awareness, and urban, modern occupations in government, education, journalism, and industry.[80] In urban Protestant churches they found space to grapple with these concepts and roles and with the related ideas of progress and society. Urban Protestant churches thus allowed attendees to engage with the discursive authority of the West, cementing its association with Protestantism in a manner that distinguished it from Buddhism, its primary rival in the Meiji and early Taishō periods. Nowhere were these trends more evident than in the capital, the national epicenter of government, media, business, and educational institutions, of the new middle class that animated them, and of Protestantism in imperial Japan.

This book studies the development and impacts of Tokyo's largest and most influential Japanese Protestant congregations and argues that their urban emplacements and built and social spaces were instrumental in the processes that bridged Christianity and society in modern Japan. The story unfolds through an examination of the Reinanzaka, Banchō, Hongō, and Fujimichō Churches between 1879 and 1923. Utilizing a variety of sources—from maps and architectural sketches to autobiographies and letters, sermons and speeches, and Protestant newspapers and journals—the chapters that follow offer the first scholarly analysis of the interconnected locational, built, and social spaces of the urban Japanese Protestant church. This examination reveals that the use of urban emplacement, architecture, pastoral and lay discursive space, regular meetings and gatherings, and other events worked together to make churches accessible and relevant for Japanese attendees. Furthermore, as the final chapters of this work will demonstrate, Japanese attendees internalized new ideals and built new networks within the church space that many used to impact society beyond the church.

Through this process, attendees broke through many of the remaining barriers separating Christianity from Japanese society. By the turn of the twentieth century, these spaces had come to offer valid Japanese pathways to social awareness and change. Just as they did in the United States, Latin America, and colonial Korea, Protestant churches in Japan came to serve as loci of social empowerment.[81] These churches' strong social focus stemmed in part from their Japanese pastors who firmly believed that Christianity held the key to not only personal but also national salvation. Like most attendees, they had come of age amid the unprecedented socioeconomic change and cultural displacement of the Meiji period (1868–1912). In their youth, they learned to apply Protestantism's combination of religious morality with social awareness and reform-mindedness to their spiritual and intellectual crises. Ebina Danjō (1856–1937), Yokoi Tokio (1857–1927), and Kozaki Hiromichi (1856–1938), for instance, all encountered Christianity as students of Janes at the Kumamoto Yōgakkō in the early 1870s. These boys from the rapidly disbanding samurai class found hope and moral structure in Christianity.[82] Like these members of the so-called Kumamoto Band, Uemura Masahisa (1857–1925) had suffered from the economic and moral dislocation of the era as a son in a samurai family. Beginning with his classes in the English preparatory school of Presbyterian missionary James Ballagh (1832–1920) in Yokohama, Uemura also resolved his moral uncertainty with Christianity.[83] Uemura, like Ebina, Yokoi, and Kozaki, was convinced that this foreign religion, capable of helping him to understand himself and his relation to the cosmos, could also help fix his struggling nation. They and lay attendees combined new perspectives, ideals, and ethics to create a new Protestant social vision.

Physical Space

The physical space of the capital's largest Protestant churches, comprising their changing locations within Tokyo and their buildings, enabled novel and transformative social spaces. As historian of religion Allan Grapard has argued, scholars must think spatially about religion in Japan.[84] In particular, he emphasizes "the notion of place," defined elsewhere as a form of space imbued with meaning by people's actions and words.[85] In his study of Sensōji in the Edo period, historian Nam-Lin Hur has done this well. Hur adeptly incorporates physical space into his narrative on the development of this famous Buddhist temple as a site for religious and more worldly gratification. For instance, he has his eye on the competition for economic and political power occurring between the shogunate and the merchant elite through the maintenance and rebuilding of the temple space.[86] Likewise making space central to her analysis, Sarah Thal masterfully describes and analyzes the development of the popular pilgrimage site Konpira while paying close attention to the declining fortunes of neighboring Buddhist temple Matsuoji. From retracing in beautiful detail the steps of a pilgrim to the shrine in 1858 to recounting the shrine's transformation into a "site for rituals of imperial subjecthood," this work maintains a spatial lens throughout.[87] In deploying it, Thal reveals the convergence of religion, politics, and ideology over time at Konpira and their connections with regional and national developments.

Inspired by these studies of Buddhist and Shinto space and the larger spatial turn in Japanese history, this book's first section presents the first historical study on the physical space of the urban Japanese Protestant church. This study of physical space forms the basis for the larger project of the book. Later chapters build on it to examine the process by which the physical space of the Japanese Protestant church became endowed with the "people, practices, [and] objects" as well as words and interpretations that made it the place it was.[88] It seeks to shed light on the ways in which women and men passed through, utilized, and appropriated the church space and gave it its true character. In other words, it delineates how they "practiced" space at church, to borrow a phrase from multidisciplinary theorist Michel de Certeau.[89]

This new narrative of the development of Japanese Protestant churches in Tokyo begins by tracking their formation within national, regional, and local space. Chapter 1 maps out the movement of Protestant Christian leaders from treaty ports and provincial capitals to key areas in Tokyo before 1906. During the 1860s and 1870s American missionaries and Protestant teachers established bases from which they successfully spread the Western religion. In these Christian strongholds, Japan's first Protestant conversions took place and modern Japan's first Christian churches took shape. By the early 1880s, however, young Japanese pastors had begun to appropriate and give new direction to Protestantism. As they graduated from Christian institutions in Sapporo, Kyoto, and Yokohama, several of them aimed to make the national capital into Japan's capital for Protestant Christianity as well. The idea of Tokyo as *teito* (imperial capital) took shape in the minds of these young Japanese Protestant leaders, awed by the capital's transformation into the national nerve center, and largely guided this trajectory and their spatial choices within Tokyo.[90] So these men created some of the country's first Japanese-led Protestant churches near the city's prestigious educational and governmental institutions. They made conscious use of specific types of urban space in Tokyo to realize their conceptions about and ambitions for Protestant Christianity in the capital. Pastors planned, built, and rebuilt churches in areas abuzz with Japan's new modern class of national leaders, from the wealthy Reinanzaka neighborhood within blocks of the Imperial Diet to the bustling cafés and boardinghouses around the Imperial University in Hongō Ward. Concurrently, some innovative religious and secular leaders affiliated with Shinto, Buddhism, and new religions such as Tenrikyo strove to mobilize the space of the capital. However, because they were very few in number and largely out of sync with the trajectories of their national organizations, these efforts did not challenge the implantation of Protestantism in the heart of Tokyo.

Moving from location within the built environment to the architecture of built space, chapter 2 narrates the origins and development of the distinctively Japanese Protestant church space before 1923. From the 1880s, the Japanese pastors and congregations of the capital's largest churches sought to create their own church buildings. In chorus with a nationwide shift beyond Westernization and toward appropriation and invention, they hoped for churches that would not be simply Western buildings copied and imported by Western missionaries. Instead, they developed structures through a more complex process involving significant Japanese contributions. From conception to design to funding or fundraising to construction, church members increasingly placed church-building projects under Japanese control. Yet the result was inevitably a hybrid space. The buildings of Tokyo's largest Japanese Protestant churches benefited from the special, protected status of Christian space and their associability with the West, while churchgoers endowed them with distinctly Japanese meaning.[91] These edifices evolved to possess distinct, eye-catching exteriors and functionally designed but impressive interiors that could bring Japanese religious seekers together in new and meaningful ways. In doing so, churchgoers exercised a legal and administrative freedom that distinguished their sites from those of their religious competitors. Much more than Buddhist temples, sect Shinto shrines, State Shinto shrines, the gathering spaces of new religions like Tenrikyō, or even mission-funded churches, they possessed a certain spatial "heterogeneity" among religious gathering spaces.[92] The appropriation of Western architectural styles for the creation of religious gathering spaces by and for Japanese individuals was critical in Protestant Christianity's indigenization.

Social Space

The physical space of the Japanese Protestant church facilitated the creation of a distinct social space with strong ties to the social and political realms in Japan. This relationship confirms the conclusions of scholars such as Peter Berger who have come, sometimes hesitantly, to recognize that separation of the religious and the secular realms is by no means a necessary condition of modernity.[93] In fact, many secular, and, even political, themes and activities characterized the social space of the Japanese Protestant church at the turn of the twentieth century. Arming attendees with a relative freedom of assembly and expression about political concerns, churches acted as a "theater . . . in which political participation [wa]s enacted through the medium of talk."[94] Like the cafés, salons, and public squares of Enlightenment-era Western Europe, Japanese Protestant churches hosted and contributed to the public sphere.[95] This stood in contrast to Buddhist temples and Shinto shrines. These sites had brought Japanese together for centuries and also served as sites for community members to deliberate on important local matters, and this remained the case to some extent in imperial Japan (1868–1945). However, the subordinate and relatively precarious position of these sites vis-à-vis the state, combined with Meiji-era restrictions on discourse and assembly and official efforts to isolate religion from politics, made them primarily spaces for the promotion of conformity, obedience, and the embodiment of state-approved ideals.[96] Protestant churches hosted discourse and activism that targeted the social and the political, and they did so in the context of laws that had significantly curtailed freedoms of expression, assembly, and organization.[97] The social space that developed within these Japanese Protestant spaces grew out of discourse and activities that linked the churches with the social and political issues facing greater Japan. Working together in largely untraditional ways, Japanese women and men brought pressing social issues from far afield into the church community. In doing so, they explicitly connected the social space of the church to that of the capital, nation, and empire. These churches also included an array of events that are not examined here. Taking part in Sunday school and singing hymns were integral parts of the church experience in Tokyo's largest congregations, but attendees left little evidence that these activities were directly relevant to the study of the relationship between church attendance and social change. Therefore, this book focuses primarily on those forms of discourse and social interaction that most demonstrably connected church and society.

In the largest room within the church, the sanctuary *(reihaidō)* or worship hall *(sankaidō),* the heart of the church experience for many attendees took place. This was the Sunday sermon, in which Japanese Protestant pastors presented their perspectives on the social reality they shared with listeners. Far from limiting themselves to explicitly religious issues, the most popular and prominent among them regularly addressed social and political themes. These sermons contained conceptualizations of the individual, society, nation, and world that were deeply rooted in the mainstream socio-moral frameworks and government rhetoric. Yet distinctly Protestant interpretations of social awareness, justice, responsibility, and activism and of the nation and nationalism set them apart. These Japanese pastors, like their elite, well-educated listeners, walked between the world of Western ideas and traditions and that of an increasingly self-aware and proud Japan. So situated, they were well placed to act as ideological interpreters and to lead members of Japan's new middle class in their challenging quests for identity. They were also contributors to the rise of modern oratory in Japan and became some of the most distinguished Japanese orators in the Meiji period.[98]

Within the privileged space of the Protestant church, Japanese pastors exercised an empowering, albeit relative, freedom to speak on social and even political themes that distinguished them from most clergy in Japan's traditional and new religions. After serving in the early 1870s as deputized ideological indoctrinators for the state with a government-approved script, shrine and temple priests were granted a conditional, "subjectified" autonomy. The freedom to preach granted Shinto priests in 1875, for instance, came with the requirement that they advocate patriotism and both service and obedience to the emperor.[99] New religions like Tenrikyō and Ōmotokyō that were granted status as shrine Shinto sects in the Meiji period frequently invoked social and political change in the Meiji period. But their new status came with both doctrinal and discursive adjustments that brought their words and practices more in line with the dictates of State Shinto.[100] Meanwhile, Buddhist clergy largely turned away from controversial social and political topics. Buddhist discourse largely respected a separation between "'morality,' 'ethics,' and culture," which lay and ordained Buddhists discussed vigorously, and "politics," which those speakers and authors typically avoided.[101] More generally, scholars have noted a "hardening of the distinction between private religious concerns and the public realm" among Buddhist leaders brought on by the Meiji government's invasive making and remaking of policies regarding Buddhist clergy.[102] Before 1900 both groups also remained administratively subject to the Shrine and Temple Bureau (Shaji Kyoku).[103] In the extremely rare instances when clergy spoke openly about major political and social issues, their sect headquarters sought with success to silence or to defrock them. Sōtō Zen priest and abbot of Rinsenji Uchiyama Gudō (1874–1911) criticized the landholding system in Japan, the imperial institution, and the conscript military. Similarly, Shin priest Takagi Kenmyō (1864–1914) advocated social activism and socialist-style reform to address the *burakumin* problem in Japan. Both were defrocked by the leadership of their sects during the development of the High Treason Incident.[104] The progressive, socially aware New Buddhism movement that gained steam in the latter half of the Taishō period would be primarily a lay movement.

Japanese Protestant pastors operated with greater autonomy, however, and their sermons therefore constituted a distinct form of socioreligious discourse in Meiji Japan. In no small part, this latitude derived from the special status of the church space. Although officials and censors occasionally fined or banned material published in church organs—material that included sermons—the official reach of the state seemed to stop at the door to the church.[105] In the Meiji and early Taishō eras, leading Japanese pastors in Tokyo and more rural areas were not arrested, and their sermons were not interrupted, even when they discussed or held events relating to controversial topics like the High Treason Incident.[106] As chapter 3 demonstrates, pastors used this freedom to encourage attendees to locate themselves communally and globally and battle differentiation and discrimination based on socioeconomic status, gender, and even ethnicity by acting on Protestant ideals. At the same time, however, these same men possessed and advocated a sincere patriotism for their country and, as is clear from chapter 4, exhorted their audiences to develop a Japanese national identity and awareness. This involved cultivating Christian nationalisms built around the particular national imaginary or vision of the national community that Japanese pastors conjured for their listeners each Sunday. Although these nation-views were not fully centered on the official nationalism propagated by government officials and ideologues in the service of the state, they remained embedded in an ideological context dominated by those perspectives. The pastors of the capital's largest churches, like most of their attendees, generally took for granted their mandate of imperial loyalty and service and the primacy of Japan's national destiny. However, they advocated the fulfillment of these imperatives simultaneously with the implementation of Protestant universal values and calls for social improvement. Together these chapters illustrate the prominent role that Japanese Protestant sermons played in the transmission of social ideals at church and in equipping listeners to see themselves as more than the "metaphorical foreigners" that many Japanese considered them to be.[107] Their words shed light on the complex ideological acrobatics through which Japanese Protestants formulated their distinct place in the nation-state and on the manifestation of a pervasive "Shinto secular" even in Christian discourse.[108]

Starting around 1900, sermons often appeared where nonattendees could also read them. Nonetheless, the fact that they were a form of spoken discourse is extremely important. With their words, each Japanese Protestant pastor defined the character of his church space as a place, framing the meaning that not only he but the congregation would give it. As these chapters show, this aspect of pastoral activity was intrinsically linked with the location, shape, and functions of urban Protestant church spaces. It was at times the mutually reinforcing nature of the relationship between church space and the pastoral discursive space that drew the attention, and ire, of religious leaders from other faiths, such as Buddhist priests.

While sermons provided much of the fundamental contours and color of the discursive space in leading Protestant churches, lectures and speeches on social and political themes by laypersons constituted a major part of the space as well. Chapter 5 examines these events and the words spoken there and integrates them into the story of Japanese Protestantism's development as a religion of social consciousness and reform. Utilizing the different types of spaces within the church, and benefiting from the special status of those buildings, such presentations brought important topics of the day into the church. From academic talks to reports of labor disputes and environmental issues, the church space was host to a wide range of talks that went well beyond strictly religious subjects. The "woman question" attracted audiences with particular frequency and consistency. Speakers expressed their opinions on the definitions and rights of modern Japanese womanhood as well as the institutions in imperial Japan most associated with it: marriage, family, and the home. Although still exceedingly rare, there were speech and lecture events featuring women as well. Churches belonged to the small group of spaces in the late Meiji period in which "public women" were encouraged not only to gather and participate but also to be heard.[109] Women educators in particular took advantage of the lay lectern at church to express their points of view. Behind these events were local branches of social reform organizations like the Japan Woman's Christian Temperance Union as well as various church *seinenkai* (youth groups) and *fujinkai* (women's groups), who all sought to encourage churchgoers to think about society beyond the church. However, churchgoers also strove to engage with the real problems facing Japanese society and affect positive change.

Attendees at Tokyo's largest Japanese Protestant churches mobilized the space of the church to organize words and actions aimed at reforming society. In addition to lectures and speeches, church-based *seinenkai* and *fujinkai* made particularly effective use of the church space to respond intellectually and concretely to social problems and participate in secular projects. Chapter 6 describes the efforts of churchgoing women and men who organized themselves and took action to address the social issues they considered most pressing. Within the church, women administered programs of public welfare, education, and social reform that transformed the social perspective of Japanese Protestantism into concrete action. They also used the church to participate in activities aimed at serving the local and national community, from providing regional disaster relief to providing moral support for Japan's imperial military. *Fujinkai* were among the busiest and most popular organizations in Tokyo Protestant churches, arguably the first modern Japanese religious gathering space to consistently encourage women to serve as leaders. They helped legitimize public roles for women and set the stage for the significant increase in women's public activism throughout the first half of the twentieth century. *Fujinkai* stood out in the context of new, explicit policies excluding women from political associations and assemblies after 1890 and a decline in the momentum generated by early secular groups seeking to address the oppression of women in Japan.[110] Meanwhile, church-based youth groups were also involved in a number of relief projects. In contrast with *fujinkai,* however, male-led *seinenkai* were primarily focused on making an intellectual contribution to the moral cultivation of Japanese society. The processes of writing and speaking that characterized youth group activities helped many young Japanese to crystallize ideas and stances that eventually formed the basis for more concrete activism and reform.

For men and women alike, events organized and words exchanged inside the church space played very critical roles in helping churchgoers find their way to social activism and engagement outside the church. From public intellectuals and journalists to social reformers to college professors to politicians to businessmen, thousands of Japanese Protestant church attendees consciously carried experiences from church attendance with them into their secular endeavors. Attendees at Reinanzaka, Hongō, Fujimichō, and Banchō Churches had notable impacts on Japanese society that were closely related to their experiences at church. Members of the new educated elite, born in the second and third generations of Meiji youth, were particularly drawn to Tokyo's largest Protestant churches.[111] Faced with the popularity of Protestant churches among this attractive demographic, even Buddhist priests noticed and responded. After describing larger trends in the composition and size of these congregations' attendance data, chapter 7 examines the path from church into society for a small sample of churchgoers in the capital's leading Protestant congregations. The women and men examined are not meant to be representative of all or even most of the attendees at the Reinanzaka, Banchō, Fujimichō, and Hongō Churches between the 1880s and the early 1920s, who would together number a few thousand. Rather, they are included because they represent a range of distinctly modern professions, they made notable contributions to modern Japan, and their stories demonstrate the relationship between church attendance and social change. Furthermore, most provide insight beyond the handful of extremely well-known and oft-studied Japanese Protestants involved in major movements in social reform and thought. The chapter is illustrative of an underexamined process that occurred in the lives of hundreds of churchgoers throughout Japan and that significantly affected modern Japan.

CHAPTER ONE

Placing Japanese Protestant Churches in Tokyo

The brain and the heart of Japan had been separated by nearly three hundred miles for over two and a half centuries, when a coup in 1868 to "restore" supreme imperial authority took place. Among the new Meiji government's first initiatives was the effort to resolve this bifurcation by unifying Japan's political and economic capital, Edo, with its symbolic and cultural capital, Kyoto. With a single imperial proclamation on 3 September 1868—made in the middle of a civil war between Tokugawa loyalists and imperial restoration forces—Edo became the new national capital.[1] In the following month the emperor moved from his palace in Kyoto into the former shogun's castle in Tokyo.[2] The solution to one major problem, however, also created new dilemmas, particularly for institutions deeply entrenched near the former cultural center of Japan. Religious organizations most densely concentrated in the Kinki region, near Japan's ancient imperial capitals, were suddenly forced to deliberate about the significance of Tokyo for their organizations.

The responses of several major Japanese religious movements to the rise of Tokyo had important consequences for the development of their respective sects in imperial Japan. Religious leaders and evangelists made choices about establishing a stronger institutional and representational presence in the new capital, and about where within the city that presence should be located and focused. More broadly, they also struggled with the question of shifting their existing bases in the religious heartland of Japan to the capital, thus aligning the geography of their religious organizations with the new government's conceptualizations of center and periphery. The traditional Japanese religions of Shinto and Buddhism, both then engaged in substantial processes of redefinition and repositioning, dealt with these issues, but they were not alone. Protestant Christianity and Japanese New Religions like Tenrikyō had thrived best in that same shared corner of Japan. And Roman Catholicism's main stronghold was far from the capital in Nagasaki. These movements too, therefore, were confronted with the rise of Tokyo. Each of these diverse groups sought access to target populations in the capital and to use the city to broadcast their religious movement's beliefs and ideals more widely throughout Japan. Ultimately, however, the relationships with the capital of particularly active Japanese religious movements including sect Shinto, an ostensibly suprareligious State Shinto, True Pure Land Buddhism, and Tenrikyō proved ambiguous. Furthermore, their bases remained firmly grounded in the Kansai area. Roman Catholicism meanwhile continued to prioritize Nagasaki over other mission sites.[3] Protestant Christian leaders, by contrast, moved early and decisively to make Tokyo the capital of Japanese Protestantism and to mobilize urban space in the city to reach Tokyoites and broader Japanese society. These efforts distinguished it from other groups in the religious landscape of Meiji Japan.

The movement of Protestant Christianity, a religion previously confined to and identified with the Japanese periphery, toward and then within the nation's center proved fundamental to its growth and, more significantly, its influence. Beginning in the late 1870s, the first generation of Japanese Protestant pastors made their way to Tokyo from various points in Japan. The city had an understandable magnetism for this group. As home to hundreds of Western Christians hired to work as experts by the government and other institutions, Tokyo was necessarily a tolerant place for the religion and therefore appealing. However, the capital also offered access to individuals occupying, or destined to occupy, seats of social, cultural, political, or economic power. Often possessed of an avid interest in Western knowledge that softened their attitudes and opened their minds to the foreign religion, these men and women of Japan's new educated elite represented an ideal target audience for Christianity. Early Japanese pastors made spatial decisions that took their congregations away from Tokyo's foreign settlement and its environs and in the direction of the zones where these potential attendees lived, studied, and worked. This was the process at work within the founding and development of the capital's largest and most influential Protestant congregations in Meiji- and Taishō-era Tokyo. The decisions, spatial priorities, and understanding of urban space of these congregations' pastors guided the Reinanzaka, Banchō, Hongō, and Fujimichō Churches as they laid down enduring roots near the nation's premier institutions of education and government, leading the way in Tokyo's transformation into the center of Protestantism in Japan by 1890.[4]

Religious Leaders and the Rise of a New Capital

Already during the Tokugawa period (1600–1868), all roads literally led to the capital city, then called Edo. Four of Japan's five major constructed routes ended in Edo from the early seventeenth century onward.[5] With a population of 1 million in the early 1700s, the shogun's capital was in all probability the world's largest city, far surpassing Europe's largest city, London, for decades to come.[6] But in the tumultuous years immediately preceding and following the Meiji Restoration of 1868, much of the old Edo collapsed in on itself as a national civic government disassembled the Tokugawa family's feudal regime. In its place, the new leadership sought to build a centralized, modern nation with a new capital city. Edo lost over half its population, tens of thousands of servants and employees of the military elite lost their positions, and the local and regional economy suffered dramatically during the years that saw the new capital's birth.[7]

With great effort and excitement over the next three decades, however, national and city officials and Tokyoites transformed Edo into Tokyo, Japan's *teito* (imperial capital). By the mid-1880s, the capital began to recover its pre-1868 population. The new glitzy Ginza district took center stage and came to represent modernization, Western learning, and the new Japan.[8] Tokyo residents like famous entrepreneur Shibusawa Eiichi (1840–1931) and scholar-politician Taguchi Ukichi (1855–1905) conjured the image of a true capital that, like Paris or New York in their respective countries, symbolized the bright future of Japan.[9] Although the return of the recently departed former daimyo, the arrival of the old Kyoto aristocracy, and the persistence of the true and relatively constant *Edokko* (Edo native) population all contributed, the most significant population vector in Tokyo's recovery came from elsewhere. It would be the waves of urban newcomers rushing on central Japan's major roads to Tokyo that would give new life to the city as the administrative, financial, and symbolic capital of the Japanese nation and the residence of its emperor.[10] Men and women of all classes from all over the country came to the capital during the 1880s and 1890s. Tokyo was especially attractive for members of the new intellectual elite who came from Japan's countryside and treaty ports with aspirations of pursuing careers as intellectuals, bureaucrats, and even religious leaders in the nucleus of the nation.[11] They left their ancestral homes all over Japan and arrived in Tokyo with what contemporary authors coined as "city fever," *tokainetsu*.[12]

Among this great influx of arrivals and returnees were Japanese religious leaders, evangelists, and lay proponents seeking to enroot their sects in the soil of the new capital. Some of the earliest such efforts came from promoters of Shinto and Buddhism just after the transition from shogunal to imperial rule in 1868. Daimyo Kamei Koremi of Tsuwano domain and his retainer, Shintoist scholar Fukuba Bisei (1831–1907), came to Tokyo in 1869 to hold leading positions in the newly resurrected Jingikan (Ministry of Rites) within the new Meiji government. These intellectual heirs of Kokugaku luminaries Ōkuni Takamasa (1793–1871) and Hirata Atsutane (1776–1843) sought to implement a policy that reunified the religious and secular roles of imperial rule. For Fukuba in particular, the symbolic and pragmatic functions of the capital as a focal point for Shinto and as the home of the Meiji emperor were especially important. And more specifically within Tokyo, Fukuba worked to move the newly installed Hasshinden (altar to the eight protective deities of the imperial house and the state) from within the Jingikan to the central locus of imperial power in Japan, the new imperial palace itself.[13] In 1870, this Shinto advocate and administrator also announced the launching of the Great Promulgation Campaign, a program of which he was a chief architect.[14] In its efforts to widely instill respect for and loyalty to the Meiji emperor, patriotism, and traditional Confucian morality, this campaign developed by Fukuba would eventually locate its headquarters, the Great Teaching Institute, in Tokyo in 1873.[15] Fukuba worked there as an administrator.[16] The institute was reconstituted as the main Office of Shinto Affairs in 1875.[17] Then, in the wake of the Pantheon Dispute that divided leading Shinto officials in the institute over the question of including Izumo Shrine's *kami* Okuninushi no Mikoto in the state pantheon, the Shinto Honkyoku became an independent Shinto sect in 1886. Under the leadership of former daimyo and priest Inaba Masakuni (1834–1898), this organization used its position in the capital to bring together and oversee Shinto-derived sects not yet recognized as religious groups.[18]

Originally working with Shintoists to establish the Ministry of Doctrine, the more religiously inclusive successor of the Shintoist Ministry of Rites was a Buddhist priest and advocate also seeking to place his religion on a firmer basis in the capital. Kyoto's Higashi Honganji, headquarters of True Pure Land Buddhism in Japan, sent Shin sect cleric Shimaji Mokurai (1838–1911) to Tokyo in 1870. He was tasked with using his social capital among Meiji government officials to soften the new regime's anti-Buddhist position and promote the inclusion of Buddhism in the religious architecture of the new state.[19] While the broadened ministry was ultimately a failure, Shimaji was successful in turning the anti-Buddhist tide still then impacting priests and temples and in demonstrating the intellectual and practical value of freedom of religion for Meiji officials in the capital.[20] His work was instrumental in paving the way for participants in the Buddhist Enlightenment and New Buddhism movements that would develop and emanate from Tokyo in subsequent decades.

Japan's more traditional religious movements were not alone as they moved relatively quickly to target Tokyo in their campaigns for political and spiritual influence in the first years of the Meiji era. During the second decade of the Meiji period, leaders and advocates of newer religious movements also moved into Tokyo. Tenrikyō, an especially dynamic Japanese new religion founded by Nakayama Miki (1798–1897), began evangelism in the capital in 1885. Passing through on his way to Nara from a ministry trip in Niigata, missionary Kōda Chūsaburō (1828–1903) appears to have stopped in Tokyo and begun the first Tenrikyō preaching there in 1882.[21] And two years later, in 1885, Uehara Sasuke (1850–1912) traveled specifically to minister in Tokyo, where he established the Azuma Branch Church, the first Tenrikyō church in the capital.[22] In particular, Uehara was drawn to the Yoshiwara pleasure district in Shitaya Ward, where many people suffering at the bottom of society lived and worked. This mission would become the base for two-thirds of the thirty-nine Tenrikyō churches in Tokyo by 1896, while missions throughout Japan also continued to blossom. With several hundred thousand members and an increasing need for the security provided to official Shinto sects, in 1888 Tenrikyō leadership decided to seek that status.[23] Interestingly, the newly created sect Shinto Honkyoku made their recognition of Tenrikyō's affiliation with it conditional in part on the religious movement's transferal of its headquarters to Tokyo, and the spiritual head of the organization, Iburi Izō (1833–1907), acquiesced.[24]

Also coming to the capital from its regional and national peripheries were the first generation of Japanese Protestant pastors. Although Protestantism had a shorter history in Japan than Buddhism, Shinto, or even Tenrikyō, its reaction to the rise of Tokyo had much in common with its longer-established religious competition in imperial Japan. In the brief time since its introduction to Japan in the late 1850s, Protestant Christianity had developed an especially strong base in the greater Kansai region, the same area where Buddhism, imperial (Koshitsu) Shinto, and Tenrikyō flourished, and in the treaty port of Yokohama. For all these groups, the move to Tokyo also represented a move toward the national center and nearer to specific populations and institutions in the capital. And for Protestant pastors, like leaders and promoters of Buddhism, Shinto, and Tenrikyō, a mixture of purposeful and serendipitous encounters and decisions brought them to embrace the unprecedented opportunity and potential of Tokyo. Yet focusing such administrative and evangelistic attention on Tokyo inevitably led to a tension between root and branch. The energetic development of offices and churches in the capital meant both reinvigoration and competition for long-standing headquarters in and around the Kansai area.

Japanese religious institutions largely resolved this tension by preserving or returning to their original strongholds, primarily in the Kansai region. Efforts to centralize Shinto's various sects through a main seat in the capital ended in failure. Ise Grand Shrine in Mie Prefecture took over direction of the Great Promulgation Campaign in 1875, combining the positions of Ise chief priest with that of head for the Office for Shinto Affairs.[25] Arguably, the administrative organs overseeing Shinto from the capital after 1877, the Shrine and Temple

Bureau (Shaji Kyoku, est. 1877) and the Shrine Bureau (Jinja Kyoku, 1900), in fact served more and more to limit the social and political influence of Shinto religious movements.[26] Buddhist evangelism in the capital continued to expand. However, while Buddhism would continue to devote considerable resources to evangelism in the capital, leaders of its most dynamic sects, the Higashi Honganji and Nishi Honganji, chose to maintain their headquarters in Kyoto, where they still are today.[27] And despite agreeing to relocate its headquarters to Tokyo in 1887, Tenrikyō leadership was ultimately unwilling to abandon its most sacred site as its national headquarters. The *jiba,* a site in Nara Prefecture marking an *axis mundi* where God created humankind, served as the location for the group's original church, and in 1888 Tenrikyō reestablished its headquarters there.[28]

Facing a parallel dilemma, however, Protestant Christianity came to target Tokyo and continued to do so until the city became the capital of the religion in imperial Japan.[29] Building on the presence and influence of Western Christian educators and other foreign experts in Tokyo after 1869, Western missionaries rushed to evangelize in the capital after the removal of the boards proscribing Christianity in 1873. Within five years, Presbyterian, Methodist, Episcopalian, and Congregationalist missionaries from the United States and Canada founded fifteen congregations outside the former settlement in Tsukiji.[30] During that time Western missionaries worked closely with the earliest Japanese Protestant evangelists in Tokyo to launch churches in busy neighborhoods in central Tokyo wards such as Asakusa and Kōjimachi.[31] By 1900, the second year in which Japan's Home Ministry included churches in its statistics on religious spaces, there were 103 Protestant churches in the city of Tokyo.[32] The growth since the 1870s had been predominantly fueled by Protestant Christianity. This contrasted sharply with Roman Catholicism, which boasted only 8 established churches in the capital at the time. Like its Shinto, Tenrikyō, and to some extent Buddhist counterparts, the mission had in fact focused most of its attention and funds on its stronghold far from Tokyo. For the Catholic movement, this was Nagasaki, which had 54 churches in 1900.[33] This is not to say that Protestantism ignored the foundations already erected in its own stronghold in the Kansai region. Indeed, the area's larger urban centers saw significant growth in the quantity of Protestant congregations. From the low single digits in the 1870s, the number of Protestant churches in Osaka had risen to 46 by 1900, and the trend was echoed in the cities of Kobe (Hyōgo) and Kyoto, with 33 and 32 Protestant churches, respectively. However, with more than twice the number of Protestant churches than anywhere else in Japan, Tokyo had already emerged by the turn of the twentieth century as the movement's capital.[34] This remained the case in 1912, when Tokyo's 125 Protestant churches still greatly outnumbered the 65 in Kobe

(Hyōgo) and 59 in Osaka.[35] And as the growth in the number of church buildings in Tokyo continued to outpace that of other cities in the subsequent decades, this trend continued.[36] An instrumental element within this trend was the predominant role that Japanese pastors played in founding and leading churches beyond treaty ports, a development most prominently taking place in Tokyo.

In 1877 and 1878 Japan's first Protestant pastors, Okuno Masatsuna (1823–1910), Ogawa Yoshiyasu (1831–1912), and Yasugawa Tooru (d. 1908), were ordained, ushering in a new era in the development of Christianity in the capital. During the decade after 1877, the first generation of Japanese Protestant pastors took the primary role in planting and directing new churches in Tokyo and concentrated unprecedented evangelistic effort on the capital. Leading this movement was a younger subset within that first cohort who had come of age during Edo's rebirth as Tokyo. These recent graduates, the first Japanese to receive dedicated instruction in Protestant theology, biblical exegesis, and Christian leadership, had pursued higher education in order to fulfill their ambitions of contributing to the new nation.[37] Accordingly, they developed clear and defining ideas about the importance of the nation's new capital for Christianity and set about implementing them. Rather than continuing church-founding projects initiated by Western missionaries, these men assumed full responsibility for establishing and leading churches right away. Their efforts shifted the thrust of Protestantism from its strongholds in Kyoto and foreign settlements in Osaka, Kobe, Yokohama, and Tokyo to a new nexus in the heart of the capital. These pastors, as their missionary mentors were well and often enthusiastically aware, would set the course for the Japanese Protestant movement, and their ideas of Tokyo would be fundamental as they founded Meiji era Tokyo's largest congregations.

Japanese Pastors and Tokyo

In the mid-1870s, when young Japanese converts began secondary schooling in Protestant Christian strongholds to become pastors, the primacy of central Tokyo for their religion was by no means a foregone conclusion. The closest gateway into the interior of the capital for Protestant pastors was in Tokyo's foreign settlement, Tsukiji. While technically a part of Tokyo, Tsukiji was delimited by canals, gates, and the expansive Navy Meadow, all of which set it apart from the rest of the city.[38] Although many Westerners moved out of Tsukiji during the decade after its opening in 1869, the vast majority of Christian missionaries and teachers remained there and maintained it as the principal base for evangelism and education in the area.[39] They and their churches, schools, and homes gave the area a distinctly Westernized air.[40] Among those structures was the Union Seminary. This institution at Tokyo's fringe came to welcome young Japanese arriving from Aizu in the North, Oita in the South, and many points in between. Under the tutelage of American missionary educators such as William Imbrie (1845–1928), David Thompson (1835–1915), Guido Verbeck (1838–1898), James Amerman (1843–1928), James H. Ballagh (1830–1920), and Edward Rothesay Miller (1843–1915), these young men developed into some of Japan's most prominent Protestant leaders. The school opened in 1877 and grew considerably within months thanks to its merger with other existing schools. These included the Brown Preparatory School, run by American missionary Samuel Robbins Brown (1810–1880), and the Seishi School of Reformed missionary Martin Wyckoff (1850–1911), both originally located in Yokohama.[41] Most graduates of Union Seminary opted to go establish churches beyond the capital in locations ranging from Sendai in the North to Kagoshima in the South to Kōchi on the Pacific coast of rural Shikoku.[42] Still, a handful of young Presbyterian pastors, including Ibuka Kajinosuke (1854–1940), Uemura Masahisa (1858–1925), Tamura Naoomi (1858–1934), and Kitahara Yoshimichi (1846–1894), chose to establish new church congregations in the capital between 1877 and 1880.

In Tokyo, these leaders encountered young former samurai from the other main stronghold of Protestant Christianity in Japan who had made the less popular decision of going to the capital. Niijima Jō and Congregationalist missionaries founded Dōshisha Eigakkō in 1875 in distant Kyoto. From the start, this English school was an institution of Christian higher education, as its Buddhist detractors were well aware.[43] It was this aspect in particular that drew Japanese Christian young men like Yokoi Tokio, Kozaki Hiromichi, and Kanamori Michitomo of Kumamoto and Fukuoka native Ebina Danjō. All four were graduates of the Kumamoto Yōgakkō, where American educator Leroy Lansing Janes instilled Christian values and beliefs in his pupils between 1871 and 1877.[44] At Dōshisha these members of the Kumamoto Band joined other students receiving formal training from Niijima Jō and American Congregationalist missionaries such as Jerome D. Davis (1868–1923) and Dwight Learned (1848–1943) in the spiritual and academic/theological foundations of Christianity and preparation for careers in the ministry. Though not a single one of them was assigned to the capital in 1879, by 1887 all had made their way to Tokyo and begun developing new Protestant congregations there. The graduates of Tokyo Union Seminary in the capital likewise remained in Tokyo, although by the mid-1890s Uemura was the only one among them still pastoring for a church that he had established.[45]

Uemura, Kozaki, Yokoi, and Ebina were responsible for establishing the four largest and best-known congregations in Meiji-era (1868–1912) Tokyo, and for each man the capital possessed a special attraction. Coming with the flow of Japanese into the city, they, like so many of Japan's other religious leaders, saw in it new opportunities to reach and influence people and institutions capable of facilitating the propagation of their beliefs and the moral improvement of Japan. For these pastors in particular, the elements that attracted them to the capital and impressed them on their arrival between 1879 and 1887 proved fundamental to the development and location of the churches they would found. As each of these pastors went about founding new congregations, he carried with him his respective "idea of Tokyo."

For Uemura Masahisa, Tokyo represented both the past and the future. Having grown up in Edo in the 1850s and 1860s, the young pastor nurtured strong sentimental ties to the city. He expressed this clearly in a piece he wrote in late 1883 for the *Tokyo maishū shinpō* after attending the funeral ceremony for the former shogun's widow, Tenshōin, in Tokyo. His heartfelt essay described the beauty of old Edo, which had been severely damaged by the violence accompanying the Meiji Restoration. Writing about Tōezan Kaneiji, one of the Tokugawa family's two funerary temples in Edo, as it stood in 1876, Uemura recalled the "grand pagoda" that was largely destroyed by fire during the Boshin War in 1868. He also wrote with regret of the golden shogunal mausoleum, which "shined through the verdant forest day and night" until it was reduced to ashes in the Battle of Ueno.[46] Clearly, Uemura held deep and "slightly admirative emotions" about Tokyo as the former Edo.[47]

His strong feelings about the city extended from Edo to Tokyo as the new national capital. Uemura initially saw potential for Christianity in Gunma, Aichi, and Mie Prefectures and made evangelistic tours to these areas. By the start of the 1880s, however, he had made Tokyo the base for his ministry.[48] Uemura stayed in Tokyo throughout his career because he sought to target the students and the new intellectual elite in and around the capital who were progressive, inventive, and untraditional.[49] Tokyo in general and the young members of the educated elite living there in particular represented the future for Christianity and for Japan. Uemura therefore established both his household and his first church congregation, Shitaya Itchi (Presbyterian) Church, squarely within that city in 1877. The capital was a central, connecting concept for Uemura. On the one hand, it bridged his vision of Japan's past and its future, and on the other, it brought together his often conflicting roles of evangelist and social leader.[50]

Even before he moved back to the city, the intellectual currents in Tokyo caught and held Uemura's attention while he was still a student. Uemura was deeply affected by the thinkers of the so-called Meiji Enlightenment.[51] He was especially interested in Fukuzawa Yukichi (1835–1901), referring to him in September 1881 as "a rare, great scholar of our country," widely admired around the world: "We must subscribe to each of that author's publications."[52] This opinion dated from the future pastor's self-study curriculum back in Yokohama, indicating a long-standing fascination with the impressive figure and his Keio Institute in Tokyo. While working as an English teacher in 1876 and 1877 at the Brown School, Uemura studied not only theology but also the same works of moral science and political economy that Fukuzawa had assigned to students at Keio Institute.[53] Beyond proving fundamental to his academic development, these readings and Fukuzawa's many works clearly helped to draw Uemura further into the intellectual orbit of the capital.

Just as Uemura was settling down in the capital, Kozaki Hiromichi arrived in 1879. He was originally dispatched to northern Japan, while his eleven fellow graduates went to places ranging from less metropolitan areas such as Gunma and Ehime Prefectures to large cities such as Kobe, Osaka, and Kyoto.[54] Forces from a number of vectors were compelling Kozaki to ministry in Mizusawa in Iwate Prefecture. First, he had traveled to evangelize in the summer of 1878.[55] And there was a tendency for graduates to return as pastors to areas where they had gone earlier as student evangelists—areas chosen for their presumed potential as mission sites. For instance, Ebina Danjō returned to Annaka, the hometown of Niijima Jō, where he had been an evangelist during his vacations from Dōshisha.[56] Second, Niijima had clearly demonstrated his belief in the importance of developing this mission site. During Kozaki's several weeks in Mizusawa, the Dōshisha graduates' revered spiritual and intellectual leader, school founder Niijima Jō himself, came to assist in spreading the gospel.[57] Reinforcing evangelistic efforts at this site—one significant enough to merit the personal attention of such an influential figure in the Japanese Protestant movement—became even more important in 1879. After accepting a teaching position at Dōshisha, Kozaki's classmate Yamazaki Tamenori (1857–1881) could no longer return to proselytize in his hometown of Mizusawa. So he implored Kozaki to go and evangelize there after graduation that year.[58] The weight of precedent then combined with Yamazaki's request and the support of Niijima led to the departure of Kozaki, the only as-yet-unassigned member of the Dōshisha's first graduating class, for the far northeastern coast of Japan's main island that October.

The call from Tokyo proved too strong for Kozaki, however. He never made it to Mizusawa on that voyage; instead, he "decided to go to the capital for the time being."[59] However, as Yuasa Yōzō (1902–1977), a future pastor who attended Reinanzaka Church as a child from 1910 and was baptized there by Kozaki in 1919, asserted, this development that "looked like chance was not chance."[60]

Rather, several converging factors drew Kozaki to the capital. First, Yuasa doubts that Kozaki, who "aspired to be a government minister or the prime minister," could really have been "satisfied with a ministry in the remote countryside of Ōshū."[61] Like his fellow Kumamoto Band members, Kozaki was deeply interested in the fate of the Japanese nation. In his case, this concern represented a line of continuity between the adolescent Kozaki's fervent Neo-Confucianism and his deep faith in Christianity as a young adult. Originally a strong believer in Confucian morality, Kozaki became convinced during his time at the Kumamoto Yōgakkō that this ancient, hierarchical ideology was ill-suited for modern Japan. He viewed Christianity, with its advocacy for the rights, freedoms, agency, and morality of individuals, as a worthy replacement for Confucian ideology. In the end, however, his arguments that the spirit of Christianity in Japan and the adherence of Japanese citizens to Christian beliefs and values would make Japan stronger, more modern, and more advanced shared with Confucian thought a clear emphasis on the persistence and stability of the state.[62]

Even for those of his classmates who sought to more completely free themselves of conservative Neo-Confucian morality, there remained a "strong public, or political, commitment" rooted in "the Confucian ethical structure in which they had been socialized."[63] Rather than deprive the students of these vestiges of Confucianism, their lessons and interactions with the school's headmaster Captain Janes reinforced them. It is surely for this reason that, as fellow pastor Ebina Danjō recalled, "political ambitions were extremely strong" among the Yōgakkō students.[64] It is perhaps for this reason too that by the late 1890s, Kozaki's former classmates Ebina, Yokoi, and Kanamori had all taken positions as pastors in Tokyo. In 1879, however, from this group only Kozaki had gone to minister in the capital.

It required more than his ambition and dedication to the nation to convince Kozaki to diverge from the plan that Niijima Jō had set for him. Kozaki had in fact set out for Mizusawa, even as an opportunity to go evangelize in Tokyo materialized. That summer, he had received a letter from Okada Matsuo (1858–1939), a fellow Dōshisha graduate working in Tokyo as a teacher at the Gakunōsha agriculture school of Tsuda Sen (1837–1908). After discussing the matter with Tsuda, Okada drafted a letter urging Kozaki to come begin his ministry in the capital.[65] This letter had not changed his mind. As he traveled northeast along the Nakasendō, however, Kozaki encountered friends and classmates who shared Okada's enthusiasm for the capital. From his autumn stopover in Annaka, where he stayed with fellow pastor and classmate Ebina Danjō, to his arrival in Tokyo's Kyōbashi Ward that winter, Kozaki learned more and more about the nascent

Japanese Christian community taking shape in the capital. Once there, he saw that "a group of Doshisha graduates and church members from the Kansai region had formed an organization" around Tsuda's Gakunōsha and begun "holding meetings."[66] It was only after arriving in Tokyo and receiving a direct request from them, the Gunyosha or "Flock of Sheep," that Kozaki decided to stop and evangelize in the capital.[67] He and approximately ten others, including Okada Matsuo and Gunyōsha leader Katsura Tokiaki, founded Shinsakanachō Church, the core of the future Reinanzaka Church, on 12 December 1879.[68] Clearly, as Yuasa concluded, the pastor's decision to stay in the capital indicates that his resolve to go to Mizusawa was not that firm to begin with.[69] However, the combination of fellow pastors' advice and communication with Christians in Tokyo constituted a call to the capital that Kozaki was ultimately unable to resist.

Tokyo offered Kozaki arguments for staying that were both strongly convincing and relevant to his priorities. Whatever his original notions about the capital were, Kozaki's activities after arriving show that he quickly developed an appreciation for the city's potential. He immediately demonstrated his ambitions for Christianity in the capital as he frequented the intellectual and political circles molding the new Japan. Within weeks, he deliberately "sought the acquaintance of influential men" in the capital. Among them was the same Fukuzawa Yukichi who so enchanted Uemura.[70] In addition, Christian educator Tsuda Sen introduced him to other members of the well-known intellectual Meiji Six Society, the prominent group of intellectuals at the forefront of the so-called Japanese Enlightenment.[71] He even attended some of their meetings at Mikawaya Café in Kanda.[72] In this way, Kozaki met leading figures who advocated Western philosophy, law, and mathematics, as well as Western-style education on philosophical as well as practical grounds. They included famous men such as Nishi Amane (1829–1927), Nishimura Shigeki (1828–1902), Nakamura Keiū (1832–1891), Tsuda Mamichi (1829–1903), Mori Arinori (1847–1889), Sugi Kogi (1828–1917), and Sakatani Shiroshi (1822–1881).[73] He also recalls that thanks to Nishimura, he was able to speak with Tokyo imperial university professors in depth about Christianity.[74] As part of his efforts to spread Christianity, Kozaki consciously sought out leaders who embodied Tokyo's status as the modern intellectual and political center of the nation. It was through interactions such as these in his early years in Tokyo that he became convinced that the city truly was not only "the seat of the Imperial Residence and Imperial Government" but also "the center of culture and progressiveness of our land."[75]

Even if they did not make their way to Tokyo as soon after graduation as Uemura and their classmate Kozaki, pastors Ebina and Yokoi also eventually came to the capital. Each would arrive carrying his own idea of Tokyo's significance, and these visions together would greatly shape Hongō Church, the congregation these two founded and led. Ebina was the first to arrive. After serving as pastor of Annaka Church for some six years and Maebashi Church for two, Ebina had just built a house and was putting down roots in Gunma Prefecture.[76] Yet he reluctantly decided to leave.[77] He recalled that many Christians surrounding him strongly encouraged him to make that decision, and he also felt an important calling to go to Tokyo in 1886.[78] By that time, there were not one but two Congregationalist churches in Tokyo, and they were located near one another in the same ward. In choosing where to begin his ministry in Tokyo, Ebina selected the Hongō Ward. This area was several neighborhoods away from the other two churches of his denomination already established in the capital and was filled "with many students."[79] Within a year, Ebina was leading a congregation of approximately thirty members in Hongō's Yushima neighborhood.[80] The following year Ebina left the congregation and Tokyo for family reasons and his brother-in-law, fellow Kumamoto Yōgakkō and Dōshisha alumnus Yokoi Tokio, came to lead the young church in Tokyo.[81] Hoping to help Yokoi, whose wife had just died suddenly and whose mother had soon after suffered a stroke, Ebina volunteered to change places with him. He went down to Kumamoto to found schools and continue his ministry.[82] Nevertheless, in coming to Tokyo and acting on his attraction to the student-filled Hongō Ward, Ebina was fundamental in shaping the character of the church—a character he would continue to shape after returning to the church as its pastor again a decade later.

Despite the difficult circumstances that brought Yokoi and his family to Tokyo, he quickly made clear his conceptualization of the capital. He highlighted in particular the opportunities it could afford Christianity to cultivate not only Christian belief but also moral fortitude and social awareness among the Japanese. Perhaps no Japanese Protestant pastor expressed his positive views on Tokyo in more frank terms than Yokoi. As the oldest son of renowned Neo-Confucian scholar and reformer Yokoi Shōnan (1809–1869), he was born into a family directly connected to the most influential political ideologies shaping the late Tokugawa and early Meiji eras.[83] Right after graduation from the Kumamoto Yōgakkō, where he, Ebina, and Kozaki famously converted to Christianity, Yokoi went to Tokyo and enrolled in the Kaisei Gakkō, the forerunner of Tokyo Imperial University.[84] There he spent a year studying in the excitement of the capital before joining his Kumamoto classmates at Dōshisha in Kyoto in 1877. He became the founding pastor of Imabari Church, in Ehime Prefecture, a predominantly rural area on the island of Shikoku, and by the time of his departure for Kumamoto led a congregation of 370 members. Missionary educator

William E. Griffis (1843–1928) asserted that the church was at the time the largest Protestant church in Japan.[85]

As he left for Tokyo, Yokoi left this promising mission field and subsequently the opportunity to evangelize in his hometown. Within a year, however, he had visibly embraced the capital city's possibilities. Yokoi wrote his missionary mentors a letter attempting to enlighten them about Tokyo: he left for the capital, he stated simply, because he "felt and the church [at Imabari] felt that there was a very loud call from Tokyo."[86] While the city, with its growing Christian community, needed more pastors, Yokoi justified his move in terms of the capital's potential. He reminded his Dōshisha professors that the "national parliament [would] be opened" soon in 1890, accompanied by a well-attended "Asiatic Exhibition" that he believed would draw people from all over Asia.[87] In a tone that bordered on admonishment, the Japanese pastor argued that while it was indeed "wise for [the Congregationalist mission in Japan] to have confined their entire efforts in regions about Kioto, Osaka and Kobe," the time had come for Tokyo.[88] From Yokoi's perspective, as home to "three law schools . . . two or three medical schools, five or six English Schools," Tokyo First "Higher and Middle schools," and other institutions, Tokyo was not only the political but also the educational center of the nation.[89]

This was a perspective shared by more and more of the leaders and proponents of religions in Japan. Uemura continued to expand his congregation in the midst of many of the same institutions mentioned by Yokoi. The work of missionaries like Canadian Methodist Charles Eby (1845–1925) and Russian Orthodox priest St. Nicholas of Japan (1836–1912) during the 1880s focused increasingly on the city and its intellectual center in Hongō Ward.[90] Meanwhile, lay reformer Inoue Enryō (1858–1919) also established a new foothold for Buddhism in Tokyo. Although organized Buddhist evangelism in the capital began in earnest in the late 1890s, the Imperial University professor and former priest made inroads for the religion earlier among the elite students of the capital. Through the Tetsugakkan, a center he established to explore the links between Buddhism and modern philosophy in 1887, and his publication *Nihonjin,* he became a popular leader in the Meiji Buddhist Enlightenment.[91] Similarly, in the years since its start in 1885, the Tokyo ministry of Uehara Sasuke had blossomed to include several other evangelists and thousands of Tenrikyō adherents. By 1896, the mission claimed some thirty-nine churches in the capital.[92] Shintoists too showed a renewed interest in Tokyo, particularly after Shinto priests lost their roles as doctrinal instructors for the Great Teaching Campaign and conductors of funerary rites and civic shrines lost state financial support in 1882.[93] Prince Arisugawa no miya Takahito (1813–1886), former director of the

Bureau of Shinto Affairs, as well as priests tied to that office, along with scholars and others, established the Kōten Kōkyūsho in 1882.[94] This center for the education of shrine priests would soon attract the sponsorship and leadership of leading Meiji statesmen like Yamada Akiyoshi (1844–1892), Hijikata Hisamoto (1833–1918), Sasaki Takayuki (1830–1910), and Takasaki Masakaze (1836–1912). Then, in 1890, as a destination for graduates of this dormitory and school in Iidabashi, Kokugakuin was established as a center for research and education focused on the history, literature, and law of Japan with a particular emphasis on Shinto thought.[95]

While religion as a whole seemed to have finally awakened to the capital by 1890, the decade that followed revealed the fragility of the roots planted by Japanese religious movements in Tokyo. In the case of Protestantism, several events tested the primacy afforded to the city. Uemura's Ichibanchō church, the predecessor of Fujimichō Church, thrived, and the Unitarian mission led by Clay MacCauley (1843–1925) grew, erecting Unity Hall as its new headquarters and meeting space in 1894. However, the congregations of their most successful Congregationalist colleagues were suddenly struggling in the mid-1890s.[96] First Kozaki stepped down from his pastor and associate pastor positions at Reinanzaka and its branch congregation Banchō Church, respectively, in 1890. That year he returned to Dōshisha to serve as its second president. His departure was followed by that of the dynamic pastor Yokoi, who left Hongō Church to study at Yale University in 1894 and later became an educator and journalist.[97] Soon after his departure, his church had all but dissolved, with one group of members joining other churches, and another group choosing not to join any church at all.[98] In the same year, pastor Tsunajima Kakichi (1860–1935) ended a brief stay as pastor of Reinanzaka Church to go study at Yale as well.[99] Destabilizing Christian leadership in Tokyo even further at that time was pastor Kanamori Michitomo, a former pastor at Banchō church, who wrote critically about Christianity before publicly renouncing his faith in 1898.[100]

These events that seemed to weaken the very foundations of Protestant Christianity in Tokyo echoed difficulties faced by other religious movements in the capital. Tenrikyō, then recognized as a "first-class" church within the Shinto Honkyoku Sect, began to suffer from its high profile in the 1890s.[101] The Home Ministry's Shrine and Temple Bureau issued Secret Directive 12 in April 1896 to impair the growth of this religious movement by dramatically increasing its surveillance of the group.[102] Making matters worse was the removal by Tenrikyō headquarters of one of Tokyo's leading head ministers, Ueda Zenbei. A power struggle had erupted in 1895 between the spiritual leader *(honseki)* of Tenrikyō Iburi Izō (1833–1907) and a rival claimant for his position, Iida Iwajirō (b. 1858), and Ueda sided with Iida. Of particular importance, however, was Ueda's decision to follow Iida's instructions and replace the sacred Shinto mirrors with paper swords as main objects of worship, potentially inviting persecution from the state.[103] Meanwhile, the relationship between Tokyo and Shinto also suffered in the 1890s as the initiatives in education and spiritual guidance that had given birth to the Kōten Kōkyūsho and Kokugakuin lost momentum. Despite the establishment of a network of branch offices throughout the country, headed by the Tokyo institute, and efforts to elevate the standards and prestige of the new Kokugakuin, the other competing center of Shinto in Japan prevailed. Ise Shrine's Jingū Kōgakkan, established in 1882, maintained its independence from the Kōten Kōkyūsho and quickly came to overshadow that school. The Kōgakkan managed to secure substantial donations and the support of the Home Ministry and the Imperial Household Ministry, whereas until the government reinstated funding for shrines in 1906, Kokugakuin struggled to survive.[104]

Despite such difficulties, a burst of dynamism in Tokyo during the last years of the nineteenth century occurred among the Japanese religious movements most focused on addressing and engaging with modernity. The maintenance of Kyoto as the base for Shin Buddhism did not preclude the continued development of Buddhism in the capital. Building on the momentum created largely by scholar-clerics like Inoue Enryō and fellow Imperial University professor Murakami Senshō (1851–1929), priests and other advocates finally made a concerted effort to target the capital in the 1890s. Instrumental in this process was Furukawa Rōsen (1871–1899), a young priest trained in Buddhist as well as Westernized forms of knowledge at the Nishi Honganji sect's recently opened normal school, the Futsū Kyōkō, in Kyoto.[105] In Tokyo, he launched lay organizations such as the Buddhist Youth Association (1899), Tokyo Buddhist Youth Society (1892), and the Warp and Woof Society (1894) in an effort to promote a new, revived, modern form of Buddhism. Members of his groups such as fellow Shin priest Sakaino Kōyō (1871–1933) would go on, after Furukawa's untimely death in 1899, to form the Buddhist Pure Believers Fellowship that year (renamed New Buddhist Fellowship in 1903) and its influential journal *New Buddhism* a year later. Through these media, Buddhist laymen and clerics developed and propagated a Buddhism of belief, rationality, and dynamism that distinguished it from the traditional Buddhism of the past.[106]

The other major strand in the movement to revitalize Japanese Buddhism in Tokyo was led by True Pure Land priest Kiyozawa Manshi. After studying with Inoue at the imperial university on a scholarship from Higashi Honganji headquarters and actively participating in the Tetsugakkan, Kiyozawa became an outspoken critic of institutional Buddhism. Like Furukawa and Sakaino, the priest emphasized faith as the fundamental element in the way that Buddhists saw and interacted with society. His *seishinshugi*, or spiritual activism, differed from and competed with the ideas and beliefs of the New Buddhist Fellowship, but they shared a strong desire to make Buddhism capable of responding to the promise and perils of modernization.[107] And like its rival, Kiyozawa's group focused its attention on the capital, especially the area near the imperial university where he established the Kōkōdō, a communal residence and school for his followers.[108] The site, owned by Shin priest Chikazumi Jōkan, would continue to host efforts to use strategies borrowed from Protestant Christianity to make Buddhism more modern, socially relevant, and popular in the capital.[109]

Greatly inspired by Protestantism in the West, Kiyozawa and Chikazumi confronted and competed with a revived Japanese Protestant Christianity in Tokyo at the turn of the twentieth century. After a brief but devastating downturn, the capital again became a priority of Japanese Protestant pastors in the closing years of the nineteenth century. In 1896, Tsunajima Kakichi had returned to Tokyo from New Haven to become pastor of Banchō Church.[110] And the following year Kozaki, who had stepped away but not resigned from his pastoral duties, returned to act as pastor of Reinanzaka Church in 1897. He was joined in Tokyo that year by Ebina, who finally returned to the Hongō Church he had founded, citing the importance of the capital for Protestantism and for the future of Japan. Since first undertaking summer evangelism in Annaka on the advice of Niijima, Ebina had been influenced greatly by others and by what they believed was necessary or preferable.[111] This applied to his appointments as head of the Japan Evangelical Alliance, as an educator and institution-builder in Kumamoto, and as pastor of Kobe Church; the latter required him to forgo a long-awaited trip to the United States and Europe.[112]

In making the decision to leave Kobe Church and go to Tokyo, however, Iwai Fumio explains that Ebina "compellingly expressed his own free will."[113] He made this clear in his letter of resignation to the Kobe Church congregation in May 1897. His attachment to the church members and their faithfulness and hard work made leaving difficult. In a sense, he did not welcome the prospect of going to Tokyo, a "desolate wasteland" compared to the warm, sizable Christian community in Kobe.[114] But Ebina would nevertheless take "the road to Tokyo without anxiety about the future and with resolve." In doing so he hoped to truly "open up a new direction for evangelism in Tokyo."[115] It troubled Ebina that after such auspicious beginnings, Protestant Christianity in the city with the most economic, cultural, and political wealth in Japan had gone into decline. In writing about his decision to go to Tokyo, he noted his intention to join forces with Yokohama Band member Oshikawa Masayoshi (1852–1928) and Christian educator Iwamoto Yoshiharu (Zenji 1863–1943) to implement a "restoration plan" for Tokyo.[116] On returning to Tokyo in 1897, Ebina picked up where he and Yokoi had left off and began reestablishing the congregation in Hongō. In very little time, Ebina succeeded in transforming the moribund church into a leading religious institution in the capital, where he remained as pastor until his acceptance of the presidency of Dōshisha in 1920.

Although each of these pastors took a different path to Tokyo, their reasons for founding and leading churches in the young capital were similar and related. As Tokyo assumed its new identity as the nation's political, economic, intellectual, and cultural capital, they sought to make the city a spiritual capital as well. Uemura, Kozaki, Yokoi, and Ebina established churches through which they implemented their respective ideas of Tokyo as the focal point for Protestantism in Japan. To that end, these enterprising Japanese pastors built their new religious gathering spaces near the institutions of the intellectual and political elite most engaged in conceptualizing and implementing the projects of modernity in Japan.

Locating Japanese Protestant Churches in the Capital

In terms of their geographical location, the capital's largest Protestant churches embodied a common trend. The oldest of these congregations, Fujimichō Church and Reinanzaka Church, which trace their histories back to the late 1870s, moved progressively toward the heart of the city. On the other hand, the various sites that the pastors of Banchō Church (est. 1885) and Hongō Church (est. 1886) chose changed very little. In the end, however, all four churches eventually settled and gained prominence in strategic, central locations that reflected their pastors' priorities and ambitions in the capital. Convinced that the location of their religious space could impact the interactions of its neighboring residents and attendees and in turn affect the fate of the nation, Protestant pastors prioritized spatial considerations as they conceived and built churches in areas densely populated by the country's new educated elite.

The approach of Japanese Protestant pastors to urban space contravened the long-standing norms of Japan's traditional religions. For over two centuries, the prevailing set of spatial priorities for religious sites in Edo aimed to give Buddhist temples and Shinto shrines an "aura of the nonquotidian, the sacred, and the ceremonial."[117] To accomplish this, the founders established such sites separate from the rest of the city.[118] In Edo's crowded, busy Shitamachi (Low City), all of the major temples were built on sites that projected out into a river, pond, or sea inlet.[119] In the green, spacious Yamanote (High City), where the warrior nobility and their families resided, temples and shrines were built on wooded hills situated well above the commotion of the city.[120] In both settings, the visitor was (and is still) typically drawn up a narrow path or staircase across a threshold separating profane and sacred space and into the "interiority" *(oku)* offered by the religious site.[121] This type of arrangement is still visible at sites like Kentaisan Hojo-in and Tomioka Hachiman Shrine in the Fukagawa area, or on the hills in Shiba and Ichigaya where Zōjōji and Kameoka Hachiman Shrine, respectively, are located. In the first half of the Meiji period, however, a small number of dynamic Japanese religious leaders and laymen showcased a different set of spatial priorities as they founded new religious gathering spaces in the capital.

Like Tenrikyō ministers in Tokyo and General Ōmura Masajirō (1824–1869), Japanese Protestant pastors utilized urban space with the explicit intention of drawing a crowd. Tenrikyō evangelist Uehara Sasuke founded his first congregations in the midst of the Yoshiwara, not on its edges, where Buddhist temples stood. And as the religion grew in Tokyo, ministers like Ueda Zenbei targeted areas where the political and intellectual elite congregated. Similarly, General Ōmura Masajirō (1824–1869) commissioned the Tokyo shrine for the war dead *(shōkon-sha)* in 1869 on the hill Kudan-zaka in northern Kōjimachi Ward, because it was an ideal site for all classes to come together for shrine worship, in a sense rejecting the seclusion and interiority that characterized Edo's major religious spaces.[122] Soon after, the addition of a straight, broad causeway leading to the shrine's main gate only accentuated this openness.[123] Ōmura also felt that this shrine on Kudan-zaka would represent the new "spirit of the land," in part because it was so centrally situated, at the intersection of the lower-class Shitamachi and the upper-class Yamanote.[124] Ōmura's project was singular, with no parallels among traditional Japanese religious spaces in Tokyo, but his thinking did parallel that of Japanese Protestant pastors.

The founding leaders of Tokyo's largest Protestant congregations were also convinced that a religious space's location could be conducive to attracting nearby residents, facilitating the interactions of visitors, and assuring their message a prominent place in the broader national consciousness. Accordingly, they constructed churches amid the highest concentrations of Japanese members of the educated elite in the capital. In particular, Tokyo's newest Protestant churches targeted the students, graduates, and educators of the country's top public and private universities and higher schools, bureaucrats in national ministries and city government, elected politicians, and leaders in industry, nationwide mass media, and other distinctly modern categories. The capital, whose lack of zoning and land use regulations is treated in more depth in the next chapter, provided Japanese pastors with the freedom to place their churches as they saw fit.[125] And they did. By the end of the nineteenth century, Tokyo's most popular churches would all be purposefully located in the midst of the upper-class Yamanote neighborhoods that provided them with access to many of the strongest minds and pocketbooks in Japan.

Within the Yamanote, Kōjimachi Ward became the nerve center of the capital, and consequently the nation, from the early 1880s. This zone was therefore particularly attractive for the pastors who founded Tokyo's largest Protestant churches. The earliest two were Uemura Masahisa and Kozaki Hiromichi, who, after beginning their ministries in the Shitamachi, soon established their ministries in that ward. In both cases, their original church locations in the lower city had offered significant advantages as well, but Uemura and Kozaki both recognized the potential of Kōjimachi.

In 1877, Uemura chose to begin his Tokyo ministry in Shitaya Ward's Neribeichō neighborhood (plate 1). This zone above the Kanda River was adjacent to the up-and-coming intellectual center of the new capital.[126] Tokyo was still very much a provincial capital, dominated by commoner culture and lacking modern political and cultural centers.[127] Nevertheless, the Imperial University was rapidly coming to define the culture of Hongō Ward, as well as the nearby Kanda and Shitaya Wards. There, in the shadow of the Imperial University, new educational institutions abounded, from a private medical school—the Kōju-in of Takashina Tsunenori (1834–1889)—in Neribeichō[128] to Tokyo Higher Normal School (1873) and Tokyo Women's Higher Normal School (1875) in Ochanomizu.[129] Situated at the edge of the more densely populated Shitamachi, these wards also offered students affordable housing options. Shitaya was therefore a dynamic, youthful ward. As pastor Saba Wataru (1881–1958), Uemura's former theology student and son-in-law, explained, "Students lived in his vicinity, there were also private schools, [and] there were of course many houseboys."[130] In this area, Uemura's church was relatively successful, with a membership of seventy-six in 1883.[131] Wanting to move on and feeling that the church was on solid footing, however, Uemura tendered his resignation early that year and turned his attention to evangelizing and other projects in Tokyo. Among them was his contribution to the translation of the Old Testament that James Hepburn and Guido Verbeck supervised in 1884.[132]

In 1885, an invitation by American dentist Vernon Eastlake and his Japanese Christian wife to come lead Bible study at his home in Kōjimachi exposed Uemura to the possibilities of that area.[133] With the rapid growth of this study to over one hundred men and women, Uemura soon chose to concentrate his evangelization efforts there in the Banchō neighborhood (plate 2), some four miles from Neribeichō. From the late 1880s, Kōjimachi was also becoming home to many Westerners who worked as foreign experts for the government and as diplomats in the ward's many embassies and consulates, but also as professors, journalists, and even dentists. And, of course, many of them were fervent Protestant Christians like Eastlake. As the request of the American dentist makes clear, however, the presence of American and Canadian Christians in the northern part of the ward had not led to large, successful churches. By 1887, Uemura had moved his household to the ward. He then founded Ichibanchō Church, the predecessor of Fujimichō Church, in the Ichibanchō neighborhood.[134]

In choosing to stay and found a church in Banchō, Uemura made a crucial decision that defined the type of urban space in which his new congregation would develop. This upland district just outside the castle walls had housed the Tokugawa shogunate's direct vassals *(hatamoto)*.[135] The relatively large residences, the topography, the view of Mount Fuji, and the centrality that made this area a prime location in the Edo period persisted into the Meiji period. High officials, aristocrats, and business leaders replaced the *hatamoto*, leasing and then purchasing the mansions from the new government in the 1870s.[136] By the time Uemura established Ichibanchō Church, the neighborhood boasted a high concentration of figures who possessed substantial political, financial, and social capital. The official residence of the Imperial Household Minister Hijikata Hisamoto (1833–1918) stood across the street from the church.[137] Imperial Councilor and physician to the Meiji emperor Iwasa Jun (1835–1912) also lived very nearby in Ichibanchō.[138] The official residence of the minister of agriculture and commerce, an office occupied by famous statesmen like future prime ministers Kuroda Kiyotaka (1840–1900) and Ōkuma Shigenobu (1838–1922) in the late 1880s and 1890s, was located a block from the church in Fujimichō Itchome.[139] Leaders of major companies like Mitsui Takayasu (1850–1922), the president of Mitsui Bank, who lived only four blocks from Ichibanchō Church, also called the neighborhood home.[140]

In addition to the wealthy and powerful, Banchō was home to another important demographic to which Uemura attached particular importance. Uemura set down roots for his new church in close proximity to students at prominent educational institutions. Students, whom Uemura viewed as progressive and open-minded, flocked in large numbers to Banchō, where schools were a central identifying element. In Ichibanchō, for instance, well-known literary figure Mishima Chūshū (1831–1919) founded the Nishogakusha Kangaku Juku, a school for Chinese and Confucian studies that managed to thrive amid the more modern Western schools opening in the capital in the Meiji period.[141] Forces promoting the Christian education of Japanese women were also especially strong in Banchō, and this greatly influenced the neighborhood and Ichibanchō church. Located nearby in Naka-rokubanchō was Sakurai Girls' School, also known as Banchō Girls' School.[142] Later, Tsuda Women's English School—founded by the youngest member of the Iwakura Mission (1871–1873) to the US, Tsuda Umeko (1864–1929), after her return from over a decade there—was located two blocks away in Gobanchō.

Clearly, however, the establishment of one particular school in the neighborhood weighed positively in Uemura's decision to establish a permanent church in Banchō.[143] Meiji Girls' School opened in 1885 through the work of Kimura Kumaji (1845–1927) and his wife Toko (1848–1886).[144] Both had close ties to Uemura and to the church he had led previously in Neribeichō: Kimura had replaced Uemura as pastor of Shitaya Church, and his wife had founded the women's group of that church before assuming responsibility for the daily management of Meiji Girls' School.[145] Also affiliated with Uemura's former church was Christian educator Iwamoto Yoshiharu (1863–1942), a teacher and, from 1887, vice principal at Meiji Girls' School who had been baptized by Kimura there in 1884.[146] Iwamoto then became one of the ten founding members of Uemura's new Ichibanchō Church.[147] The proximity of such schools and the lines connecting the faculty at these schools contributed to the rapid growth of Ichibanchō Church to 145 members by March 1887.[148]

When the congregation had outgrown the Ichibanchō Church building and decided with Uemura to build a new church, they chose to maintain the benefits of this location. In 1898, the Ichibanchō Church congregation began planning to erect a new, larger church building in the adjacent Fujimichō neighborhood (plate 3).[149] Situated to the north of Ichibanchō, the new site in Fujimichō rokuchōme shared with the old site the access to students that Uemura had prioritized since beginning his ministry. While remaining relatively close to the schools in Banchō, only a few blocks away, locating the congregation in Fujimichō placed the church closer to a new set of educational institutions as well. They included First Middle School, a school for the brightest male students, and the Imperial Army Tokyo Arsenal, where young cadets studied and drilled throughout the Meiji period, as well as Hōsei University, Tokyo University of Science, Senshū University, Nihon Law University, the military medical college, Kokugakuin University, and the Japanese Red Cross. Beyond these institutions, however, the northern area of Kōjimachi Ward was attractive because it was a focal point in the capital, situated on the edge of the Musashino Plateau, above the Shitamachi areas just across the imperial palace. It was, after all, this location that motivated the founder of the neighborhood's most famous landmark, Yasukuni Shrine, to establish the religious site there. In its locations in both Ichibanchō and Fujimichō, Uemura Masahisa's church was always within two large blocks of Yasukuni Shrine, indicating that he and his congregation valued that particular section of Kōjimachi. The proximity also hints at the fact that Christianity had successfully made its way into the cultural and spatial core of the capital.

Traditional Japanese religious institutions did respond to the inroads made by Christianity in the capital. During the 1870s, Shinto priests and lay adherents occasionally demonstrated their displeasure. In one instance in 1878, as the tutelary *kami* being carried in a procession from Yotsuya Shrine neared a Christian church, the *kami* just happened to become so active that its portable shrine rammed into the building.[150] For the most part, however, the reaction by Shinto priests and Shintoist scholars to Christianity's encroachment was an ideological one. In the same year that Ōmura's Tokyo Shōkonsha was built, the Ministry of Doctrine (Kyōbushō) launched a religious offensive aimed at revitalizing the nation's native religion and bolstering it against the perceived foreign threat of Christianity.[151] Through the Great Teaching Campaign, the Meiji government sought to elevate Shinto above the realm of contestable religion and enhance the legitimacy of the emperor and his government.[152]

Buddhist institutions mounted a primarily ideological opposition to the spread of Christianity in the capital. Reeling from the negative impacts that the official promotion of Shinto wrought for their religion, Buddhists and Buddhist institutions were preoccupied with finding a secure place among Japan's traditional religions.[153] First the official separation of Buddhism from Shinto (Shinbutsu Bunri) mandated by the new Meiji government in 1868 left Buddhism economically and politically bereft, and then it was subjected to attacks carried out under the Haibutsu Kishaku (Abolish Buddhism and Destroy Buddha) movement.[154] Nevertheless, several Buddhist leaders saw the growth of Christianity as a dangerous threat to their religion's survival. The Yaso Taiji (Extermination of Christianity) movement that gained steam and prospered between 1883 and 1885 throughout the country was a direct reaction to Christianity's development in Meiji Japan outside the country's treaty ports.[155] Ideological in nature, the movement consisted of Buddhist opponents of Christianity giving lectures, forming societies, and inciting protests against the religion. The movement lost momentum, however, as the national government increasingly emphasized Westernization and after Buddhist priests lost their roles as "official" priests for state rites in 1884.[156]

Despite the relatively minor nature of the resistance posed by traditional Japanese religion, Kozaki Hiromichi began his ministry in the capital's safest zone for Christianity. Arriving in 1879, two years after Uemura, Kozaki first evangelized in an area of Tokyo very familiar with and relatively friendly to

Protestant Christianity.[157] He and fellow Dōshisha graduate Okada rented a classroom in Tsuda Sen's Gakunōsha for services and prayer meetings in Kyōbashi Ward (plate 4). The school, run by well-known Christian agricultural educator Tsuda Sen (1837–1908),[158] was in the Shinsakanachō neighborhood of the Ginza district—the district where the city government had built a modern, "prefabricated Western urban space."[159] This area, meant to prominently display Japanese modernization with its brick buildings, sidewalks, and gaslights, was especially popular with Westerners and pro-Western Japanese, making it a natural haven for Christianity.[160] Tokyo Union Seminary graduate Tamura Naoomi also lived and preached in Shinsakanachō. That same year, Tamura had moved his Ginza Church to that neighborhood and renamed it Kyōbashi Church.[161] Adding to the palpable, welcoming presence of Christianity in Shinsakanachō and greater Kyōbashi Ward were strong links with Christian people and institutions in Tsukiji. A dozen short blocks away stood the former foreign settlement at Tsukiji, an area that boasted an even higher concentration of Christian institutions, including Shinsakaechō Church, Tsukiji Methodist Church, and missionary schools such as Tsukiji College and Kaigan Girls' School.[162] The first three locations for the new Shinsakanachō Church that Kozaki founded were near Ginza and within Tsukiji's sphere of influence. After giving up the space at the Gakunōsha, the church held services nearby in Minami Kajimachi and then in Ginza's Sukiyabashi neighborhood.[163]

Although this zone's relative openness to Westerners and Christianity offered advantages that led many churches and pastors to remain there, Kozaki's nascent congregation soon moved on. As had been the case for Uemura in student-filled Neribeichō, Kozaki moved away from promising sites in the Shitamachi, and increasingly shifted his focus toward the Yamanote in general and Kōjimachi Ward in particular. Between 1882 and 1886, Kozaki's church located itself much nearer to the center of national government in the capital. In 1882, the still-small congregation moved to a residence in the Shinsakurada-chō neighborhood in Shiba Ward (plate 5).[164] Although this new location was only a dozen long blocks away from the original site, it marked the beginning of the church's progressive shift away from Tsukiji and toward the political heart of the capital. Shinsakurada-chō lay adjacent to the government offices and embassies outside the Sakurada gate of the imperial palace. Within the year, the Shinsakurada Church moved yet again, to Nakano-chō in Azabu, where it merged with the Nippon Church. Imperial Naval Academy teacher and Christian Awatzu Takaaki (1838–1880) established this very small, independent Japanese church on his home's property in 1876.[165] Although it had persisted, the church's future had become increasingly uncertain since his untimely death in 1880.[166] The 1882 merger gave birth to Tokyo Dai-Ichi (First) Church, a growing congregation under Kozaki's leadership. Like his friend and colleague Uemura, who quickly came to appreciate the advantages of Banchō, Kozaki clearly valued the possibilities of this corner of the capital. They remained in Nakano-chō for three years, the longest period of stability up to that point. And when a larger building was required, the congregation moved a final time to a new permanent location that was located even closer to the seats of power in the capital.

In April 1886, the Tokyo Dai-Ichi Church moved to its current location on Reinanzaka, a hill in the Akasaka district of Kōjimachi, and changed its name to Reinanzaka Church (plate 6).[167] Reinanzaka represented an ideal location for the growing church because it was even closer to members of the nation's economic and political elite than the Nakanochō site had been. Kozaki recalled that during the late 1880s, when Baron Katō Tomofusaburō (1861–1923) was vice minister of the Imperial Navy, he lived directly opposite the new Reinanzaka Church.[168] This was far from an isolated instance, and the church was in fact surrounded by illustrious neighbors. Baron Ikeda Kensai (1841–1918), imperial physician and founding chair of Tokyo Imperial University's medical department, and Tanaka Fujimarō (1845–1909), who served as vice minister of education and as a Ministry of Justice official, lived one block northwest (plate 6).[169] Members of the imperial family even graced this area with their presence when they visited the imperial villa across the street from these residences. To the southeast lay the residence of Ōki Takatō (1832–1899), chairman of the *genrōin,* the imperially appointed national assembly that preceded the Imperial Diet.[170] Business leaders such as Ōkura Kihachirō (1837–1928), head of the Ōkura armaments and trade zaibatsu and a nearby commercial school, also resided near the church.[171] A block to the north stood the personal residence of the same Marquis Kuroda Kiyotaka who, during his short tenure as minister of agriculture and commerce, had resided in Banchō.[172] High-profile residents made Reinanzaka a prime location for a pastor aspiring to influence the nation's top figures.

Reinanzaka was also optimal because it offered access to the government offices with which these figures were associated in the diplomatic and political nerve center of Japan. The adjacent Nagatachō neighborhood was the location of the Education, Justice, Military, Foreign, and Home Ministries. Two years later, Nagatachō would also be home to one of the most influential institutions in Japan, the Privy Council, a secretive, imperially appointed board that provided counsel to the emperor on state affairs.[173] Of the utmost significance in 1886, however, was the well-known fact that construction on the new Imperial Diet would begin there in Nagatachō in the next couple of years—a project that came to completion in 1890. That same year the US Embassy would move from Tsukiji to a plot right across the street from the church. The new Reinanzaka Church, then, was well situated near the nation's key political organs and the neighborhoods where their high-ranking officials resided.

In 1886, as the Tokyo Daiichi Church settled on Reinanzaka, a small group of the growing church's members suggested that the congregation support a satellite church closer to their particular homes and offices.[174] Among them was Supreme Court judge and future attorney general Miyoshi Taizō (1845–1908), who lived in Banchō.[175] Also playing a central role in this enterprise was young Tokyo Imperial University law professor Wadagaki Kenzō (1860–1919). At the time, he was also acting as commissioner for the Ministry of Education and incidentally lived in nearby Nagatachō.[176] They were joined by others with close ties to ministries and other government institutions in the heart of Kōjimachi. These included Okabe Nagamoto (1855–1925), who began work at the British embassy in Japan not long after helping establish the church.[177] With the vocal support of Pastor Kozaki, in 1886 these men formed the Banchō Lecture Hall, the institution that would soon develop into Banchō Church, in the Naka-rokubanchō neighborhood (plate 2).

Given that it was located near the homes and workplaces of the new aristocracy, Banchō Church had much in common with the older Ichibanchō and Reinanzaka Churches in Kōjimachi. Unlike these churches that arrived at permanent locations after several long moves across the capital, however, Banchō began its existence in the neighborhood where it would remain. Located only a few blocks away from Uemura's Ichibanchō Church, Banchō Church had access to many of the same institutions that initially drew Ichibanchō pastor Uemura to the area. In particular, the church was not far from Meiji Girls' School and was even closer to Joshi Gakuin. Kozaki recalled that students from these schools "thronged to the church" and that there were never less than "four or five hundred people" gathered.[178] This estimate is in accord with attendance figures for Banchō at the time. As I will discuss in subsequent chapters, Banchō and Tokyo's other three largest Protestant congregations each regularly drew hundreds of men and women in the late nineteenth and early twentieth century.

Student attendees also largely fueled the growth of the youngest of Tokyo's most popular Japanese Protestant churches. This was the Hongō Church, founded and led by Ebina and Yokoi—a church that, like Banchō, never strayed more than a few blocks from its original location. In October 1886, Ebina began his ministry in a rented, poorly kept, leaky room in a former daimyo residence in Yushima Yonchōme within Hongō Ward (plate 7).[179] The church moved frequently in its first years, like Kozaki's early congregation. Leaving their first space that winter, the congregation relocated to a small, rented home in

Nishikatachō and then to a rented lecture hall in Kinsukechō the following spring. Between Yokoi's assumption of the pastorate in August 1887 and the congregation's move into a new facility in Hongō's Higashi Takecho in 1891,[180] the church also met in a Presbyterian church in Harukichō and then in a home in Morikawachō.[181] Yokoi resigned to pursue other, more academic opportunities in 1894. However, the church persisted in that location under his successor Ebina Danjō until 1898, when the Hongō Fire destroyed over a thousand buildings, including the church, and forced the congregation to move again.[182] The year before, Ebina had returned as pastor of Hongō Church and would remain there in that role for over two decades. During that time, the church would make Ikizaka in the Yumichō neighborhood its long-term home. After renting space for afternoon services in yet another church, the congregation finally settled into a new building of its own in Yumichō Itchōme in October 1901.[183] Despite all this movement, the Hongō Church had in fact remained relatively close to its spatial origins. This site was only a few small blocks from Yokoi's 1891 Higashi Takechō building, and the various temporary sites the church occupied all lay within a kilometer of that location.

The leaders and members of the Hongō Church decided again and again to gather in an area of the capital that held great strategic importance. This persistent insistence on the Hongō Ward reflected the priorities of both Ebina and Yokoi, who purposefully established and maintained this congregation within a very short walking distance from Tokyo Imperial University. This school, however, was not the only element that had attracted the pastors. In fact, the portion of Hongō Ward surrounding the Imperial University in the 1880s was filled with the individuals both Ebina and Yokoi hoped to attract as well as the places where those persons assembled. Located at approximately the same walking distance from the Hongō Church was the famous First Higher School for the nation's top high school boys. After the construction of the iconic Hongōkan in 1905, the church was also never far from this wooden boardinghouse in Morikawachō for Imperial University students.[184] In addition, a mere block away from the 1891 Hongō Church building lay the Saisei Gakusha. Founded by Hasegawa Yasushi (1842–1912) in 1876, this institution became one of imperial-era Tokyo's three leading private medical schools.[185] Nearby in Yushima Yonchōme were the Tokyo Higher Normal School and Tokyo Women's Higher Normal School. Ogino Ginko (1851–1913), the first Japanese woman to be licensed as a Western-style physician, was a teacher there in late 1886 when she became a member of Hongō Church.[186] Her fellow teacher, pioneering children's educator Furuichi Shizuko (1848–1933), began attending the church at that time as well.[187] In addition, just up the road from the 1891 Hongō building was Japan Women's School, forerunner of Sagami Women's University. So Hongō too, like Fujimichō and Banchō, benefited from its close proximity to women's schools.

As Ebina and Yokoi realized from the start, Hongō Ward was an ideal place from which to reach Japan's brightest young minds. In his essay "Hongō kaiwai" (The Hongō neighborhood), historical novelist Shiba Ryōtarō captures the vibrant dynamic that animated the area in the Meiji period. Along the way, he walks the reader past many well-known areas and buildings, including the homes of zoologist Edward S. Morse (1838–1925) and art scholar Ernest Fenellosa (1853–1908), two of the numerous foreign educators who lived and taught in Hongō.[188] This ward proved a crucial source of attendees for Hongō Church, from dedicated members to passersby, and soon Hongō became an integral part of the church's identity. It is easy to see why missionaries and Japanese religious leaders targeted Hongō with more frequency after 1886. Methodist missionary Charles Eby, who also sought to attract Japan's top intellectuals and their students, erected the ultimately less successful Central Tabernacle Church (Hongō Chūō Kaidō) in Hongō in 1890.[189]

By the turn of the nineteenth century, Japanese religious movements beyond Protestant Christianity had also come to more fully mobilize the space of the capital, including the intellectual hub in Hongō Ward. Building on the momentum of Buddhistic education in Tokyo, the True Pure Land sect entrusted priest Chikazumi Jōkan with a prime site in Morikawa-chō, the neighborhood directly across the street from the famous red gate of Tokyo Imperial University. Kiyozawa Manshi's Kōkōdō occupied part of the lot, but as his health declined precipitously around 1902, Chikazumi opened a Buddhist dormitory there. This Kyūdō Gakusha (Way-Seekers' School), a dormitory and teaching space, would serve as a primary locus of Buddhist education and proselytization in the capital. Based on the success of this initiative, Chikazumi commissioned a novel, adjacent Buddhist gathering space in 1915 as well.[190] The Kyūdō Kaikan (Way-Seekers' Hall) was so popular that it managed to compete with neighboring Protestant churches, a competition that the priest clearly embraced as he adopted Christian religious activities like the weekly Sunday sermon to enhance Buddhism's social relevance, appeal, and impact.

Shinto administrators and priests also renewed their efforts to mobilize space in the capital for the promotion of their ideology and ideals at the dawn of the twentieth century. After the creation of a Shrine Bureau as a separate entity distinct from the Bureau of Religion within the Home Ministry in 1900, shrine space in general and in the capital in particular became a central focus. This, the last of the five major administrative separations of religion from the Meiji state, created a government office explicitly devoted to the use of religious gathering spaces to foster national identity, nationalism, and both obedience and service to the state.[191] In Tokyo, the bureau concentrated special attention on Yasukuni Shrine. Already back in the early 1870s, the combination of official ceremonies for the war dead attended by government dignitaries and popular entertainment such as sumo, horse racing, and peep shows had emblazoned the Tokyo *shōkonsha* in the popular consciousness of the residents and tourists in the capital. Then the site gained imperial patronage and recognition as an "imperial shrine of special status" *(bekkaku kampeisha)* in 1879, receiving the new name "Yasukuni" from the Meiji emperor.[192] But it was only under the new Shrine Bureau's fresh emphasis on shrine space after 1900 that the shrine became a nationally sacred mnemonic site that would draw millions of visitors each year. Meanwhile, the Army and Navy Ministries controlled the shrine, and funding came from the Home Ministry.[193] Images of and references to that space literally permeated Japanese culture throughout the first half of the twentieth century, with particular force at times of military conflict. In 1905, during the Sino-Japanese War, the Japanese Navy *Seamen's Manual* included not only the assurance that if they died they would be enshrined at Yasukuni but also a drawing of a sailor at salute before the giant metal *torii* of the shrine.[194] Yasukuni represented an exception among Shinto religious gathering spaces because of its particular funding and administration and its position outside of, and above, the highest category of state-supported Shinto shrines.[195] Yet a great part of what made the shrine so special was its location in the capital—a site from which the imperial government increasingly broadcast Shinto nationalism, militarism, and national identity. Like the capital's most popular Protestant churches, some Shinto and Buddhist religious gathering spaces defied many of traditional Japanese religion's spatial priorities. Their founders and leaders purposefully located them near the people and institutions in Tokyo that were advantageous to the distinctly modern local and national ambitions they had for their religious movements.

The rise of Tokyo as the new national capital attracted many who sought to harness the city's energy and influence for their religious movements. Shinto advocates first sought to transform the capital into the ritualistic and administrative center of imperial Shinto. They then worked to make it the base for a nationwide campaign to promote Shinto and imperial loyalty and a national hub of Shinto-focused educational institutions. Buddhists mobilized the capital to procure the protection of Buddhists and their beliefs, assert the religion's deep compatibility with modernization and Westernization, and reform its spirituality, hierarchical institutions, social awareness, and appeal. Among Japanese New Religions, Tenrikyō made especially notable efforts to evangelize in Tokyo, then sought umbrage within Shinto by relocating its headquarters to the capital. It was in this context that Protestant Christian pastors too made their way to Tokyo, and they shared much with their fellow religious leaders. Like these other figures, Uemura Masahisa, Kozaki Hiromichi, Ebina Danjō, and Yokoi Tokio (figure 1.1) arrived in the city from local and national peripheries to which their religious movements remained firmly attached. In addition, they were all drawn to the city for its importance to their religious movement and its application to the issues facing Japan. For this reason, Protestant pastors, Buddhist scholars and priests, Shinto priests, administrators, and educators, and Tenrikyō ministers targeted zones in the capital where their evangelism would reach a specific target audience and also reverberate more broadly beyond Tokyo.

Figure 1.1. Japanese Protestant leaders at the Third All-Japan Christian Conference, augmented with ovals marking the faces of Kozaki Hiromichi, Uemura Masahisa, Yokoi Tokio, and Ebina Danjō, from left to right. Source: Suzuki Shinichi, "1883 nen 5 gatsu 12 nichi ni Tōkyō Kudanshita de satsuei sareta dai 3-kai zenkoku Kirisutokyō shinto dai shinbokukai no kanbu no shūgō shashin" [Photo of the 3rd national gathering of Christian leaders on 12 May 1883]. (Courtesy of Wikimedia Commons)

While religious leaders in these diverse movements all set their sights on Tokyo, their evangelism there encountered notably different fates. Two substantial obstacles impeded the efforts of both new and traditional Japanese religions to capitalize on the city. First, Shinto, Buddhism, and even the dynamic Tenrikyō movement suffered from powerful tensions between Tokyo and their headquarters in the Kansai. The victory of Ise over Tokyo in Shinto, the reassertion of Kyoto as the seat of Buddhism's most popular sects, and Tenrikyō's return to the sacred *jiba* near Nara had long-lasting impacts on evangelism in the capital. Second, the relationships between the capital and the headquarters of Shin Buddhism and the Shinto sects with the strongest ties to Tokyo, including Tenrikyō, were complicated by their subordination to and dependence on the state. The separation of the "transcendent and mundane" prescribed by Nishi Honganji's Abbot Konkyō (d. 1871) in his "Testament" was vastly influential in formulating a relatively apolitical Shin Buddhism.[196] But it also pointed to a broader "subjectification" of Japanese religion as a whole to the demands of the national government. This process only reinforced the spatial demotion of the national capital from a position of central importance for these movements and the promotion of headquarters in Kyoto, Nara, Ise, and elsewhere that were unmistakably separate and distant from the seat of the national government.

However, the relationship between Protestant Christianity and the capital was less encumbered by such factors than these competing movements. Japanese pastors proved capable of resolving the pull between root and branch. Purposefully moving away from the security and stability of missionary strongholds, they founded their congregations in the nation's center, declared Tokyo the capital of Protestantism in Japan, and put down roots in strategic, promising neighborhoods (plate 8). Through their work, Tokyo became host to the core rather than the margins of Protestant Christianity in Japan and to the churches that defined rather than defied the larger Japanese Protestant movement.

Table 1. Church Foundation Dates

Pastor	*Original Church Name*	*Final Church Name*	*Year*
Uemura Masahisa	Shitaya (Itchi) Church	Shitaya Church	1877
Kozaki Hiromichi	Shinsakanachō Church	Reinanzaka Church	1879
Kozaki Hiromichi	Banchō Church	Banchō Church	1886
Ebina Danjō	Hongō Church	Hongō Church	1886
Uemura Masahisa	Ichibanchō Church	Fujimichō Church	1887

This is one particularly significant way that leading Japanese Protestant churches in the capital differed from the few, anomalous, norm-defying Buddhist and Shinto institutions there that harbored similar ambitions and targeted the same neighborhoods. In founding their churches, these men also benefited from Christianity's particular relationship with Japan's government. Historically, diplomatically, and culturally, Protestant Christianity and its ties to the Meiji state were distinctly weaker than those of Shinto, Buddhism, or Japanese New Religions. Ultimately these same two factors—the relative autonomy of Tokyo's leading Protestant churches from missionary control and Christianity's position vis-à-vis the state—proved decisive for the built spaces of the capital's largest congregations as well.

Shitaya Key

1 Tokyo Higher Normal School

2 Kojū-in

3 Shitaya Church

4 Hongō Church, 1886

5 Hongō Church, 1891

Plate 1. Shitaya Ward. GIS-created map of Tokyo's Shitaya and eastern Hongō Ward, ca. 1880, with key landmarks and churches.

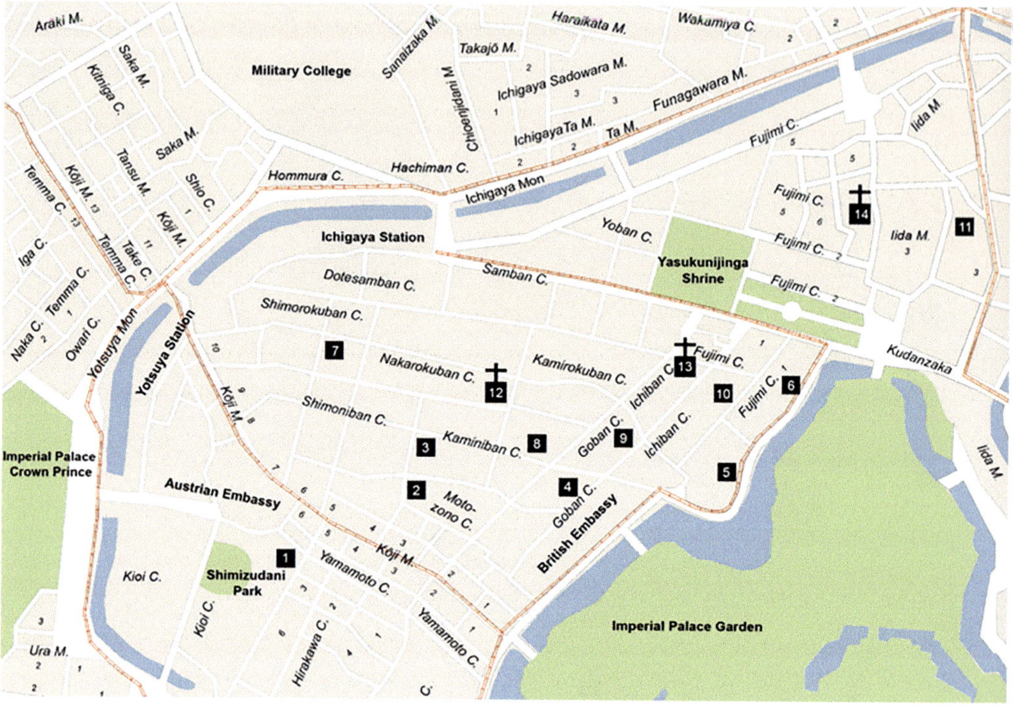

Banchō Key

1 Tokyo Pharmacy School	8 Mitsui Takayasu Residence
2 Jissen Girls' School and Polytechnic	9 Dr. Iwasa Jun Residence
3 Sakurai/Banchō Girls School and Joshi Gakuin	10 Nishōgakusha Kangaku Juku
4 Tsuda Women's English School	11 Meiji Girls' School, 1887
5 Imperial Household Min. Official Residence	12 Banchō Church
6 Min. of Agriculture and Commerce Official Residence	13 Ichibanchō Church
7 Meiji Girls' School, 1892	14 Fujimichō Church

Plate 2. Kōjimachi Ward. GIS-created map of Banchō neighborhood in Tokyo's Kōjimachi Ward, ca. 1880, with key landmarks and churches.

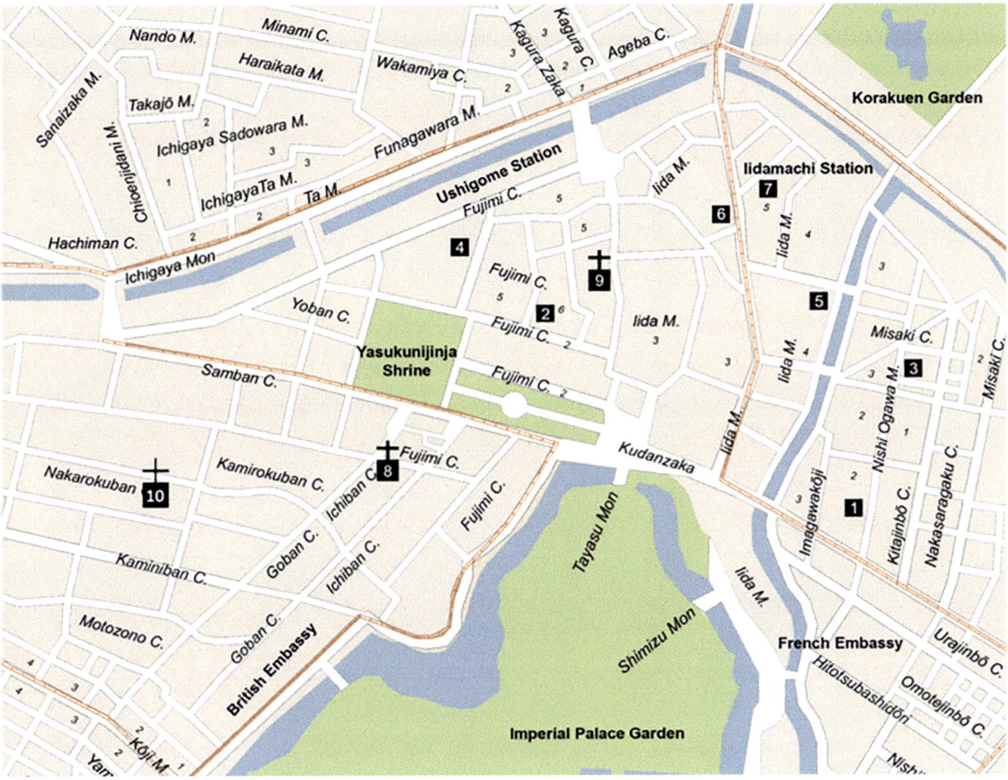

Fujimichō Key

1	Senshū University	6	Red Cross Japan
2	Hōsei University	7	Kokugakuin
3	Nihon Hōritsu University	8	Ichibanchō Church
4	Military Medical School	9	Fujimichō Church
5	Tokyo Rika University	10	Banchō Church

Plate 3. Kōjimachi Ward. GIS-created map of the Banchō and Fujimichō neighborhoods in Tokyo's Kōjimachi Ward, ca. 1880, with key landmarks and churches.

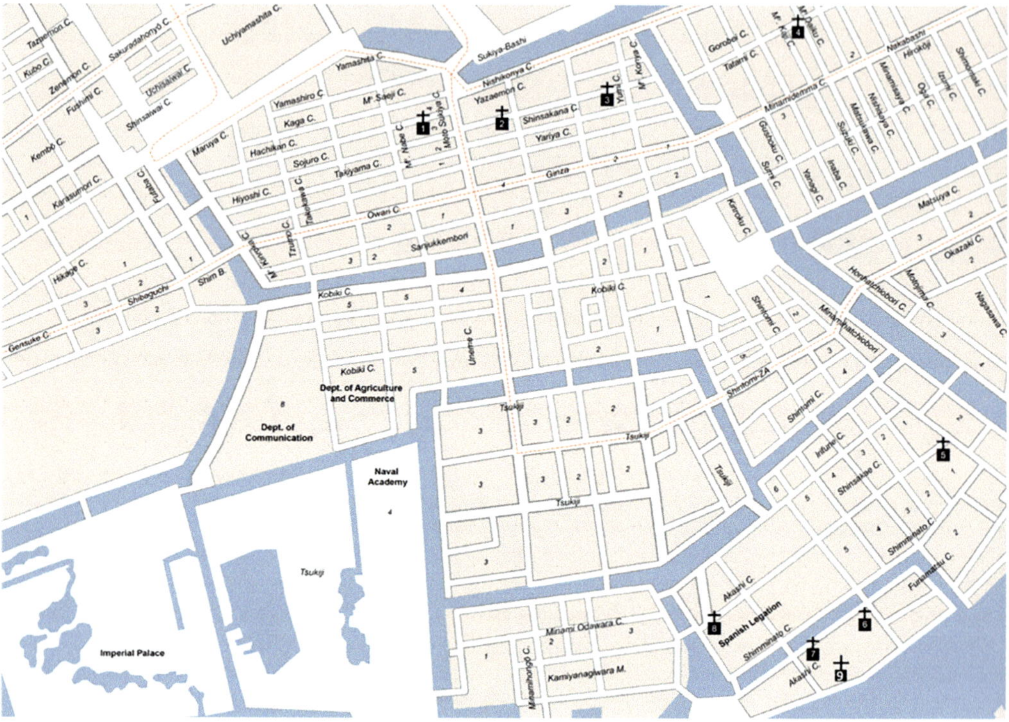

Kyōbashi Key

1. Sukiyabashi Church
2. Shinsakanōchō Church (in the Gakunōsha)
3. Kyōbashi Church
4. Minami-Kajichō Church
5. Shinsakaechō Church
6. Kaigan Jogakkō and Tsukiji Methodist Church
7. Tokyo Union Church and Tokyo Itchi Shingakkō
8. Rikkyō (St. Paul's Church) and Trinity Divinity School and Tsukiji Methodist Church
9. Tsukiji College

Plate 4. Kyōbashi Ward. GIS-created map of the Tsukiji and Ginza neighborhoods in Tokyo's Kyōbashi Ward, ca. 1880, with key landmarks and churches.

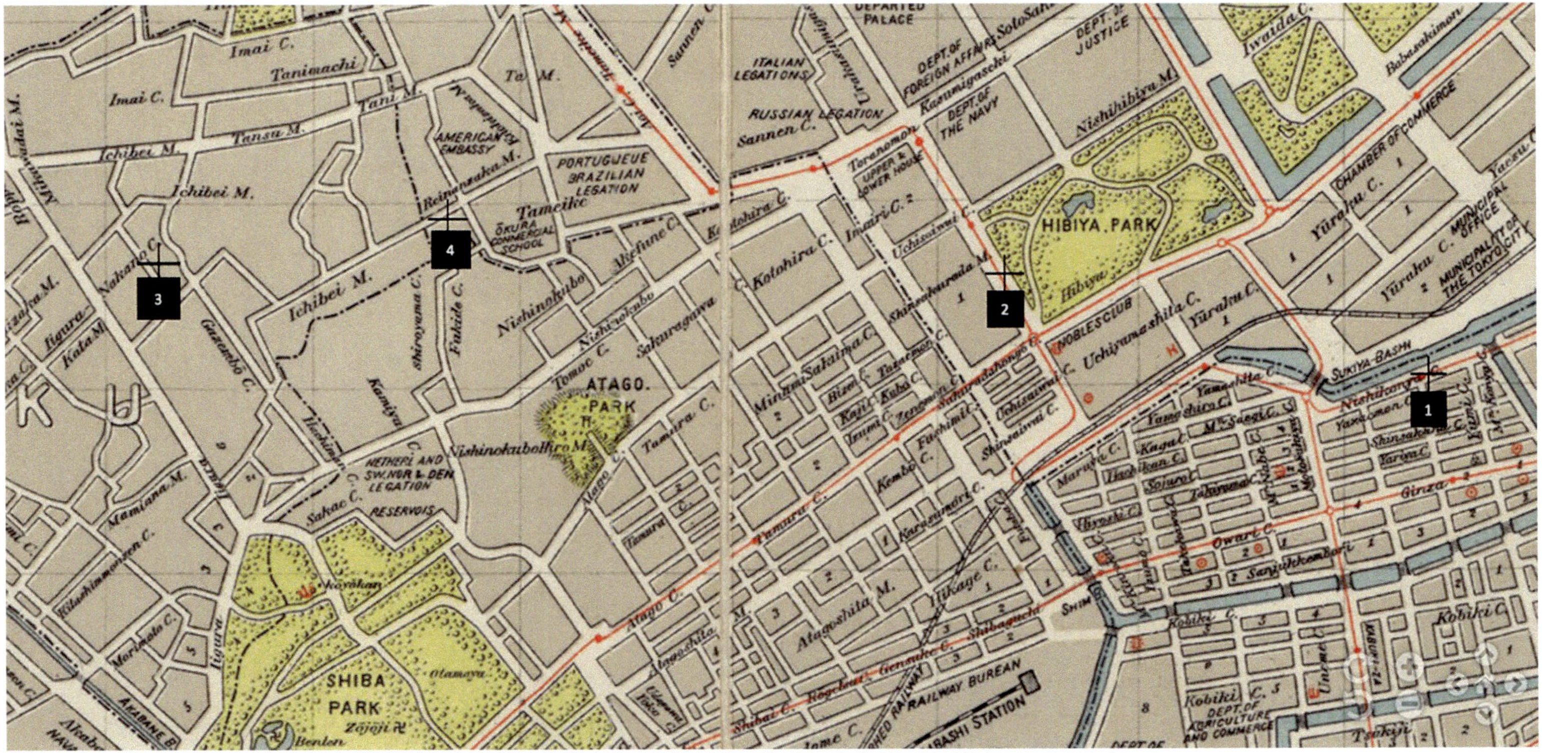

Azabu and Shiba Key

1 Shinsakanachō Church, 1879

2 Shinsakuradachō (Tokyo Dai-ichi Church), 1882

3 Nippon Church (Tokyo Daiichi Church), 1882

4 Reinanzaka Church, 1886

Plate 5. Azabu and Shiba Wards. Map excerpt showing sections of Tokyo's Azabu, Shiba, and Kyōbashi Wards, ca. 1880, augmented with churches. Source: S. Nishinomiya, *The Revised Map of Tokyo* (Tokyo, 1907).

Reinanzaka Key

1 Ōki Residence

2 Ōkura Commercial School

3 Ōkura Residence

4 Imperial Villa

5 Ikeda Residence

6 Tanaka Residence

7 Kuroda Residence

8 Reinanzaka Church

Plate 6. Azabu and Kōjimachi Wards. GIS-created map of the Reinanzaka neighborhood in Tokyo's Kōjimachi Ward, ca. 1880, with a church and key landmarks.

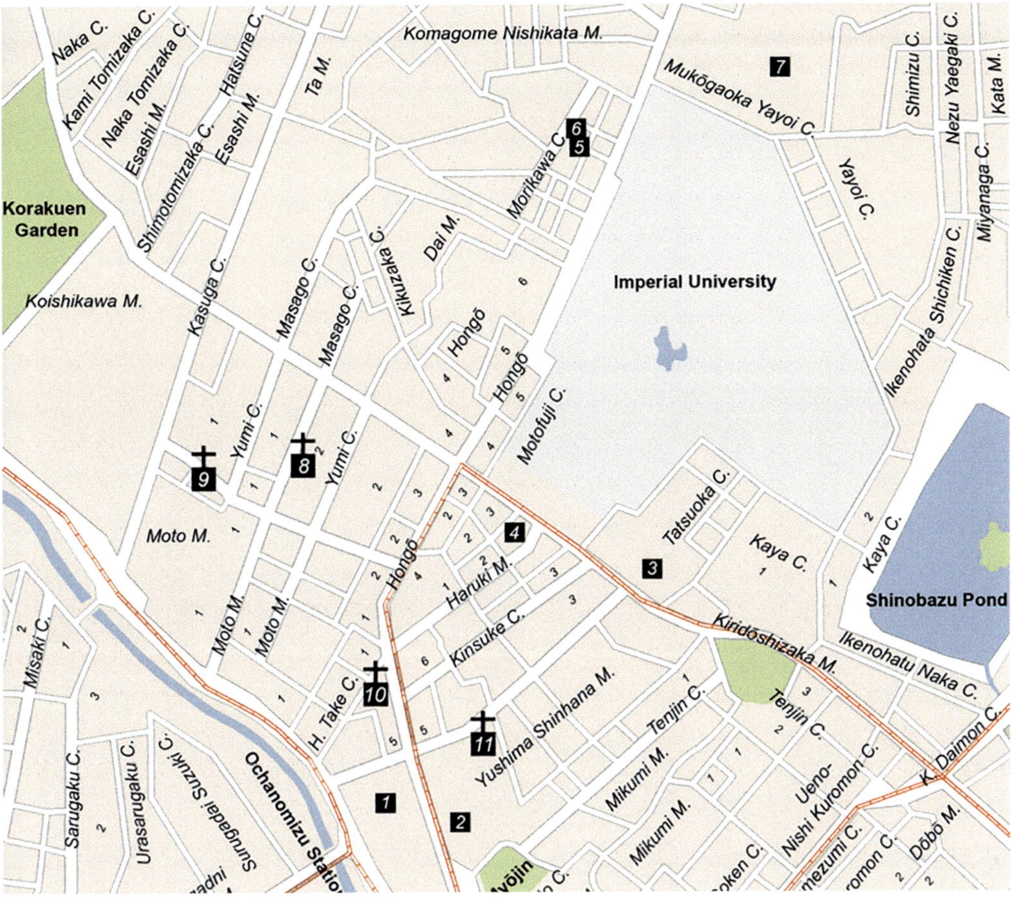

Hongō Key

- 1 Tokyo Higher Normal School/Tokyo Women's Higher Normal School
- 2 Saisei Gakusha
- 3 Japan Women's School
- 4 Chūō Kaidō
- 5 Kyūdō kaikan and Kyūdō gakusha
- 6 Hongōkan
- 7 Tokyo First Higher School
- 8 Hongō Church, 1926
- 9 Hongō Church, 1901
- 10 Hongō Church, 1891
- 11 Hongō Church, 1886

Plate 7. Hongō Ward. GIS-created map of Tokyo's Hongō Ward, ca. 1880, with key landmarks and churches.

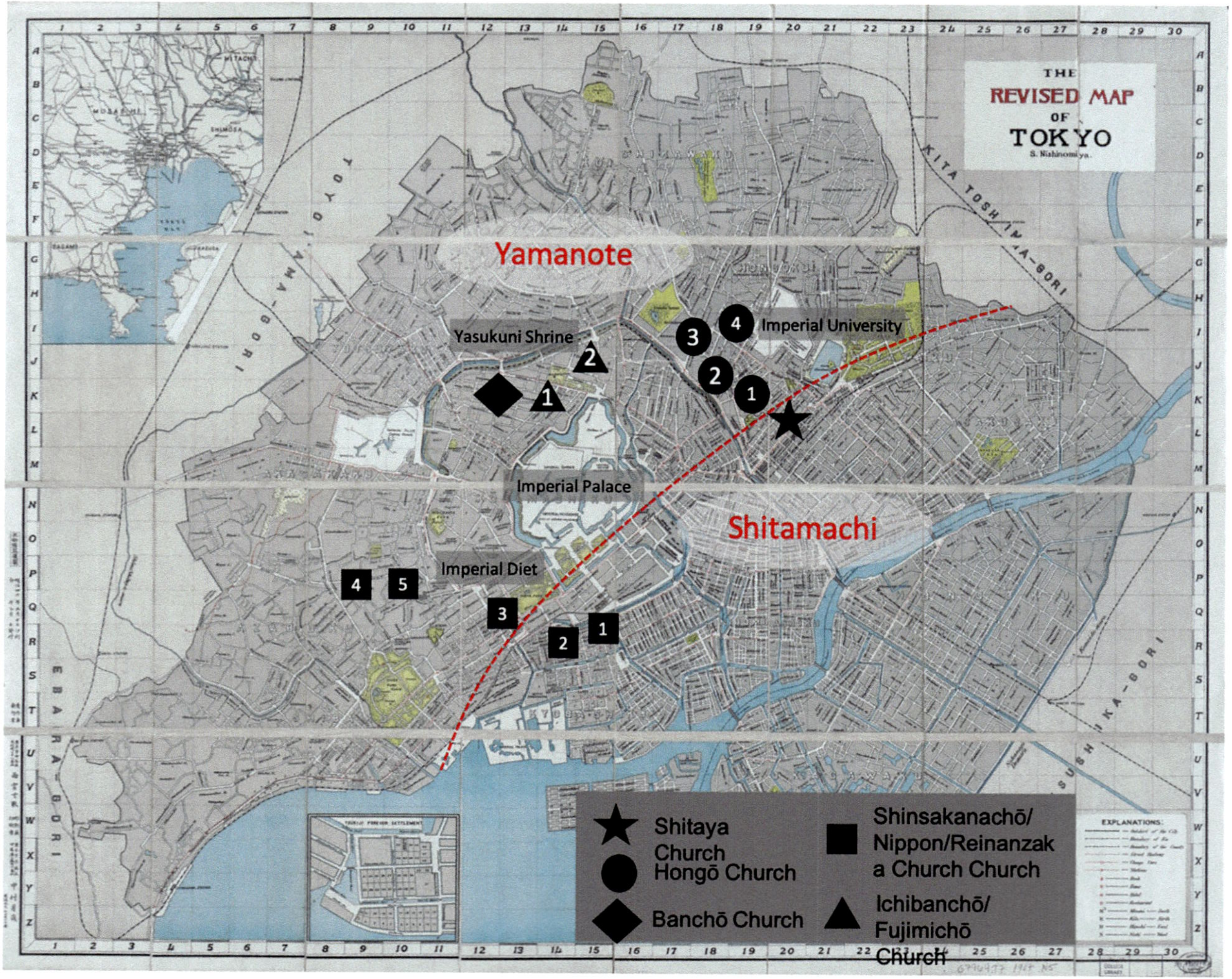

Plate 8. Map of central Tokyo in 1907, augmented to show the placement of leading Japanese Protestant churches over time. Source: S. Nishinomiya, *The Revised Map of Tokyo* (Tokyo, 1907).

CHAPTER TWO

Building the Japanese Protestant Church in Tokyo

The same whirlwind of modernization and Westernization that transformed the urban geography of Japan's major cities and ports during the Meiji period also dramatically changed their built environments. Japan's new urban built spaces reflected an array of tastes and objectives that often set them apart from their predecessors. An integral part of this trend was the development of new religious gathering spaces in Tokyo. In particular, Westerners and Japanese with significant knowledge of the West built spaces that further diversified the Japanese religious landscape. Even the proudly Japanese Yasukuni Shrine owed its creation in part to Ōmura Masajirō's extensive reading about the Napoleonic army and British navy.[1] The Christian church space in particular exemplified the changing religious landscape of Bakumatsu Japan, a country suddenly inundated with Western thought, religion, and expatriates.

In a small number of cases this flow of Western people and ideas led to new and unique church architecture combinations, but for the most part it resulted in architectural importation and transplantation. During the Meiji period a handful of Catholic churches appeared in today's Nagasaki Prefecture that represented radical departures from Western models. They included the former Gorin Kyōkaidō (1881) and Ōno Kyōkaidō (1893), both characterized by their distinct and eclectic designs.[2] During the first two decades of Christianity's new incarnation in Japan, however, most churches were the fruit of a unidirectional process of stylistic transmission. This involved the copying or slight modification of existing Western models in the Japanese context at the behest of Westerners. Ōura Cathedral (Tenshudō) in Nagasaki was the work of Japanese master carpenter Koyama Hidenoshin (1828–1898). However, Koyama essentially reproduced a Catholic basilica that catered to the preferences of the resident priest, Father Bernard Petitjean (1829–1884), and the Paris Foreign Mission Society, which funded the project.[3] When Dutch Reformed missionary James Ballagh erected the first freestanding Protestant church building in Japan in 1872, a similar process of reproduction was at work. The structure was a small single-room stone chapel, and his Western cultural background and architectural preferences were apparent in the chapel's design. Similarly, the designers of the newly completed Yokohama Kaigan Church building the small chapel's congregation moved into in 1875 essentially transplanted an American church structure to Japan. Presbyterian missionaries James Ballagh and Samuel Brown, those responsible for this church, commissioned an edifice that resembled New

Figure 2.1. The Roman Catholic basilica Ōura Tenshūdō in Nagasaki, completed in 1864. Source: "Sōken tōji no Ōura Tenshudō" [Ōura Cathedral at Establishment], *Nihon no bijutsu*, no. 446 (July 2003): 23. (Courtesy of Wikimedia Commons)

England churches from its gabled main building to its square side bell tower with a crenelated parapet.[4] Western missionaries building churches that closely imitated existing Western models epitomized the movement of ideas, styles, and shapes from an amalgamated West to Japan.

Also coming from the West were the funds that gave missionary boards ownership and design prerogative over those spaces and endowed them with the

Figure 2.2. The first Presbyterian chapel in Yokohama, often referred to as Sei no Inuya ("Sacred Doghouse") Chapel, completed in 1872. Source: "1887 nen no Nihon Kirisuto kyōkai Yokohama Kaigan Kyōkai 15 shūnen no kinen satsuei" [Photo of the 15th anniversary of Nihon Kirisuto kyōkai Yokohama Kaigan Church], Yokohama Kaigan Church Archives. (Courtesy of Wikimedia Commons)

Figure 2.3. Yokohama Kaigan Church, completed in 1875. Source: "1887 nen no Nihon Kirisuto kyōkai Yokohama Kaigan Kyōkai 15 shūnen no kinen satsuei" [Photo of the 15th anniversary of Nihon Kirisuto kyōkai Yokohama Kaigan Church], Yokohama Kaigan Church Archives. (Courtesy of Wikimedia Commons)

special symbolism and privileges of Western spaces in Japan. The new Protestant churches in the foreign concession in Tsukiji and, later, in central Tokyo that were established just after Yokohama Kaigan Church depended primarily on the financial support of foreigners. The missionary organizations belonging to nine different Protestant denominations raised and provided the means for the founding of eighteen churches and the construction of fourteen church buildings during the 1870s.[5] These small structures were built along Western lines with those funds. The earliest Protestant churches in Tokyo were, in this sense, similar to Roman Catholic churches in Tsukiji and Nagasaki in this same period. Because the new congregations lacked the resources for construction and self-support, funds from the Paris Foreign Missionary Society paid for the establishment and building of churches.[6] This remained the case even in the early twentieth century, when French political upheaval decreased the availability of financial resources and unselfish priests covered the costs of their missions out of their own pockets.[7] Likewise, the Russian Greek Orthodox mission remained closely bound financially to its benefactor, the Russian government, building its new church in 1891 on land owned by the Russian legation.[8] And despite early progress toward self-support in northern Japan, efforts to develop strong Japanese financial support for the Orthodox mission and its church buildings ultimately fell far short of their needs.[9] There were already indications, however, that the importation of foreign resources, and the influence this arrangement had on the shape of churches, would not continue indefinitely to define Christianity in Japan.

As Japan's first generation of native Protestant leaders began to establish new churches in Tokyo, the religious gathering space of the church took on new meaning that reflected a changing relationship between Japan and the West. From the early 1880s, many in Japan's urban educated elite began to move beyond Westernization and, instead, to engage with and appropriate, modify, and challenge Western ideas. Meanwhile, government officials came to assert Japan's autonomy in the face of Western presumptions of hegemony and superiority. Well attuned to, and participating in, this situation, Japanese pastors increasingly sought to create new church spaces that, in addition to being outside the foreign concessions and treaty ports, were more than Western buildings copied and imported by Western missionaries. Rather, they imagined church spaces that evinced a more complex process involving significant Japanese contributions. As such, these churches could cater to the Japanese Christians and potential converts in Tokyo who conducted government, studied, wrote, taught, and worked at other occupations in the midst of these shifting cultural and power dynamics.

It was in this context that the first Japanese Protestant church built without funding or assistance from Western missionaries took shape. In 1876, Imperial Naval Academy teacher Awatzu Takaaki (1838–1880) founded and built a church in the Azabu neighborhood of Tokyo. Awatzu, a student and convert of Ballagh, had recently returned from an observational tour of the United States. Awatzu proceeded to use his own capital to transform his earthen-walled storehouse into a small thirty-seat stone chapel. Looking to encourage this undertaking, Presbyterian missionary David Thompson and others in Tsukiji generously offered to donate pews, a table, and an organ to his new enterprise. Awatzu, however, was determined that the Nippon Kyōkai building, down to the furniture inside, would be an entirely independent, Japanese religious gathering space, so he refused these gifts. He thereby contested the unidirectional nature of the Christian architectural interaction between the West and Japan, and the broader pattern of cultural intercourse of which it was a part. Through these efforts and choices, Awatzu also built the country's first "Japanese" Protestant church. Looking at the development of Christianity in Tokyo during the subsequent decades, this small gesture of polite declination was in fact a watershed moment. It both set a precedent for and foreshadowed the Japanese pastors and congregations in the capital who consciously commissioned church buildings that were Japanese on the inside and outside. Furthermore, it highlighted the increasing priority that Japanese churches would place on establishing and exercising their autonomy.

The pastors of what would become Tokyo's largest Protestant congregations in the late Meiji and early Taishō periods shared Awatzu's desire for truly "Japanese" churches. Rather than signifying the incorporation of traditionally Japanese architectural design elements, although this did at times occur, the term "Japanese" here refers to the cultural "meaning" or "signification" with which the built space of the church was endowed.[10] Through this process, a mass of stones, wood, and glass constituting an unnamed "thing" in the Vitruvian sense, "open to endless significatory possibilities," gained an identity and meaning. While many in Japan associated churches with the contemporary and medieval Western cultures whose architectural forms and styles were evident in the churches' composition, these elements held no monopoly on meaning. Instead, several other factors also determined the signification of the church space in Japan, including the designers' and commissioners' intentions, both the occupation and utilization of the built space, and the relations of ownership and control that characterized the space. From the mid-1880s onward, a handful of Protestant churches in the capital developed a distinctly Japanese meaning in all of these areas—a meaning that combined the Western connotations and symbolism of these spaces with inconstant and myriad elements of "Japaneseness." That meaning also mirrored the complex cultural synthesis occurring in Japanese society at the time.[11]

This emphasis on making churches in Japan "Japanese" in fact developed out of a convergence of Japanese and foreign missionary priorities. From the first years after the decriminalization of Christianity, Japanese Protestant leaders expressed their desire to administer their own churches.[12] One early and remarkable manifestation of that desire was the creation of the Nihon Kirisuto Dendō Kaisha (Japanese Evangelical Alliance) in 1878 by Japanese delegates from the nine nascent American Board (Congregational) mission churches.[13] The organization aimed to foster independence for the Japanese Congregational (renamed "Kumiai" in 1886) churches from both foreign control and foreign aid.[14] Such views only grew stronger from the 1890s as ethnic nationalism and anti-Western sentiment increased. In that context, Japanese Protestants became even less willing to let foreign missionaries determine the shape of their faith.[15] Long-standing ambitions for independence among Japanese Presbyterian leaders led in 1891 to the establishment of the Nihon Kirisutokyōkai (Japan Christian Church), a Japanese organization distinct from the three Presbyterian missions in Japan.[16] And in 1906, this body of approximately seventy-five churches made church membership and recognition conditional on freedom from mission support.[17] Japanese pastors affiliated with these two movements, and particularly those in Tokyo, evinced an early, strong, and contagious interest in establishing independent churches.

Importantly, however, Protestant missionaries largely shared the enthusiasm of Japanese Christians for Japanese churches. As early as 1876, American Board missionary John H. De Forest (1844–1911) and others had committed themselves to developing a Japanese pastorate. Adhering to that vision, De Forest even cited it in explaining his reasons for declining the pastorate of Kobe Church. He felt that "their truest growth could be secured in no other way than by getting at the earliest possible date a native pastor."[18] In addition to Japanese leadership, American Board missionaries also viewed the achievement of self-support as central to the indigenization of Protestant churches in Japan. The American Board wrote in 1906 that it had encouraged the founding of the Japan Evangelical Alliance precisely because the endeavor aligned with its "time-honored policy of" promoting "a self-directing, *self-supporting,* and self-propagating native church."[19] While some churches had already devoted themselves to self-sufficiency in the early 1880s, all Kumiai churches had ceased receiving funds from the American Board by 1897.[20] The American Board frequently displayed its approval of this movement for self-support, noting specifically in each annual report and mission histories the number of independent Japanese churches and often the number of partially self-supporting churches as well. For instance, in 1893, 42 of the 60 Congregational churches in Japan were self-supporting, and in 1915, of the 104 Congregational churches in Japan, 80 were fully self-supporting and 17 were supported only by the Japan Evangelical Alliance. Presbyterian missionaries too supported Japanese churches' drive for self-support. E. Rothesay Miller (1843–1915) of the Presbyterian and then the Dutch Reformed missions wrote in 1901 to express approval that the three leading churches in the Tokyo-Yokohama region were self-supporting. He and his fellow missionaries were "devoutly thankful" for this.[21] It was, after all, their goal "to bring the Japanese church as quickly as possible into a state of entire independence of foreign money, being self-supporting and self-propagating."[22]

Missionaries of the Episcopal Church, on the other hand, were less unified in embracing the then predominant principles of self-support. These had been first clearly enunciated in the mid-nineteenth century by Henry Venn (1796–1873), mission secretary of their denomination's close English sibling, the Anglican Church, and American Board foreign mission secretary Rufus Anderson (1796–1880).[23] While most Episcopal missionaries in Japan agreed with the idea of Japanese churches achieving financial self-support, influential mission figures feared the prospect of a self-governing Japanese Episcopal body. Bishop of Tokyo John McKim (1852–1936) did not "think it safe to give the first generation of Christians in a heathen land complete autonomy as a Church."[24] Many thought, like McKim, that although the "spirit of consecration and independence . . . so largely prevail[ed] in the Japanese churches," it was still true that "the infant church in Japan, needs our influence and help."[25] Consideration of self-support and self-direction were largely a response to the threats of Japanese nationalism and only led to the naming of the first Japanese bishops in 1923, Joseph Motoda (1862–1928) and John Naide (1866–1945).[26] This lack of institutional and moral support for self-support helps to explain why the Nihon Seikokai, the joint Episcopal-Anglican body in Japan, claimed very few self-supporting churches and no substantial Japanese-owned church buildings.[27]

Ultimately, the backing of missionary organizations for true Japanese leadership and financial self-sufficiency quickened the vision and ambitions of Japanese Protestant pastors. For the two leading denominations in prewar Japan, the Nihon Kumiai (Congregational) and Nihon Kirisutokyōkai (Presbyterian), this meant independence at the church, regional, and national levels of organization, but it also had important spatial implications. Japanese church buildings—commissioned, owned, animated, and controlled by Japanese Christians—held the potential to redefine Japanese Protestantism. They could assert the Japanese identity, racial equality, and intellectual and theological parity of their pastors with their Western mentors, altering the dynamic between Japanese convert and foreign missionary. At the same time, Japanese Protestant churches also held the potential to broadcast images and discourse that would underline the modernity, appeal, and Japaneseness of Christianity to their compatriots. The decade after the erection of Awatzu's Nippon Kyōkai saw the building of other self-supporting and self-governing churches like the 1885 edifice that Congregational pastor Kanamori Tsūrin's (1857–1945) Okayama Church had built.[28] Tokyo, however, was the capital of Protestantism in Japan and home to the large congregations that increasingly directed the Japanese Protestant movement. Leading them were Japanese pastors who imagined church buildings that they and their growing church bodies could fully claim, from the first sketches to the last interior detail. Pastors Kozaki Hiromichi, Yokoi Tokio, Ebina Danjō, and Uemura Masahisa, and the congregations they led conceptualized, helped design, owned, and operated Japanese Protestant church buildings that could bring Japanese religious seekers together in new and meaningful ways.[29] The reality of Japanese ownership, in the figurative and literal senses, meant a degree of autonomy in choices about adapting, expanding, and abandoning the building and in creating buildings capable of catering to the priorities and ambitions of Tokyo's new cosmopolitan educated elite. Over time, these spaces evolved to possess distinct, eye-catching exteriors and functionally designed interiors that were situated at the intersection of architectural innovation, cultural eclecticism, and the functionalist tradition.

For passersby and church attendees alike, however, the Japanese Protestant church building was irrevocably connected to the people and ideas of the West. From their steeples to their windows to their bricks, churches were recognizably Western. Such traits inevitably summoned associations with Protestant churches in the United States and in England. They therefore belonged to the group of buildings in Japan that projected auras of Westernization and modernity. No matter how Japanese the meanings of these churches became, it was literally impossible to ignore those churches' Western features.

Rather than undermine the Japanese nature of the churches, however, this chapter will demonstrate how these elements complemented each other. The Japanese Protestant church was a special type of Japanese-Western hybrid gathering space in imperial Japan. It combined Japanese design, ownership, priorities, and usage with a distinctively alluring Western-style architectural form—and the explicit and implicit protections and privileges that accrued to such built spaces. Just as the modern dwelling in imperial Japan was central to the development of bourgeois culture, the hybridity of the Protestant church space would contribute to the formation of modern identities by Japanese churchgoers.[30] The home and the church embodied the intersection of Japanese and Western styles and functions for men and women in Japan who were seeking a path between the two.[31] The consciously Japanese, reform-oriented social spaces that would later take shape in Protestant churches depended significantly on these foundations. Furthermore, these facets distinguished Protestant church space and what they could offer members of Japan's educated elite from traditional Japanese religious space.

The Church as Privileged Space

Generally speaking, new urban built spaces in the Meiji and early Taishō periods benefited from a notable freedom from cumbersome building restrictions, and new urban religious gathering spaces were no exception. New church buildings in large cities operated in a relatively open regulatory environment. And despite the sometimes limiting influence of traditional norms of emplacement and architecture, the same was true for new shrines and temples in major metropolitan areas. In contrast with modern model cities in the West, such as Haussman's Paris and Hobrect's Berlin, Tokyo did not take shape through careful top-down urban planning. To be sure, leading intellectuals, officials, and entrepreneurs in the Meiji era often wrote and spoke about the need to apply Western urban design principles.[32] But the resistance of cost-wary large landowners, a lack of local government resources for implementation and enforcement, and little popular support blocked these efforts.[33] The only major urban planning reform relevant to buildings that resulted from Home Ministry and Tokyo governor's initiatives before 1919 was the institution of fire-prevention measures for central Tokyo. An 1882 regulation required that all new buildings in central Tokyo be equipped with fire-resistant tile roofs and that older buildings in that zone conform to this requirement within seven years.[34] The Meiji Cabinet-approved Tokyo City Improvement Ordinance of 1888, however, contained no additional building code or measures to regulate the design or construction of buildings.[35] And campaigns beginning in 1889, 1903, and 1906 all failed to apply Western models and create a comprehensive body of city or national building ordinances.[36] Finally, in 1919, the Home Ministry's newly established City Planning Section under Ikeda Hiroshi (1881–1939) drafted the City Planning Act and Urban Building Act.[37] Together, building on the work of the Tokyo mayor's office, the Home Ministry, and the Society of Architects, these acts introduced government oversight of zoning, unified building lines, density and height limits, and fire-safety-related restrictions.[38] In the absence of such basic guidance as height control, designers and commissioners of religious spaces in Tokyo and other large cities were free to build as they saw fit up until this point.[39]

There were also other factors in urban Japan that held the potential to dictate and limit the forms of religious gathering space in the decades before 1919. Even before the first bricks were laid, Protestant church buildings in Japan were a relatively privileged form of religious gathering space in imperial Japan. This was in part because the processes of designing and building churches occurred in conditions that were markedly less restricted than those surrounding the creation and alteration of Shinto and Buddhist space in imperial Japan. From the start of the Meiji period, Shinto shrines and Buddhist temples were increasingly and forcefully relegated to subservient roles within government strategies to control the re/construction of Japanese religious space. Temples, which had benefited from consistent government sponsorship for over two hundred years under the mandatory *Danka* or temple registration system, were left reeling in the early Meiji era. They were suddenly deprived of funding and institutionally separated from adjacent Shinto shrines by the *shinbutsu bunri* edict of 1868.[40] Between 1860 and the early 1870s, temples were even the subject of deliberate vandalism and hateful protest during the nationwide Haibutsu Kishaku (Abolish Buddhism and Destroy the Buddha) campaign.[41] Scholars estimate that thirty thousand Buddhist structures had been demolished by 1874.[42] Although Buddhist institutions such as the Higashi Honganji staged an impressive comeback later in the Meiji period, Buddhist religious gathering spaces struggled to establish public legitimacy and private funding in the new Japan.

On a legal level, traditional Japanese religious gathering spaces in general came under the jurisdiction of a new, unprecedentedly powerful, and invasive national government from the early 1870s. Decisions involved in maintaining, creating, or expanding Buddhist and Shinto spaces were at best subject to the approval of the prefectural and national government, and at worst dependent on the political and financial support of the state. This was made abundantly clear when, with the passing of the Koshaji Hozon Hō (Law for the Protection of Ancient Shrines and Temples) in 1897, the government explicitly asserted its right to regulate Japanese religious space in order to better preserve them. The law ordered the restoration of religious structures over four hundred years old as well as all buildings associated with the emperor or otherwise nationally significant under the aegis of the national government.[43] In addition to empowering the national government, this regulation signaled a disempowerment of sites that lacked the proper forms of national significance and age, and countless temples and shrines fought in vain for government recognition. Among those religious sites considered nationally significant and sufficiently historic, the law placed the task of raising funds to repair and rebuild shrines and temples entirely at the mercy of local officials or officials within the Home Ministry.[44] No such mercy was forthcoming when the head priest of Matsuoji sought permission to repair the temple in an effort to avoid obsolescence as neighboring Kotohira, a nationally sponsored Shinto shrine, received extra funding, personnel, and space. In this situation, as in countless other cases of religious construction and repair, the prerogatives of the state were clearly paramount.[45]

While this law clearly favored them, Shinto shrines suffered, too, from the Meiji government's efforts to unify and mobilize for the sake of modern nation-building.[46] The *jinja gappei* or "shrine merger" policy decreased the number of shrines in towns and villages from 190,000 to 100,000 between 1905 and 1910.[47] Performed as part of the Home Ministry's Local Improvement Movement, shrine mergers were meant to make Japanese citizens aware of their membership in districts *(gun)* as opposed to their smaller hamlets.[48] Another objective was to elevate the dignity of true, significant shrines by removing those that were less significant.[49] Whether it accomplished these objectives or not, the outcome was a dramatic reduction in the agency of Shinto priests and parishioners regarding their shrines. The sight of shrines being demolished and their venerated objects of worship being transferred must have underscored this reality with painful clarity.[50] In fact, however, the disentitlement of Shinto shrines began in the early 1870s when the Meiji government confiscated most shrines' landholdings.[51] With the advent of a new national hierarchy of shrines during the Great Promulgation Campaigns, the position of *minsha* (or people's shrines) became weaker as their class was denied any national government funding.[52] Furthermore, the shrine bureau set narrow eligibility conditions dictating which *minsha* could receive prefectural and municipal offerings.[53] In the era of the development and implementation of modern State Shinto, a paradoxical situation arose in which shrines were nationalized and obligated to promote state and emperor but were deprived of property and denied funding by that very state. The making and modifying of Shinto religious gathering spaces were greatly restricted in this context that combined government supervision and dominance with government neglect.

Christianity's religious gathering spaces, on the other hand, operated in a very different environment that gave Christians more freedom to build, repair, and rebuild their churches as they deemed appropriate. Indeed, the protection that enabled this relative autonomy came from the same national government whose protection imposed such dependence and restrictions on other religious spaces. The Treaty of Amity and Commerce signed by the United States and Japan in 1858 committed Japan's government to specifically protect the rights of Americans in Japan to freely exercise their religion and "to erect suitable places of worship." It further stipulated that "no injury shall be done to such buildings."[54] While such obligations clearly applied in the context of churches in treaty ports, they continued to apply after the Meiji government decriminalized Christianity in 1873. Furthermore, and as some Western governments had made exceedingly clear, Japanese treatment of Christians was under particularly close scrutiny by the West—a scrutiny that extended to new churches appearing and multiplying outside Japan's foreign settlements. By the late 1870s, as new churches were built beyond the concessions, they inherited this legacy as well as the benefits of Christianity's new legal standing in Japan. It is unfortunately not clear to what extent this standing or local reactions against it applied to the lots on which churches were built.[55] However, it is abundantly clear that Christianity's new status and the protection of the treaty port system created an environment that was particularly conducive to the building of new churches.[56] This protection applied to church-building projects of Westerners affiliated with the Roman Catholic, Russian Orthodox, and Protestant missions. It also extended to the churches taking shape through the initiative, leadership, and fundraising of Japanese Protestants and the distinct social spaces that, despite government limits on press, assembly, and organizing, developed inside.

Exterior Architectural Space

Japan's first generation of Protestant pastors and their congregations proved particularly capable of utilizing this special latitude to create new religious gathering spaces in the capital. After spending three years moving its meetings from private residences to rented classrooms to a purchased home, Kozaki Hiromichi's Shinsakurada Church finally acquired a building in 1882.[57] It achieved this by merging with Awatzu's Nippon Church in its one-room chapel to form Tokyo Dai-ichi (First) Church.[58] By the mid-1880s, however, as the number of churchgoers began to rise, the spatial needs of the Tokyo Dai-ichi Church surpassed the size of the building. The church became so full for the Sunday sermons that many people were forced to stand outside, and the congregation began making plans to build a significantly larger, more visible and functional church.[59]

Like the Nippon Church building that preceded it, the new Tokyo Dai-Ichi Church building was a primarily Japanese endeavor. Rather than adopt the existing blueprint of a Western church or acquire the services of a missionary, pastor Kozaki Hiromichi and three other church leaders designed the simple building themselves. Yamazaki Kaiichi, Wada Seiki (1859–1933), and Iwazawa Mitsuteru were elected to the New Construction Committee on 28 August 1883 and spent months collecting and studying various church designs. Finally, on 24 February 1884, they unveiled a design that corresponded to their vision for the new church building.[60]

The construction costs for the new church amounted to 2,300 yen, significantly exceeding the resources of the congregation. In agreement with the American Board of Commissioners for Foreign Missions' new policy of encouraging autonomous, independent native churches, Tokyo Dai-Ichi Church had adopted the principle of independence and autonomy in 1883.[61] So Kozaki and the church members set out to raise all of the funds themselves, embodying the increasingly prevalent view among the American Board that native churches' "self-support [was] the condition of the best spiritual life."[62] It was therefore a surprise when the Japan Mission of the American Board made a significant donation of 500 yen to the building project in the last year of fundraising. Combined with church members' contributions of 1,000 yen, former members' contributions totaling 170 yen, a donation by an American named Mr. Porter, and the church's two-year loan for 500 yen, this boost allowed the church to meet its goal.[63] So although their new building was conceived and designed by Japanese Christians, the 27 percent of total costs paid for by Westerners played a critical role in making Tokyo Dai-Ichi Church's new building possible.[64] On 1 August 1886 the Tokyo Dai-ichi Christian Church celebrated the completion of the new meeting hall *(kaidō).* They named the building Reinanzaka Church after the Tokyo neighborhood in which it was located.

Reinanzaka Church was a plain, relatively simple, single-story building measuring 1,618 square feet.[65] Like the sources that financed its construction, the church's exterior was neither completely Western nor completely Japanese. Instead, Kozaki and the other members of the New Building Committee helped design a building that belonged to the Japanese-Western Compromise *(wayō setchū)* architectural category.[66] This style was particularly popular in the Meiji era for government offices, mission schools, and churches—all noticeable buildings with strong, visible associations with Western-style modernity in Japan. Reinanzaka's design incorporates American-style clapboard siding and Japanese-style roof architectural elements like the *ichimonji-gawara* tiles and the raised hips and ridge, and this fusion characterized Japanese-Western architecture in the Meiji period.[67] When one compares the church as pictured here with a police station in Kagawa prefecture's Sakaide city, built in 1891, and Kiryū city's Meijikan (formerly the Gunma Prefectural Health Office), built in 1879, many of the elements of *wayō-setchū* architecture that these buildings share are evident.[68]

Two years later, in 1888, Uemura Masahisa's congregation completed its first building in the *wayō setchū* style as well. Like Kozaki, Uemura had borrowed and rented spaces before erecting a building. Uemura and his congregation built the "roughly built" and "temporary" wooden Ichibanchō Church building, which was notably smaller and more modest than the building of his Congregationalist colleague.[69] The structure measured only 854 square feet (24

Figure 2.4. Reinanzaka Church, completed in 1886. Source: Ii and Fugami, *Reinanzaka Kyōkai 100-nen shi*, vi. (Courtesy of Reinanzaka Church)

Figure 2.5. Reinanzaka Church Sunday School, ca. 1900, showing a side exterior wall. Source: Ii and Fugami, *Reinanzaka Kyōkai 100-nen shi*, x. (Courtesy of Reinanzaka Church)

Figure 2.6. Meiji-era Police Station in Sakaide, Japan. Source: Photo by author.

Figure 2.7. Kiryū Meijikan, restored former Gunma Prefectural Health Office: Source https://commons.wikimedia.org/wiki/File:Kiryu-Meijikan-2013012603.jpg (accessed 31 May 2020). (Courtesy of Wikimedia Commons)

tsubo), cost only 600 yen, and had an uncomfortably low ceiling.[70] The size of this "snug" building was surely attributable to Uemura, who insisted from the start that his "church [be] self-supporting, a vital principle for me!"[71] But none of these factors kept the church congregation from continuing its persistent growth throughout the late 1880s and 1890s. Churches like Ichibanchō and Reinanzaka and other Japanese-Western Compromise buildings broadcast their associations with both the West and the official architectural styles of the new Japanese nation.

When another church, the "leading Congregationalist church of Tokyo," went about creating a new building in 1891, however, there was no sign of stylistic compromise.[72] Instead, the Banchō Church congregation preferred elegant, Western-style architecture. The building that the congregation dedicated in January 1892 was a "substantial . . . brick edifice," according to Daniel Greene, one of two American missionaries present at the ceremony.[73] Demonstrating the Victorian Gothic Revival style, the church had a front-gabled structure with Gothic arched windows, engaged square columns that framed the entry, and other features that served to qualify Greene's assessment. If the structure earned

Figure 2.8. Ichibanchō Church, completed in 1887. Source Saba Wataru, *Uemura Masahisa to sono jidai,* 3:83.

such praise from this Western missionary who was particularly familiar with church architecture, it must have evoked an even more significant response from Japanese onlookers and attendees. The building was large enough to hold more than four hundred people.[74] After renting space in the Mitsubishi Club Assembly Hall in 1885 and building a simple lecture hall *(kōgisho)* in 1886, the congregation chose to erect this very visible and dignified Western-style edifice at a cost of 2,000 yen.[75] Of that sum, "the whole expense was borne by the members of the church" except for the small amount of 100 yen "contributed by a few outside friends."[76] So while the building was not truly an architectural or funding compromise between Japanese and Westerners, the church remained a hybrid space that combined Japanese and Western elements: the visibility and appeal of late nineteenth-century Western architecture coalesced with the church's Japanese ownership and membership. Such appropriations of Western architectural styles for the creation of religious gathering spaces by and for Japanese individuals characterized many Protestant church buildings in the Meiji period.

Perhaps no Tokyo Japanese Protestant church embodied this trend in the 1890s, however, more than Hongō Church. Not long after arriving in Tokyo in 1887, Yokoi Tokio led the congregation of the young church in Hongō Ward in envisioning a building that would accommodate hundreds of attendees and impress those inside and out. Because the congregation had more than sixty members[77] and very "lively" Sunday services, its rented lecture hall became too small.[78] Even more ambitious than Banchō's construction project, Hongō Church members aimed for their first church edifice to be a custom-designed, modern, Western-style church building. Like his classmate Kozaki, his colleague Uemura, and many Japanese pastors throughout Japan, the missionary organization with which Yokoi was affiliated could only provide modest support. The Japan Mission's contribution amounted to 180 yen. Unlike the congregations of his fellow Tokyo pastors, however, the growing membership at Hongō was entirely unable to pay for this undertaking. As mentioned in chapter 1, Hongō Ward had enormous appeal because it was full of bright college students. As students, though, they still had little money, and the 100 yen that they mustered up was clearly inadequate.[79] Despite the challenges dampening his grand ambitions, Yokoi was unwilling to dream smaller. He traveled to the United States, where he met with the American Board and traveled all over the country for ten months in a successful effort to raise funds for the proposed church.[80] Returning with US$10,000 in 1889, Yokoi and the Hongō Church congregation then had the capital to commission a church of the highest caliber.[81]

This church building was funded almost entirely by Americans and Japanese in the United States, yet only 1 percent of that support came from a missionary organization. Instead, those contributions resulted in the construction of a Japanese Protestant church that would reflect the priorities and vision of pastor Yokoi. He imagined a Protestant church for Japan's best students and young professionals that was free from the specific objectives of any foreign body, secular or religious. With the resources accumulated, Yokoi and his congregation made decisions that point to an appreciation for impressive Western-style architecture at the forefront of modern design in Japan. These choices foreshadowed the

Figure 2.9. Banchō Church, completed in 1892, with unnamed members standing on the stairs. Source: Itō Kiyoshi, *Banchō Kyōkai 100-nen shi*, 25. (Courtesy of Banchō Church)

stylistic and spatial priorities for other Japanese Protestant churches in Tokyo in the late Meiji period and beyond.

First and foremost among these choices was that of the architect. A number of cost-effective options were available for church design in 1890, and hiring a well-educated and skillful missionary would have been one of them. Daniel Greene, who, as mentioned above, attended the unveiling of the Banchō Church building, had designed the beautiful redbrick chapel of the Dōshisha School, Yokoi's alma mater, only four years before.[82] The Hongō Church congregation did not, however, choose someone like Greene, who was frequently in the capital and whose enthusiasm about the potential for this new Congregationalist church in the capital would surely have been reflected in his fee. Instead, Yokoi and church leaders selected a Japanese architect whose name was widely known and carried strong associations with modern Western-style architecture. The Hongō Church hired Imperial University architecture professor Tatsuno Kingo (1854–1919), one of the first Western-style Japanese architects, to design and oversee the construction of their first permanent building.[83] Tatsuno was a star student of the British architect Josiah Conder (1852–1920), who founded the architecture department of the Imperial University's Engineering School. Although Conder spent very little time on Japan's architectural heritage with this first cohort, Tatsuno and the other four students were very much engaged in a search for balance between the modern Western and the traditional Japanese styles.[84] In fact, Japanese Protestant pastors and the first Japanese Western-style architects were kindred spirits in a way. Both were constantly involved in the complex borrowing, appropriation, interpretation, and creation processes through which foreign knowledge and culture passed into Japan, making their collaboration in church design very logical. Tatsuno is remembered for designing the Bank of Japan (Nihon Ginkō) headquarters in 1896 and iconic Tokyo Station in 1914.[85] He was also, however, the main architect for many other spaces, including the Hongō Church building.

With the drafting work of his student assistant Ishii Keikichi (1866–1932), a Hongō member who was destined to become a modernist architect in his own right, Tatsuno designed a large church that was noticeably modern and eclectic.[86] The new building, completed in April 1891, was an imposing two-story, redbrick, one-hundred-square-foot building that displayed Tatsuno's signature combination of Gothic Revival and Neoclassical architecture. So although the elements such as the large rose window, prominent front gable, and the numerable buttresses point to the influence of Conder, who was "at his most expressive and adroit when designing in the Gothic idiom," the stamp of the Japanese architect remains pronounced.[87] Tatsuno's stylistic preferences shine through in his combination of these features with the Neoclassical low hip roof and the Romanesque rounded arches.[88] Such elaborate design work along with the land and construction costs came to the enormous sum of 14,042 yen and 54 sen (approximately US$10,500 in 1892).[89] Thus, rather than simply utilize the considerable amount that Yokoi had raised, the Hongō Church chose to spend even more, evincing a high prioritization for modern Western-style architectural grandeur.

Like so many buildings in Tokyo before World War II, however, the Hongō Church edifice was short-lived. The building perished during the Hongō Fire of March 1898, which destroyed over one thousand homes.[90] The congregation chose to build a large but more modest and standard church in 1901.[91] Although the construction for the new edifice in nearby Ikizaka only cost the church

Figure 2.10. Sketch of the exterior of Hongō Church, completed in 1891. Source: *Kirisutokyō shimbun*, no. 405 (1 May 1891): 9.

members 1,600 yen, the result was a functional two-story wooden church building with a footprint of approximately 1,440 square feet.[92]

In 1906, Uemura's Ichibanchō church dedicated its new Fujimichō Church building. Uemura continued to equate the independence and autonomy of his church with almost no foreign aid. Just as Awatzu Takaaki had deliberately opposed the unidirectional process of religious, cultural, and stylistic

Figure 2.11. Hongō Church at Ikizaka, completed in 1901, with annex added in 1913. Source: *Yumichō Hongō Kyōkai 100-nen shi*, 925. (Courtesy of Yumichō Hongō Church)

transmission, Uemura refused to depend on missionary organizations. Over the course of three years between 1899 and 1902, Uemura and a handful of members worked with a Japanese architect, likely affiliated with the Josiah Conder school, to plan the new church. The group continued developing the initial plans for an 8,000-yen church until the total cost for the project reached the high sum of 30,000 yen.[93] Like Yokoi in the United States, Uemura set out on a fundraising tour, but unlike his colleague, he pursued this campaign only in Japan. In the end, he raised 16,000 yen from individuals associated with his Ichibanchō Church, 1,500 yen from members of other churches in Japan, 230 from foreign friends, and 270 from individual missionaries.[94] Then, when a missionary in the United States proposed to solicit funds from the Presbyterian Churches of America amounting to as much as $5,000 (or approximately 10,000 yen), Uemura and the congregation politely refused. Church elder Uzawa Fusaaki (1872–1955) reported in April 1906 that they felt very compelled "to build it ourselves."[95]

Church members, galvanized by the women's group, raised funds to supplement those raised by Uemura. The very building materials used to construct the church came from members. One Ichibanchō member who owned a lumber business donated "good timber" from which the church was constructed. The gift was made in honor of his recently deceased parents, both committed members of Ichibanchō Church. And his father had been one of the planners for the new building.[96] The final product was an impressive two-story, cross-gabled wooden church building with a dramatic rose window, multiple extended eaves, and rounded arches. In the end, the massive donated ridgepole proved so large that the builders were unable to tile it, leaving it exposed.[97] Nearly two decades had elapsed since the church members had built the temporary structure in Ichibanchō, intending for it to act as their church space for no more than five years. Finally, this new Fujimichō Church edifice was the large, impressive building for which the church members had so ardently hoped. It is likely that the Fujimichō Church was the most expensive church built in Japan up to that point.[98]

During the same years that Uemura and the Ichibanchō Church planned and built the Fujimichō Church, pastor Kozaki was also actively envisioning a new and much enlarged Reinanzaka Church building.[99] During the late 1890s, the church had narrowly survived, but Kozaki believed that a new building could hold the key to a revival. In order to raise funds for and build what was most surely among the most expensive Japanese Protestant churches in Japan, Kozaki clearly required a vision. He made that vision clear to his congregation, leaving evidence of the objectives and priorities behind the new Reinanzaka building project. In a 1908 sermon titled "The Necessity of a Great Church," he underlined this need and expressed his dream to have a church with "1000 attendees for

Figure 2.12. Fujimichō Church, completed in 1906, with photo of Uemura Masahisa in the top right corner. Source: *Uemura zenshū*, vol. 2, n. p.

[Sunday] service."[100] He said, "It has been 9 years since I again became pastor of this church, and in [my] thinking at the time I was determined at all costs to advance this church and to make it into a great church. Even if it took ten years, I was going to produce a visible result."[101] Evidently, the time had come to achieve that result, and he worked with the same Professor Tatsuno selected by Yokoi and the Hongō congregation in 1890–1891 to make this building a reality. Rather than imitating a particular American church structure or one of the several impressive Western churches that missionaries had designed in Japan, Kozaki's contribution to the plans for the new structure was based on the functions he hoped the church building would fill. Kozaki especially idolized the iconic Broadway Tabernacle of New York, a large and spectacular church he had visited while studying at Yale in 1893 and 1894. The pastor's vision centered around a highly visible church building that would entice and cater to hundreds of educated Japanese. While this building served as a physical representation of Kozaki's objectives, the Metropolitan Tabernacle of the Reverend Charles Haddon Spurgeon (1834–1892) in London represented the essence of those goals.[102] Spurgeon had constructed and filled the sort of large, urban religious space in London to which Kozaki himself aspired. The Southwark London congregation had swelled from "313, with only thirty percent attendance, to 6000," and to house so many attendees, in 1856 he had the tabernacle built, including an immense sanctuary.[103] In Kozaki's case, the fruit of the ten-year planning project was indeed a great church for Japan.

The newly completed Reinanzaka Church was a three-storied, cross-gabled, redbrick church. It rose above the other buildings in the area, leading one paper to refer to the church as the city's "highest tower" *(saikō-tō)* in an article that included a sketch done by Usui Izō (figure 2.15).[104] Like the spires that adorned most Protestant church architecture in the United States during the nineteenth century, Reinanzaka's bell tower was clearly one of the most notable and identifiable features of the new church.[105] The tower, with Gothic Revival features such as its hip roof, connecting buttresses, and rose window, contrasted gently with the Romanesque rounded arch windows that covered the main body of the church building. As I mentioned before, this architectural mixture was one commonly known characteristic of Tatsuno's work. To add to the grandeur and appeal of this structure, the congregation opted to have Czechoslovakian stained glass in the arched windows.[106] This was the same type of "Bohemian" glass that adorned the palaces of European royalty like King Edward VII of England and Emperor Franz Josef I of Austria.[107] So this choice of glass placed Reinanzaka Church in the company of some of the West's most sumptuous residences, and complemented the other architectural elements that made the new building so conspicuous and identifiable.

To make the transition from planning to the construction of the new church building, Reinanzaka Church members had to dig deep into their pockets. While this congregation proved more willing than Uemura's Fujimichō Church to accept Westerners' contributions, the burden of funding the majority of the project fell upon the church body. Although Kozaki led a campaign that raised

Figure 2.13. Exterior *(top)* and interior *(bottom)* of the Metropolitan Tabernacle in London, completed in 1861. *Survey of London*, vol. 25: *St George's Fields (The Parishes of St. George the Martyr Southwark and St. Mary Newington)* (London: London County Council, 1955), 104. (Courtesy Wikimedia Commons)

Figure 2.14. Exterior of Reinanzaka Church, completed in 1917. Source: Kojima Akio, *Reinanzaka Kyōkai—Kojima Akio shashinshū* [Reinanzaka Church: Kojima Akio photo collection] (Tokyo: Kyōbunkan, 1984), 8. (Courtesy of Kojima Akio)

Figure 2.15. Sketch of Reinanzaka Church, 1917, by Usui Izō. Source: Yuasa Yōzō, *Nobiyuku kyōkai*, ii.

50,000 yen between 1910 and 1917, he insisted that a sum closer to 100,000 yen was closer to what would be required.[108] To help with the difference, the church put together an English-language fundraising pamphlet that Kozaki distributed to potential donors in the United States.[109] The most substantial contribution came through the conversations of former member Nakaseko Rokurō, a Kyoto Imperial University chemistry professor, with an American named C. L. James and his mother.[110] In the end, each of them donated 10,000 yen to the project, and the total sum raised amounted to 73,000 yen.[111] Still, the American generosity had not come from missionary organizations, allowing Kozaki and the congregation to envision and realize the church that they desired.

These church bodies also made the maintenance and improvement of their buildings high priorities. Unlike traditional Japanese religious sites such as Yasukuni Shrine, for which Japan's Home Ministry oversaw all proposed repairs and modifications, church congregations exercised considerable freedom.[112] In 1906 the Hongō congregation widened the left side of the Ikizaka building by eighteen feet.[113] Then in 1913 they added a two-story, 890 square-foot (25-*tsubo*) annex with a modern slate-tile roof.[114] The addition cost approximately 2,700 yen.[115] Given the consequence of these structures, it is perhaps unsurprising that some of these churches chose preeminent modern Japanese architects to design their expansions. A significant, continued increase in membership forced the Fujimichō congregation to envision expansion, and they selected Sone Tatsuzō (1853–1937), another member of the Imperial University's first graduating class in architecture who, like Tatsuno, had studied with Josiah Conder.[116] Sone, along with Tatsuno, Satachi Shichijirō (1857–1922), and Katayama Tokuma (1854–1917), developed and applied an inclusive, combinative approach to diverse architectural styles.[117] He was particularly interested in reconciling Japanese styles with Western styles. Sone in fact devoted attention to this topic in his senior thesis, arguing for the fusion of styles and materials from the West with forms native to Japan.[118] Sone would also build Shiba Church in Tokyo the following year and Sapporo Independent Church in 1922.[119] In the case of the new and improved Fujimichō Church, concrete replaced wood and the building was expanded by an extra 3,985 square feet at a cost of 3,800 yen in 1915.[120]

By the early Taishō period, Protestant churches had lost their monopoly on impressive, functional modern religious gathering spaces in Tokyo as Buddhist temples and halls took shape. In the same year as Sone Tatsuzō completed his renovation of Fujimichō Church, fellow Tokyo Imperial University graduate Takeda Goichi (1872–1938) completed the True Pure Land sect's Kyūdō Kaikan (Way-Seekers' Hall). Priest Chikazumi Jōkan commissioned the hall as a building that would compete with popular Protestant churches near the Tokyo Imperial University like Hongō Church.[121] This building, which blended modern, Western-style architecture with iconic Buddhist design elements, is evidence of traditional Japanese religion's engagement with impressive modern architecture in the national capital.

Even with the success of that building, however, such Buddhist sites in Tokyo were relatively rare, particularly in comparison with Japanese Protestant churches. This was clearly related to the severing of Buddhist temples from Shinto shrines, the destruction of Buddhist temples in the Haibutsu Kishaku movement, and the inferior position of temples in the hierarchy of nationally significant Japanese religious spaces. These vectors did lead a few Buddhist thinkers to grapple with the religion's intellectual, spiritual, and institutional relationships with the state and to modernization and social problems, including Kyūdō Kaikan founder Chikazumi. The overarching result, however, was that institutional Buddhism adopted a defensive, reactive stance and fought for survival by "actively ingratiating itself with the new state authority."[122] Considering this context is crucial for understanding the failure of Buddhist sects to provide significant institutional initiative or support for new, modern Buddhist gathering spaces in Tokyo. It is also essential for appreciating the efforts of those few Buddhist priests who sought to mobilize new forms of built space to make Buddhism modern and relevant.

Interior Architectural Space

The distinct and privileged position of Christianity also gave Protestant congregations the power to shape and reshape their church building interiors as they saw fit. Between the 1880s and 1910s, the interior of the capital's most popular Protestant churches transformed dramatically. From simple spaces with few rooms, churches became complex, compartmentalized, multiroom spaces. Through this metamorphosis the Japanese Protestant church building emerged as a collection of diverse gathering spaces that accommodated a gradual increase in the number and variety of functions that the buildings could host.

While the church space changed significantly, the heart of that space and the primacy it was given in the design and use of the building was consistent. The interiors of the buildings developed by Tokyo's largest congregations centered around a large open room—a type of space that was common to the vast majority of churches throughout the world. This was the sanctuary *(reihaidō),* the room that hosted regular and special worship services *(reihai).* In the Japanese case, the space was also sometimes alternately referred to as the meeting hall *(shūkaidō).*[123] As has been the case since late antiquity, when the earliest Christian church buildings were constructed, this was an open gathering space intended to bring people together, provide them with ample seating space, and foster a sense of belonging.[124] From the oldest single-room chapels to the most grandiose churches, the *reihaidō* was the centerpiece of the church space in Japan, and this was evident in the size and seating capacity of these rooms. Reinanzaka Church's 1886 (Tokyo Dai-Ichi) building boasted a 1,464-square-foot *shūkaidō* with a seating capacity of 150, a significant improvement over the 30-seat *shūkaidō* of the Nippon Church.[125] The *reihaidō* of the new 1891 Banchō Church building had seating for 450.[126] In 1901 and 1906, respectively, Hongō Church and Fujimichō Church erected large gathering spaces with seating capacities of 500.[127] Even larger was the 600-seat *reihaidō* included in the design for Reinanzaka Church's new 1917 building.[128]

More than just a large space, the *reihaidō* increasingly came to constitute an impressive and attractive hall. The congregation and pastors of Tokyo's largest churches expressed, and made manifest, the importance that they placed on the *reihaidō* through their design and decorative choices. Among the more visible and practical elements that these churches included in their large halls were the galleries that looked down toward the centered pulpits *(seidan* or *kyōdan).* The 1886 Reinanzaka *reihaidō* had just such a gallery on its second floor, and the congregation included an even more striking three-sided gallery in their new 1917 *reihaidō.*[129] Hongō Church's 1891 building contained an ornate second-story gallery, and after the great Hongō Fire of 1898 destroyed it, the simpler and cheaper 1901 building included a gallery as well.[130] Fujimichō Church's *shūkaidō* had a three-sided gallery. As Ichibanchō Church's New Building Project Committee explained in early February 1899, "The sanctuary is the house of God." So it was necessary for the congregation to adopt a "suitably impressive architecture" for such a space, and this would be "extremely expensive."[131] In the end, the *shūkaidō* of Fujimichō Church definitely met both of these expectations.

The design features throughout these large gathering spaces also reveal an array of impressive techniques and styles, particularly beginning in the late nineteenth century. Flanking the pulpit of Banchō's *reihaidō* were engaged square columns with ornately embellished capitals. The consciously more modest Fujimichō *shūkaidō* was, from the ceiling bordered in subtly crenulated trim to the Victorian railing with thick balusters enclosing the gallery, also a striking and impressive space.[132] On entering the 1917 Reinanzaka's *reihaidō* and stepping onto the terracotta-tiled floor, church attendees would have encountered a particularly eye-catching wooden triple-height ceiling above the central aisle of the nave. It was composed of five-sided arches and was supported by a special wooden truss configuration of multiweb, radiating member beams. Extending outward from the central aisle on both sides, there was a wooden barrel-vault-type arched surface and then a wooden rib groin vault ceiling above the side galleries. The *reihaidō* and *shūkadō* of these churches also benefited from a marked luminosity. The great halls of Banchō (1892), Fujimichō (1906), and Reinanzaka (1917) featured large, elegant chandeliers that hung above the congregation. And the large windows that adorned the exteriors of most of these buildings illuminated their large interior gathering spaces and made them seem even larger. Reinanzaka (1886) and Banchō (1892) both featured rows of large elevated windows. The *reihaidō* and *shūkadō* of Hongō (1891), Fujimichō (1906), and Reinanzaka (1917) all included rows of large clerestory windows that gave light and added to the impressive Western Christian air of those churches.

In some ways, these formal spaces shared much with the large halls of traditional Japanese religious sites in the capital. Yasukuni Shrine and Kanda Myōjin, located very near Fujimichō Church and Hongō Church, respectively, each offered several large gathering spaces. At Yasukuni, there was the Nōraku-dō

Figure 2.16. The *reihaidō* (sanctuary) in the interior of Banchō Church, completed in 1892. Source: Itō, *Banchō 100-nen shi*, 56. (Courtesy of Banchō Church)

(Nō Performance Hall). Another famous shrine, Kanda Myōjin, contained the Hōōden (Firebird Goddess Hall), where visitors watched performances of Kagura (Ceremonial Dance).[133] Moving to Buddhist temples in Tokyo, Zōjōji's *hondō* (main hall) was large enough to accommodate large gatherings.[134] However, these spaces carried strong associations with the "traditional" Japanese moral order and the state that aimed at once, paradoxically, to redefine and uphold it. In contrast, the modern Western-style interiors of Protestant churches connoted not only the West but also concomitant forms of modern Western belief and knowledge.

Figure 2.17. The *shūkaidō* (sanctuary) in the interior of Fujimichō Church, completed in 1906. Source: Fujimichō Church Records Room. (Courtesy of Fujimichō Church)

Japanese Protestant churches in the national capital and elsewhere were not simply sanctuaries and assembly halls. While those rooms constituted the core of every newly constructed Protestant church space in modern Japan, churches also increasingly included smaller informal spaces that were adaptable for multiple types of small gatherings. This represented another key difference between traditional Japanese religious spaces and Protestant churches. Major traditional Japanese religious spaces in Tokyo, including those established in the late nineteenth and early twentieth centuries, prioritized ritual and commemorative spaces, and even smaller edifices had specific, formal purposes. Completed in 1920, Meiji Shrine included smaller buildings such as a worship hall *(haiden)*, the emperor's sojourn hall *(benden)*, and ritual offerings hall *(shinseiden)*, but had no interior spaces for informal, small group activities such as classes or meetings.[135] Buddhist temples also lacked adaptable, informal small gathering spaces. The main hall *(hondō)* of Buddhist temples during the Meiji and early Taishō periods were often flanked by small buildings, but these were dedicated to specific formal activities. The temple Zōjōji, whose buildings were appropriated for the Great Teaching Campaign in the 1870s to train proselytizers to preach a fusion of Shinto, nationalism, and emperor worship, offers a case in

Figure 2.18. The *reihaidō* (sanctuary) chancel *(top left)* and gallery *(top right and bottom)* in the interior of Reinanzaka Church, completed in 1917. Source: Kojima, *Reinanzaka Kyōkai—Kojima Akio shashinshū*, 15–17. (Courtesy of Kojima Akio)

point. A scripture hall, a teahouse, and a belfry occupy the primary precinct of the temple along with the *hondō*.[136] Temples and shrines alike continued, of course, to act as gathering spaces for groups of all ages. However, such gatherings had to take advantage of the generous outdoor spaces in which these religious sites were situated. It is worth noting that temples and shrines in the capital did eventually grow to include auxiliary spaces for small, informal gatherings during the early Shōwa period.[137]

Tokyo's Japanese Protestant churches, on the other hand, evolved around the turn of the twentieth century into open, multifunctional spaces conducive to several forms and scales of social interaction. Their spaces embodied the new emphasis on full and active participation by the laity that has been progressively altering church architecture since the start of the Protestant Reformation.[138] Protestant churches in particular have increasingly evinced a high prioritization of the inclusion of additional, smaller gathering spaces in the church that could foster various forms of group activity and exchange. This combination of multifunctional spaces of varied sizes and dimensions constitutes a key element in the distinct spatial character of Protestant church interiors.

An important source of evidence regarding the diverse functions of the Japanese Protestant church space in the early 1900s comes from the 1890s, when many Tokyo churches were particularly constrained by spatial limitations. Even in a decade that Sumiya Mikio and missionary-historian Otis Cary agree was typified by Protestant Christianity's so-called retarded growth, Tokyo Protestant churches quickly proved too small for their congregations.[139] This lack of space was particularly evident in spaces beyond the sanctuary. The small Ichibanchō *shūkaidō* was sufficient for the eighty church attendees who came each Sunday for the service in 1890, for instance, but it lacked auxiliary spaces for groups such as the church's women's group. Predictably, the church's women's group was at the forefront of the drive to draw attention to and find a solution to the church's space dilemmas.[140] After the Hongō Fire, as the congregation of Hongō Church waited for the completion of their new church in Hongō Ward's Ikizaka neighborhood, members were optimistic that the new building would facilitate the resuscitation of the women's and youth groups.[141] The new church only began to fulfill those hopes. As one member recalled, the 1901 building lacked a dedicated space for Sunday school, and he had to teach the sessions in a nearby kindergarten.[142] As Hongō had done in 1891 and would do again in the late 1910s, however, the growing congregations of the capital's leading churches often prioritized spaces that could accommodate a mixture of events and gatherings simultaneously.

Tokyo's largest Japanese Protestant congregations were building multifunctional churches that combined large and small gathering spaces and invited churchgoers to actively engage in social interactions with one another. In his sermon titled "The Necessity of a Great Church" about the realization of a new church building in 1908, Kozaki explained what he meant by the adjective "great" in his sermon title. His models were, again, large church buildings with multiple types of interior space such as the Broadway Tabernacle of New York and the Metropolitan Tabernacle of London. Like their pastors, Kozaki sought to build a church that was more than simply the sanctuary. A great church also needed "Sunday school rooms, rooms for the youth group and women's group, a library, a cafeteria, a bathing room, a game room, and other important spaces," he explained.[143]

More than a vision limited to Kozaki, Japanese Protestant pastors shared similar objectives for the diversity and functionality of their space. The 1891 Hongō Church had a meeting hall behind the sanctuary and two smaller rooms for meetings and classes. Pastor Ebina recalled with regret that when the Hongō Fire destroyed their building in 1898, they "did not have a Sunday school . . . a women's group, elders group, or youth group, either."[144] The Hongō Church's 1901 Ikizaka building was unable to entirely fulfill these needs, so the annex the church built in 1913 included meeting rooms, Sunday school rooms, and a secondary sanctuary.[145] The eight rooms in the main space upstairs were separated by thick linen curtains that could be removed to transform the space into a second sanctuary.[146] Also, as one member recalled, they were equipped with movable wooden benches of different age-appropriate heights.[147] These rooms served the needs of the whole congregation and of the various church-based groups that met in the church.[148] The addition that Fujimichō Church built onto their 1906 building in 1915 contained the same types of auxiliary spaces and fulfilled the same range of functions. Some were equipped with movable chairs and tables.

At the time of Kozaki's sermon, the 1887 Reinanzaka Church building had functioned much like the great churches he had idealized for over two decades—even without the same types of auxiliary spaces. The new building he and the congregation began planning for around 1908 took nine years to come to fruition. So rather than a space for the beginning of something new, the new Reinanzaka that opened its doors in May 1917 was a space for the continuation and expansion of the dynamic church that the congregation had been developing for some thirty years. It was full of various types of interior spaces. In addition to the sanctuary, the building contained some eighteen large and small rooms complementing the *reihaidō,* enabling the church to hold a total of some thousand people at a time.[149] While this floor plan uses the label *kyōshitsu* (classroom) for the nine rooms specifically meant for social interaction, these spaces served a

Figure 2.19. A *kyōshitsu* (classroom) in the interior of Fujimichō Church, completed in 1906. Source: Fujimichō Church Records Room. (Courtesy of Fujimichō Church)

larger range of purposes than this label implies, and this was the objective from the beginning. For this reason, when the *Tokyo Yūkan shimbun* reported on the church's interior, it described a church with "an elders' hall, youth hall, women's group hall, Sunday school rooms, evening school rooms, kindergarten rooms, a choir room, study room, and a cafeteria," among others.[150] The Reinanzaka Church had a building that fit the description of the "great church" Kozaki

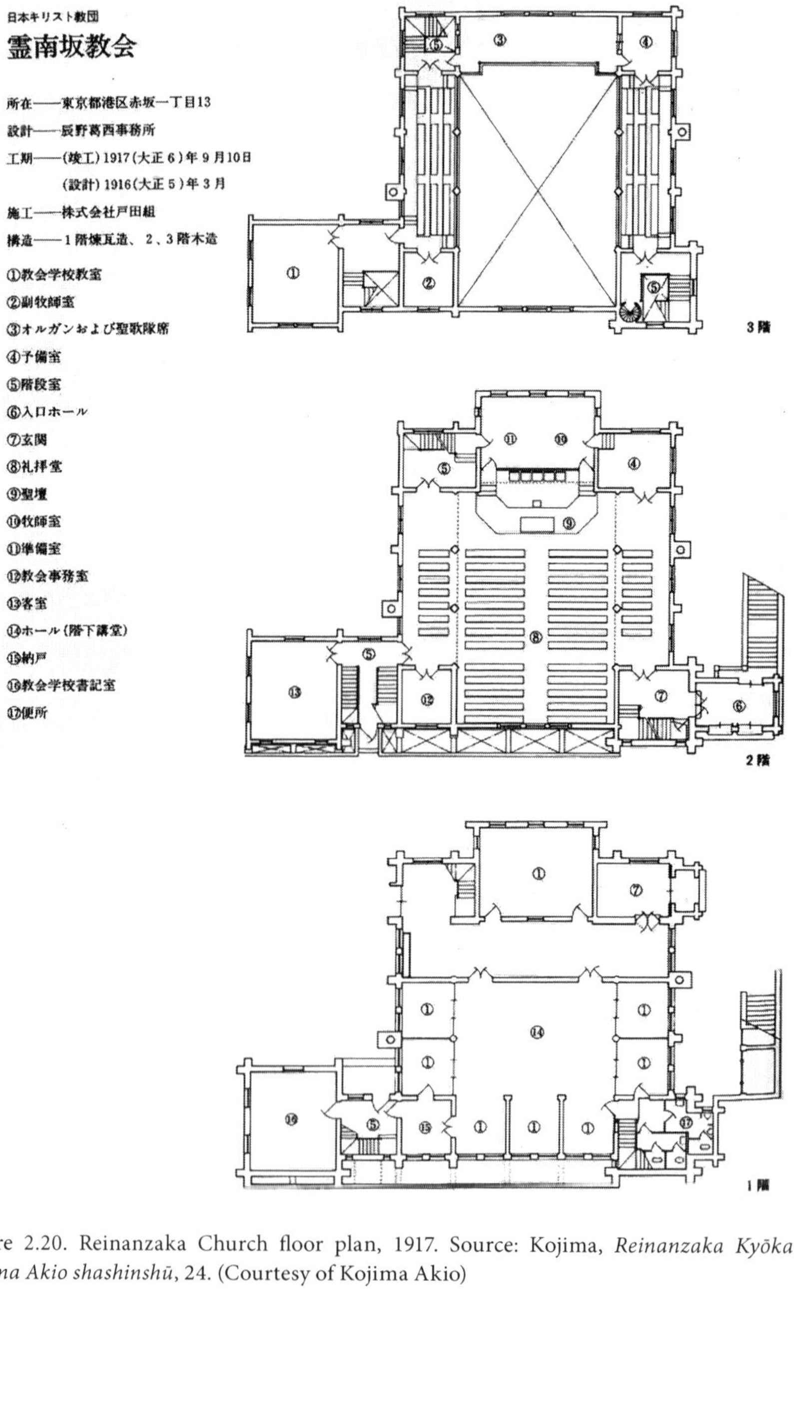

Figure 2.20. Reinanzaka Church floor plan, 1917. Source: Kojima, *Reinanzaka Kyōkai—Kojima Akio shashinshū*, 24. (Courtesy of Kojima Akio)

envisioned, but also an appropriate one for the great church he and churchgoers had already formed and cultivated.

Tokyo's largest Protestant congregations commissioned buildings that reflected their ambitions and priorities but also mirrored trends in the indigenization of Christianity in turn-of-the-century Japan. Initially, these churches' founding pastors sought to build simple, practical religious gathering spaces. From the 1890s, however, these pastors and lay church leaders envisioned large, modern churches to accommodate their growing congregations and facilitate attendees' social interactions. To realize their grand visions, they often looked to renowned Japanese architects. Increasingly, funds for their design and construction came solely from Japanese resources and resources raised by Japanese pastors without assistance from mission organizations. The pastors of Reinanzaka, Banchō, Fujimichō, and Hongō Churches in fact prided themselves on their institutions' financial autonomy from mission organizations, as did the missionaries with whom they were affiliated. With Japanese ownership, Japanese architects, and Japanese congregations, these growing churches each came to possess a notably Japanese meaning. Even with its new Japanese signification, however, the church building retained its associability with Westernization, the most dynamic sociocultural, economic, and political change happening in imperial Japan. It was precisely this quality that shielded the church building from many of the limitations and requirements of the new imperial government's religious reinvention and regulation project. The Japanese Protestant church building, then, constituted a truly hybrid form of religious gathering space in imperial Japan.

Church interiors in Japan grew and developed in conjunction with their exteriors to fit the needs and objectives of their congregations and pastors. The simple *reihaidō* of early church buildings were replaced by larger and larger worship halls with second-story galleries and seating for hundreds of attendees. In these interior spaces, the innovative and impressive design work of eminent Japanese architects was also on display and contributed to the modern, Western-style aesthetic of those rooms. In addition to the *reihaidō,* churches grew to include functional, adaptable, and informal gathering spaces as well. These rooms served as classrooms as well as meeting rooms for various church-based groups. It was through the addition of such spaces that the well-traveled, cosmopolitan pastors in the first generation of Japanese Protestant pastors realized "great" churches—churches modeled in spirit if not in form on the large, dynamic urban Protestant churches of London and New York.

Yet these churches were located in Tokyo and represented a new and distinct type of religious gathering space in Japan. The Western appearance and associations of their exteriors assured them the status of privileged, protected spaces. Like all Christian churches in Japan, the capital's Japanese-led Protestant churches were not subject to the new ritual participation imperatives issued by national and local authorities in the way that Shinto spaces were. Financially or organizationally, churches were not nearly as challenged by the rise of State Shinto as Buddhist spaces or sect Shinto spaces were. However, mission-dependent church buildings in Japan persistently suffered from other financial and organizational constraints associated with their foreign funding sources. By contrast, self-supporting and autonomous churches in Tokyo and later in other major metropolitan areas did not. Japanese Protestant pastors and congregations there truly managed to capitalize on the special status of the church space and their relative institutional independence. With them, they commissioned distinct, impressive, Western-style Japanese church edifices built by the foremost among modern Japanese architects. While these Japanese Protestant churches might have mostly blended in on the streets of a major US or English metropolitan city, they were visually and functionally distinct in imperial-era Tokyo. Tokyo's well-educated, cosmopolitan religious seekers in the late nineteenth and early twentieth centuries were drawn to these churches and the social space that developed inside.

CHAPTER THREE

Preaching Self and World in the Capital

For the throngs of Japanese in the nation's largest cities, the 1880s ushered in a new, thought-provoking sensation: public oratory. From the floor of the new National Diet to large university lecture halls to a small but growing number of assembly halls, speakers offered talks on an array of important topics to urbanites. During the 1870s, the well-traveled and multitalented Fukuzawa Yukichi (1835–1901) lamented the lack of proper discussions in Japan, by which he meant not only the properly organized meeting but also, and more pertinent to this essay, the public speech.[1] Only thirty years later, however, there were almost too many orators to count. In his *Ensetsu zappō* (Various Speeches) of 1903, author-journalist Nakajima Kisō (1863–1936) published interviews with individuals on his short list of Japan's most distinguished speakers. Among them were political figures such as recent prime minister Ōkuma Shigenobu (1838–1922), National Diet vice speaker and newspaper magnate Shimada Saburō (1852–1923), and recent minister of education Ozaki Yukio (1858–1954), and scholars such as legal expert Takata Sanae (1860–1938) and economic law specialist Amano Tameyuki (1860–1938).[2] Well aware that secular orators were not the only individuals rousing public interest with speeches, however, Nakajima also highlighted several of Tokyo's most prominent religious leaders, including Presbyterian minister Uemura Masahisa.

In the Meiji and Taishō periods, new centrally located, modern, functional Protestant religious gathering spaces in the capital played host to Uemura and other well-known Protestant orators. The most popular among them animated the *shūkaidō* and *reihaidō* and preached to several hundred listeners on a weekly basis. From the early 1890s, hordes of Meiji Japan's students, professionals, and other elites descended on Fujimichō Church, where Uemura Masahisa was head pastor. A similar phenomenon was occurring in Tokyo's largest Protestant churches. Reinanzaka, Hongō, and Banchō Churches hosted the sermons of Congregationalist pastors including Kozaki Hiromichi, Yokoi Tokio, Ebina Danjō, and their fellow Doshisha graduate Tsunajima Kakichi. While they contributed significantly to the growth and dynamism of Japanese

Figure 3.1. Uemura Masahisa, ca. 1920. Source: Aoyoshi, *Uemura Masahisa den* [Biography of Uemura Masahisa], n.p.

Figure 3.2. Kozaki Hiromichi, ca. 1920. Source: Nakamura Satoshi, *Nihon Purotesutanto Kaigai senkyōshi* [History of Japanese Protestant overseas missions] (Tokyo: Shinkyō shuppan, 1945), n.p.

Protestant churches in imperial Japan, sermons vitally underlined the relevance of Protestant beliefs and ideals to Japanese society and reinforced the links between them.

The efflorescence of socially concerned Japanese pastoral discourse within the capital's Protestant churches took place in an environment that, in many ways, should have been unfavorable for it. During the Meiji period, the new government exerted three interconnecting types of pressure on Japanese subjects that worked to significantly impair the relationship between religion and society. Anticipating and then responding to calls for broader popular participation in governance, the Home Ministry and later the prime minister himself instituted relatively strict limits on expression and assembly. Regulations such as the 1875 Press Ordinance, the 1880 Ordinance on Public Meetings, and its successor, the 1890 Law on Assembly and Political Association, dramatically curtailed any freedoms that the people of Japan had gained under the 1889 Meiji Constitution.[3] Women in particular were prohibited from taking part in public assembly for political purposes or joining political parties.[4] Finally, the 1900 Public Order and

Figure 3.3. Yokoi Tokio, ca. 1900. Source: Hongō Kyōkai, *Hongō Kyōkai sōritsu 50-nen*, n.p.

Figure 3.4. Ebina Danjō, ca. 1910. Source: *Yumichō Hongō Kyōkai 100-nen shi*, n.p. (Courtesy Yumichō Hongō Church)

Police Law consolidated pervasive restrictions on speech, assembly, association, and organization into one tool for stifling debate and suppressing dissent.[5] These regulations had many clear implications for religious organizations and, importantly, for the ability of priests and pastors to address social topics in their religious discourse.

Furthermore, the Meiji government also targeted the relationship between religion and social discourse more directly. Between 1890 and the early 1920s, officials and bureaucrats worked diligently to sever the ties between religion and the "political" realm. During the Great Teaching Campaign in the early 1870s, the state had endorsed the pastoral roles of religionists affiliated with Shinto, Buddhism, and New Religions and deputized them to explicitly connect public orthodoxy with the religious creeds and beliefs of their respective denominations.[6] Although evangelists were instructed to essentially speak from script and officials often warned Buddhist priests to make the style and content of their lectures conform to those of the greater campaign, their public sermons and lectures were nevertheless connecting the religious and the political.[7] The result of such oversight was that Shinto and Buddhist spoken discourse tended to conform with the entirety of the *saisei itchi* (unity of rule and

Figure 3.5. Tsunajima Kakichi, ca. 1910. Source: Ii and Fugami, *Reinanzaka Kyōkai 100-nen shi*, n.p. (Courtesy of Reinanzaka Church)

doctrine) ideal.[8] By the early 1880s, however, Meiji leaders realized the utility of elevating emperor-centered Shinto above the contested realm of religion and of separating religion, and religionists, from politics.

Changes to the status of Buddhist clergy during the Great Teaching Campaign had, by the campaign's end in 1884, imposed a definite rift between private religious concerns and the so-called public realm for clerics.[9] They were aware that their religious status in the new Meiji grammar of religion at least theoretically excluded them from the secular social domain.[10] And while Shinto priests, as state officials and private religionists, remained briefly able to justify intervening in the political world in word and deed, the nationalization of Shinto in 1900 ended their ambiguous status. In that year the newly created Shrine Bureau ordered Shinto priests to return to their ritualist functions and step away from their preaching and proselytizing duties.[11] Through legal and administrative moves, the Meiji government dissociated religion from politics and religionists from political discourse—a category that increasingly included topics dangerously adjacent to politics such as social reform, improvement, and reorganization.

Although most Japanese religious leaders clearly avoided discussing social issues with strong political associations in relation to religion, a small number did not. Chikazumi Jōkan along with a dozen scholars and activists affiliated with the New Buddhist Fellowship argued that Buddhists needed to concern themselves with modern social and political problems.[12] Yet this priest and these lay Buddhists constituted a small countercurrent to mainstream Buddhism, and their influential efforts were marginalized and opposed by the greater Buddhist establishment.[13] In addition, their meetings and speeches were often shut down through the Public Order and Police Law of 1900.[14] Whereas these figures were exceptions in their denomination, many Japanese

Protestant pastors evoked the social and the political in their sermons each Sunday. In contrast to their Buddhist and Shinto counterparts, Protestant pastors maintained their principal role as preachers and used their pulpits to address explicitly and implicitly political subjects. The pacifist pastor Kashiwagi Gien, for instance, openly criticized political and social oppression and the Japanese imperialist project before his small congregation in Annaka.[15] Yet despite his controversial stances and the fining and frequent suspension of his church's monthly periodical, the *Jōmō Kyōkai Geppō,* during the 1930s, Kashiwagi was never even arrested or impeded from giving sermons at church.[16] And in the capital of Protestantism in Japan, it was even more evident that the walls of churches and the new institutional liberties of the Protestant movement gave pastors an empowering, albeit relative, freedom of speech. These leaders utilized this latitude to contravene government efforts to depoliticize and disempower religion, openly connecting religious with the social and political in their sermons.

These pastors took aim at the unprecedented moral confusion that followed the dismantling and reconstruction of the Japanese sociopolitical system during the mid-nineteenth century.[17] Uemura, Kozaki, Tsunajima, and Ebina drew on local, national, and international events transpiring distinctly within the this-worldly realm and Protestant Christian religious morality to demonstrate the nature and significance of each listener's social responsibilities. Furthermore, they consciously wedded their modern messages to Enlightenment ideals such as human equality, progress, and reason that could not but resonate with the well-informed, multilingual urban elite of late nineteenth- and early twentieth-century Japan.[18]

Sermons as Distinct Discourse

Pastors' sermons at the Reinanzaka, Banchō, Fujimichō, and Hongō Churches left lasting imprints on their Japanese attendees. Feminist author Hiratsuka Raichō (1886–1971) and radical anarchist author Ōsugi Sakae (1885–1923) both wrote of the strong impression that Ebina made on them from the pulpit of Hongō. Hiratsuka recalled that she "listened attentively" to Ebina, who was "very popular among the young students" because he was such "an eloquent and polished speaker with a commanding presence."[19] Ōsugi agreed, recalling, "I liked [Ebina's] sermons best. . . . I was completely entranced by the preacher's eloquence. His wonderful voice enthralled me whenever, pushing back his gray hair and stroking his long beard, he would thrust up his hands and invoke God."[20] Ōsugi and Hiratsuka, who both attended Hongō for less than a year, were famous figures drawn to the pastor as orator and the sermon as spectacle. Even such passers-through, however, took important messages and ideals away from the sermons of the *reihaidō*. Recalling one sermon, Ōsugi was struck by "Ebina's contention that religion was cosmopolitan, that it superseded national boundaries, and that it was libertarian in its denial of all earthly authorities."[21]

The recollections of long-term members of Tokyo's largest Japanese Protestant congregations also reveal a strong appreciation for both the performance and the content of the sermon. Hongō member Yoshino Sakuzō, a Tokyo Imperial University professor famous for his new conceptualization of constitutional popular democracy *(minponshugi),* had strong memories of Ebina's sermons. He remembered that Ebina "once attempted to explain this problem [the nature of socialism] from Hongō Church's lectern. Unexpectedly, this single sermon had an enormous influence inside and outside of the church."[22] Less captivated with Ebina than Yoshino was, future theologian and Shinanomachi Church pastor Takakura Tokutarō (1885–1934) left Hongō in 1906. He chose to attend Fujimichō Church because pastor Uemura gave impressive and thought-provoking sermons.[23] Editor, pioneering journalist, and educator Hani Motoko records that she was "spellbound" by Uemura's sermons.[24] At Banchō Church Tsunajima Kakichi also gave sermons that were both relevant and powerful, earning him a reputation well beyond the walls of his church. To demonstrate the newly fashioned electronic record player at the National Industrial Exposition in Osaka in 1903, organizers chose to broadcast a recorded sermon by Tsunajima dealing with the famous suicide of Fujimura Misao (1886–1903) at Kegon Falls (in the Nikkō temple complex).[25]

While Tsunajima's recording was lost during Banchō Church's evacuation and repeated relocations during World War II, many sermons by Meiji and Taishō Tokyo's most prominent Japanese Protestant pastors are extant and accessible.[26] One can read such sermons in many places. They range from these pastors' collected works to short sermon anthologies to the *kyōdan* (pulpit) section of church-published monthly journals. They were also often transcribed in *Rikugō zasshi* (Cosmos Journal), a leading Christian periodical edited by Kozaki, Uemura, and others; *Kirisutokyō shimbun* (Christian News); Uemura's *Fukuin shimpō* (Gospel News); church-published journals such as *Shinjin* (New Man) and *Shinjokai* (New Women's World) that were edited by Ebina and Hongō Church members; and even secular newspapers such as *Kokumin no tomo* (Nation's Friend) and the daily *Mainichi shimbun* (Daily News).[27]

Aware of this, several scholars writing about particular pastors' intellectual development and stances have made reference, here and there, to Japanese Protestant sermons. A handful of sermons by these pastors, including most recently one by Tsunajima, have been incorporated into articles and books dealing with these pastors' respective perspectives on theology as well as topics such as Confucianism, nationalism, and imperialism.[28] Clearly, sermons, which were often transcribed in such print publications, formed an integral part of the Japanese Christian leaders' discourse through which "Christianity began to be absorbed into the intellectual life of Japan" from the late 1870s onward.[29]

Yet sermons differed in one major way from most of the printed matter of the publications in which they appeared: sermons were a form of spoken discourse. Pronounced during services held at midmorning and often also in the evening by eloquent Japanese religious interpreters in large, ornate *reihaidō* and *shūkaidō*, sermons largely defined each church's culture and the experience of church attendance.[30] In contrast to various forms of written discourse that only originated and finished on the page, sermons were actually "communicative events" that took place. These events were made up of spoken language "used by a real speaker in an attempt to affect the beliefs and behavior of other real people in a particular socio-historical setting."[31] Sermons, then, have typically been persuasive in nature.[32] And to achieve this objective, religionists have been able, like other public speakers, to avail themselves of rhetorical and paralinguistic devices that are most possible in speech. These range from the use of anecdotes or parables and repetition to the use of pitch, pause, and pace.[33] It is also important to understand sermons as part of a "communicative link" connecting them with the larger context of events and activities taking place within the church.[34] While these included other events during the service and religious education, they also encompassed socially focused lay discourse, regular meetings of church-based groups, and other less regular happenings at church. In the context of a government working to solidify the distinction between private religion and the politicized public sphere, spoken, public discourse linking religion and social issues was relatively rare and significant. When seeking to understand the new allure, relevance, and impact of the discursive spaces within Japanese Protestant churches, therefore, sermons deserve consideration as a subject of their own—consideration that no other scholar has given them.

The following paragraphs examine the content and context of some forty-five sermons given between 1893 and 1920 by the pastors of the Reinanzaka, Hongō, Banchō, and Fujimichō Churches. This chapter argues that the leaders of Tokyo's largest Protestant churches offered original and meaningful perspectives on the individual, society, and the world through their sermons to the privileged segments of Japan's new educated elite. This comparative analysis of sermons reveals that, despite their frequently cited theological and ideological differences, the pastors of the capital's largest churches preached on shared socio-moral ideals.

In particular, Kozaki, Ebina, Uemura, and Tsunajima advocated progress, brotherhood, equality, and moral activism.

Four Tokyo Japanese Pastors

The pastorates of Kozaki, Uemura, Ebina, and Tsunajima each spanned decades, and certainly their theological and political stances evolved over that time. But the relationship between those changes and their pastoral discourse is far from straightforward. While there is insufficient information on Tsunajima's perspectives, those of Kozaki, Uemura, and Ebina have been well examined using an abundance of sources. While Kozaki's position changed little throughout his career, those of Ebina and Uemura both underwent major shifts during their time as pastors in Tokyo. Interestingly, the transition that occurred in Uemura's thought seems to have impacted the tone and message of his sermons more than the shift in Ebina's thought did his. Ultimately, however, it is more important to note that within each respective pastor's body of sermons, the same themes and moral imperatives prevail for the decades that make up the majority of his pastoral tenure. Church attendees, therefore, who attended Hongō or Reinanzaka between 1900 and 1920, or Ichibanchō/Fujimichō between 1890 and 1910, would have encountered a relatively consistent set of values and ideals. Based on the twenty sermons given by Tsunajima Kakichi between 1912 and 1924 and published as a collection by Christian publisher Fukunaga Bunnosuke (1861–1939), the same was true for Banchō Church during that time and likely the decade before.

Although many influences from Ebina's youth and young adulthood had already greatly informed his theological and social perspectives when he again became pastor at Hongō Church in 1898, his thinking continued to evolve. His upbringing in a samurai family that had supported the Tokugawa shogunate had endowed Ebina with a strong, sacrificial devotion for his lord that ultimately translated into loyalty and devotion to God.[35] Through his interactions with Janes at the Kumamoto Yōgakkō, Ebina also encountered, intellectually, the broader expanses of Japan, the world, and the universe for the first time, and this exposure also proved formative.[36] Missionary educators at his next school, the Dōshisha Eigakkō, taught but also at times limited Ebina and disparaged Japanese culture. Both sides of those encounters motivated him to develop his own understanding of God and God's relationship to humankind and to strive for institutional independence.[37] Furthermore, from the late 1880s, Ebina was greatly influenced by the so-called New Theology or Liberal Theology preached by German Evangelical Missionary Society missionary Wilfred Spinner

(1854–1918) and others in Japan.[38] In particular, he was quickly impressed by the "liberal ethics and social engagement based on the benevolent fatherhood of God and the brotherhood of man" embodied in this form of theological thought.[39] Combining these elements, Ebina developed a theology that built on rather than deviated from his Neo-Confucian, samurai intellectual foundations.[40]

In sermons between 1900 and his assumption of Dōshisha's presidency in 1920, Ebina showed many different colors. As Japan's involvement in Korea and conflict with Russia escalated during the early 1900s, the pastor emphasized nation, patriotism, the Japanese race, and empire. Following the death of the Meiji emperor in 1912, however, his sermons more frequently emphasized the themes most prominent among the progressive trends of the day. These included the equality and contributions of women and the importance of the modern family unit, for instance. And in his final years at Hongō, Ebina more often and clearly embraced liberal ideologies and movements such as internationalism, democracy, universal suffrage, and women's rights. In this phase that coincided with the final years and aftermath of World War I, terms such as "the people" *(kokumin),* "humanity" *(ningen),* and "the world" *(sekai)* appear in his sermons with more frequency. As with his other writings during this era of unprecedented global conflict and then international cooperation, his sermons promoted a global Christianity.[41] His perspectives were definitely more progressive in this period. In fact, however, Ebina's sermons throughout his pastorate at Hongō Church consistently contained imperatives and ideals that promoted conscience-driven activism, social awareness, and social change.

Kozaki, like Ebina, drew on a wealth of experience and education in Kumamoto and Kyoto in developing his worldview and the galvanizing sermons that he built on it. Made head of his samurai household in Kumamoto at age fourteen following his father's death, Kozaki developed a strong sense of responsibility and significant management skills.[42] By then Kozaki had also been thoroughly trained in martial arts and Confucian political philosophy at the Jishūkan in preparation for an important domain administration position.[43] In his time as an honors student at this elite domain-sponsored school, he was particularly drawn to Yokoi Shōnan's new formulation of Jitsugaku (Practical Studies), a proactive Neo-Confucian use of rationality and science to solve Japan's problems.[44] Then at the Kumamoto Yōgakkō under Janes's tutelage, Kozaki interpreted Christianity through his foundations in Confucianism.[45] Like Ebina, he embraced Christianity as a belief system but also as a path to modern, practical, political action.[46] Then at Dōshisha, Kozaki studied science, mathematics, history, law, and religion alongside Ebina with Western missionaries who reinforced some of these tendencies while working to temper others.[47]

In terms of Western teachers, Kozaki was particularly indebted to figures like American Board missionary Dwight Learned (1848–1943), who advocated ideals such as liberty, popular rights, and equality in his courses on political economy.[48] Of utmost significance, however, was Kozaki's Japanese mentor and teacher at Dōshisha, Niijima Jō, who impressed on Kozaki that Christianity required radical social responsibility.[49] As Kozaki began his pastorate in Tokyo in 1879, he carried with him a Christianity that combined religious beliefs with his duty to the Japanese nation, an appreciation for rational, proactive Confucian ethics, and a commitment to both liberalism and modernity. It permeated his various endeavors in the capital, from founding and leading the Japan YMCA and editing its organ *Rikugō zasshi* to writing on the ideal relationship between religion and society in Japan.[50] His 1886 book *Seikyō shinron* (A New Theory of Politics and Religion) articulated this synthesis, arguing that Christianity perfected the shortcomings of Confucianism and was necessary for the success of the new Japan.[51]

Similarly, Kozaki's sermons were characterized by their emphases on the rights of individuals, social improvement, and nationalism—even as his theological and philosophical positions continued to develop. Kozaki was deeply affected by the same wave of Liberal Theology as Ebina beginning in the late 1880s. He advocated the historicization or higher criticism of the Bible and disagreed with his missionary mentors' view that the Bible was by definition infallible.[52] Liberal Theology also allowed Kozaki to adopt a theistic view of evolution that left room for new scientific knowledge and God's divine intervention.[53] Ultimately, however, Kozaki upheld the truth of the gospel and wrote and preached in defense of evangelicalism against what he saw as the excesses of the New Theology.[54] Kozaki continued to argue, as he had in 1886, that it was the literal sacrifice of Jesus that united all humans as equal.[55] And he held that it was the immanence of the Holy Spirit, not subjective reason, that guided Christians working in the political and cultural spheres to improve the world.[56] Clearly indebted to his Confucian intellectual origins, Kozaki's pastoral discourse remained preoccupied with the correct relationship between the enlightened, forward-thinking, moral individual and society until his retirement from Reinanzaka Church in 1922.

His sermons over the years also maintained his commitment to the modernization and improvement of the Japanese nation and national identity and to the institutions he considered crucial to realizing those goals, such as the family, the state, and the church.[57] Sermons between 1902 and 1904 focused on themes such as "Faith and Life," "Active Religion," "Family Religion," "Diligence and Faith," and "The Origins of Social Reform."[58] And some notably similar themes appear in later sermons, including "Life and Faith" of 1908, "Christ's Social Perspective" of 1911, and "Labor Ideals" of 1916.[59] This does not mean that Kozaki's sermons were unchanging. In the years following the Russo-Japanese War, themes that simply received attention within Kozaki's sermons became the titular focus of his pastoral discourse. These included sermons on the nation and nation-state, such as "Our Country's Great Weakness" of 1907, "The Terrible Spectacle of our Country's Spiritual World" of 1910, "The State's Invisible Foundations" of 1913, and "Patriotism and Faith" of 1913.[60] And this trend is also particularly evident in 1920, when Kozaki's sermons on topics including "Pioneering Popular Ideals" (a sermon promoting universal suffrage) and "The Brotherhood of Christianity" prominently highlighted ideals already present in his previous sermons.[61] However, these slight shifts did not amount to noteworthy trends, and Kozaki's ideals did not change significantly. In a 1919 sermon titled "The Ideal Church," Kozaki highlighted three institutions that God provided for the edification of humanity. These were "the family . . . the state . . . [and] the church."[62] Looking back to his *Seikyō Shinron,* we see that these were the same institutions he emphasized back in 1886.[63] Kozaki was one of the two leading pastors best-known for their efforts to maintain theological orthodoxy.[64]

Long before he befriended his fellow pastor and cofounder of the Japan YWCA in 1881, Uemura Masahisa had a great deal in common with him. Like Kozaki and Ebina, Uemura derived from a samurai family on the losing side of the Meiji Restoration and held a strong attachment to the ideologies of his youth. Born into a *hatamoto* (Tokugawa bannermen) family, he learned as a child to adhere to a Confucian code of warrior ethics that emphasized duty, honor, diligence, perseverance, and honesty.[65] The young Uemura came, in large part thanks to the encouragement of his mother, to idolize daimyo Katō Kiyomasa (1562–1611) in particular.[66] This figure was famous for his military exploits under the command of Hideyoshi and Tokugawa Ieyasu and for his book of precepts outlining samurai ideals, often referred to as *bushidō.*[67] The importance of *bushidō* grew for Uemura as the Tokugawa-era samurai order crumbled on the eve of the Meiji Restoration. He watched his samurai family, which traced its lineage back to Tokugawa Ieyasu, as they were reduced to using a single bucket to wash and prepare rice.[68] In this context, his mother's entreaty for him as the "son of a samurai" to go out and "become a person of prominence, raise his family's reputation, and make a name for himself" held especially powerful significance.[69] Motivated by these factors, Uemura went on to study English and other Western subjects under James Ballagh.[70] In that context, Uemura added new knowledge and experience that he would carry with him as a Christian and as a pastor. The passion of missionary educators James Ballagh and Samuel Brown proved contagious and convincing for Uemura and a dozen other young Japanese converts. But the same was also true of Ballagh's deep commitment to Japan and the Japanese and his respect for the traditions and position of the former samurai.[71] Finally, the founding of Japan's first Protestant church in Yokohama had a great influence on Uemura. He helped draw up a charter that made the new church intentionally nondenominational, financially independent, and staunchly Bible based.[72]

Many of these principles stayed with him for the rest of his career as a professor at Meiji Gakuin, founding president of Tokyo Shingakusha, author, editor, and pastor. Uemura championed a broadly defined independence for Japanese individuals and for the Japanese church.[73] Such independence ideally gave each Japanese the freedom to train and then utilize his or her conscience, the wellspring of social and moral values.[74] As Uemura and Kozaki made clear in the inaugural issue of *Rikugo zasshi,* ideals such as equality, human rights, and love ranked especially high among these.[75] Uemura also believed that Christians had a duty to develop social consciousness and to engage with and comment on society.[76] His position on this in 1884, when he published his book *Shinri ippan* (An Outline of Truth), called on Christians to embody noble ideals, improve society, and even confront the state if their consciences dictated it.[77] In arguing for the existence of God and for Christianity's usefulness for Japan, this philosophical work also evoked Japan's cultural heritage and marked continuity with Uemura's samurai education and values.[78] From the 1890s, he introduced the concept of "baptized Bushidō" to characterize the transformation of his old faith and culture by Christianity.[79] As for Uemura's evangelical theological position, he made even fewer concessions to the new Liberal Theology that came and challenged conservative Protestant Christianity in late nineteenth-century Japan. He ceased to insist on the direct verbal inspiration of the Bible, but maintained a strong belief in the divinity and sacrifice of Jesus and most other major tenets of evangelical Christianity.[80] The single question on which Uemura's views appear to have shifted is that of the relationship between religion and the state. His insistence on separating loyalty to country from loyalty to God and on keeping the church distinct and independent from the state evolved into something that many have seen as a disillusioned acquiescence to the state.[81] Uemura increasingly encouraged Christians to turn inward toward themselves and the church and away from the world and confrontation with the state.[82]

While Uemura's sermons after the death of the Meiji emperor in 1912 reflect this change in theme and tone, his sermons during the two previous decades highlight a consistent set of objectives with clear connections to the pastor's earlier works and upbringing. During those years in the latter half of the Meiji era, Uemura often spoke of the affinities between *bushidō* and Christianity and about the nature of Japanese Christian patriotism.[83] In doing so, he sought to reconcile his samurai and Christian identities. The pastor also often preached on the responsibility of Christians to be aware of pressing social issues such as the labor problem in Japan as well as women's rights and the Japanese marriage system.[84] Furthermore, Uemura's sermons in this period are filled with calls to independent thinking and Christian moral activism as well. In thought and action, key ideals such as brotherhood and equality feature prominently as desired objectives.[85] It was in preaching on these types of topics that Uemura's church attracted hundreds and eventually more than one thousand attendees each week, and these themes provide lines of commonality between his sermons and those of his fellow pastors in the capital.

In spite of their differences, these pastors worked together diligently to promote many shared Protestant Christianity social ideals in Meiji- and Taishō-era Tokyo and beyond. In addition to different opinions on the proper distance of religious leaders from the greater Japanese sociopolitical arena, heated disagreements broke out over the question of New Theology. The conflict between Uemura and Ebina that has received the most attention occurred during a series of debates in 1901 over theological differences surrounding issues of the divinity of Christ and the contrast between the thought-based and experience-based types of conversion and belief. As early as 1930, Anesaki Masaharu began a long line of historiography, including works by Unuma Hiroko, Takeda Kiyoko, Dohi Akio, and Yosuke Nirei, which depicts a relatively conservative Uemura and a liberal Ebina.[86] Yet even at their most divergent, Uemura and Ebina shared a great deal in their worldview and their pastoral discourse.[87] Uemura, who disapproved of the Protestant minister leading social reform as an activist, believed that the church should send freely, independently thinking reform-minded men and women out into the world to respond to the needs of society.[88] This echoed the attitude of Christian service and reform that Niijima Jō cultivated in students like Ebina, Kozaki, and Tsunajima at Dōshisha.[89] Indeed, despite their vast differences, there were fundamental similarities in the broader meanings in the messages of all four pastors that may help offer explanations for the similar type of socially conscious Japanese individuals who attended their churches. With their Sunday sermons inside Tokyo's largest Protestant churches, Congregationalist pastors Ebina, Kozaki, and Tsunajima, and Presbyterian pastor Uemura all presented a value system that centered much less on the state and its prerogatives than on their conceptualizations of individual and collective social responsibility, social and intellectual progress, and Christian brotherhood in Japan and beyond.

Themes in Japanese Protestant Pastoral Discourse

Eyes Ahead

In contrast to the national government and its proponents that implored the public to remember a distant historical Japan and its timeless lessons, Tokyo Protestant pastors aimed to turn their listeners attention to the realization of a new and better Japan in an improved world. Beginning in the 1880s, ideologues writing in or on behalf of the Meiji government transformed elite nativist ideas of the late 1700s into a vigorous, modern campaign to construct, codify, and popularize a Japanese national past.[90] In 1890 the Ministry of Education and the emperor announced the Imperial Rescript on Education (Kyōiku ni Kansuru Chokugo), calling on Japanese to "render illustrious the best traditions of your forefathers" by practicing "loyalty and filial piety."[91] Nearly two decades later, in 1908, the Ministry of Education issued the Imperial Rescript on Diligence and Thrift (Boshin Shōsho), propagating the "the teachings of our revered ancestors" on the ideals of filial piety and the mandate to continue the "record of our glorious history."[92] That year Itō Hirobumi commemorated the twenty-year-old Meiji Constitution with talk of "the grandeur of Japan's ageless past."[93]

Tokyo Protestant pastors emphasized not the past but the future of Japan and the assertive role that each listener should take in shaping it. On 5 July 1908, just three months before the issuing of the Boshin Rescript, Kozaki spoke of a society based on ideals that directly contradicted the rescript's wistful spirit. Tokugawa morality was based on a reverence for the idyllic past that he considered unequal to the modern tasks of contemporary religion. Kozaki described Tang China (618–906) as Neo-Confucianism's ideal before contrasting that ideology with Protestant Christianity. Unlike this and other moments in the real or mythical past that are idealized by "other teachings . . . planning for revival," Kozaki made clear that Christians look to the future for the "realization" of their ideal society.[94]

The opinions of other Protestant pastors resonated with those of Kozaki, and both Ebina and Uemura concurred entirely on the importance of looking forward. In March 1896, speaking in words from the New Testament, Uemura reiterated that "Jesus does not intend for us to look towards the trivial things that lay behind, only to pursue what is ahead."[95] Similarly, Ebina told his congregation in the fall of 1902 that all classes were "needed for the future Japan" that he and other Christians hoped to realize.[96] Weeks after the end of the

Russo-Japanese War in 1905, Ebina asked the crowd to be encouraged and "full of hope regarding the future."[97] Protestant pastors in Tokyo, despite their numerous differences, agreed that Christians must fix their eyes forward instead of looking backward.

The "future Japan" that Japanese Protestant leaders saw off ahead in the distance was a nation that was modern in not only material but also spiritual terms, made possible by Christianity. There was among Japanese Christians concern that economic and technological progress in Japan were being accompanied by moral decline rather than improvement.[98] Recognizing this sentiment, leading pastors in the capital used their pulpits to promote deep, meaningful spiritual change to accompany Japan's modernization. Ebina explained in a 1905 sermon that in Japan, although "the times have changed, [and] civilization has advanced," only Christianity could make the superficial appearance of civilization into an internalized moral reality. So in order to push Japanese morality forward to the advanced level of the other parameters of civilization, he repeated throughout his sermon that "now it is time to pray."[99] Likewise, Kozaki told his listeners in 1913 to think hard about the "spiritual fate of each individual along with the future prospects of our nation."[100] With a more pronounced optimism, Uemura surveyed the evidence of progress in many different areas of Japanese endeavor and took heart. "Not a few of the elements of our new code are to be attributed to the influence of Christianity," he said, and he harbored a strong "hope" for the moral advancement of Japan.[101] For these pastors, a better "future Japan" required a new moral system to replace the Neo-Confucian teachings they themselves had studied so carefully in their youth. They advocated melding the good elements from traditional Neo-Confucianism with a new, self-consciously "modernist" and socially progressive morality of Protestant Christianity.[102]

Brotherhood

The national unity that the Meiji government was working so diligently to foster continued to prove elusive, and Protestant Christian pastors purported to have the remedy. The Five Charter Oath (Gokajō no Goseimon) of 1868 laid the foundations for the Meiji state, and in it Japan's new national leaders wrote that "all classes, high and low, shall be united in vigorously carrying out the administration of affairs of state."[103] The goal was a tight-knit national community of brothers and sisters, connected by their common relationship to the Japanese emperor. In defining the content and boundaries of Japanese subjecthood, the 1889 Constitution of the Empire of Japan, drawn up by Itō Hirobumi and Inoue Kowashi (1843–1895), was firmly establishing the basis for a nation of unified citizens. With the abolition of feudal domains and the status system, and the creation of a conscript army, compulsory education, and both national and prefectural assemblies, Japan had quickly and decisively cut the barriers separating the nation's 40 million countrymen.[104] Yet as the national government produced rhetoric on national unity, events throughout the nation demonstrated dissatisfaction and disunity. From the Freedom and People's Rights movement of the 1880s to the 1907 Ashio Copper Mine riots to the Rice Riots that engulfed Japan in 1918, men and women across Japan drew attention to the divisive conflicts within the so-called national brotherhood.[105] Japan, like so many other nations at the time, had failed to institute the type of unity outlined in its political charter. But Japanese Protestant Christian leaders argued that Protestant morality could change all that.

Protestant Christianity presented itself as a religious ideology that promoted deep and strong connections between all people, and its advocates in Japan promised that Protestantism's ideals would help unify all Japanese and indeed all mankind. Japanese Christian intellectuals saw in Protestant Christianity a specific "concept of human brotherhood."[106] In describing the roots of this contention, several scholars have drawn attention to the "Christian humanism based on universal brotherhood" that characterized the religious morality of Yoshino Sakuzō and many other social reform-minded Tokyo Protestants.[107] Nowhere was this rhetoric more alive than in the Sunday sermons of Protestant pastors in the capital.

Although the ideals of universal brotherhood and human unity were not limited to Protestant Christianity, several Protestant pastors in Tokyo were convinced that only the Protestant conceptualization of brotherhood could truly bring about the unity of all people. Kozaki pointed out that "brotherhood" *(kyōdai-shugi)* was a virtue that could in fact be found in many places, from the *Analects of Confucius* to the cries of the French Revolution. Although Confucius had written, Kozaki explained in 1920, of a "Brotherhood of All between the Four Seas," this ideal really only applied to the Chinese.[108] In France, the success of and social progress since the French Revolution promised to realize brotherhood. But none could deny the gap between the industrialists and the workers so readily apparent in that country at the time. In reality, the brotherhood so often spoken of was much less often seen: "True brotherhood is difficult to find outside of Christianity; the one reason for this is that without the recognition of a single [heavenly] father, the basis for brotherly friendship to occur is lacking."[109] From the Old Testament to the French National Convention's Proclamation to the Nations, the ideal of brotherhood without Protestant Christianity lacked conviction, in Kozak's opinion.

Kozaki, Uemura, Ebina, and Tsunajima all considered the father-child relationship of Protestant Christianity to be central to the development of brotherhood. The connection "between God and man is [like that of] father-to-son, and [that] between people . . . is [like] the perfection of love between siblings," Kozaki preached in 1908.[110] Likewise, Ebina explained that "God is the father of all men . . . [and] all men are God's children."[111] This outlook permeates much of his sermons and appears in his many writings and speeches calling for international brotherhood.[112] Even within the family, proper filial and brotherly relations depended on Christianity. Using his own case as a model, Tsunajima explained that a Christian's love for God had to function as the cause of his or her love for actual parents and siblings.[113] He told listeners that "following the heavenly father's command," a broad mandate that included living a "life of service [and] a life of sacrifice," was a higher priority for the Christian than love for brothers at the national or even family level.[114] Rather than focusing on one's love "for [one's] children, for [one's] wife or husband, for [one's] parents . . . for the national society," the Banchō pastor implored Christians to focus on their love for God the Father, which would then radiate outward to real and imagined brothers. Uemura specifically criticized atheism because it lacked such a God as father figure. In a sermon in Taiwan that encapsulated his views, he explained that the world of atheism "would be no different than an assembly of orphans." In such a world "the spirit of brotherhood would completely disappear."[115] By contrast, Christ's vision, Kozaki argued in 1911, was a "society connected together with love as an organism. . . . The term that demonstrates this relationship is sibling."[116] Ebina, some years earlier, had expressed his own conviction that, in the final analysis, Christianity was the only world ideology that taught that "all . . . children of God . . . [are] linked together as one."[117] In 1897 at Ichibanchō, Uemura preached that "it is Christianity that teaches the way for people of the world to believe together in one heavenly father and [live] as brothers and sisters."[118]

The pastors of Hongō, Banchō, Reinanzaka, and Fujimichō, despite their considerable differences, agreed that Protestant conceptualizations of brotherhood could address the shortcomings of Japanese colonial policy. While the Japanese expansionists also spoke of brotherhood as they colonized and annexed other nations, Uemura sought to show the insufficiency of their inclusiveness. The Japanese sense of brotherhood was in fact based on the "blood group" *(kettō dantai),* and Uemura asked them rhetorically, "What then is to be done about the people of Taiwan?"[119] These men and women could never be truly considered siblings under the blood relative definition that began to gain popularity in Japan during the late 1890s. Only the brotherhood of God's children could cross such boundaries. Among these pastors Uemura was the most openly critical of the

Japanese annexation of Korea and often expressed respect for the nationalism and independence of Japan's colonized subjects.[120]

However, the words of fellow pastors also urged caution. The Kumiai Kyōkai began a mission to Korea in 1911 with the dual goals of the salvation and assimilation of Koreans, largely based on the ideas of pastor Ebina Danjō.[121] He at times wrote and spoke approvingly of annexation and the collaboration of his denomination's mission with the Japanese imperial project, and he was fundraising chairman for the mission in the early Taishō period.[122] However, scholars have identified in his rhetoric a call for "ethical imperialism."[123] He argued, for instance, that while Japan should send farmers and merchants to Korea and the government should "facilitate this migration," they should avoid "transporting armed troops and instead send "warriors of peace."[124] And in a 1912 sermon he provided a model for maintaining "genuine patriotic feeling" and Christian ideals while living abroad. For the pastor, Paul had embodied such a love for his country Israel by proudly taking the message of "God's chosen people" to the Romans. Ebina explained that Paul suffered enormously to spread Christianity in that hostile environment in order to fulfill the Jewish God's "promise of bringing happiness to the world."[125] To endure such hardship for the sake of another country was in fact a reflection of the apostle's deep pride in his own. This perspective echoes those he gave in a sermon in Seoul in 1915 in which he promoted all people viewing each other as siblings under the compassion and egalitarianism of Christ.[126] Like Ebina, fellow Kumiai pastor Tsunajima Kakichi evinced approval and pride at the Kumiai mission in Korea. However, in a sermon given in a church at the first annual conference of the Kumiai Kyōkai in 1913 in Seoul, Tsunajima explained that the brotherhood of Christianity extended beyond ethnic, cultural, and linguistic bonds. So while the Japanese state had annexed Korea and conducted the Naisen Ittai (Japan and Korea as One) policy, it was only through the spiritual power of Christ that these different peoples could become compatriots.[127]

As the government ideologues propagated the concept of the ethnically based national body *(kokutai)* to stand for the entirety of the Japanese people under the rule of the timeless emperor, Protestant Christianity promoted a distinct, more active type of unity. It was precisely this type of conceptualization that literary scholar and government adviser Inoue Tetsujirō targeted as he sought to discredit and weaken Protestant Christianity. He specifically complained that filial piety and loyalty did not appear among Christianity's key tenets and that, furthermore, the religion preached universal love.[128] For Christians, the emperor did not constitute the center of a Japan-specific Neo-Confucian loyalty structure that fostered a sort of official brotherhood for the national benefit. Instead,

Christians pointed above the emperor to a universal God who commanded all people, as his individual children, to cooperate in a brotherhood based on the Christian concept of boundless love. While Inoue singled out this particular value as a threat to the Japanese *kokutai,* he was in fact taking on a much larger set of values that were deeply intertwined with Protestant Christianity's Western heritage. First was the rebirth of the ideal of brotherhood in late eighteenth-century Western European and American philosophy as the claim that all men, across national boundaries, possessed certain common characteristics. Second, the new conceptualization of brotherhood came attached to the revolutionary ideal of *égalité* that French and British philosophers had derived from abstract brotherhood and standardized as a natural human right during the European Enlightenment. While it appeared to have existed in many different cultures and epochs, it was the Enlightenment version of brotherhood, and its ancillary of equality, that many of Japan's most well-read and intellectually diverse Japanese Protestant pastors knew well and intended to spread.

Equality in Theory

Japanese Protestant pastors frequently encouraged their listeners to think about the meaning of both brotherhood and equality in ways that added depth to Meiji government laws and rhetoric. By the late 1890s, when Protestant churches in Tokyo began to see unprecedented, sustained growth and their popular pastors became well-known figures, Japan could present itself as a nation of equals, in theory. Japanese citizens became commoners with new freedoms of occupation and marriage, including most of the former samurai class.[129] Even the lowest class in Japan, the *burakumin* who worked in ritually or physically impure occupations, were freed from their official class and elevated to commoner status in the 1871 Eta Emancipation Edict (Eta Kaihōrei).[130] Taken together, people across Japan were referring to the "equality of the four classes" *(shimin byōdō)* that the new national government had established.[131] Japanese Christian leaders sought to provide a religio-moral basis for this legal equality, creating a theoretical foundation for a community of equals that new social and economic differences would not undermine.

When Japanese Protestant Christian pastors imagined brotherhood, they included in their worldview a strong call for the adjacent value of equality that disregarded the various forms of hierarchy implicit in most existing forms of the concept. For Kozaki, any so-called brotherhood not premised on equality did not contain the powerful mandate of Christianity's brotherhood. In a 1920 sermon, he explained that "equality" was a prerequisite of "true brotherhood."[132] The brotherhood that Kozaki saw most frequently in Japan was one of "paternalists . . . [who] insult the weak." The Protestant values of "equality and democracy oppose" this type of condescension.[133] He saw the incongruity of the lectures on social equality that lower-class workers in Tokyo heard from various progovernment ideologues and their actual socioeconomic reality.[134] That day, Kozaki told his congregation of professors, teachers, Diet members, and other community leaders that none of them were to be called master (rabbi), citing Matthew 23:8. For this reason, Kozaki denounced Hinduism and the socioeconomic divisions of the "four-caste system" *(shi-zoku no seido)*.[135] Despite the persistence of notions of hierarchy and class superiority in Japan and elsewhere, he contended that all were brothers and sisters with a common master, the Lord, and that none of them was superior to any other.[136]

Kozaki, Ebina, and Tsunajima emphasized Protestant Christianity's disregard for socioeconomic distinctions and privilege. Christians' belief in a single father meant that "regardless of race, nation, or social rank, everyone can have a sense of brotherhood," by Kozaki's reckoning.[137] Likewise, Ebina declared that "Jesus makes no distinction between rich and poor, no differentiation between old and young, male and female, and considers all people as equal."[138] In a 1920 sermon, Ebina took aim at social stratification by demonstrating that unlike the Old Testament situation that required "intermediation," the covenant of the New Testament meant there was no need for mediatory agents between God and man. Christians required no help from "angels" or earthly intercessors because each was his or her own "priest." In this system, Ebina concluded, Protestant Christianity had both introduced and defined "true equality" as a situation in which "not a single person could have control over another."[139]

The same leveling process also applied beyond the sphere of religion as well. For Kozaki, brotherhood meant the leveling of all, making "even the brave hero" or "the great sage" just another brother.[140] In Japan's expansion, Uemura worried about the status of the colonized, such as the people of Taiwan, who were not capable of being included in the tight, homogeneous blood-related Japanese brotherhood. Between extermination and second-class citizenship, Uemura considered bleak the outlook for efforts to integrate Taiwanese into the Japanese sociocultural polity.[141] In fact, he explained, they deserved to be treated as equals. Even one's closest associates and family, these pastors argued, were not above the other members of the universal brotherhood of mankind. And as Tsunajima's recapitulation of Mark 3:33 made clear, anyone in the brotherhood of man was just as important and close to Jesus as his own mother and brother.[142] While pastors spoke often of the ideal of equality as it appeared in the Bible, they also highlighted examples of egalitarianism at work in the modern world.

In many of their sermons, Tokyo's Protestant pastors praised strides taken in applying the ideal of equality. In the final years of World War I, Tsunajima pondered optimistically that good things would come of those events, just as "equality" had been born out of the "French Revolution . . . after the tragic bloodshed."[143] In 1911, Kozaki also praised the equality sought by both the French Revolution and the US war for independence.[144] Looking to yet another instance of national violence, Ebina said of the US Civil War that "there was in the history of the world, never a war as honorable." The "pure motive" for which the Union army fought was the liberation of "an enslaved foreign people" and the endowment of these men and women with "equal freedom and rights."[145] Even Japan was to be applauded as a nation that had, in Kozaki's opinion on that Sunday in 1912, "reformed feudalistic Old Japan in the span of less than half a century" by "widely imposing the equality of the four classes."[146] Protestant pastors contended that the world had made laudable progress in trying to realize a brotherhood of equals, and pushed their listeners to continue the march. Such references were also, however, a reminder for listeners of the difficulties inherent in achieving that goal and of the righteousness of extreme measures for such a cause.

In focusing on such recent revolutionary moments, Tsunajima, Kozaki, and Ebina were clearly stating that inequality was not something to be wiped away by positive thinking. From the nation of so-called Christian charity that officially condoned slavery until 1863 and continued to maintain striking racial divisions to the dramatic middle- and lower-class revolts of 1848 across a Europe that purported to represent and uphold liberty, equality, and brotherhood, individuals were clearly not all treated as equals in reality. In Japan, several remnants of class inequality would continue to persist well into and beyond the twentieth century. Specifically, both the gender and class inequality that characterized the rapidly modernizing United States and Western Europe were rife in Japan as well. Yet these pastors presented both the possibility and the mandate of imagining a worldwide brotherhood of equals through Christianity. Beyond reifying the definitions of brotherhood and equality, they considered all Christians responsible for developing and applying specific Protestant ideals of equality in their daily lives.

Gender Equality in Practice

The Meiji period witnessed an unprecedented interest in questioning, defining, and propagating definitions of Japanese womanhood, and Tokyo's Protestant pastors were actively involved in this process in both word and deed. Liberal and conservative thinkers clashed in Meiji journals, newspapers, and books, and at lecterns and even pulpits, over the definition and political rights of the Japanese woman. All of these voices agreed that the behavior and treatment of Japanese women would stand as an indicator for Westerners of Japan's level of civilization.[147] Furthermore, they were all convinced that Japanese women had an enormous role to play in the establishment and maintenance of a modern Japan that was a rich country and strong nation.[148] Much more numerous than these assumptions, however, were the points of disagreement centering around women's rights to participate in the political arena, assemble in both women's and mixed groups for intellectual exchange, access higher education, and receive protection by law from being divorced on frivolous grounds.

To state it more directly, intellectuals, activists, and administrators were debating women's right to understand and influence their own position in Japanese society. On the liberal end of the spectrum of the debate were a number of Japanese theorists calling for great improvement in the position of the Japanese woman during the 1870s. Educator and author Mori Arinori (1847–1899) did just that in several articles in *Meiroku zasshi* (Meiji Six Journal) and contributed to a growing body of writings that included works by author and social critic Fukuzawa Yukichi, translator and educator Nakamura Masanao (1832–1891), and others who echoed such ideals.[149] Taking these claims even further were men and women who called for complete gender equality, such as Freedom and People's Rights movement leaders Ueki Emori (1857–1892) and Kishida Toshiko (1863–1901).[150] More conservative opinions at the other end of the spectrum, while they supported women's public appearance in elite charity bazaars and sophisticated ballroom events at the Rokumeikan,[151] used contradictory depictions of women as mentally weak and immature beings, potentially disruptive activists, and unofficially deputized civil servants to justify their exclusion from the broadly defined public sphere.[152]

Despite the confusing mixture of opinions circulating around the issue in the closing decades of the nineteenth century, the basic contours of the new definition of the Japanese woman were often strikingly clear. From the early 1870s onward, the Meiji state increasingly brought women's gender-based roles, which previously had differed according to class and status and were, in many cases, regulated by customary practice, under the control of its newly established national administration and body of laws.[153] With the promulgation of Meiji Japan's long-awaited constitution in 1889, Japanese women were emphatically and officially recognized as a unitary group and denied, along with 99 percent of the male Japanese populace, the right to vote.[154] In 1890, the Imperial Diet elected by status-based, limited manhood suffrage opened. Women were quickly forbidden to organize or participate in political activities, including attending sessions in the Diet, by that year's Shūkai oyobi Seisha Hō (Assembly and Political

Organization Law).[155] The Meiji Civil Code of 1898 enumerated the right of a husband but not, in most cases, a wife to sue for divorce on grounds of adultery, thus perpetuating and reinforcing a customary sexual double standard that facilitated the existence and prosperity of licensed prostitution.[156] Two years later, the Home Ministry issued Article Five of the Chian Keisatsu Hō (Public Order and Police Law) of 1900, further prohibiting women from assembly.[157] While this legislation made it apparent that women were not to be public, various government policies and initiatives also provided Japanese women with several ideas of the proper roles that they were supposed to fill.

From the 1870s onward, the *ryōsai kenbō* (good wife, wise mother) ideal became the model for Japanese womanhood in both more progressive and more conservative circles, and the government took action to provide women with all of the resources necessary to fit this role. Initially, well-traveled, liberal thinkers drew from experience in the West to develop an ideal of Japanese women as "good companions for their husbands, good teachers for their children, and good citizens who could help to create a strong and powerful nation."[158] Seemingly convinced, the government construed the first two roles as fulfillment of the third and mandated first elementary education for both girls and boys in 1873 and then one higher school for girls or more in each prefecture in 1899.[159] Through schooling, women exercised their right and ability to achieve literacy and acquire an array of practical skills. The purpose and sphere for the use of these capacities and knowledge, however, remained limited to the creation, maintenance, and improvement of the home and family for the benefit of the nation. The Ministry of Education's 1887 publication of *Meiji Onna no daigaku* (The Meiji Greater Learning for Women) once and for all established the government line that the public space for women was the private space of the home.[160]

It was in the context of and in opposition to this image and its repercussions that Protestant pastors advocated for a much more public role for women that contrasted with more restrictive norms and policies. Many Tokyo pastors made strong statements in favor of women's rights and their suitability for public roles that began with affirmations of the "distinct" strengths of the female gender. At many points both Ebina and Kozaki placed strong emphasis on the value of the woman. Drawing from the four Gospels, Ebina explained in 1916 that women were just as important as Jesus's male followers during his time on earth. They were "partners in Christ's ministry from start to finish," and Ebina provided examples of their distinctive contributions. It was indeed the women who went to see Christ's "last moments and prepared the body for burial," while Jesus's actual disciples were broken with sorrow and confusion. In the final moments, on cutting open Jesus's garments, the soldier found "seamless undergarments," a sign of high-quality craftsmanship. Only Jesus's female followers could have made such "precious" clothing.[161] In a sermon before the national Christian Women's Conference (Fujin Taikai) in 1909 at Reinanzaka Church, Kozaki asked his congregation to identify the persons who took care of the "necessities of life" *(ishokujū)* for Jesus and his disciples. He also asked them who it was that "always gave comfort and encouragement to Jesus and the disciples." In both cases, he answered, it was Christ's women followers.[162] And just as they held a place of high esteem within Jesus's entourage, Tokyo Protestant pastors posited that women also deserved proper consideration within the family.

Japanese pastors were particularly interested in elevating the position of women within the household. The state situated married women below the male heads of household and routed the transmission of the head's indivisible inheritance past the wife to the oldest male heir. Furthermore, the Meiji era saw the continuation of unpunished adultery and even polygamy by the husband.[163] It was in this context that Kozaki asserted that Jesus held a high regard for the position of the woman in the family. As evidence, he cited Christ's words on the holiness of marriage, insistence on the unity between one man and one woman, and repudiation of divorce.[164] Similarly, Uemura emphasized in 1895 the importance of the woman's position as "wife" by promoting the ideal of marriage and marital monogamy. He condemned the frequency, even among Japanese Christians, of husbands who all too readily divorced their wives and remarried numerous times.[165] The pastor called to mind for his listeners the Old Testament "moral teachers" *(dōtoku no sensei)*, ancient Israel's male and female judges, who so eagerly strove to demonstrate the wrongfulness of polygamy to the people of Israel.[166] It was these individuals who were responsible for instilling in their fellow countrymen the moral foundations for a marriage system in which a husband had only one wife.[167] Like Christ in relation to the Christian church, a husband must sacrifice himself for his wife, making it impossible to truly provide such love for more than one wife.[168] Clearly, denominational and theological differences aside, Protestant pastors in Tokyo viewed Japanese women as primarily wives, mothers, or daughters. Yet they called for women to receive greater respect and value in these roles, and such perspectives applied beyond the home as well.

In Protestant pastoral discourse, the woman in the world and in Japan was undeniably capable of occupying roles within the public sphere that were both equivalent to and as important as roles filled by men. Protestant pastors questioned the unnecessarily large gap separating the sexes and advocated women's public participation. In 1902, Ebina insisted that even in the past, samurai wives were nonetheless samurai, and he praised the Meiji Restoration for repudiating "the differentiation between man and woman."[169] Speaking of gender relations in France, Kozaki lamented the persistent examples of the "distinctions between man and woman" and labeled such practices "unjust" and "unnecessary."[170] For Uemura, the male examples of St. Paul, St. Francis, St. Bernard, and even Christ clearly demonstrated that God condoned legal and professional independence for men. In his sermon in 1916, however, he extended this conclusion to women as well.[171] Such views are consistent with Uemura's reputation for criticizing "the sexism in Japanese society" and efforts aimed at "improving the status of women."[172]

Tsunajima noted that while England's men were sent to the battlefield to serve the nation in World War I (1914–1918), women very ably filled a variety of public professional roles such as "post office clerks, bank employees, bus conductors, and other types of duties."[173] Ebina criticized Shakespeare, who "didn't value women much in his works." Instead, the pastor echoed the sentiments of thinkers such as the selectively progressive Fukuzawa Yukichi and lauded John Stuart Mill, who "paid women a great deal of respect and contributed to the female emancipation movement."[174] In 1913, he offered an interpretation of the place that New Testament–based Christianity afforded women in the sociopolitical realm. Ebina explained that "in the world, the great power of the woman was not confined to the house, instead transcending the home, [and extending to] the building of the nation of God."[175] He, like his Protestant colleagues, believed that women could hold places of leadership and should value and develop their enormous capacity to impact society and the world.

In their sermons, Protestant pastors allowed for the possibility that women could do the same tasks as men and perform as well as or better than men. Furthermore, no matter what vocation women chose, Protestant pastoral discourse included a strong call for women's right to choose their paths in life and to do so publicly to the same extent that men held these rights. Embedded in these speeches, there remained an assumption of the separateness of a distinct women's sphere and a visible approbation of the good wife, wise mother construct, yet these roles were not to exclude women from the public sphere. Instead, these pastors' views on Japanese womanhood differed significantly from the Meiji government model and placed a high value on women's public existence and participation. By the end of the Meiji period, these pastors and others like Presbyterian Tamura Naoomi added considerable weight to their arguments for the benefits of the elevation of women's status from firsthand experience gleaned from sojourns in the United States and other Western countries. Using their experience among elites in the US and Western Europe, these pastors argued that women in modern Western countries were indeed accorded a much higher status and better treatment than their Japanese counterparts.[176] In order to make way for the modern, educated, sociopolitically active new Japanese woman, it would be necessary to leave behind the underprivileged, sequestered housewife of Japanese custom and rethink Confucian gender roles. In fact, Ebina, Kozaki, Uemura, and Tsunajima's dissatisfaction with the role of the woman in Japan was only part of a much larger and more emphatic critique of an East Asian religio-moral tradition that they ranked as inferior to a more enlightening and civilizing Protestant Christianity.

Eastern Morality

Japanese Protestant pastors claimed emphatically that Eastern religious morality in general and Japanese religious morality in particular could not lead to moral revolution in Japanese society. Evaluating the moral situation in Japan, Kozaki lamented the endless violence, including the "triple and quintuple murders," "suicides," and "infanticide and parricide" that filled the burgeoning daily newspapers in the late Meiji period. Uemura noticed with regret that over the past century, the Japanese people had developed "conceit," "materialism," and "hopeless pessimism."[177] Having lost the ability to practice their well-learned religious morality, Kozaki saw that his fellow countrymen were turning to "alcohol, lust, greed for wealth, [and] greed for fame" and harboring "jealous, grudge-holding, and vengeful hearts."[178] As opposed to other countries faced with "materialism, skepticism, naturalism, and a pessimistic outlook," however, Kozaki said that Japan lacked a religion capable of minimizing the spread of these dilemmas.[179] In fact, by his reckoning the premodern ideologies of "[Neo-]Confucianism, Buddhism, and Shintō fell with the Tokugawa Bakufu," along with their ability to meet the moral needs of the nation.[180] Echoing this view, Ebina cautioned in the same year that constructing the new Japan on Japanese religiosity would be like "building on a truly insecure foundation."[181] As a religion for the making of a modern Japan, Tokyo Protestant pastors vehemently argued that Buddhism and Shinto were woefully inadequate because of their alleged inability to foster pertinent religious morality and moral action.

From the late 1890s, the pastors of Tokyo's largest Protestant churches made frequent, strong critiques regarding the lack of real-world applicability that they perceived in Japanese religion. According to Ebina, some religious men in Japan "draw near only to the Buddha, separating themselves from man, and separating themselves from the world."[182] Uemura spoke in 1911 of seeing in Buddhism a quest for "becoming a priest and reaching nirvana" that left the masters very separate from and far above the practitioners and that emphasized too heavily the "religious path" over religious action.[183] In 1906, Ebina concluded that any religion that isolated itself from the secular world paved the road to "society's destruction."[184] Five years before, in a 1901 sermon titled "Religion and Morality," he had also decried the rift separating religion from active morality in Japan's traditional religions. He told of a tragic incident in China, perpetrated by Japanese soldiers during the Sino-Japanese War, that illustrated the men's lack of a moral compass. In it, Ebina provided listeners with a vivid example of the consequences of shallow religious morality. Their conduct, he said, was "truly like the behavior of ghoulish beasts," and as a consequence "several hundred women, severely frightened at the possibility of having their bodies disgraced, dove head first into an irrigation barrel and died. . . . Try to imagine that this were Japan, try to imagine that these were our mothers, our daughters, our older sisters, our younger sisters."[185] Ebina clearly believed that these servicemen's religious convictions did not run deep enough to appear in their everyday actions, and the image of inactive religion went well beyond such extreme examples.

Also critical of Eastern religion, Tsunajima spoke out against religions that were so literally and figuratively sedentary that they were, in his view, incapable of making an impact on the behavior of adherents. In particular, Tsunajima targeted Buddhism as a religion that lacked energy. Even to the impartial observer, he said, Buddhism would appear to lack the characteristics of a "dynamic religion." Relating the treatment of sacred objects and symbols to the inactivity that he saw as inherent in the religion, Tsunajima mocked Buddhist statues in particular.

> Buddhism is a religion that teaches Nirvana, a religion of stillness. Doesn't everyone just sit and meditate when they look at a Buddhist statue? At a Buddhist statue, one cannot possibly find a dynamic place. . . . In Numazu, I saw . . . the Sleeping Buddha [Neshaka] Mountain. . . . These are just harmless things, but . . . they speak to the essence of what Buddhism is.[186]

To place an even blunter point on his argument, Tsunajima posited that while it was indeed "admirable that Daruma spent nine years meditating before a wall, a wall is useless as a partner."[187] Religious learning and doctrines that stopped at the nearest wall or at the motionless edges of the Sleeping Buddha's robes could not reach the religionist's everyday life or society at large.

What Japan needed, these Protestant pastors claimed, was a religion that focused its attention away from such stagnation and toward application and action. Tsunajima said it best when he explained that most of the Japanese religions of the past strove for "stillness" and that a "religion of stillness is . . . a religion of deadness."[188] He wanted his listeners to realize that their religion was the much-needed alternative. "Christianity is an active religion whereas Buddhism represents an unadventurous religious approach. In contrast to a Buddhist country which decays and, in vain, deeply desires indolence, a Christian country [is] lively, energetic, and flourishing."[189] Uemura viewed Christianity in the same light, equating "Christianity" with "life" in more than one of his sermons. In an 1894 sermon on Christian morals and Christian faith, he borrowed the phrase "Christianity is life" from England's former prime minister William Gladstone.[190] Again, this time in 1898, Uemura explained that, like the Greeks and Romans whose point of pride was the "[foot] race," Christians took pride in their "ability," "vigor," and "life."[191] Although in this and other sermons Uemura pointed to the parallel importance of doctrine and belief, he also considered Christianity a guide to moral action. Christianity was, for these pastors, the quintessential religion of life, and this connection between religiosity and moral action carried over into the various aspects of daily life where doctrine-centered religion could not go.

Whereas traditional Japanese religious convictions never actually made it into the practice of everyday life, according to Ebina, the Christian religion was very much a part of the common daily lives of believers. Japanese altars (Shinto *kamiza* or Buddhist *butsudan*) in the elevated alcove *(tokonoma)* constituted, he explained in 1916, "a family's sacred place, [and thus] the family members naturally act with restraint."[192] The daily interaction that Christians have with Christian symbols and the spirit of Christ, however, was very different. The American practice of hanging Christian symbols in the dining room brings the family together as they welcome "someone very close to the family." This sermon sends a clear message that Ebina made on several occasions: Christianity teaches believers to take religion and apply it to even the most unsacred elements of your life. And he was also conveying an underlying message that the American Protestant tradition, from which Japan's major denominations had developed, placed religious morality in the center of ordinary life.

In several instances, these Protestant pastors held up American Protestant Christianity and its role in everyday life to demonstrate the potential relevance that the religion could have for taking moral action in Japan. Tsunajima, for instance, spoke about New York businessman Charles Nelson Crittenton (1833–1909), who started an organization in 1883 for the financial and moral assistance of young unwed mothers and troubled women.[193] Crittenton and his wife were devastated by the sudden death of their beautiful daughter Florence in a violent storm. After some time, rising out of their grief, the couple thought beyond the ill fate of their privileged young daughter to the numerous "fallen girls" who were alive but living in less fortunate circumstances. The wealthy couple exercised their Christian charity in an exemplary way by selling all their valuable possessions and devoting the proceeds to the "rescue of pitiful women."[194] By choosing to tell this particular story, Tsunajima made clear his contention that Christianity was a religion of life and action, even in the face of death.

Similarly, Uemura utilized a figure from American Protestantism to illustrate Christianity's potential as a religion of real-world morality with the capacity to guide the world's troubled youth. In August 1893, he told the story of an American Christian teenager who acted on values found in both Japanese and Western religious morality. He dressed the adolescent George Washington (1732–1799) in the archetype of the ideal, Christian moral youth, capable of making the right choice. When confronted with the consequences of his decision to leave his widowed mother and begin his career in the naval military immediately, Washington decided to stay home. While Washington's actions clearly embodied the Confucian virtues of "filial piety" *(kō)* and "devotion" *(kenshin)* for many Japanese listeners, Uemura could also cast him as a devout adherent of the Bible, obedient to the important command to "honor thy father and thy mother."[195] It is also significant that the filial piety praised here differed considerably from the state-centered filial piety enshrined in documents on morality issued by the Meiji government. Washington did not offer himself "courageously to the state," as required by the Imperial Rescript on Education of 1890. And, as many of Uemura's well-educated and well-traveled listeners surely knew well, the youth would in fact lead a new independent country in revolt against the state to which he owed his loyalty. The choice of Washington was far from neutral, even if the sermon did not elaborate on this potentially subversive element of the story. Uemura did emphasize that by choosing not to "climb the ladder of lofty ambitions" and by "throwing aside great [future] achievement," Washington displayed the Christian morality necessary to become a great leader in the secular world. For Japan's youth who, despite ample moral instruction in Neo-Confucian ethics, still often sought a more practical type of morality, Washington's life had much to teach about the relationship between morality and action.[196]

Tokyo's Protestant pastors treated Eastern religion as morally weak and often used American Protestantism as a measuring stick against which to evaluate traditional Japanese religion. Furthermore, Uemura, Tsunajima, Kozaki, and Ebina all tied the past and present of Japan to Shinto and Buddhism while issuing a call to their audience to make Protestant Christianity the religion of an improved and modernized future Japan. Kozaki told Reinanzaka attendees in 1907 that it was their "urgent task" to reflect on how to "deal with moral education in schools . . . ; family morality . . . ; the morality of society . . . ; the inertia of the feudal era's morality."[197] These and similar messages by Protestant leaders in the capital gave congregations the responsibility of defying the trend apparent in Japan's other religions by applying religious morality to their lives each day.

While these pastors' views clearly contained biased generalizations about Japanese religion, there were shades of truth in their critiques. In conversation with Unitarianism in Japan, some members of the so-called Buddhist Enlightenment aimed to address the shortcomings of Buddhism in the modern Japanese context. Buddhist reformers such as educator Nakanishi Ushirō (1859–1930) and activist Ōuchi Seiran (1845–1918) strove to render Buddhism more progressive, social, and spiritual. During the 1890s, both the New Buddhism movement that drew inspiration from these figures and the *seishinshugi* movement of Shin priest Kiyozawa Manshi promoted a more transformative, applied, and socially aware form of Buddhism.[198] In his sermons in Tokyo and various articles, Kiyozawa's junior colleague Chikazumi Jōkan explained that Buddhism in Japan lacked experience applying its ideals to society and working for the realization of social reform. To respond to this issue, Chikazumi underlined the importance of Buddhists turning toward society rather than away from it.[199] These priests and laymen sought to remedy the very lack of activism and social engagement of Buddhism that Tokyo's leading Protestant pastors criticized. Ultimately their efforts and message were largely circumscribed by the Kyoto headquarters of the Higashi and Nishi Honganji sects of Shin Buddhism. However, the voices of these figures would continue to inspire moderate and radical Buddhist reformers in the early twentieth century and the Buddhist socialist movement beyond the Pure Land school.

To attend a sermon at one of Tokyo's largest congregations in the Meiji and early Taishō periods was to think about the nature of the individual, the world, and the moral relationship between the two. Pastoral discourse each Sunday brought global issues and guidance on self and social improvement into the *reihaidō*, impressing on listeners the significance and attainability of values that transcended denomination, local priorities, and national circumstance. The complex mixture of religious and social discourse was a key factor in these pastors' ability to offer listeners pieces with which they could form their individual worldviews and courses of social action. On the one hand, Protestant pastors in the capital asked their audiences to embrace modernity and the individuality, individual responsibility, and the subjective reasoning that came with it. On the other, they made strong cases for both the theorization and realization of the Enlightenment vision of a universal brotherhood of equals. With their sermons and actions, these pastors opened the doors of the Protestant church wide to all types of

Japanese, regardless of gender or class, and explained why they should all exchange ideas as equals. They also encouraged listeners to internally reflect and externally act on Protestant Christian morality. In achieving all this, pastors consciously distinguished their sermons from the simplified civil morality taught by many state agents and the doctrinal preaching, abstract religious philosophies, and inactivity that they perceived in Eastern religiosity.

Protestant pastoral discourse depicted Protestant Christianity as the religion best suited for the future of Japan and its people. These pastors frequently highlighted their religion's close association with the origins of the modern world and contrasted it with what they perceived to be the past-centered stagnancy of other Japanese religions. The greatest modern nations, such as the United States, England, and even predominantly Catholic France, had after all been recently constructed and reconstructed on the very humanistic bulwarks present in the Protestant Christian worldview, and in the eyes of Uemura, Tsunajima, Kozaki, and Ebina, Japan could share in their prosperous fate. In addition, their nation's colonial acquisitions were also destined, as Japan's spiritual periphery, to reap the benefits of both Japan's material and spiritual achievements. For these pastors, the promise of Christian ideals for Japan were also especially important to Japanese individuals as they constructed identities and worldviews and exercised the agency to act on them. Sermons at leading churches in Tokyo gave each listener a social mandate to think deeply about and work to improve society.

In Sunday sermons at these dynamic churches, the large portion of Japan's intelligentsia who had spent time in Western Europe or the United States or had immersed itself deeply in Western thought could hear a perspective that was relevant to their issues of identity. The themes and questions that preoccupied the literate, active public in the West also interested these curious Japanese minds, and the pastors' sermons often allowed listeners to come into contact and wrestle with these very quandaries. Japanese Christians and nonmember churchgoers all became citizens of the world when they attended church.

Yet neither the sermonizer nor the sermonized could escape the fact that they were also citizens of the nation of Japan, faced with the challenges and euphoria of national consciousness that was changing at a pace perhaps unparalleled among the modernizing nations of that time. Without addressing this other facet of identity, the Protestant sermon would not have achieved the popularity or notoriety that it did among the well-traveled, well-read, nationally minded men and women who peopled Protestant churches in the capital at the turn of the twentieth century.

CHAPTER FOUR

Preaching the National Imaginary

Beginning in the mid-nineteenth century, Japan embarked on a feverish quest to reach the promised land of modernity. To more fully understand this objective and the means of achieving it, many of the most socially and politically active Japanese looked to the advanced nations of Europe and the United States. Through encounters with Westerners and Western sources, they sought and found formulas and models for dramatically improving the condition of the Japanese people and their systems of governance. Taken together, several of the most frequently repeated elements of this blueprint emphasized that the teleological destiny, and pinnacle, of mankind was the sovereign nation-state. The ideal modern nation would be led by civilized individuals, strengthened by heavy industry and expansion, and peopled by loyal citizens.[1]

While the new national government continuously strove to make the populace aware of their membership in the Japanese nation and to instruct them of their duties to that entity, questions about the nature of the nation persisted and even multiplied for the citizenry. The modernizing people of Meiji Japan were increasingly literate, well-versed in the recently standardized national language, formally educated, linked by a growing national mass media, and connected by the expanding national network of railway and telegraph lines.[2] Thus armed, they often dealt with this challenge by adding their own interpretations to government rhetoric. Struggling to make sense of their national community and their respective places within it, many Japanese reacted by creating and tuning in to a multiplicity of discourses on the nation.

More than ever before, being Japanese became a challenge for all classes, and an array of ideologues quickly appeared in the late nineteenth century offering explanations and guidance. Through the strong language of decrees and pronouncements and the softer language of advertising campaigns and imperial visits, the Meiji government aimed to instill in the public an appropriate Japanese national identity and pride.[3] Government-affiliated ideologues and publicists were not alone, however, and complementing their efforts were popular *(minkan)* ideologues who made themselves increasingly available to the Japanese public.

They surfaced "all around, plying different interpretive trades in different social places."[4] Making use of a variety of old and new gathering spaces, from the floor of the new Imperial Diet to lecture halls at the Imperial University, Keio University, and Waseda University's predecessor, Tokyo Senmon Gakkō, to Hibiya Park after 1902, nation-minded activists and orators enhanced, reinterpreted, reduced, and refuted the views promulgated by the state.[5] The new religious gathering space of the Japanese Protestant church figured among these forums, providing thousands of attendees with new meeting spaces and discursive tools for imagining and coming to terms with the new nation.

Urban Japanese Protestant churches were particularly attractive to the cosmopolitan new educated elite as its members worked to define and embody Japaneseness. Converging in large numbers on the new national capital in the 1880s, 1890s, and early 1900s, they often discovered within Tokyo's largest Protestant churches words and interactions that addressed their dilemmas. The nation's intellectual elite typically possessed superior education, broad travel experiences, proficiency in one or more Western languages, and ambitions to shape Japan's future. Yet these very characteristics made the task and process of constructing a workable nation-view all the more complex for these individuals. The country's new intelligentsia could not but be troubled by the difficulty of navigating between the moral hierarchies of loyalty and status of the Tokugawa period, the new national morality espoused by the imperial government, love and respect for Japan in general, and Western forms of knowledge and culture. The *shūkaidō* (meeting hall) and *reihaidō* (worship hall) of Tokyo's most influential Protestant churches played host to ideologues and rhetoric that spoke directly to the concerns of those searching for a solid sense of national belonging and individual purpose within the nation. In the midst of a concerted ideological push to privatize religion and weaken its ability to connect with and impact the political sphere, these churchgoing seekers flocked to church spaces that eschewed such categorization and separation.

Front and center in Protestant church *shūkaidō* and *reihaidō*, these Japanese cosmopolitans could find a highly qualified popular ideologue in the person of the Japanese Protestant pastor. These church leaders too were well educated, often familiar with English or German, experienced in studying under Western experts or living abroad, and preoccupied with the essence and fate of the nation. Tokyo's Protestant pastorate was therefore particularly well-positioned to respond to the questions and anxieties of nationally aware and concerned attendees from the new educated elite. While the leaders of Tokyo's leading congregations were authors of weekly and monthly articles in Christian and secular periodicals, they were also pastors who gave sermons at church. In contrast to the experience of reading alone, Sunday sermons in the largest churches of the capital addressed hundreds of women and men together who sought spiritual as well as moral guidance. In their pastoral role, ministers gave sermons that could appeal to Japanese caught between universal ideals, Western learning, and national identity. This was especially valid in the social, economic, and political center of the nation, where the need for and visibility of such cultural interpreters remained high until the 1930s. For those grappling with the increasingly complex set of topics surrounding the definition of Japan and national citizenship, spoken pastoral discourse presented a supplemental and highly relevant set of national imaginaries. For those concerned with the relationship between the nation and religion, pastoral discourse situated Protestant religio-moral guidance in a distinctly Japanese cultural context.

During the Meiji and early Taishō periods, multiple Japanese religious movements struggled to demonstrate their legitimacy as Japanese and their specific relevance to the people of Japan. While administrative and funding decisions greatly weakened sect Shinto, government initiatives and Shintoist ideologues ensured that the religion became especially associated with modern, well-curated conceptualizations of Japaneseness in the national consciousness. And arguably, the many Japanese new religions that took shelter under the aegis of the approved Shinto sects were recognizable as Japanese movements suitable for the Japanese. The centrality of the Jiba in Tenri City, Japan, for Tenrikyō rites, for instance, has guaranteed that believers around the world still ground their faith in the space and events that take place around the *kanrodai* (a pillar) in Nara Japan.[6] However, persecution, vilification, and xenophobic criticisms made it imperative that Buddhism and Christianity demonstrate their status as Japanese religions. In intensifying anti-Christian rhetoric that treated Christianity as foreign, Buddhists in fact played a prominent role in making this process more difficult for Christians.[7] And disparaging Christianity also became one of the ways that Buddhist clerics and laymen worked to enhance Buddhism's standing in Japan.

Buddhist individuals and groups underlined their religion's cultural and historical connections to Japan as well as its usefulness to the Japanese state.[8] Citizenship, loyalty, and patriotism were key discursive emphases of the New Buddhism movement that developed from the 1890s onward.[9] Shin priest Kiyozawa Manshi wrote and spoke about Buddhists' duties to the nation, calling readers in one case to take up arms for the nation if necessary.[10] Pure Land priest–turned–preacher Tanaka Chigaku (1861–1939) was perhaps the most outspoken public voice highlighting the interconnectedness and interdependence of Buddhism with the Japanese national polity. The Nichirenism proselytizer gave frequent and regular lectures in the Central Assembly Hall (Chūō Kōkaidō) at

Risshō Ankokukai headquarters in Osaka's Nakanoshima neighborhood, at Emperor Jimmu's mausoleum in Nara, and at hundreds of preaching spots throughout Japan. In his talks, he pointed to the deep connections and congruity of Nichiren's religious outlook with Japan's historical emperors, Japanese expansionism, and nationalism.[11] His particular Buddhist-Shinto synthesis would prove instrumental for the nation-views of influential nationalist radicals including Ishiwara Kanji (1889–1949), Inoue Nissho (1886–1967), and Kita Ikki (1883–1937) from the last half of the Taishō period onward.[12]

Buddhist priests, scholars, and officials were part of a sea of critics who placed Christianity under siege, forcing it to define its relationship with the state and the Japanese people in the 1890s and afterward. Protestant Christianity was all but compelled to act by the failure of a few Protestant Christians to adequately demonstrate their nationalism and Japanese national identity in ceremonies and in written and spoken discourse. However, Japanese Protestant pastors were not passive in this regard. Rather, many among them embraced the opportunity to explain how they and their beliefs were Japanese and exuded patriotism and concern for the Japanese national polity. Leaders presented their Christianity as the ultimate example of "western learning with the Japanese spirit" *(yōsai yamato damashi)* and often argued that their faith and actions were "for the sake of Japan."[13] Especially in the capital, this rapprochement was highly visible. The fervent patriotism of Ebina Danjō in particular has come to represent the most extreme form of Japanese Protestant nationalism. Though his patriotism did not prevent him from criticizing government policies from time to time, scholars have rightfully characterized him as the epitome of the "Christian nationalist leader."[14] By the outbreak of the Russo-Japanese War, a small minority of Japanese pastors and leading Protestants expressed their reservations about Japanese militarism and imperialism. However, even they often strove to emphasize their love for the Japanese nation and the centrality of Christian faith and morality for the improvement of Japan. The least jingoistic among Tokyo's leading Japanese Protestant pastors, for instance, explained in 1906 that "true Christianity" in fact considers "the idea of patriotism . . . to be very noble."[15] On these grounds, in part, Uemura Masahisa approved of his government's recent war with Russia.[16]

Among the varying shades of nationalistic Japanese Protestantism that emerged in turn-of-the-century Japan, the modern construct of the "nation" as national community was a common denominator. Prasenjit Duara has demonstrated that although the modern nation unites the affections, worries, and ambitions of its citizens, the shapes and shades of "nationalism" among the members of any modern nation can be varied and multiplicitous. While the object of nationalism, the nation, is constant and shared, "nationalism" is in fact the "site where different representations of the nation contest and negotiate with each other."[17] Even within the confines of the "Shinto Secular," a fairly unified ideological and semantic field that centered around the imperial institution and the Japanese nation-state, varied Protestant Christian nationalisms were possible.[18] This definition helps explain how Protestant churches in Tokyo were able to act as loci for the formation and transformation of Japanese nationalisms.

This chapter illuminates the types of nation that Tokyo's most popular Protestant pastors helped their listeners imagine from the pulpit. Congregationalist pastors Ebina Danjō, Kozaki Hiromichi, and Tsunajima Kakichi and Presbyterian pastor Uemura Masahisa were busy building and propagating specific nationalisms. They selected elements from within their personal reflections on Japan to project a specific image of the nation to their audiences. Furthermore, these pastors consciously blurred the line between religious and social discourse each week as they addressed topics ranging from the national identity, responsibility to and love for the nation, the definition of the national body *(kokutai),* and the glorious national past and future. Their special "nationalisms"[19] diverged significantly in direction and depth from the forms of nationalism most prevalent in Meiji and Taishō Japan, and their sermons went to the heart of the pressing nation-related questions of the day.[20]

Taken together, these men constituted a sociopolitically conscious Tokyo pastorate sensitive and responsive to those walking between the world of Western ideas and traditions and a Japan rapidly becoming aware and proud of itself. As such, the pastors equipped Japanese Christians within the space of the church to assert their Japaneseness to themselves and to those who considered them "metaphorical foreigners."[21] In other words, it shows how pastors offered attendees ranging from the far left to the far right tools for reconciling Japanese national identity and patriotism with Christian spirituality and social ideals. The chapter also identifies the divergent but proactive, patriotic, and socially engaged nation-views that characterized the pastoral discourse in the Reinanzaka, Banchō, Hongō, and Fujimichō Churches and helped form the perspectives on which a variety of well-known and lesser-known Japanese churchgoers built their own impactful nationalisms. For all four, the Japanese nation comprehended a set of meanings and responsibilities that went above and beyond official nationalisms and government dicta. They each firmly believed that their audience could only truly make sense of the problems and potential of the Japanese nation through the prism of Protestant belief and action. Each Sunday, these pastors and others like them negated the claims of Christianity's many detractors that the religion was unnationalist by offering the Japanese educated elite unprecedented, pertinent, empowering ways of seeing their nation and actively contributing to its present and future.

The Nation, Obvious and Elusive

The nation and its destiny were at the heart of many Tokyo pastors' sermons. Each week listeners at each of Tokyo's largest Protestant churches were exposed to variations on this theme. As one might expect, the nation played a decisive role in the vast majority of sermons that Ebina gave at Hongō. He made frequent and clear reference to the Japanese nation in the titles of his sermons, often using the suggestive diction of "our nation" *(waga kuni, waga kokumin,* or *waga kokutai).* Ebina's tendency to focus on the nation continues to interest many different types of religious scholars, and sermon titles such as "The New Way of the Warrior" (Shin bushidō) and "The Meaning of a Virtuous Country" (Kunshikoku no igi) offer evidence as to why he has been singled out so prominently by scholars such as Shuma Iwai and Dohi Akio.[22] From making criticisms and suggestions about Japan as a whole to outlining strategies for Japanese Christians to act as catalysts for national change to locating the Japanese national past in Western rubrics of race, sovereignty, progress, and expansion, Ebina consistently and directly engaged the nation. His close colleague Kozaki too spoke explicitly on the nation. The trend is easily visible in sermon titles such as "The Great Weakness of Our Nation" (Waga kokumin no daiketten), "The Terrible Spectacle of Our Nation's Spiritual State" (Waga kuni seishinkai no sanjō), and "Patriotism and Faith" (Aikokushin to shinkō).

In contrast to these more overt references and emphases, the nation is often only present at a subtler level in the sermons of the much less sensational Tsunajima Kakichi and the outspoken, popular, and more theologically focused pastor Uemura Masahisa. Only two of Uemura's several hundred extant sermons, "The Christian Family and the State" (Kirisutokyō no ie to kuni) from March 1898 and "Christianity and the Way of the Warrior" (Kirisutokyō to bushidō) from July 1897, testify to his interest in nation-related themes and topics. In the case of Tsunajima, it would also seem from a distance that few of his surviving sermons appear to deal with the "nation" directly. An analysis of the content of these pastors' sermons reveals, however, that both aimed to affect the shape of the Japanese nation imagined by their listeners through their mention and use of nation-related rhetoric. They drew on images, symbols, figures, events, and ideologies linked to the national past of Japan and other countries in order to put the messages of Protestant Christianity in terms more familiar to the Japanese audience. At a deeper level, Uemura and Tsunajima utilized these discursive tools to lift out certain elements within the Japanese national imaginary that they considered most compatible with Christianity and to suppress others, valorizing certain ideals they judged as crucial for the creation of a new and better Japan and avoiding or discarding others.

Despite their substantial dissimilarities, Tokyo's Protestant pastors clearly shared a strong interest in the fate of the Japanese nation-state and its people. Tsunajima, Uemura, Kozaki, and Ebina were all, regardless of their differences in theological or political orientation, self-aware members of and advocates for the Japanese national community. As such, they, like their listeners, were increasingly surrounded on all sides by the national narratives and moral injunctions prescribed by the national government. Ultimately, these religious leaders and their audience members would each have to flesh out government rhetoric with his or her sociopolitical and religio-moral preferences and knowledge. With their sermons, these pastors crafted and propagated specific nationalisms that they considered beneficial to Japan. In these constructions, the men also proposed elements with which listeners could craft their individual nation-views and work to actualize them. Each of the four subsequent sections of this essay will explore the nation in general and the Japanese nation in particular that popular Protestant pastors in Tokyo conjured from their pulpits. The first section will examine the nation-view of Tsunajima Kakichi, one of Meiji- and Taishō-era Japan's most prominent pastors who has been almost entirely ignored by scholars. The subsequent sections will describe and analyze the nation-views of his much more historically recognized colleagues Uemura Masahisa, Kozaki Hiromichi, and Ebina Danjō.

The Nation of Tsunajima Kakichi

In his role as pastor of one of Tokyo's four largest Protestant churches, Tsunajima Kakichi spoke to a congregation of more than three hundred each Sunday morning between late 1896 and 1931, and he often clothed his rhetoric in the motif of the nation. Speaking directly in his sermons to the citizens of a nation characterized by domestic and international wars during the nineteenth and early twentieth centuries, Tsunajima often borrowed metaphors and paragons from the Japanese military past and present. He singled out the patriotic soldier as a model for Christian behavior. The pastor paid specific attention to military men in Japan and elsewhere who had fought for their national community and demonstrated qualities such as sacrifice, leadership, and self-mastery. Tsunajima considered these ideals translatable to the Christian and his or her task for Japan.

Tsunajima argued that the Christian, like the soldier, was motivated by and responsible for the triumph of the nation. At the root of the soldier's courage lay his conviction that he is fighting "on God's side" for "sincere loyalty and patriotism, truth, a righteous death . . . [and] his fellow countrymen."[23] In particular, Tsunajima pinpointed some Western military leaders who exemplified this combination of patriotism and Christian righteousness, designating them as "the ideal for people who believe in God." He spoke of English general Oliver Cromwell (1599–1658), who chanted "psalms in a loud voice," and "Union Army generals [who] advanced while singing psalms" during the US Civil War.[24] In a sermon titled "The Lord Is My Castle" (Kami wa waga shiro nari) and several others, Tsunajima idealized both literal and figurative Christian soldiers who had exerted themselves for the good of their respective countries. In order to impress upon listeners the type of dedication that would allow the Japanese Christian soldier to fight successfully "for the moralization of his fellow countrymen," he described the efforts of the British to save their homeland during World War I: "Men in the prime of their lives were sent to the battlefield to serve the nation. . . . They sacrificed everything for the survival of Great Britain; they offered up their whole heart, whole soul, and whole life without looking back. Our spiritual battle is also like this."[25] Tsunajima asked his listeners to develop a similar "resoluteness" as they carried out their roles as "Christian soldiers."[26]

For Tsunajima, the Japanese Protestant was not akin to just any soldier but instead constituted a member of a small elite specifically charged with a mission for the nation. In a sermon titled "Gideon's Elite Troops" (Gideon no seihei), Tsunajima likened his listeners to two groups whose members disregarded their own lives in order to fight for their respective nations: biblical judge Gideon's select, three-hundred-man elite troop *(seihei)* and the Japanese suicide corps *(kesshitai).*[27] The well-known term "suicide corps" had existed for centuries. In the aftermath of a famous and successful *kesshitai* operation in 1905 during the Siege of Port Arthur by a *kesshitai,* however, the term gained new significance and visibility.[28] Tsunajima told his listeners that "we Christians are God's chosen suicide corps" in Japan's spiritual battle, and then told the story of one such unit formed bravely and spontaneously to eliminate a major threat to the new Japan at any cost.[29] On a train ride from Osaka to Kobe in 1883, a stranger with a "commanding face and powerful physique" told Tsunajima that he had "personally taken the initiative of forming a suicide corps [of] sixteen volunteers" during the Satsuma Rebellion of 1877. The self-selected band of healthy, strong, young soldiers, "vigorous" and "full of life," swooped down on the "rebels" like an "irresistible force," and "of the seventeen, not even a single one was killed or injured."[30]

Tsunajima was confident that his listeners were capable of such victory for God in Japan.

Like the members of Gideon's elite troop or the Japanese suicide corps, the Japanese Christian was a member of a select, proactive, and well-equipped few who were responsible for positively impacting the nation's destiny. Just as many Japanese students hoped to become influential, wealthy, or famous, many men and women sought to guide Japan's spiritual development. In the spiritual realm as in the secular, however, only a select group would "take the lead": "Of the countless students who harbor high ambitions . . . how many really attain the success they expect? Every year, among the hundreds and thousands of graduates, how many take the lead in the business world, the political world, the intellectual world? There are truly not many." This small group was composed of individuals who were selected, at least in part, because they each possessed the necessary qualities for leadership. These ranged from the "dignity [required] of a high-level executive" to the respective appropriate qualities of a "school principal . . . company president . . . prefectural governor . . . [or] cabinet minister."[31] In a similar fashion, he encouraged church attendees, many of whom belonged to the socioeconomic group that Tsunajima's sermon purposefully targeted, to assume their roles of spiritual leadership in the nation just as they had in sociocultural, educational, political, and economic affairs. These members of the new educated elite were endowed with the traits and skills to remold Japan.

As with all of those positions, the responsibility of the Japanese Christian community to the nation required the development and possession of a special set of characteristics. The Japanese Christians' "duty as the chosen" was to "save our fellow countrymen," and for the completion of this task Tsunajima recommended a distinct combination of practical virtues. He looked not only to Western Christian models but also to some particularly empowering elements in Japanese Neo-Confucian moral teachings. As the "face of the church," the Japanese Christian needed to learn "self-respect, self-appointment, self-confidence," and the quality from which all of these other virtues derived, the all-encompassing Neo-Confucian virtue of "self-cultivation."[32] For the sake of the nation, then, Tsunajima's recommendation focused not on those authority-related Neo-Confucian virtues that the Meiji government was advocating most strongly, namely loyalty and filial piety, but on the personal, reflective virtue of self-cultivation and its capacity to inspire individuals to effect substantial change.[33] In his view as expressed here, Japan needed cultivated leaders more than obedient subjects.

In his spoken pastoral discourse, Tsunajima clearly argued that Japanese Christians were designated to play an important role in the continued existence and amelioration of Japan. Even in a sermon in which he argued that Christianity transcended the linguistic, ethnic, and cultural elements of national identity—an argument that ostensibly advocated brotherhood across national boundaries—he did so to promote the nation. In that case, the nation was the expanded Japanese nation-state constructed by the imperial policy of *naisen ittai* to include colonized Korea.[34] In comparison with his fellow leading pastors in Tokyo, far fewer of Tsunajima's sermons have survived, and the single collection of his sermons clearly reflects the preferences and biases of Christian Fukunaga Bunnosuke (1861–1939), who published twenty of them. Yet these sources demonstrate that Tsunajima Kakichi formulated and expressed a form of nationalism. The pastor utilized Japanese morality, national consciousness, military metaphors, and patriotic Christian models to galvanize his listeners to think about and contribute to the nation.

The Nation of Uemura Masahisa

In his sermons each Sunday at Fujimichō Church, Uemura Masahisa intended to be neither critic nor proponent of the prosperity of the Japanese nation. He sought to encourage individual Christians to develop moral strength and apply it in the secular world, whether or not it benefited Japan. On certain occasions, however, fundamental disagreements with particular formulations of the Japanese national polity clearly motivated Uemura to enter the realm of political discourse. When we examine two such instances, it becomes clear that Uemura's more doctrine-based religious morality could in fact have direct sociopolitical application. In 1890, in the first issue of his new religio-political journal *Nippon Hyōron,* Uemura wrote that he thought of his ministry "in terms of Japan." He explained that, like other Japanese, "I have critical opinions about politics, literature, social issues, economics and education."[35] While scholars have shown that Uemura demonstrated a certain interest in and passion for Japan in his action and written words, none have remarked that he also spoke on the Japanese nation aloud in his sermons at his Ichibanchō and Fujimichō Churches.

In 1897, Uemura challenged one of the theoretical foundations for the Japanese national polity that was beginning to gain popularity during the 1890s with its unprecedented linkages between religious belief and nationalism. Several political ideologues in the nineteenth century told Japanese citizens that under the guidance and protection of the Japanese emperor, they were a body of brothers and sisters. Japanese Protestant Christians, who were aiming to construct a new society based on the principle of brotherhood for all under Christ, agreed with many elements of this discourse. By the end of the decade, however, some of them had become wary of the type of brotherhood that conservative nationalist Hozumi Yatsuka wrote of in his 1897 work *Kokumin kyōiku: Aikokushin* (National Education: Patriotism). While many voices praised the ethnicity-based concept of the Japanese family-state that Hozumi developed, advocated, and placed at the center of a nascent State Shinto ideological constellation, some writers and speakers in Japan, including the least politically active Protestant pastors, encouraged their audiences to reevaluate Hozumi's claims about the true Japan.[36]

Uemura claimed that Hozumi's ideology contained a blurred vision of the nation and its foundational elements. First, the Tokyo Imperial University legal scholar had misunderstood the origins of patriotism. He viewed patriotism as both analogous to and a natural outgrowth of ancestor worship, Uemura explained. According to Hozumi's version of Shinto cosmology, all Japanese were blood relatives of the same race *(minzoku)* simultaneously practicing "reverence for one's mother and father . . . reverence for the family's ancestors . . . [and] reverence for the common ancestors of the Japanese race."[37] By loving one's country, as a collective body of blood relatives (living and deceased), one was showing the ultimate level of "love and respect" for all of these individuals.[38] This was how Uemura summarized Hozumi's argument before presenting several reasons for his listeners to refute it.

Uemura argued that the relationship between patriotism, familial love, and supernatural religion constructed by Hozumi was backward. To begin with, the idea that "if he does not worship and trust in an invisible supreme being, man is unable to govern himself or raise a country" was completely false.[39] Religion and the nation-state did not and should not depend on one another, a sermon contention that echoes the division between church and state found in Uemura's writings by Takenaka Masao and, more recently, J. Nelson Jennings.[40] Second, Uemura argued that it was instead by loving one's family members that one could be most patriotic, and not vice versa. On this point Uemura found the poem "Hermann and Dorothea" by Johann Wolfgang von Goethe (1749–1832) to be both poignant and pertinent.[41] In this story set when Napoleon had extended his control over all of Europe in the early 1800s, "German customs and manners were being destroyed, [and] a young married man and woman, Hermann and Dorothea, built a family and from it patriotism sprung forth. . . . Love for the family needs to become . . . love [for] the country."[42] Furthermore, while Hozumi equated the family with the country, Uemura imagined an entirely different set of familial relationships.

Uemura also took issue with the delimitation of Hozumi's family-state and the consequences that such definitions would have inside and outside Japan. The all-inclusive family-state developed by Hozumi and other late Meiji ideologues enveloped all Japanese, but as mentioned in the preceding chapter, Uemura expressed concern about the fate of Taiwan's inhabitants, who, as of 1895, were residents of Japan's first official colony. The Taiwanese could have no place in bloodline-based nationalism, leaving the Japanese only two choices of treatment. Given the impossibility of assimilating such people into Hozumi's Japanese race-based family-state, the invading Japanese would have to "completely slaughter this people or if not make them all into slaves."[43] Although Uemura shows no awareness of the inferior treatment afforded the Taiwanese (Chinese) and even more inferior treatment of the territories' aborigines *(seiban),* his dire vision proved prophetic. The hard labor, severe punishment and repression, low and infrequent wages, and other conditions of the aborigines were in many ways similar to slavery. The Musha Incident of 1930, during which 134 Japanese were slain by Taiwanese aborigines, testified to the contradictions between Japanese imperialism and the Japanese ethnicity-based family-state. In punitive revenge, the Japanese killed some 500 Taiwanese.[44] As Uemura drew this sermon to a close, he spoke of "confusion" and "pity" as he expressed strong reservations about "Japan's expansion" across the North Sea into the Shandong Peninsula as well.[45]

Within the international and philanthropic constellation of Uemura's nationalism, there remained room, nonetheless, for a strong emphasis on ameliorating the situation of the Japanese people at home. He idealized the "burning patriotic passion" of the "Old Testament prophets" who were deeply saddened by the "immorality and sin of [their] country." "In Japan too," he said, "this [type of] patriotism is desirable."[46] In particular, Uemura lamented the situation among the young men and women coming of age in Japan's urban centers. In the Japan of Uemura's time, love suicides, depression, and other problems among the capital's maladjusted young adults served as daily reminders of the identity issues that this age group faced.[47] Uemura's love for Japan led him to work toward replacing the insufficient ideologies and worldviews popular among this age group with the promises and ideals of Protestant Christian morality.

Around the turn of the twentieth century, as Meiji youth sought to identify and understand their lack of cultural certainty and navigate Japan's complex new loyalty structure, *bushidō* or "the way of the warrior" experienced a discernible resurgence.[48] Confucian philosophy scholar and professor Inoue Tetsujirō (1855–1944) was the strongest voice promoting *bushidō* in imperial Japan.[49] He held up the ideas of Yamaga Sokō (1622–1685), one of the original theorists of this ideology, and disseminated his own interpretations of *bushidō* in various forms.[50] Inoue was of the state's most influential ideologues, and his vision of *bushidō*—one loudly advocating nationalism and imperialism—permeated much of Japan's cultural landscape. Yet Meiji youth were drawn to this ideology by their own needs and priorities. By Uemura's estimation, this was because that ideology drew images that resonated with those youths' emotional state and offered directives that simplified moral dilemmas. In some ways, Uemura sympathized with "the many in today's society [who feel] aloof from the world, like a rootless floating plant, transiently passing through life." He understood how they could read Tokugawa-era samurai Daidōji Yūzan's (1639–1730) *Budō shoshinshū* (Initiation into the Warrior Way) and identify with phrases such as "In general man's life is transient, like the evening dew [and] the morning frost."[51] After repeating these lines aloud in his sermon "Christianity and Bushidō" (Kirisutokyō to bushidō) in 1898, Uemura explained the attraction that the allegedly uncomplicated value system of the samurai, whose "highest aim is to . . . fully accomplish loyalty and filial piety," could have for young wonderers at the turn of the century.[52] Despite this ideology's attractiveness, however, Uemura urged caution.

Japan's youth could not solve the modern problems that they and their nation faced by simply following Bushidō's prescriptions, because the ideology overemphasized obedience and disparaged liberty, love, and the individual. According to Uemura, the Bushidō that pursued the very filial piety and loyalty that the Meiji state preached so diligently viewed all of these elements as greatly inferior to the shared obligations of all Japanese citizens to their nation and its leaders. On the other hand, religion, while it admittedly "implies obedience to someone with control over you," in fact "also implies developing and maintaining oneself." Religion improves on behavioral codes like *bushidō* by addressing the individual and placing "obedience and love and liberty . . . parallel to one another," Uemura declared. For him, Christianity in particular was the "religion that harmonizes, arranges, and most beautifully fulfills this [set]."[53] Uemura was characterizing Protestant Christianity as a religion that established balance between the Western ideals of love and liberty, the modern category of the individual, and the Meiji era's most touted Neo-Confucian virtues of obedience and duty to authority. Without Christianity, *bushidō* and the nationalistic ideologies linked to that belief system would inevitably lead Tokyo churchgoers and other Japanese down a dangerous path.

On the opposing side of Uemura's argument were the many Japanese whom, through the language of *bushidō,* were inflating the national pride of Japan beyond its healthy limits, he complained. Worried that *bushidō,* "our nation's bright flower . . . is now gradually losing its loveliness . . . and no longer wields the power it did in the past," many "work hard . . . to maintain *[bushidō],* to promote it." Those days, he remarked, "the Japanese are a people whose hearts' blood jumps when they hear the words prestige, popularity, acclaim, glory, etc."[54] As evidence,

Uemura called listeners' attention to the fact that children sang the stanzas of "At the Foot of Mount Fuji" at the middle school near Fujimichō Church, where he was pastor, promoting the "sense of honor" *(renchi)* valorized by Bushidō rhetoric.

> Gathered at the foot of the mountain,
> The towering peak of Mount Fuji,
> Looking up in the morning and at night,
> Let us lift honor up high.[55]

The situation had become so acute that the preservation and enhanced glory of "the country's national honor" had become the top priority in Japan's foreign diplomacy, he explained.[56] During the late 1890s, as Japan sought diligently to step out from under the heavy financial and emotional burden of its various unequal treaties with Western nations, calls for national dignity reached an unprecedented high.[57] The recent repopularization of *bushidō* was at once a product of and a contributing factor to this trend that sought to rediscover and praise Japan's indigenous past. Even Christians, such as Quaker Nitobe Inazō (1862–1933), represented the Japanese past and present through the lens of *bushidō*.[58] All of this attention, however, had ignored the fundamental question of the origins and distinctiveness of *bushidō* for the Japanese people.

In response to the rise of national pride surrounding this ideology, Uemura set out to analyze and demystify the long-lived cultural link between *bushidō* and Japan. He criticized outright the glorification of *bushidō* as a specifically Japanese moral system. To demonstrate the errors in such a claim, Uemura highlighted the various sightings of the *bushidō*-type ethos in non-Japanese settings. He derided the millions of Japanese

> who chant *Yamato damashii* [the Japanese Spirit] . . . and have a habit of being proud that *bushidō* is something that [they] exclusively possess. This is nothing other than favoritism. It cannot be said that *bushidō* is entirely our nation's tradition [alone]. It exists in Turkey; it exists in Tartary; if we think back to the foundation of the Ottoman Empire, that ethos is very similar to that of our nation's Bushidō spirit. . . . And even perusing Greek [and] Roman history, there are many of their manners and customs that, when considered in comparison with our nation's warriors, would be viewed admirably.[59]

This insight was meant less to insult Japanese tradition than to free Japanese minds from what he considered baseless chauvinism. Rather than focusing on the Japanese nature and origins of *bushidō,* which in fact were limited, or seeking to accumulate honor and glory by practicing the old warrior way, Uemura encouraged Japanese to think more carefully about *bushidō* as a moral code.

Despite some apparent disapproval of elements within *bushidō,* Uemura was in fact more of a reformer than an enemy of the ideology. As an advocate of "Baptized Bushidō," the fulfillment of Neo-Confucian morality with Christian elements, it should come as no surprise that Uemura found a great deal of value in many portions of *bushidō* thought.[60] He looked positively on the self-sacrifice (literal and figurative), adherence to a moral code, respect for truth and honesty, appreciation for teachings and reason over emotion, and development of self-control advocated by *bushidō.* These elements were worth upholding. He hoped listeners would see that the best things within *bushidō* could be developed and achieved by "pouring into our nation" the tenets of Christianity. Christianity is, above all, a religion that values "doctrine," "self-sacrifice," and the search for "truth over profit."[61] To make these characteristics clearer, Uemura drew on an example of *bushidō*-inspired bravery from the recent Japanese past.

In 1877, several men in Kōchi Prefecture, a seaward coastal area on the island of Shikoku, were plotting with Saigō Takamori to "betray the Meiji government" as part of the same rebellion mentioned by Tsunajima above.[62] A young national tax official named Watanabe Kunitake (1846–1919) received and accepted a government commission to come from Tokyo to deal with this situation. Politician Ozaki Yukio recalled that in 1877 this man was "sent to Tosa [Kōchi Prefecture] as governor, though he must still have been only in his twenties. . . . Watanabe arrived alone to take office in an uncertain land without even a bodyguard."[63] He resolutely declared, as the old story goes, that the Meiji government could not permit the prefectural army to join Saigō's forces, and in obedience the leadership in Kōchi did not fight alongside the so-called rebels in the famous war.

While some claimed that by nature Watanabe was just a brave man, Uemura insisted that only through training had he developed into a man capable of such a task. Uemura, like Ozaki Yukio, demonstrated a certain admiration for Watanabe's thorough training in Zen Buddhism and strict regimen based on *bushidō.* In order to achieve this level of self-mastery, Uemura emphasized, Watanabe had employed the same portions of *bushidō* that resonated with the virtues of Christ and his most successful followers. By "cultivating morality, studying knowledge, and exercising discipline," both Watanabe and numerous courageous Christians had developed the will necessary to overcome the challenges that stood before them.[64] For in *bushidō,* as in Christianity, "genuine bravery can only be reached through the cultivation of character."[65] The other overemphasized elements of *bushidō* paled in comparison, and by replacing the objectives of fame and pride with the empowering imperative to "act with love," Christians could in fact elevate *bushidō* into a world-changing moral code.[66]

Rather than an effort to sell his vision of Japan to listeners, it would seem that he sought to encourage them to reflect carefully about their own nation-views before taking action outside the church. As historian Dohi Akio has explained, Uemura aimed to empower freethinking, responsible Christians to take action for the improvement of the nation.[67] By this understanding, it would ultimately be up to these active, thoughtful Japanese Christians to determine the nature and function of the nation as well as its future. Therefore, by concentrating on the definitions of the Japanese national polity and the value systems that would guide and motivate its citizens, Uemura was in fact playing an active role in their sociopolitical preparation. There were of course other pastors in Tokyo who addressed the nation and its destiny much more directly and more often than either Uemura or Tsunajima.

The Nation of Kozaki Hiromichi

Whereas Uemura made allowances for certain elements within Japanese cultural constructs at Fujimichō Church, Reinanzaka pastor Kozaki Hiromichi wholly embraced the glorious Japanese past and present in sermons at his church. In notably passionate tones, Kozaki described Japan in his sermons as a well-guided, culturally superior, great nation whose path to prosperity lacked only the spirituality and moral values of Protestant Christianity. For all those criticizing the imported religion as un-Japanese and incongruous with Japanese nationalism, Kozaki retorted with a patriotic Christianity. His sermons could not but serve to help awaken the national consciousness of church attendees, offering them elements with which to both deconstruct and rebuild their national identities. But in a manner reminiscent of Uemura, Kozaki encouraged his audience to transform their justified love for country into active religious morality for the sake of the nation.

The third decade of the Meiji period was filled with debate surrounding the Japaneseness and patriotic qualities of Protestant Christianity, fueled by Neo-Confucian and Buddhist scholars who opposed the religion. As Kiri Paramore has demonstrated, that opposition was strongly rooted in a tradition of academic anti-Christian discourse whose main objective was the reinforcement of the Japanese sociopolitical order rather than the oppression of actual Christian practice.[68] In the 1890s, however, the opponents of Christianity found concrete evidence for their claims. First there was the "Uchimura Kanzō lèse-majesté incident," in which Protestant Christian Uchimura Kanzō refused to bow to a special copy of the Imperial Rescript on Education, stamped with the imperial seal. This infamous event occurred at the Tokyo First Higher School, the nation's premier boys' secondary school, where he was a teacher in 1891.[69] This was followed by speeches and publications by Inoue Tetsujirō, the staunchly Neo-Confucian scholar in "service to the government" *(goyō gakusha).*[70] Inoue immediately and harshly condemned Uchimura. Over the following two years, he published his anti-Christian work *The Clash between Education and Religion* (1892–1893) and led an assault on Christianity. He used the 1890 Imperial Rescript on Education to demonstrate that the religion's morality was at odds with the law and political order of both old and new Japan.[71] He argued that "Christianity lacks nationalistic spirit" and that "Christianity is incompatible with the national rescript."[72] Anti-Christian articles in Buddhist journals only served to fan the flames, leaving Japanese Protestant Christianity's nationalist credentials in doubt.[73] Over the next several years, a number of Protestant pastors responded by affirming their love for Japan.

Kozaki Hiromichi represented a group of pastors who, much more than Uemura and Tsunajima, exhibited in their sermons a special national pride. He preached in 1907 about the spiritual morality that Japan was missing, but only after describing precisely what type of nation Japan was, and the aspects that the nation did not lack. By his reckoning, Japan could boast of having the world's second-strongest infantry and naval power, as well as remarkable progress in education and science that equaled the highest levels found in the West. While many in the United States and Western Europe failed to recognize the achievements of Japan, a non-white nation, and its legitimate place among the world's great powers, Kozaki offered listeners a list of reasons for celebrating their Japaneseness. In response to those who claimed that "our race will never reach the level of the white man," the pastor explained: "Not only is it in no way true that we are inferior to whites, but on the contrary it seems that we surpass them. From the example of war, we understand this; from the racial competition on America's Pacific coast, we can very well understand this."[74] Here Kozaki was referring to the success of the Japanese Imperial Navy against Russia, a Western nation of "white" people, in the recent Russo-Japanese War from 1904 to 1905. Kozaki was also alluding to the so-called Japan-US Gentlemen's Agreement (Nichibei Shinshi Kyōyaku) of 1907, which informally bound Japan to cease emigration to the United States.[75] More specifically, he spoke of the academic and career success of Japanese immigrants in California who, often outperforming their white American colleagues, had engendered the ill will behind anti-Japanese nativism in the state.[76] All in all, Kozaki summarized these positive elements by asserting that the Japanese were a "people [who] will never lose to another nation."[77] While he aimed to show that religious morality was "our nation's great weakness"—the phrase used as the sermon's title—Kozaki also believed firmly in the nation of Japan, just as his (and Hongō pastor Ebina Danjō's) first Western teacher, Captain Janes at the Kumamoto *Yōgakkō,* had taught him to do three decades before.[78]

By the end of the Meiji period anyone seeking to portray the entirety of the Japanese Christian movement as unnationalist would have had a hard time overlooking the open nationalism displayed by some Protestant religious leaders. Christianity had shed its foreign image and become very Japanese. Kozaki's rhetoric, like that of many of his colleagues, had not only come to successfully defend Christianity but had even begun to evoke some of the same claims, concerns, and points of national pride as the religion's ideological enemies in Japan. A cursory comparison between the widely distributed commentary on the Imperial Rescript that Inoue composed at the behest of the Ministry of Education in 1891 and Kozaki's 1913 sermon "Patriotism and Faith" (Aikokushin to shinkō) reveal a number of common elements surrounding the topic of the nation. Inoue warned his compatriots that

> in the world today Europe and America are of course great powers, while the countries settled by the Europeans have prospered as well. Now only the countries of the East are capable of competing with the progress of these nations. Yet India, Egypt, Burma, and Annam have already lost their independence; Siam, Tibet, and Korea are extremely weak and will find it difficult to establish their autonomy. Thus in the Orient today Japan and China alone have an independence stable enough to vie for rights with these powers. . . . Only in Japan does the idea of progress flourish, and Japan has it within its means to anticipate a glorious civilization in the future.[79]

Two decades later, the situation in Japan had improved greatly, and Kozaki reiterated many of the points that Inoue had used for the purpose of instilling fear and fostering patriotism:

> Our nation is drawing the world's attention as the sole strong nation in Asia, based on the Sino-Japanese and Russo-Japanese Wars. Among the nations of Asia, only one has preserved the dignity of independence. India lost its independence to the Turks. Burma and Annam in a short time, followed in those tracks and lost their independence. Four years ago, Chosen [Korea] was joined to our nation. Persia, too, in the near

> future will be divided up between England and Russia. . . . Our nation excels far above the rest, easily . . . preserving our independence, but we must [also] be thankful that our military strength can be compared to that of the West's strongest countries.[80]

These phrases clearly served to demonstrate and rejoice in Japan's status, effectively challenging Protestant Christianity's image as an unpatriotic religion. Such words left listeners at Reinanzaka with a picture of Japan as a strong, successful empire poised for a prosperous future. Kozaki, however, also aimed in this sermon to show the cracks in Japan's success, such as "corruption scandals" and other forms of "depravity," and to recommend the spiritual and moral guidance of Christianity as part of the solution. The Japan that the Meiji government and its citizens had built so well and so quickly was, after all, very much worth saving.

In September 1912, the passing of the Meiji emperor at the age of sixty gave millions of Japanese an occasion to mourn a national leader and emblem while praising his accomplishments. Voices across Japan reminded the Japanese at home and abroad of Emperor Meiji's contribution to the modern transformation of Japan. During the emperor's last days, journalist and political critic Yamaji Aizan (1864–1917) wrote in *Kokumin zasshi* (People's Magazine) about Emperor Meiji's success in unifying the Japanese people and promoting the cause of democracy, among other achievements.[81] Everywhere one looked in Japan, the people were lugubrious, and even those possessing strong nationalisms that opposed the existent Japanese political order expressed deep regret and sorrow.[82] Given that Christian leaders such as Uchimura Kanzō, who harbored both sentiments against the current government and a strong sense of nationalism, "felt as if he had lost a father," it should come as no surprise that less reservedly patriotic pastors utilized the emperor's passing as a moment to celebrate the rapid metamorphosis of Japan.[83]

In two sermons eulogizing the Meiji emperor, Kozaki spoke in patriotic admiration of the ruler, who, like ancient Israel's legendary leaders Moses and King David, had led Japan in its fruitful quest for nationhood. "Moses was the founder of Israel," explained Kozaki in June 1912, and "Emperor Meiji was the founder of the new Japan."[84] It was Moses who first gave the people of Israel a "national awareness" *(kokumintaru no ishiki),* specifically referring to his role in transmitting to them their new law. Similarly, after the Meiji Restoration, Emperor Meiji "bestowed upon our nation the organization for the new Japan . . . [and] the consciousness of the new Japan." That September, in a second sermon on the Meiji emperor, Kozaki highlighted the steps taken many centuries after Moses by David to assure the persistence of the nation of Israel. "King David conquered neighboring enemies . . . [and] greatly expanded the territory," stabilizing the country of "Judea" (Yudaya) as a fixed and sovereign physical space.[85] In Japan, Emperor Meiji brought about "the restoration of the imperial institution, the abolition of the feudal fiefs, the creation of prefectures," and other things that likewise established Japan as a true nation. Taking the parallels further, he noted that "abroad, in both wars, against China and Russia, the military power [of Japan] shined upon the world and . . . expanded the territory."[86] Like Moses and David and their native Israel, the Meiji emperor had established and secured the future of the new Japan in terms of both governance and territory.

In building their nations, Kozaki drew attention to the fact that all three of these exemplary men had accomplished this task while seeking to maintain "pious minds."[87] While this insight shows that Kozaki, like Tsunajima, considered it not only natural but commendable for pious individuals to work for the existence and the survival of the nation, it also served to separate his viewpoint from that of many other Meiji ideologues. When Kozaki specified the type of nation that Japanese Christians should work to construct and maintain on Empire Day (Kigensetsu; 11 February) in 1912, he focused most of all on the type of spiritual foundation that any healthy nation should possess.[88] Whereas political ideologues such as Meiji statesman Ōkubo Toshimichi (1830–1878) and political adviser Yano Fumio (1850–1931) argued that in order for people to gain wealth, the nation must first become wealthy, Kozaki assigned a lower level of priority to such goals.[89] Although he wholly agreed with those calling for Japan to embody the "Rich Country, Strong Army" ideal, Kozaki argued that one "cannot create a nation with these material things only."[90] "No matter how mighty the army and navy are, no matter how well the constitution is made, no matter how prosperous commerce and industry are," Kozaki urged his listeners to consider the importance of "the nation's religious cultivation." Despite all of the important elements for constructing a new Japan and helping it to prosper, he argued that the "intangible [element of] faith must be placed at the foundation of the nation."[91]

As an important manifestation of that Christian faith, Kozaki highlighted the concept of "universal love" in Christianity, arguing that, contrary to the contentions of anti-Christian detractors, this virtue had everything to do with Japan and its future. While Inoue Tetsujirō construed universal love as incongruous with love of country, positing that "it was difficult for universal love and love for country to coexist," Kozaki strongly disagreed.[92] He explained that, "conceptualizing love as something available in only a fixed amount," Christianity's opponents felt that if one were to "pour love out to the world, one would completely extinguish one's love of country." But in fact, according to the Reinanzaka pastor, these two goals were highly compatible because "love is not a quantifiable thing." Instead, Kozaki conceived of universal love as something felt and expressed on an individual level, regardless of separations such as family or nationality. "One loves his own child and also loves the children of others. And as for those with one child or with several, the love that those children receive is no different."[93] Paul, for instance, was one of the "most fervent members of the Israeli independence faction" and "worried about the future of the people of Israel." However, in comparison to his concern for the political fate of Israel, an occupied and "ruined country," Paul "came to lament even more the spiritual fate of his fellow countrymen, that is to say their individual salvation."[94] By focusing one's love on individual Japanese rather than on the "nation," a Christian could demonstrate patriotism and universal love at the same time.

Kozaki Hiromichi considered the fate of the nation to be of the utmost importance, and he frequently addressed the most pressing national issues facing Japanese listeners. He urged his congregation to develop and express an active love for Japan. That nation was full of industrious and capable individuals who were at that very moment proving that Japan was worthy of inclusion among the great nations, and Kozaki made no apologies about reminding his listeners of this. However, these same individuals were also men and women afflicted with the social problems that were plaguing their quickly modernizing country: deficient levels of religious consciousness and insufficient exposure to the promise of eternal salvation through Christianity. Kozaki called for his congregation and others to work together to improve their very worthy nation by thinking about and dealing with these issues. In his religious discourse, Kozaki Hiromichi propagated a nationalism that was at once very aware of the existence and significance of the Japanese people and at the same time dedicated to their spiritual and social improvement.

The Nation of Ebina Danjō

Among the Protestant pastors in Tokyo during the Meiji and Taishō periods, none have been treated as "nationalist" or "patriotic" as frequently as Hongō Church pastor Ebina Danjō. Although other pastors such as Tsunajima, Uemura, and Kozaki also evinced concern and excitement for the present and future condition of their nation, Ebina's sermons addressed more often, and made bolder statements about, the nature and primacy of the Japanese nation and Japanese national identity. From making positive reflections on national heroes to isolating the core qualities of the nation and its citizens, he promoted a Protestant

Christianity that could claim to be both Japanese and patriotic. Yet somehow Ebina's sermons appealed to a mixed audience that included not only right-wing politicians and conservative thinkers but also left-wing students and activists. An investigation of the nation that he constructed in his sermons reveals a complex mixture of Christian humanism and nationalism that in fact held attractive elements for various types of listeners and defies simplistic categorizations.

Ebina imagined certain elements of Japanese national identity in terms reminiscent of some of Meiji Japan's most conservative nationalist thinkers. In his 1901 sermon titled "Our Moral Cultivation," he explained that each Japanese individual's identity was inevitably derived from that person's lineage and ancestors. Contradicting the old Japanese proverb that "breeding more than birth makes a man," Ebina argued that "birth more than breeding makes a man."[95] To determine our nature, "we must know our lineage; knowing our lineage is, namely, knowing what type of thing we are. What kind of parents do I come from? What sort of character do my parents have[?]"[96] For Ebina, this road of genealogical inquiry inevitably led back for all Japanese to the "founding ancestors of the [Japanese] nation."[97] Like Imperial University constitutional law professor Hozumi Yatsuka, who conceptualized the Japanese state as an ethnic group of "blood relatives of the same womb," Ebina linked all Japanese to the country's legendary founding emperor Jimmu and his descendants.[98] While Hozumi employed this logic to place all Japanese under the hereditary rule of the Japanese emperor, Ebina had a different legacy in mind.

For Ebina, the most important element transmitted to his listeners through their ancestors was the "national historical spirit" *(kokumin rekishiteki seishin)* that touched each and every Japanese and made them members of the Japanese nation.[99] To be Japanese was to be "linked to the flow of the pulsing of that great spirit." At home or abroad, "no matter where we go, we are Japanese; the Japanese nation's spirit is our spirit; our spirit is Japan's spirit," he proclaimed. Japanese men and women would always be possessed of the "national historical spirit" that made them typically Japanese, just as historical figures from other countries remained part of and shaped by their respective original national cultures. "Great men transcend their times, but certainly they cannot escape being the product of their nation's character. Plato, Socrates, Aristotle were born in Greece . . . and they remained children of Greece's [national] character. Cicero [and] Caesar built Rome, and they came to be creatures of Rome's [national] character."[100] Just as Rome and Greece had national characters that produced great men, Ebina was quick to show that Japan did as well.

The national historical character of Japan had laid the foundation for the "great character" *(daijinkaku)* of the admirable men of Japan's recent and distant past.[101] Although Ebina offers no definition for this term, *daijinkaku* was clearly a popular term in prewar Japan.[102] In usage, *daijinkaku* carried a similar connotation to that of "the Japanese spirit" *(Yamato damashii),* the inner force bequeathed to the Japanese people by their long line of powerful ancestors and particularly referenced in times of war.[103] In a sermon titled "The Beauty of War" made while Japan was in the midst of the Russo-Japanese War in August 1904, Ebina recalled certain paragons of military bravery who embodied *daijinkaku.* He called to mind ultraloyalist Satsuma samurai "Saigō Takamori's bronze statue in Ueno Park."[104] He spoke of the monument to the founder of Japan's modern military, "the bronze statue of Ōmura Masajirō [standing] before Yasukuni Shrine" with reverence.[105] Looking back to the Gempei War (1180–1185), Ebina praised the bravery and acumen of Minamoto loyalist samurai Nasu no Yoichi (1169–1232), who so famously "shot down the fan target with just one shot."[106] These men represented the embodiment of the *daijinkaku* that had been available to all Japanese since the original founders' first manifestations of this trait. While anyone could claim to personify *daijinkaku,* Ebina proceeded to explain why these men and the many like them in Japan's history had truly come to possess this characteristic.

In an age of increasingly large and damaging wars, Ebina used the examples of these military figures to demonstrate that war, a real crucible of "purification," provided Japanese with an "opportunity to develop the great national character."[107] For both soldiers and civilians, Ebina argued that it was in war and such moments of national crisis that "Japanese patriotism . . . was so strikingly manifested" in those Japanese who exerted themselves for the nation.[108] After all, "war is not just a soldiers' war; the whole nation is fighting. . . . After victory, soldiers cannot be proud of themselves alone."[109] Looking around him, he remarked that in this particular instance, he saw the Russo-Japanese War "beginning to produce the great character" in the Japanese. Nearing the end of his sermon, Ebina proclaimed that "seeing the splendid [national] character now being born within our nation, I truly cannot suppress my happiness."[110] It would take a lot more than patriotic displays of *daijinkaku,* however, for Japan to become one of the world's great powers. Ebina called his listeners' attention to other pertinent inherited elements within the Japanese national historical spirit that would serve Japan as it continued marching forward onto the international stage.

Ebina explained that within that same "national historical character," his audience's ancestors had also passed down a certain expeditionary spirit into which all Japanese were now able and strongly encouraged to tap. In response to the countless Westerners who insisted that "the Japanese are an island race; their spirit does not escape the island country mentality," Ebina's 1901 sermon "Our Moral Cultivation" offered a very different interpretation of Japan's history and national essence. Japan, though indeed an island nation, had reasserted its connection with the "people of the continent" under the leadership of "Toyotomi Hideyoshi" and general "Date Masamune" (1567–1636) when they invaded Korea at the end of the sixteenth century.[111] For Ebina, adventurer and explorer "Yamada Nagamasa" (1590–1630) was another good example of Japan's noninsularity, and his "departure from the island country [to Thailand] displayed our nation's character."[112] The task of uncovering and utilizing that expeditionary spirit was especially incumbent on the Japanese people of Ebina's day, and in a 1902 sermon titled "The New Way of the Warrior," the pastor outlined motivations and strategies for utilizing this spirit.

For Ebina, it was very important for Japanese to develop the related quality of *bu* (martial spirit) in order to facilitate the realization of their inherited expeditionary spirit. It was by exercising this character trait, he said, that Japanese could work for the betterment of Japan beyond its immediate frontiers. For all classes, Ebina recommended that "we thank God who gave this warrior spirit to the Japanese race" and declared that "with this [spirit], wherever the Japanese race goes, they advance, and [we] must not stop advancing."[113] He continued by specifying the applications of a *bu*-inspired expeditionary ethos for different occupational classes in Japan. "The Japanese scholar," for instance, was for Ebina "a warrior, fighting against the cosmos and the universe, conquering them and enlarging mankind's territory."[114] This extended to the Japanese merchant, intending to become "prominent in the world," and even to the "farmer."

Just as so many other voices in the Meiji media were inundating farmers with proexpansion discourse, Ebina spent a significant portion of his sermon "The New Way of the Warrior" promoting the expeditionary warrior spirit among Japanese farmers as well. He wholly endorsed Japan's growth beyond its borders and believed strongly in the Japanese people's mandate to spread prosperity and order to its neighbors. The Meiji Japanese state colonized Hokkaidō in 1869, Okinawa in 1879, Taiwan in 1895, and Korea in 1910 in an effort to make economic gains and secure their still-sovereign islands against Western colonization.[115] As the result of a "deliberate colonization policy of the Japanese government," Japanese settlers, of whom the majority were farmers, were arriving in Korea and other colonies by the late Meiji period.[116] Politician Nagai Ryūtarō (1881–1944), historian and statesman Takekoshi Yosaburō (1865–1950), and other ideologues depicted glowing images of paradisiacal lands in Japan's overseas territories that Japanese farmers could come and cultivate without limit.[117] In agreement, Ebina preached that it was the task of Japan's agriculturalists to subdue the "savage wastelands" of "Hokkaido, Taiwan, Manchuria, and Korea . . . taking up their hoe, with their shovel on their shoulder, conquering nature with our hand."[118] Beyond disparaging those lands, the pastor here was highlighting Japan's imperial imperative to dominate nature in its colonies. This mandate was deeply grounded in Western Enlightenment-era assumptions about nature and race, and Ebina's expansionist discourse built on this legacy to glorify Japan.[119] If they did not go to these places and "cultivate that warrior spirit and plan expeditions, [then] our national agricultural policy . . . is just useless talk," he explained.[120]

As one might expect, Ebina also had a great deal to say about the recently repopularized ideological constellation of "loyalty" and "filial piety" *(chūkō)* that had become intimately linked with the Meiji revival of *bushidō*. One would also expect that, given his reputation for patriotic Christianity, his pronouncements on these two ideals would coincide with the nationalist discourse of progovernment Meiji ideologues. Indeed, he clearly grasped and supported the conservative ideological understanding of the concept in which "the Japanese people's spirit manifests loyalty to [their] sovereign. . . . Loyalty to the monarch is direct loyalty to the state and love for country." Here and elsewhere, he repeatedly emphasized moral values that the Meiji government had enshrined and propagated in both the 1890 Imperial Rescript on Education and the commentaries and glosses of the text that appeared during the last decades of the Meiji period.[121] In his 1902 sermon on new *bushidō*, Ebina admitted to thinking immediately of loyalty and patriotism when he thought of *bushidō*. In the words that followed these statements, however, the Hongō pastor demonstrated that he had a lot more to say about true patriotism and loyalty than the vague language of the Meiji government's moral directives, and that his nation-view was in fact very different from that propagated by the state.

Mixed in with all of his praise and admiration for the Japan of yesterday, today, and tomorrow in this sermon, Ebina built a working definition of loyalty that clearly incorporated elements of his influential Christian humanism and tempered his nationalism. The Hongō pastor signaled an upcoming deviation from the mainstream nationalism of his previous sentences when he told listeners, "We must remember not to narrowly limit loyalty to the monarch and filial piety to parents."[122] Using his expanded understanding of loyalty, Ebina then went on to criticize certain soldiers because "on the one hand they boast of loyalty to the emperor but on the other they inflict insults on the people; this is not true loyalty. If one loves the emperor, that love must necessarily extend to the people as well. . . . [We must] build the nation, person by person, with love for the people . . . for this is the Christian's heart."[123] As Ebina would explain three years later in an October 1905 sermon on Christianity in wartime, loyalty to the monarch meant more than obedience and respect for the imperial family, and patriotism was more than simply proclaiming love for one's country. If "the people are treated as inconsequential, where is the patriotism?" he pondered. The people of Japan together formed "one body . . . [and] without the individual, there is no national polity."[124] Going beyond reformulations of loyalty and patriotism, Ebina also addressed the goals and application of the warrior's moral code itself. "The spirit of the warrior way does not mean simply boasting of strength, but helping the weak. . . . He [the warrior] not only sacrifices himself for noble, strong, and great people, but also lends his life for the sake of the weak, small, and humble."[125] It is perhaps for this reason that Ebina placed such a marked emphasis on improving the nation for the sake of his "forty million countrymen" in 1901, 1902, and 1903, "fifty million fellow countrymen" in 1905, and "sixty million fellow countrymen" in 1920.[126] That emphasis in fact grew considerably. He left to become president of Dōshisha in 1920. By then, his pastoral discourse had shifted to topics of brotherhood and popular democratic governance. Contrary to Inoue Tetsujirō's assertion that for Japan's national success, "we can only rely on our 40 million fellow countrymen," Ebina instead believed that it was the responsibility of each Christian to serve those fellow countrymen.[127] In the end, the nationalist rhetoric that Ebina propagated from his pulpit left plenty of space for listeners to interpret, adjust, and select relevant elements into a workable and powerful mandate for Christian social activism in the name of both the Japanese nation and mankind.

If even the nationalism of Ebina Danjō is impossible to confine to a single hue, it stands to reason that Japanese Protestant nationalism in Meiji and Taishō Japan was not a single entity but many. The interplay of these four pastors' understandings of and hopes for the nation provides compelling evidence that nationalism is a body of competing conceptualizations of the meaning of the nation rather than one ideology, a debate more than a speech, a journey more than a place. The undeniably present and powerful Japanese national community was a constant within all of these shifting definitions, and official and popular ideologues alike strove to influence how the Japanese would perceive and interpret it. Although the national government aimed to create a modern nation-state and a unified and dutiful body of imperial subjects, the questions and concerns of Japan's educated elite became a sea of competing and complementary nationalisms by the 1890s. As these individuals searched for ways to think about and interact with the nation and turned to various types of popular ideologues, Protestant pastors became one important source of inspiration and new paradigms.

Tokyo's Protestant pastors formulated their nationalisms as both religious and secular responses to the socio-moral dilemmas inherent in the rise of the modern nation. In doing so, they filled important roles as cultural interpreters and popular ideologues for the most educated, ambitious, worldly members of Japan's new educated elite. Ebina espoused an intense nationalism filtered through Christian humanism, brotherhood, and individualism. Kozaki echoed many of these sentiments and expressed pride in his country while highlighting the role that Christianity in general and universal love in particular could play in fulfilling Japan's destiny. Uemura selectively criticized and promoted a *bushidō* ideology supported by but beyond the control of the Meiji government.[128] Tsunajima called his listeners to bravery, sacrifice, and self-discipline in the service of God and nation. Tokyo's Protestant pastors, considered together, offered nation-minded Japanese a set of perspectives and impetuses that were relatively difficult to find outside the church. Equipped with these original, timely and applicable fragments of these pastors' alternative nation-views, Christians and other churchgoers set about transforming Protestant national imaginaries into reality.

CHAPTER FIVE

The Lay Lectern—Discourse beyond Religion at Church

For all their eloquence and relevance, pastors' sermons were only one part of the greater discursive space fostered inside Tokyo's largest Protestant churches. These churches also hosted afternoon and evening *enzetsu* (speeches) and *kōen* (lectures) on weekends and weekdays. Just as sermons exceeded the boundaries of religious discourse, these *enzetsu* and *kōen* often dealt with social and political topics in church *reihaidō, shūkaidō,* and *kyōshitsu.* The most common occasions to hear talks beyond the sermon in Japanese Protestant churches were the *enzetsukai* (speech meeting) and *kōenkai* (lecture meeting). Although the *enzetsukai* tended toward oratory and persuasion and the *kōenkai* toward expertise and experience, the words of speakers freely transgressed the lines separating these two genres in Japan. And together these two types of events were among the most publicized and well-attended social events of the Japanese Protestant movement throughout the Meiji and early Taishō periods. The popular pastors examined in this book, and in much other scholarship, spoke at church during such events. However, it was laymen and laywomen, from both within and outside the church membership, who addressed social issues most often and who predominated secularly themed church *enzetsukai* and *kōenkai.* In hosting these events, Tokyo's leading Protestant churches provided reformists and dissidents with a privileged, relatively safe space, literally and figuratively, to think and speak about social change in modern Japan.

This trend took place in parallel, and at times in conversation with, the development of new lay-focused organizations and discourse in Buddhism as well. Seeking to assert the relevance and applicability of Buddhism to Japanese lives so transformed by modern concerns and changes, Buddhist priests, scholars, and lay leaders placed a strong, unconventional emphasis on Japanese lay-Buddhist practice as well as discourse. Advocates also highlighted the enviable social engagement of Christianity and its positive impact on the religion's reception in Japan.[1] In his Tetsugakkan and publications such as the best-selling *Introduction to the Revitalization of Buddhism,* Imperial University professor Inoue Enryō helped launch a movement to promote lay Buddhism *(zaike bukkyō).* And from the mid-1870s, *koji,* or lay Buddhist preachers, created teaching assemblies and lay societies that were parallel to and typically more secularly oriented than traditional institutional Buddhism. In addition, clerics such as Nichiren monk Nagamatsu Seifu (1817–1890) and Rinzai Zen priest Imakita Kōsen (1816–1892) promoted the expansion of Buddhism into the everyday lives of the Japanese. Imakita often led the meetings of Confucian scholar Okunomiya Zōsai's (1811–1877) Ryōmō Kyōkai (Association for the Abandonment of Concepts of Objectivity and Subjectivity) at Tokyo's Rinshōin in Yushima. The gatherings included cultural activities like poetry, games, and even open discussion of non-political ideas.[2] Meanwhile, lay Buddhist preacher-activist Ōuchi Seiran targeted the broader public with lectures, tracts, and books.[3] And Imakita's disciple Shaku Sōen (1860–1919), a Rinzai Zen priest, translated Paul Carus's influential *The Gospel of Buddha* into Japanese and aimed with his writings and teachings to promote Zen practice and reform among the lay population.[4]

By the late 1890s, efforts to incorporate more lay participation into Buddhism had gained particular momentum in Tokyo among the educated elite. The New Buddhist movement and its New Buddhist Fellowship published the journal *New Buddhism* and held frequent public meetings where speakers spoke on a wide variety of topics. Aloud and in print, lay members expressed themselves on themes like Confucianism, *bushidō,* and government edicts. Also in Tokyo, Shin priest Chikazumi Jōkan hosted meetings in his Kyūdō Gakushsa (Way-Seekers' School) and Kyūdō Kaikan (Way-Seekers' Hall), where laypersons shared in "faith conversations."[5] While Chikazumi dominated the lectern, on occasion laymen like Buddhist scholar Uesugi Bunshū (1863–1936) spoke to the assembly and addressed topics that bridged the religious and secular spheres, such as "Buddhism's Perspective on War."[6] These leaders and their groups contributed to a "general trend among lay practitioners to exert more control over systems of religious knowledge and practice."[7] And while laypersons' lectures and speeches refracting society and politics through the lens of religion did not necessarily come to define Japanese Buddhism—New Buddhist Fellowship members, for instance, often worked in secret to spread their message and promote social activism—this turn toward the laity did help contribute to the redefinition of the practice of Buddhism in modern Japan.

The Japanese Protestant movement also sought to bring together Japanese laypersons in new ways and to forge new connections between religious belief and practice and the concerns of modern daily life. And like Imakita and Chikazumi, Tokyo pastors and lay churchgoers made novel use of religious space to achieve this. By the 1890s, Japanese Protestantism was largely and openly defined by lay participation, notably including lay discourse. Lay lectures and talks at church, which encompassed talks on social, cultural, political, and scientific topics, were particularly important in determining the character of Japanese Protestant churches. Large gathering spaces within these buildings fostered the development of a distinct, relatively open lay discursive space. In this sense, the capital's Protestant church buildings grew to function like the Mita Enzetsukan (Mita Oratory Hall) that Fukuzawa Yukichi established for his Mita Enzetsukai (Mita Speaking Society) in 1875 or other new venues for speeches and lectures in the Meiji period.[8] Unlike this site at Keio University and the growing number of such halls, however, urban churches were explicitly religious gathering spaces that regularly hosted lay discourse on social and political topics. And these events occurred with much more frequency and visibility than Buddhist events on such topics. Churches came to act as spaces for discussing the application of religious ideals and ideology to the concrete sociopolitical world and for interrogating the relationship between religion and society in Japan more broadly.

Hosting lay speeches and lectures was a collective effort. Pastors and members invested tremendous energy in organizing these events, sometimes over the course of several months. While pastors were responsible for inviting laypersons to speak in the late nineteenth century, lay leaders and dynamic church-based organizations and church-based branches of national voluntary associations were increasingly responsible for such events after 1900. Japanese Protestant churchgoers invited members and visitors to give talks that brought secular knowledge and news into the space of the church. These figures kept Tokyo's leading Protestant churches busy well beyond Sunday morning worship. On Sundays at 2 p.m., Reinanzaka's *fujinkai* (women's group) and *seinenkai* (youth group) held *enzetsukai* in 1901.[9] Similarly, at 1 p.m. on Sundays in 1905, Hongō Church's *fujinkai* hosted *enzetsukai*. Evening lectures and speech meetings were also quite common. At Ichibanchō on Sundays in 1898, the *seinenkai* held *enzetsukai* in the evenings at 7:30.[10] But events organized by church-based groups were not limited to Sundays. In late 1892, a well-publicized series of *kōenkai* took place in Hongō Church's *reihaidō* on Saturdays evenings at 6.[11] The first of several *enzetsukai* hosted by the *fujinkai* of Banchō Church occurred at 2 p.m. on Saturday, 10 December 1892.[12] And as a 1:30 p.m. *fujinkai kōenkai* at Hongō Church on Saturday, 24 May 1919, illustrates, this active use of the church space for such events continued into Japan's interwar period.[13] Throughout the weekend, then, speakers came to talk about subjects such as education, psychology, literature, and philosophy, as well as current events in Japan and abroad.

One category of topic that attracted audiences with particular frequency and consistency was that surrounding the position of women in Japan. Laymen and laywomen expressed their opinions on the definitions and rights of modern

Japanese womanhood as well as the institutions in imperial Japan most associated with it of marriage, family, and the home. This chapter examines the socially and politically conscious lay discursive space that took shape in Tokyo's largest Japanese Protestant churches. To do so it analyzes the *Kirisutokyō shimbun* (Christian News), the leading Christian newspaper in imperial Japan, as well as church bulletins such as the *Reinanzaka kyōhō* (Reinanzaka Church News), *Hongō Kyōkai geppō* (Hongō Church Monthly News), autobiographies, and other sources. Through these sources, the chapter argues that secularly themed lay discourse at church, in tandem with sermons, contributed to Protestantism's correlation not only with Western knowledge and modernity but also with progressive thinking, social awareness, and reformism. As these examples in Tokyo demonstrate, urban churches worked with better-studied spaces like Christian schools and hospitals and media such as Protestant periodicals to cement Christianity's ties to Japanese society and the discursive authority of the West.

Origins of the Lay Lectern in Tokyo Protestant Churches

From 1890, in the months following the opening of the new Imperial Diet, Protestant churches in the capital regularly transformed their pulpits into lecterns. Churches strove to demonstrate Christianity's compatibility with the latest intellectual and scientific developments and its relevance to the nation's modern projects and problems. Two of the first churches to embody this new trend were the Ichibanchō Church (predecessor to Fujimichō Church) and Banchō Church. During an event at Ichibanchō that January, for instance, Tokyo First Middle School teacher Kimura Junkichi (1866–1938) spoke on physics.[14] The following month, the youth group of Banchō hosted speeches by English teacher and Amherst College graduate Koyano Keizō (b. 1852) and Treasury Department official Soeda Jun'ichi (1864–1929) in the fledgling congregation's 1886 Banchō Lecture Hall.[15] Later that month the girls' youth group *(joshi seinenkai)* held an *enzetsukai* against licensed prostitution at Banchō featuring author Ishizaka Kameharu (1865–1926) and businessman Furushō Saburō along with pastor Tamura Naoomi.[16] Then in June the church's *seinenkai* invited well-known journalist and statesman Shimada Saburō (1852–1923) to talk about the role of religion in France and Germany.[17] Shimada was also invited by the Ichibanchō Church *seinenkai* to speak in November of the following year.[18] These first invitations came only a few years after he assumed the presidency of the *Mainichi shimbun*, one of Japan's oldest and most widely circulated daily newspapers, and just after his 1890 election to the House of Representatives in the brand new Imperial Diet.[19] A lifelong member of Ichibanchō since his baptism there in 1886, an eloquent speaker, and an advocate of social reform, Shimada Saburō was a fixture in Tokyo Protestant church *enzetsukai* and *kōenkai* throughout the Meiji and Taishō periods.[20]

At Banchō Church, the *fujinkai* also actively sought lay lecturers in this early period. As Mara Patessio has demonstrated, *fujinkai* in general were much more than women's versions of men's organizations. Instead, they functioned as independent, women-led groups concerned for the most part with subjects most mundane to women. The Banchō Church *fujinkai* exemplified this trend when it announced a plan to bring lecturers who could speak on "hygiene, physiology, and home economics," in late 1892. Like the topics, the group's decision to restrict attendance of the series to women illustrates an intentional emphasis on women and women's issues. The first guest, Dr. Willis Whitney (1855–1919), addressed the audience on 10 December 1892, a Saturday.[21] This Christian physician taught physiology, chemistry, and English at the Kanazawa Middle Normal School and was well equipped to enlighten his all-female audience.[22] The talk was indicative of a wider effort in the capital to bring scientific knowledge and discourse into Protestant church spaces.

In the 1890s, Tokyo Protestant pastors and congregations fostered a stimulating intellectual environment at church by hosting talks that dealt with science, broadly defined. They essentially carried over into the church the vibrant exchange of ideas taking place in the burgeoning print media. This included the rapidly expanding newspaper media, reaching tens of millions by the late 1870s.[23] But the pastors and topics bore the closest relationships to the intellectual journals of the day. Of particular relevance were journals such as the short-lived but widely influential *Meiroku zasshi* (Meiji 6 Journal), which ran from 1874 to 1875 and popularized the ideas of leading thinkers like Fukuzawa Yukichi, Nishi Amane (1829–1897), and Nakamura Masanao (1832–1891).[24] Both enamored with Fukuzawa and interested in such intellectual pursuits, pastors Kozaki and Uemura founded *Rikugo zasshi* (Cosmos) in 1880 as a forum for scholarly articles on subjects like philosophy, religion, and science.[25] Quickly the publication evolved into one of the most highly respected journals of its day.[26] Church *enzetsukai and kōenkai* connected churches to the discursive space developing in *Rikugo zasshi* and other periodicals edited by Japanese members of Protestant networks.

And like contributors to this serial, the guests invited to give such church speeches and lectures addressed the epistemologies and purposes of science as well as science's relationship to spiritual, moral, and social thought. In 1893, Tokyo Imperial University philosophy professor Nakajima Rikizō (1858–1919), a member of Banchō Church, lectured there. He sought to counter claims that science was prospering while philosophy was increasingly in decline. As the investigation of the fundamental truth of the universe, he argued, philosophy was broad in scope and valuable to scientific knowledge.[27] Nakajima, however, encouraged listeners to consider philosophy and science as part of the same whole and promoted its study. With his speech, Nakajima was in fact addressing one of the essential problems facing young men and women in the Meiji period: the omnipotence of modern Western science. For instance, the influx of Western scientific learning in the late Tokugawa and early Meiji periods emphasized the distinction between philosophy and science, challenging the old Confucian intellectual order, and presented science as superior. Of course, the ramifications for religion were even more consequential, as debates between creationist American missionaries and their evolutionist Japanese converts made apparent.[28] Like Nakajima, many in the first generation of Protestant pastors believed that science was compatible with other forms of knowledge and belief.[29]

The Tokyo congregation that most staunchly championed the congruity between secular knowledge and the religious gathering space of the church in the Meiji era, however, was Hongō Church. Speaking events in the 1890s cemented the associations of the church space with modern academic learning in Japan. Pastor Yokoi Tokio organized a winter series of "Science Lectures" *(Gakujutsu kōen)* between November 1891 and January 1892 and another between November 1892 and January 1893.[30] The pastor invited several well-known Christian and non-Christian speakers to take the podium in the *reihaidō*. Seventeen of Tokyo's most highly regarded scholars, primarily Tokyo Imperial University professors, gave lectures on topics falling within the broad, secular category of "science" *(gakujutsu)* to mixed audiences as large as 450.[31] Many among the Imperial University faculty presenting were Hongō members. These included psychology professor Motora Yūjirō (1858–1912), who spoke on Japanese folkways; historian and economist Taguchi Ukichi (1855–1905), who lectured on Japanese history; and law professor Terao Tooru (1859–1925), who discussed the relationship between morality and law. Another member, Tokyo Senmon Gakkō professor of philosophy and psychology Ōnishi Hajime (1864–1900), addressed the conduct and character of the famous Dutch philosopher Baruch Spinoza (1632–1677). Layperson members of other churches, like Banchō's Nakajima, who spoke on Europe's pessimistic philosophy, often addressed audiences at Hongō as well.[32] Yet guest speakers, like church attendees in Tokyo Protestant churches in general, were not limited to church members or Christians.

The Hongō Church's science lectures also featured prominent non-Christians. Among them were zoologist Mitsukuri Kakichi (1858–1909); Dr. Kitazato Shibasaburō (1853–1931), founding director of the Tokyo Institute for Infectious Disease; and Tokyo Senmon Gakkō literature professor and author Tsubouchi Shōyō (1859–1935).[33] Perhaps the most famous non-Christian to regularly participate in Protestant networks and give lectures at churches was the editor, journalist, and author Tokutomi Sohō (1863–1957). A classmate of pastors Yokoi and Kozaki in Kumamoto and at the Dōshisha, and Yokoi's cousin, Tokutomi maintained a close personal and professional relationship with these men and their congregations throughout his life.[34] His connection ran so deep that in his final years Tokutomi requested that his funeral be held at Reinanzaka.[35] So it is not surprising that he accepted Yokoi's invitation and gave a speech about Yoshida Shōin (1830–1859) on 14 January 1892 that would form the basis for his 1893 work of the same name. Yoshida's failed efforts to stow away on Commodore Perry's ship, assassinate a minor shogunate official, and lead a revolt led to his imprisonment and execution. But in jail and later as a head of the Shoka Sonjuku in Chōshū domain's capital of Hagi, Yoshida taught several young ambitious samurai like the famous Itō Hirobumi and Kido Takayoshi (1833–1877), who would eventually overthrow and replace the shogunate.[36] In his talk, Tokutomi situated Yoshida's character sketch in a detailed description of the situation at the time of the Meiji Restoration.[37] On that Saturday evening, hundreds in Japan's educated elite heard Tokutomi approvingly elucidate the ideas, ideals, and actions that in part formed the foundations for the new imperial Japan in the Hongō Church *reihaidō*.

In addition to such non-Christians, pastor Yokoi and the congregation even welcomed as guest speakers well-known figures who were ambivalent about or held critical views of Christianity. On 22 January 1892, Murakami Senshō (1851–1929), the chief instructor at Asakusa Honganji and Buddhism scholar at the Imperial University, stepped behind the lectern. Dressed in his robes, he acknowledged the "extremely strange" nature of his appearing in a lecture series taking place in a "Christian church."[38] He described the astonishment he felt when pastor Yokoi, whom he had never met before, visited him at his home in November with a letter of introduction from one of the priest's close acquaintances and invited him to speak at Hongō. "Was it not unprecedented since time immemorial," mused Murakami, "that a Buddhist priest give a lecture in a Christian church . . . at the behest of the most influential man in Christianity." However, the speaker embraced the opportunity. After all, "the Buddha did not only preach to . . . Buddhists." Murakami, in accordance with the scientific emphasis of the series, lectured not on theology but on Buddhist philosophy. He focused in particular on the central importance of "idealism" in Buddhism.[39] In fact, "idealism" was a topic of great interest in the Meiji era. Japanese thinkers lamented that many Westerners perceived among the Japanese a disdain for abstract or theoretical philosophy. Prominent Japanese intellectuals such as Buddhist lay advocate Inoue Enryō aimed to remedy this with the founding of the Philosophy Association (Tetsugakkai) in 1884 and the Philosophy Institute (Tetsugakkan) in 1887.[40] Inoue was joined by budding students from the capital's top universities as well as by religious leaders like Protestant pastor Kozaki Hiromichi and Buddhist priest Shimaji Mokurai.[41] It was in that context that Murakami highlighted Buddhism's contribution to Japanese philosophy in general and abstract philosophy in particular.

The guest speaker who came on 12 December 1891, himself a member of the Tetsugakkai, was also an exponent of the soundness and profoundness of Japanese philosophy. As a figure actively engaged in debates about the distinctiveness of Japanese intellectual developments, the invitee was indeed an especially good fit for the series. Inoue Tetsujirō (1855–1944) was also, however, Protestant Christianity's strongest ideological opponent throughout the Meiji period, and this made his visit to Hongō Church surprising. That February, the Imperial University professor of philosophy had quickly become the loudest voice condemning Christian educator Uchimura Kanzō for having failed to show proper reverence to the Imperial Rescript on Education. Then in September his criticism of Christianity became embedded in the very ideological fabric of the Meiji state. In his official commentary on the Imperial Rescript on Education, he enshrined Confucian morality and obedience to the emperor above all—and argued that these values were antithetical to Christianity. His influential 1893 book *Kyōiku to shūkyō to no shōtotstu* (The Clash of Education and Religion) would soon crystallize his stance against Christianity and his conviction that the religion was "antinationalistic" and un-Japanese.[42] So the image of Inoue standing behind a pulpit at Hongō Church was an unlikely one.

However, Inoue did speak at Hongō. And both the church's invitation to speak and his acceptance of that invitation say a great deal about the relatively open nature of the physical and discursive spaces that Yokoi and his congregation hoped to engender within their church. The event also offers evidence of the relative acceptance that Protestant Christianity had gained among the educated elite in the capital. Before an audience of 450, Inoue gave a lecture titled "Discussing the Study of Ōyōmei" in which he underlined the value of the philosophy of Wang Yangming (1472–1529), a form of Neo-Confucianism that he considered seminal and foundational for East Asia and for Japan.[43] Although there were several great scholars in the Ming dynasty (1368–1644) who elaborated on the ideas of Song philosopher Lu Jiyuan (d. 1192), an intellectual rival of the more influential Neo-Confucian scholar Zhu Xi (1130–1200), "Wang Yangming alone excelled in the Ming period."[44] Then, beginning with Nakae

Tōju (1608–1648), "the earliest to revere Ōyōmei in Japan," Inoue proceeded to describe the development of the ideology in that country. Kumazawa Banzan (1619–1691), Nakae's pupil, carried on the teachings, which then continued on in the writings of "Miwa Shissai" (1669–1744) and "Ōshio Heihachirō" (1793–1837). By recounting the legacy of Ōyōmei, Inoue highlighted the Japanese appropriation and adaptation of Wang Yangming's Neo-Confucianism. In classical China, he argued, scholars had favored "materialistic" philosophy, and "concrete" thought had won out over "abstract" thought. But Wang Yangming's "idealism" or even "spiritualism" was the exception.[45] So Inoue praised Japanese scholars for selecting what he believed to be the only Chinese scholar advocating "idealism," an assertion that, like that of Murakami above, contradicted negative characterizations of Japanese philosophy as overly practical and concrete.

In the end, Inoue presented Ōyōmei as a philosophy that unified the abstract and the tangible. At the center of Wang Yangming's Neo-Confucianism was the concept of "knowledge and action as one." The ideas of the scholar, for Inoue, boiled down to the simple truth that "knowing a thing and doing a thing are the same" and that "without action, there is absolutely no knowing a thing."[46] In spite of his efforts to differentiate Christianity from "Japanese" religion that year and in the years to come, this part of his lecture praised an ideology that resonated with Protestant Christianity and with the social gospel more specifically. With its criticism of the privileged knowledge of the priestly class and the lack of individual agency in the practice of faith, the Protestant Reformation had objectives not unlike those of Wang Yangming. But more importantly, the impetus to apply Protestant religious convictions to the improvement of Japanese society—combining knowledge, in the broader Platonian sense, with action—had already come to define the Christian movement in the capital by the 1890s.[47] Among the key proponents in the movement were Hongō Church pastor Yokoi Tokio and Reinanzaka Church pastor Kozaki Hiromichi, both uncoincidentally from Kumamoto domain where Ōyōmei had thrived for centuries. In fact, Yokoi's father was Yokoi Shōnan (1809–1869), a prominent Ōyōmei scholar who argued for the complete reform of the Tokugawa shogunate and whose Shōnando in Kumamoto was a bastion for reformist thought.[48] So the anti-Christian Inoue and Protestant leader Yokoi both advocated equating knowledge with action in Japan.

The topics covered by guest speakers over the course of the two series of Hongō Church Science Lectures were highly varied, ranging from literature to philosophy to nature to medicine. But nearly all of the talks had one overarching theme in common: a focus on Japan. Experts from Tokyo Imperial University and Tokyo Senmon Gakkō as well as from the nonacademic world led hundreds of Japanese men and women in defining Japan through its history, culture, and intellectual traditions. Whereas the detractors of Christianity faulted the religion for its foreignness and its inability to contribute to Japanese national identity, these events stood as a counterargument. Japanese laymen, including several non-Christians and even some opponents of Christianity, informed Japanese listeners about the essence of the Japanese nation. The discussions unfolding throughout Japanese society in the 1890s concerning the people, ideas, and words that constituted Japan, then, made their way into the religious gathering space of the Protestant church. And this was what pastors and congregations like Yokoi and his Hongō Church intended.

The momentum of church *enzetsukai* and *kōenkai* of the early 1890s weakened in the mid-1890s as leadership changes at Hongō, Reinanzaka, and Banchō led to dwindling numbers. *Enzetsukai* on socially and politically topical subjects did continue to occur on occasion in the church, and laymen like socialist intellectual and activist Sugiyama Shigeyoshi (1867–1927), who spoke at a Banchō *enzetsukai* in 1893, still addressed audiences.[49] As Japan embarked further along the road to armed conflict with China over Korea, talk turned to war and all its implications. Hongō Church—even without pastor Yokoi, whose departure for study at Yale in 1894 left the church without consistent leadership—played a leading role in hosting speech events on this topic. The Tokyo Kirisutokyō Seinen Kaikan (YMCA Hall), completed in 1894 on the eve of the outbreak of the first Sino-Japanese War, hosted most such talks, but Hongō continued in its role as well. In between speeches by pastors Takagi Mizutarō (1864–1921) and Uemura Masahisa, for instance, journalist and official army interpreter Tagawa Daikichirō (1869–1947) spoke at Hongō in September 1894 on the economic and political background of the "Sino-Korean problem." Tagawa lamented the "unhealthy trend" of "patriotism" without "benevolence," as he was paraphrased in the *Kirisutokyō shimbun,* and he argued before an audience of two hundred listeners that the Japanese needed to act with ethical, just hearts.[50] The church also hosted a talk in October that year by German pastor and missionary H. Ritter Max Christlieb on international law and ethics in the context of the developing Sino-Japanese War to an audience of about fifty.[51]

Revitalized by the arrival of Tsunajima Kakichi in 1896 and the return of pastors Kozaki and Ebina in 1897, churches in Tokyo increased their efforts to host lay discourse on current events, social movements, and scholarly developments. Banchō held special *enzetsukai* on three Sunday nights in late June and early July 1902. Along with pastors and evangelists like Ebina Danjō, Ōyama Tōsuke (1879–1919), and Matsumura Kaiseki (1859–1939), the series featured a secular talk by a prominent layman. Katayama Sen (1850–1933) had recently been editor of the Socialist Party and labor union organ *Labor World* (Rōdō sekai), and he spoke from the perspective of Christian socialism.[52] Sugiyama Shigeyoshi, another guest with strong ties to social protest movements in Meiji Japan, was scheduled to speak but was in the end unable to appear.[53] With the reorganization of its youth group and other church groups in 1901, Reinanzaka Church turned its focus to lay *enzetsukai* as well. In May 1903 the church's *seinenkai* organized a speech meeting that featured Terao Shin (1887–1969), a student soon matriculating at Tokyo Imperial University,[54] who spoke about the biology of the flower. Then Kanda Toyoho (1884–1941), a recent graduate of Azabu Middle School and houseboy of professor and official Kume Kunitake, gave a lecture titled "A Child's View of Life."[55] In addition, socialist activist Oikawa Teiju expounded about "The Origins of Socialism."

Katayama and Oikawa's talks and Reinanzaka's new efforts to facilitate discussion on pressing social questions coincided with the dawn of the socialist movement in Japan. Although already alive as a concept for several years, the formation of the Society for the Study of Social Problems (Shakai Mondai Kenkyūkai) by intellectuals such as Katayama Sen constituted the first organized attempt to investigate the topic.[56] It was followed in 1898 by the creation of the Society for the Study of Socialism (Shakaishugi Kenkyūkai), an event that scholars agree marked the birth of the Japanese socialist movement.[57] While the Public Order and Police Law of 1900, which criminalized labor unions and unrest, and other forms of government pressure discouraged and dispersed many, a handful of activist-thinkers went on to found the very short-lived Social Democratic Party (Shakai Minshutō) in 1901. Meanwhile, the newspapers *Heimin shimbun* (Commoner News), published by Kōtoku Shūsui (1871–1911), Sakai Toshihiko (1871–1933), and Uchimura Kanzō in 1903, and *Shin kigen* (New Era), edited by Abe Isoo (1865–1949) and Ishikawa Sanshirō from 1905 to 1906, published essays by Japanese and Russian socialist thinkers.[58] The government looked with disfavor on these types of publications as well and frequently shut them down.

Socialism and Modernism in Lay Discursive Space at Church

It was in this context that Japanese interested in investigating socialism and its responses to the social problems inherent in a modernizing Japan sought safe meeting spaces. Churches as hybrid, privileged spaces were ideal for such gatherings. This is why, as scholars have noted, the Society for the Study of Socialism held its monthly meetings for discussions and lectures on socialism in the library of the Unitarian Church in Mita.[59] Socialism's ties to Protestant religious gathering spaces were, however, much broader than this single connection. Socialist groups made use of other Protestant churches, whose role in hosting such gatherings has been largely ignored. These included Methodist missionary Charles Eby's Central Tabernacle (Chūō Kaidō), where the Socialism Society (Shakaishugi Kyōkai), the successor of the Society for the Study of Socialism, held several "Great Speech Meetings on Socialism" in 1903.[60] Furthermore, Tokyo's largest Japanese-led Protestant congregations were also actively involved in hosting talks and gatherings about socialism. In July and August 1903, Reinanzaka Church lent its building to a group of socialists for the purpose of holding "Socialism speech meetings."[61] Beyond such indirect support for discussions about socialism, the church also hosted talks by outspoken socialists. The fall of the following year, for instance, the church's youth group held a *kōenkai* where Kōtoku Shūsui gave an alternative perspective on "loyalty and patriotism" to a sixty-five-person audience of mostly young men and women.[62] And Reinanzaka was not alone.

In June of the year before, Hongō Church had hosted a talk by Abe Isoo on the subject of "Socialists' View of Christ." Although the speaker was an ordained Unitarian minister, he often wore the hat of a layman. He could speak from his secular roles as a professor of political science at Tokyo Senmon Gakkō (renamed Waseda University that year), a political activist, and a newspaper editor.[63] Events featuring socialists in fact intensified at Hongō as war with Russia loomed larger and nearer, and in those years Kōtoku Shūsui and Sakai Toyohiko spoke often at Hongō.[64] Socialism continued to be a topic of interest and discussion there after the conclusion of the war as well. In May 1906, the church's youth group hosted a talk by Abe titled "The Morality of Socialism."[65] The decision to host events and discourse dedicated to this controversial ideology inside churches throws the strong relationship between Protestantism and socialism into sharp relief.

Indeed, as scholars have convincingly demonstrated for decades, socialism and Protestant Christianity were closely tied in late Meiji-era Japan. The faith of Japanese Protestants aligned well in many cases with the tenets and objectives of socialism.[66] In particular, the principles of "brotherhood" and "humanitarianism" were shared by the religious and political ideologies.[67] By the late nineteenth century, many among them saw socialism as a way to improve on an apolitical, imported Christianity and implement true social reform in Japan.[68] It was during this "brief moment of sympathy" that Christianity and socialism worked closely together in imperial Japan.[69] So as socialism became more popular, and dangerous, in the early 1900s, most Japanese socialists were Christians.[70] In Tokyo, several of them were also members of the largest Japanese Protestant congregations. Journalist, author, and socialist activist Ishikawa Sanshirō was a member of Hongō Church. Also among the members of Hongō in the early 1900s were socialist intellectual and activist Arahata Kanson (1887–1981),[71] and both Ōsugi Sakae and Abe Isoo.[72] Socialist labor organizer and editor Katayama Sen was a member of Banchō Church from 1896 until the death of his wife Fudeko in 1903, and maintained close ties to the church afterward.[73] In 1907, long before he became Japan's first socialist prime minister, the young Tokyo Imperial University student Katayama Tetsu (1887–1978) began a lifelong membership at Fujimichō Church as well.[74]

At church these men and the hundreds of others in their Tokyo congregations who at the very least sympathized with some of socialism's core ideals gave and listened to lectures and speeches about the topic. In doing so, they strengthened the bond between Protestant Christianity and socialism. Beyond the intellectual bonds, however, such events also gave the two a spatial connection. Protestant religious gathering spaces directly contributed to the development of the socialist movement. They hosted discussions and talks about the ideology at a time when most other forms of space, and especially religious gathering spaces, could not. They cultivated a lay discursive space in which investigations into contentious subjects like socialism were not only allowed but encouraged. For these reasons, even as most Japanese socialists moved toward material socialism and away from Christian socialism, the imprint of Christianity remained strong.

As present as socialism was at Tokyo Protestant churches in the first decade of the twentieth century, their discursive spaces were filled with other subjects as well. At Reinanzaka, the tradition of the scholarly meeting continued into the twentieth century. A speech meeting there in August 1903 featured Tokyo Imperial University professor of psychology Yamaguchi Sannosuke, who spoke about "hypnosis and its experiments," as well as Tokutomi Sohō, who addressed family and education in his lecture "The Power of Nurturing."[75] The following year, the church hosted another *kōenkai* featuring a talk that concerned the latest in academic theories. Journalist, lawyer, and socialist activist Kinoshita Naoe (1869–1937) lectured in December 1904 on "the world of modern thought." Also connecting listeners to developments beyond Japan, the guest who preceded Kinoshita that day spoke on his "lessons from America." This was novelist and poet Noguchi Yonejirō (1875–1947), author of a recent, well-received English-language novel about a Japanese girl living in the US.[76] Having resided in California, Chicago, and New York, Noguchi was particularly well qualified to share such insights.[77]

International perspectives and the topic of education continued to feature prominently in Reinanzaka *kōenkai* in the Meiji period and beyond. In May 1909, influential philosopher and critic Miyake Setsurei (1860–1945) gave, in the words of the church bulletin, an "original critique" in his talk titled "London and Tokyo." Miyake, like Tokutomi Sohō at the time, held views on the conservative end of the political spectrum, a contrast with many of the more liberal listeners and guests. In fact, the speaker who followed Miyake was one such progressive. Shimada Saburō gave a lecture titled "New Civilization" to a 250-person audience.[78] In addition to talks like these organized by Kozaki and other church leaders, speech events were often coordinated by the Reinanzaka *seinenkai* as well. In February 1911, noted child psychologist and educator Takashima Heizaburō (1865–1946) accepted an invitation from the youth group to come speak at Reinanzaka.[79] After tracing the development of "individualism" back to Socrates and Epicurus, he described how the theory had become fundamental to Western society and in turn the greater world.[80] Next came Shiga Shigetaka (1863–1927), editor of the nationalistic *Nihonjin,* who gave observations from his latest world travels.[81] Although most of the church's sources from the Taishō period have perished, it does appear that speech events continued into the 1920s. Tagawa Daikichirō, freshly returned from the Washington Naval Conference, where he was a Japanese delegate, spoke at an event organized by the women's group of Reinanzaka in May 1923. Reflecting on his experience in the United States and back home, Tagawa discussed differences between American and Japanese treatment of guests. In particular, he expressed a concern that the Japanese emphasis on keeping up appearances prevented them from occupying a more prominent place on the world stage.[82]

Women's and youth groups and church leaders consistently organized events featuring lay speeches and lectures on social and political subjects of great interest to Japan's new educated elite. Some of the most outspoken figures of Meiji and Taishō Japan recalled talks on key social, political, and cultural issues in turn-of-the-century Japan. Ōsugi Sakae remembered listening to "eloquent speeches" by socialist activists Kōtoku Shusui and Sakai Toshihiko in the *reihaidō* of Hongō Church around the turn of the century.[83] Tellingly, Ōsugi noted that he became familiar with these figures, men who inspired him and attracted him to socialism, through their newspaper articles and also through their talks "in the main hall of the Hongō Church."[84] Another trailblazer, the feminist author and editor Hiratsuka Raichō (1886–1971), also wrote of her experience in the audience at Hongō speech meetings. Thinking back on her brief attendance at the church, she remembered:

> After the service there were talks by famous people. I vividly remember one guest, the writer Tokutomi Roka, who spoke on Higuchi Ichiyō. . . . Another guest was Kinoshita Naoe, the author of *Confessions*

> *of a Husband* who spoke passionately about Tanaka Shōzō and the scandal surrounding the pollution caused by the copper mines in Ashio. Only dimly aware of the incident, I was much disturbed to hear the details.[85]

The founder of Japan's first all-women literary magazine, *Seitō* (Bluestocking), never became a Christian. However, Hiratsuka regularly attended Hongō Church throughout 1904 while she was a student of nearby Japan Women's University. She experienced an awakening of social consciousness at Hongō that was significant enough to merit inclusion in her memoirs. It must have also been encouraging for the future writer and editor to hear the well-known author Tokutomi Roka (1868–1927) talk about Higuchi Ichiyō (1872–1896), one of Meiji Japan's only nationally recognized female literary figures and a hero for Hiratsuka.[86] Lectures like these were an integral part of Japanese Protestant churches' appeal for the young members of the new educated elite in the capital, and for young women in particular.

The Woman Question and the Lay Lectern at Church

Among the many popular topics in lay discourse at church, few if any attracted as much attention as the so-called woman question *(fujin mondai)*. For *kōenkai* and *enzetsukai* organizers and presenters and for audience members like women's rights activist Hiratsuka, this set of questions was of the utmost importance. The "woman question" referred to the difficult questions surrounding the modern woman's appropriate place in the modern home, community, and nation and her identity as an individual.[87] Although this imported term from the West only gained currency in Japan during the Taishō period, the dawn of the *fujin mondai* in modern Japan went back much further. From the first decade of the Meiji period, government officials, Western missionaries, and Japanese intellectuals had become preoccupied with the woman question. In ideology, policy, and institutions, influential men embedded their versions of modern Japanese womanhood within the foundation of the new Japan.[88] From the 1880s, prominent women in the Freedom and People's Rights movement highlighted the dissonance between women's lack of rights and their abundant, gendered duties. During and after the movement, widow and women's rights advocate Kusunoke Kita (1836–1920) and feminist activists Fukuda Hideko (1865–1927) and Kishida Toshiko (1863–1901) pressed the new government to incorporate gender equality into its representative political processes.[89] The same decade saw members of local organizations like the Okayama Women's Friendship Society and national organizations like the Japan Woman's Christian Temperance Union (WCTU) gain access to the public sphere, where they increasingly fought to define and promote their own responses to the woman question.[90] Through public speeches, they advocated for women's rights and called for an end to institutions like concubinage and legal prostitution that in their view weakened women's position in the home and in society. While the perspectives of the women involved differed, they were connected in their conviction that women deserved the right to assemble and discuss the meaning of the woman question themselves. Efforts by the Meiji government to stifle women's voices by excluding them from Imperial Diet sessions in 1890 and prohibiting them from attending or holding political meetings under the Public Order and Police Law of 1900 met with persistent and substantial resistance.[91] Amid these struggles, Protestant churches provided a rare space for women as well as interested men to speak and exchange on the issues facing modern women in imperial Japan.

The organizations most often charged with organizing events on women's issues were church-based women's groups *(fujinkai)* and other related groups like the *joshi kyōreikai* (girls' cooperative association) at Reinanzaka. Of course, the speech meetings sponsored by these groups were not restricted to women's topics. At the Reinanzaka *joshi kyōreikai*'s science lectures in May 1903, one of the talks dealt with twentieth-century youth, a topic much broader than, although connected for many with, the woman question.[92] The speaker, Banchō Church member Iwaya Sazanami (1870–1933), was a pioneering author of children's literature and editor of *Shōnen sekai* (Youth World).[93] At Hongō, the church *fujinkai* hosted a talk on recent changes in morals and customs in the United States, England, and Germany by Motora Yujirō in December 1905. In his lecture, the Tōdai psychology professor argued that moral reform could empower Japan to fully assert its independence.[94] This topic too covered much more than women's issues.

Yet most of the church *enzetsukai* and *kōenkai* organized by women's and girls' groups did address the plight and shifting possibilities of Japanese women. After a hiatus in the latter 1890s, the Hongō Church *fujinkai* reemerged as a dynamic group that prioritized organizing *enzetsukai* with popular lay figures. They invited renowned writer Tokutomi Roka and Iwamoto Yoshiharu (1863–1942), founder of Meiji Girls' School and founding editor of *Jogaku zasshi* (Women's Education Magazine), in May 1903. The two spoke on "Miss Ichiyō" and young Japanese women's "independence and freedom," respectively.[95] Iwamoto's students, Tokutomi's female readers, and many other members of the capital's educated elite were attracted to Hongō by such prominent figures. In December 1905, Waseda University political science professor Uchigasaki Sakusaburō (1877–1947) accepted an invitation to speak at Hongō as well at the

"Tokyo Women's Speech Meeting" *(Tokyo fujin kōenkai)* hosted by the Hongō *fujinkai.*[96] Before two hundred listeners, he lectured on ten brave Western women in fields like literature and religion and commented on the rising prospects of women in general.[97] Uchigasaki highlighted the achievements of women as accomplished professionals, contradicting the strong intellectual and political currents that often defined and confined women with the gender ideology of *ryōsai kenbo.* At a Reinanzaka *fujinkai* open speech meeting, politician and Imperial Diet member Ebara Soroku (1842–1922) also underlined women's worth with a lecture on language and dignity in June 1908.[98] But as Iwaya's talk that followed, titled "How to Talk to Children," indicates, such events did not come close to escaping the "good wife, wise mother" paradigm.[99] Other talks like that by Takashima Heizaburō on "the differences between men and women" before the Reinanzaka *joshi kyōreikai* contributed to discourses that separated women from men and justified their disenfranchisement.[100] Nevertheless, running through these diverse speeches and lectures, and through the very format of the women's speech meeting itself was an affirmation that women deserved a better place in Japanese society.

A series of *kōenkai* organized by the Hongō *fujinkai* in 1909 took up the woman question in earnest, and the speakers repeatedly made this point about the social status women deserved. The timing of the series points to a church attune to debates on that topic taking place in the broader public sphere in Japan about the so-called New Woman. Modern, socially liberated, and employed outside the home, the *atarashii onna* represented a clear break from traditional gender roles in Japan.[101] Following more than two decades of debates about modern Japanese womanhood, the last years of the Meiji period year saw an explosion of interest, and contention, around the New Woman. In 1911 Hiratsuka Raichō launched the provocative women's literary magazine *Seitō,* advocating women's rights and highlighting the work of women authors and artists.[102] The editor and the women contributors represented, for both critics and admirers alike, the epitome of the New Woman in Japan.[103] Of the many sources feeding into Japanese conceptualizations of this new archetype, few were as often evoked as the figure of Dora, the self-aware protagonist of Henrik Ibsen's *A Doll's House.* The play, translated in 1910 by Waseda literature professor Tsubouchi Shōyō, premiered on the Japanese stage in a production by Tsubouchi's literary society in 1911.[104] And in 1912, *Seitō* published a feminist analysis and praise of the play by several women, contributing to a great debate among Japan's educated elite about the definition of the woman and her place, or lack thereof, in Japanese society.[105] Although the Hongō Church *fujinkai* was by no means a radical or feminist organization, it echoed some of the most basic arguments of the burgeoning feminist movement and hosted speech events that championed women's rights as individuals and as daughters and wives.

In February 1909, Hongō *fujinkai* member Yoshino Sakuzō gave an in-depth description of concubinage among the aristocracy in China in his speech "Some Words on Chinese Women."[106] The Imperial University Law professor and political theorist based his analysis on his experience in the household of General Yuan Shikai (1859–1916).[107] Yoshino explained the legally binding relationship of the secondary wives to their lord, narrated the initiation process, and even offered a descriptive tour of the household where he had worked as Yuan's tutor and recently seen these things. In his speech, however, Yoshino also drew attention to certain observations that were problematic for him. He especially lamented the situation of these secondary wives after the passing of the husband.

> The second wife, while the master is alive, receives favor and influence. After his death, however, she suddenly becomes the object of the first wife's jealousy and terrible ill treatment. . . . Even if she is not being poorly treated at the moment, it is common that she commits suicide, in expectation of such treatment. In China it is becoming popular to praise this so-called "martyrdom of the favored wife" in newspapers and the like.[108]

For his listeners, Yoshino's detailed glimpse into the *huis clos* of China's first family was accompanied by the short tale of this "tragic extreme," which warned them of the possible repercussions of polygamy.[109]

More importantly, this story was about the weak position of women in polygamous households, a situation that Japanese women activists, ranging from more conservative Protestants to radical feminists, abhorred. The decades immediately before and after 1900 in Japan saw the galvanization of both women and men around the issues of concubinage and licensed prostitution and the greater question of women's rights with which they were so clearly intertwined. The WCTU was particularly active in calling for the criminalization of prostitution, enforcement of existing prohibitions against concubinage, and procurement of legal rights for women. Thus, for Japan WCTU members listening to Yoshinō—including Iwamoto Yoshiharu, women's reform movement leader and journalist Kubushiro Ochimi (1882–1972), pioneering female physician Ogino Ginko (1851–1913), and Ebina Miya (1862–1952), Ebina Danjō's active and visible wife—the observations offered by Yoshino held a specific and powerful relevance.

Male speakers, typically invited by women leaders, dominated church *fujinkai kōenkai* and *enzetsukai*. Of course, women also spoke at *fujinkai* events.

However, only talks by the most prominent women speakers were advertised in leading Christian periodicals, and very few of those were summarized or transcribed for the broader reading public. Nevertheless, those limited sources do indicate that churches belonged to the small group of spaces in the late Meiji period in which women were not only encouraged to gather and participate but also to be heard. *Fujinkai* hosted one of the few discursive spaces in which "public women" could speak up and speak their minds.[110] And women who accepted *fujinkai* invitations appeared before mixed audiences, a newly acceptable form of social interaction in Meiji Japan.[111] Hibiki Yoneko, wife of Ichibanchō member and army lieutenant Hibiki Nobutsune (1858–1940), spoke at that church in 1898.[112] Her talk concerned Friedrich Fröbels's educational philosophy, and it touched on a theme that was among the most common in women's lay discourse.[113] Educators were in fact the most frequent women speakers, and, as in the November 1910 Reinanzaka *fujinkai* talk by Joshi Gakuin teacher Mitani Tamiko (1873–1945) on "brave women," they provided their own perspectives on the woman question.[114]

Peers' School teacher Yasui Tetsu (1870–1945) was among the most vocal women members at Hongō. Having studied abroad at Cambridge University and Wales University and taught at girls' schools in Japan and Thailand, Yasui most often spoke on women's education.[115] In a talk titled "Modern Women's Cultivation," the educator noted a lamentable dilemma concerning women's education in Japan. Neither educators nor parents actually held "very clear ideals about how to educate girls," she explained.[116] Yet it was educators and teachers, those "directly responsible for education," who filled the pages of newspapers and magazines with complaints about the state of young women's moral cultivation and were "pitilessly punishing" misbehaving girl students.[117] This system, according to Yasui, produced young educated Japanese women who were like the "bird that imitated the peacock" by "simply attaching beautiful feathers on the outside." They carried an air of sophistication and cultivation but had not developed true moral cultivation, "something that occurs from within, not something that can be attached from the outside." The fault, and the solution, lay with the parents and teachers who had failed to teach young women to think about their purpose in the world. As a remedy, Yasui suggested they teach young women to "learn as much as possible" and "do their best" for the sake of "mankind." Women with such purpose, she argued, were "brave" enough to achieve "inner peace and satisfaction."[118] Although far from confrontational or radical, Yasui's encouragement of Japanese women to seek and embrace their purposes well beyond the confines of the home was markedly progressive.

Two years later, two fellow educators who shared Yasui's moderate views on women's rights and responsibilities spoke at another *fujinkai enzetsukai* at Hongō. Educator Ninomiya Teiko (1883–1964), who the year before had become the first Asian graduate of Smith College, gave an address called "Happy Life."[119] On the same Sunday afternoon, Women's Higher Normal School teacher Okonogi Matsuko (1882–1965), a recent Wellesley College graduate, gave a lecture on "Women's Energy."[120] The young Tokyo Women's Higher Normal School teacher argued that Japanese women lacked "energy," noting that they were "criticized for having narrow hobbies and lacking self-confidence in comparison with foreign women."[121] In agreement with such negative comparisons to Western women, Okonogi explained that in Japan "ordinary women had been confined to a narrow sphere" in the past and could not aspire to much. However, now that Japanese society was changing, women were relatively freer and could undertake work that was "unattainable for the women of the past."[122] Still, she said in dissatisfaction, Japanese women continued to go about their work simply out of duty, like those who "walked reluctantly, dragging their tired feet."[123] For Japanese women to be happy and to achieve great things, it was essential to work with a "conscious will," a self-aware, agentic mentality that would engender dynamism and vitality. Like Yasui, Okonogi also spoke about the need for broader purpose in women's active lives. She urged the women in her audience to work "not only for yourself and not only for your family, but also to give extraordinary benefit to your country."[124]

Women speakers like these educators often advocated the improvement of women's status in Japan, but in gradual and subtle ways. In comparison with the incendiary rhetoric of feminists who in those very years were beginning to find their voices, the words of Yasui and Okonogi appear tame. After all, Okonogi referred with at least some approval to the view of women that G. K. Chesterton (1874–1936) put forth in his *What's Wrong with the World*. She offered no argument against his assertion that women cannot excel in first-rate jobs, instead explaining that "we Japanese women have the duty to apply great energy to even such inconspicuous jobs." Teaching, as one of the few socially acceptable career paths for educated women in Meiji Japan, was clearly one such occupation.[125] However, their words also included subtler and less complacent ideas about womanhood. Despite the strides made by Japanese society, Okonogi remarked, still "our lives generally lack stimulation"—a quiet criticism of the previous and continued negligence of women by the Japanese social and education systems and the modern, enlightened government at its head.[126] Similarly, Yasui named no names as she faulted the Japanese society as a whole for failing young women. Parents and educators with unclear and poorly informed ideas about girls' education were calling on those same girls to be paragons of virtue and to both understand and embrace their places in a rapidly modernizing Japan. It was in no small part this conviction that convinced Yasui to cofound Tokyo Women's Christian University in 1918.[127]

Occasionally there were *fujinkai* events that featured more assertive rhetoric about women's place in society. In September 1911, the Hongō *fujinkai* invited the primary benefactor of Japan Women's University to speak at an *enzetsukai* to welcome women students to the church. Head of a self-built mining, banking, and insurance empire, Hirooka Asako was one of the wealthiest women in Japan, and she used her fortune to help found the country's first women's college. Hirooka firmly believed that women deserved practical higher education and the opportunity to become professionals. A fervent, outspoken, late-life Christian convert, Hirooka addressed issues of faith in her speech "Japanese Women in the Twentieth Century." Yet the other two-thirds of her talk dealt with political and social issues of great relevance to young women in a modernizing Japan. She called on young women to be strong advocates for peace in Japan and the world, a stance that aligned with the position of the Japan YWCA, of which she was a leading member.[128] Hirooka's other injunction, however, was considerably bolder. In front of two hundred women and sixty-seven men at Hongō, she asserted that women must be involved in the promotion of industry and be economically independent.[129] In no uncertain terms, the speaker argued that women had the right and obligation to insert their voices into the political realm and participate in the business world, subverting norms that confined women to the sphere of the home.

In the years to follow, outspoken women at church continued to appear and speak before audiences. Many such talks moved increasingly to other Protestant gathering spaces intended for hosting speeches and lectures in the capital. By that time the Tokyo YMCA Hall (1894) in Kanda and the Japan YWCA Hall (1915) in nearby Jimbōchō had become the most popular locations for the large *enzetsukai* and *kōenkai* of church-based women's groups.[130] In addition, although women's groups continued to hold speaking events, they focused increasingly on explicitly religious topics. So talks like that of Iwamoto Yasuko on how to bless one's neighbor before the Reinanzaka *fujinkai* in March 1923 were the exception rather than the norm.[131] However, Japanese women did continue to address the woman question aloud at church into the Taishō period. On 26 May 1913, as part of a larger meeting of the Family Cultivation Association, Kawai Michi explained to a crowd of 150 at Fujimichō Church that "now is a blessed time."[132] In 1916, Hirooka spoke on "women's rebirth" at a September Banchō *fujinkai enzetsukai*.[133] And at Hongō, the *fujinkai* held regular speech events including women speakers in the 1910s and 1920s as well. In 1920, for instance, the group hosted a *kōenkai* and a women's conference that each drew over one hundred attendees, and among the speakers for the March *kōenkai* was Ebina Miya, who spoke on "young European and American men and women."[134]

In general, the discursive space within Protestant churches in Tokyo, and throughout Japan, became less and less heterodox during the Taishō era. This was clearly the result of an effective long-term campaign by Japanese Protestants to demonstrate their loyalty, patriotism, and national belonging through the spoken word and other forums. Government bureaucrats and ideologues legitimized Protestant social ideals as Japanese and socially constructive. As part of the effort to gain this recognition, churches largely lost the diverse mix of conservative, moderate, and liberal views that had characterized lay spoken discourse at church during the 1890s and early 1900s. However, the speech events hosted within the Hongō, Reinanzaka, Banchō, and Fujimichō Churches over those three decades underlined the associations between Protestantism and both a modernizing Japanese society and the greater discursive authority of the West. More broadly, organizers and guest speakers had succeeded in promoting a significantly new configuration of the relationship between religion and society in Japan.

In the late Meiji and Taishō periods, a vibrant lay discursive space developed within Tokyo's largest Protestant churches. In addition to countless talks on religious topics, church leaders and church-based groups purposefully organized speech and lecture events that dealt with issues directly related to politics and society. Among these were some of the most difficult and urgent questions facing the members of Japan's new educated elite. To address topics ranging from the newest findings in psychology to American society to socialism to women's education, organizers sought laymen and even some laywomen with relevant experience and expertise. Rare but especially noteworthy were guest speakers who were not Christians or who even opposed Christianity entirely. Hundreds of listeners gathered in the *reihaidō* of Tokyo's leading Protestant churches to gain knowledge, inspiration, or simply new perspectives from these figures.

Amid the rise of militarism and imperialism, this momentum slowed and eventually stalled, and this failure has, with reason, attracted significant scholarly attention. Such an approach, however, can easily obscure the legacy of the Protestant church lay discursive space. Even as the Japanese Protestant movement increasingly embraced a stance of conformity to the objectives and policies of the imperial government, many influential individuals translated the explicit and implicit messages of *enzetsukai* and *kōenkai* into action. Within the church building and beyond its walls, Japanese men and women devoted significant energy to endeavors and fights addressed at church. Furthermore, they embodied the underlying messages of so many speech events that strands of national and international fellowship connected individuals and that positive social change was possible.

CHAPTER SIX

Church-Based Groups and Activism in the Church

The myriad changes rapidly sweeping through Japan during the Meiji period destroyed long-standing local forms of belonging and community. In exchange, modern Japan offered a sense of belonging to the national community. However, society denied most Japanese a key fiber of that belonging: direct political participation. Unpropertied male youth under age twenty-five and women in general were among those who were largely excluded politically but often sought a voice in the social and political realms of the public sphere. Ironically, official rhetoric, the new flourishing mass media, and the rest of their families all strove to have those women and youth represent and embody a modernizing Japan. Then, too, controversies erupted when youth or women failed to adhere to the prevalent norms that society placed on them. These heavy and conflicting pressures helped drive women and youth, particularly those in the educated elite, to seek new forms of community and participation among their peers.

In the late nineteenth century, Japanese members of these two groups found both in the religions of Buddhism and Protestant Christianity.[1] Buddhist sects responded to the threat but also the model of Protestant Christianity in the Meiji period with movements that aimed to foster unprecedented lay participation and stronger ties between temples and the world beyond.[2] Ikeda Eishun has described the proliferation of lay societies and teaching assemblies from the 1880s that strove to strengthen the relationship between clergy and the laity and cultivate lay spirituality.[3] This same period also saw the growth of Buddhist women's groups *(bukkyō fujinkai)* and other forms of lay Buddhist women's gathering.[4] Cognizant of the times, women parishioners' desire for Buddhist education, and these groups' local success in social welfare projects, the Nishi Honganji Sect of Shin Buddhism held the first national convention of *bukkyō fujinkai* in 1908 and would create a consolidated national organization in 1933.[5] This development occurred alongside the sect's official recognition and training programs for *bōmori,* or "temple wives," whose faith and religious knowledge qualified these women to not only assist but also lead laity at the temple.[6] More broadly, from the late Meiji period all of Japan's Buddhist sects developed long- and short-term projects for helping the poor, healing the sick, and responding to natural and economic disasters.[7]

Meanwhile, a burgeoning movement of the 1880s largely rooted in Shin Buddhism came to include the young, outspoken, and articulate men of the New Buddhist Fellowship in the 1890s. And building on the educational initiatives of Inoue Enryō and Murakami Senshō in the 1880s and 1890s, leaders like Chikazumi Jōkan began implementing new ways of encouraging lay participation among the young members of the educated elite as well in the early twentieth century. However, these few movements that sought to revolutionize the message and application of Buddhism in the modern Japanese context did not significantly change institutional Buddhism.[8] The upsurges in lay participation and organization and in social welfare projects across Japan remained disconnected from the efforts of leading Tokyo Buddhist reformers like Chikazumi. For youth and for women seeking to connect religious belief with social and even political engagement and with Japanese modernity, the options provided by Buddhism were very few.

By contrast, urban Protestant Christianity in Japan was largely characterized by its ability to empower youth and women to link faith and ideals with the social and political realms. In Tokyo as in other metropolitan areas and some rural areas in Japan, Japanese-led Protestant churches offered spaces and means to gather, collaborate, speak, organize, and, through those activities, belong. Churches also provided opportunities for women and youth to develop deeper social awareness and to engage with social issues beyond the church. The principal vehicle for all these elements was the church-based group. In the *fujinkai* (women's groups) and *seinenkai* (youth groups) of the capital's largest congregations, elected group officials led regular monthly meetings about objectives, strategies, and projects. Both women's and youth groups promoted the discernible presence of lay voices speaking on real-world topics, as in the speeches and lectures analyzed in the preceding chapter—something less common in Buddhist temple space. Church members, attendees, and guest speakers bridged the divide between secular and religious discourse and brought relevant knowledge and experience to churchgoers. This social space, however, was not limited to the discourse contained within the walls of the church.

The Protestant Christian movement in imperial Japan has kept such a high profile in Japanese historiography precisely because of its connections with concrete efforts to reach and impact society. In movements for socialism and popular democracy and in efforts to improve the status of women, workers, and children in Japan since the late 1880s, Protestants have played an especially prominent role. Central to this development in major metropolitan areas were church-based groups that aimed to transform Christian ideals into new strands of social thought as well as social and political activism beyond the church. Church-based groups also constituted one of the primary ways through which church members participated in national Christian social reform organizations like the YMCA, YWCA, and WCTU. Despite this imbrication, church-based groups remained independent organizations, run according to the priorities and resources of their respective churches. From smaller groups with memberships under twenty to larger ones with hundreds of members, church-based organizations made the largest and most consistent contributions to the cultivation of the lay social space in Tokyo's prominent Japanese Protestant churches. Protestantism's relative popularity among the urban educated elite and its social influence in Meiji and early Taishō Japan were directly related to the dynamism of church-based groups. Never the subject of historical analysis, these groups were nevertheless central to the ability of churchgoers not only to listen and speak but also to act together at church. In doing so, they translated the discourse of social reform that flourished in leading churches into impactful forms of social activism.

Fujinkai in Tokyo Protestant Churches

From the early 1890s, the members of Tokyo's largest Protestant congregations increasingly took responsibility for organizing meetings and events, which significantly changed the social space of their churches. Working through church-based groups, members came to play a markedly more active and prominent role in the social life of their congregations. Women often organized the earliest church-based groups. In a related development, groups such as the Okayama Women's Friendship Society and the Kochi Women's Group met to address the oppression of women in Japan as relatively well-educated women embraced new opportunities to assemble in the 1880s.[9] However, much of the momentum these early women-only organizations generated had already diminished by the 1890s. While prefectural assemblies and the Imperial Diet had opened by 1890, women had been explicitly barred from making public speeches, joining political associations, and sponsoring or attending political discussions, including those in the Diet.[10] Protestant churches, however, afforded women room to assemble, speak on, and act regarding issues that at times bled into the political realm.

The years immediately following the prohibition of women from making political speeches and attending political meetings saw the development of vibrant *fujinkai* in Tokyo's largest Japanese Protestant churches. Already in 1891, missionary Daniel Crosby Greene remarked that "connected with the Kumi-ai churches of Tōkyō, there are several such [women's] organizations." Among them, Greene noted, "the largest is that of Bancho church."[11] While neither his account nor other sources shed light on the size of *fujinkai* meetings, there is evidence that over one hundred women attended events such as the *kanwa* (inspirational talks) hosted that year.[12] He was particularly impressed by the size of the church's *fujinkai* as well as the attention devoted in meetings not only to religion but also to "education and social reform."[13] The other two Tokyo Congregationalist church *fujinkai* to which Greene was referring had also established themselves and begun to grow by that time. At Reinanzaka, it was the elder women who formed the first church-based group in October 1888, starting the *rōjin fujinkai* (elder women's group) in part to prove that older women were of use in the world.[14] At monthly meetings, which began humbly with three or four women gathering informally to speak "freely" over tea, the women also raised money that they donated to an orphanage.[15] These gatherings became the foundation for the *fujinkai,* at times referred to as "the church's oldest association."[16] The Hongō *fujinkai,* which began in the early 1890s, was holding regular meetings of twenty attendees by 1895. Like the Banchō women's group of which Greene wrote with such approval, this *fujinkai* also featured talks with or by prominent men such as *Nichi shimbun* journalist Haneda Naminojō (1870–1917) and Iwamoto Yoshiharu.[17] Tea and conversation followed.

In their earliest manifestation, Tokyo Protestant church *fujinkai* brought women together, but in ways that conformed to relatively accepted gender norms and assumptions. When women members and other attendees assembled, they initially refrained from discussing or acting to effect significant social and political change. The choices of topics for discussion appear to have reaffirmed women's roles as nurturers, as in the instance when a group raised funds for orphans. Women, many from the samurai class, listened to male speakers and increasingly found themselves seated near male attendees in *fujinkai* meetings—a type of interaction that had already become more common in educated circles by the 1890s. Mixed gatherings had been modeled by Westerners and appropriated by many influential Japanese elites.[18] Yet early church *fujinkai* gatherings in Tokyo still appear to have respected long-standing, gendered distinctions between private and public space grounded in Neo-Confucian ideology. The meetings most often took place in the private spaces of pastors' or group members' homes. And even within that context, presentations by women seem to have been extremely rare.

As the century came to an end, however, some of these aspects began to change. After the return of pastors Ebina and Kozaki to their congregations and the installation of pastor Tsunajima Kakichi at Banchō Church in the late 1890s, the churches' *fujinkai* gained new vigor. The Reinanzaka *fujinkai* still held meetings in private residences, but those meetings included speeches and lectures by women. The appearance of Japan WCTU founding president Yajima Kajiko (1833–1925) in February 1899 at the home of Tokutomi Hisako (1829–1919) was a case in point.[19] Tokutomi Hisako, mother of renowned journalist Tokutomi Sohō and acclaimed author Tokutomi Roka, embodied the increasingly visible leadership roles of laywomen at Reinanzaka. A founding member of the *rōjin fujinkai,* Tokutomi presided over the organization until the turn of the century. In the late 1890s, her leadership was critical to the new *fujinkai* that took off and became essential to Reinanzaka's revitalization. Pastor Kozaki recalled that in the years following his return in 1897, church activities blossomed with the "resuscitation of the Women's and Young Ladies Societies."[20] Tokutomi and other elder women in the *fujinkai* were particularly influential in the church, encouraging the youth and nourishing the church's dynamism.[21]

The young women Kozaki referred to belonged to the *joshi kyōreikai,* a name rendered in English as "Young Women's Christian Endeavor Society."[22] The Reinanzaka *joshi kyōreikai* was established in July 1901 and counted seventeen members.[23] Distinct from church youth groups, which typically included both men and women, these associations were led by and made up of young women. At Reinanzaka, the *joshi kyōreikai* held regular biweekly meetings and religious activities such as prayer meetings, Bible study, and hymn practice, and it was also responsible for decisions about the use of the church space for events.[24] However, the group also held debriefings, discussions, and meetings on a range of topics, including the plight of Japan's disadvantaged working classes. In response to such talks, the group began to "undertake all kinds of work for the education of the poor."[25] In discussing and taking steps to directly address social issues, the *joshi kyōreikai* asserted young Japanese women's entitlement to be informed members of society and act as agents of social change. By the early 1900s, women's organizations were also on the rise at Ichibanchō Church, which boasted a "young women's association" *(joshi seinenkai)* of 110 members and a women's group *(fujinkai)* of 160 members, both with weekly meetings inside the church.[26] Educator-author Hibiki Yoneko and Tokutomi Sohō spoke at the women-only Ichibanchō *fujinkai* lectures on the philosophy of Friedrick Fröebels on children's education and on "women's morality," respectively, on 18 June 1898. The event attracted seventy women.[27]

In those same years, the Hongō *fujinkai* also began to undergo a metamorphosis. The attendance at *fujinkai* meetings had grown only slightly, to thirty, by 1898, and the group continued to invite "well-known men" to address "topics of interest to women."[28] Organizing *enzetsukai* continued to be one of the group's primary tasks. But the first of two key changes was underway: *fujinkai* meetings increasingly took place in the church building.[29] While there is considerable debate over the extent to which church space constitutes public space, there is consensus that church space is distinct from the private space of the home. In fact, Kelly Chong has described the contemporary South Korean church as "an arena for frequent extra-domestic social interaction in a legitimate space away from home."[30] This very precise description accurately encapsulates the nature of Protestant church space in late nineteenth-century Japan as well. Forbidden from political assembly and increasingly restricted to the duties and confines of the home, Japanese women found a social outlet at church. Tokyo's largest Protestant churches offered women space and opportunities to contravene long-standing Confucian gender norms separating the public world of men from the private world of women.[31] Even as women were prohibited from joining moral reform organizations in some parts of Japan, church attendees gathered in sizable groups, discussed social events and issues, and eventually organized for action. By 1898, the mission of the Hongō *fujinkai* had expanded to include not only speeches and informal gatherings but also "considerable work for charity," auguring the wider goals and reach of the organization in the near future.[32]

In 1900, the women's group of Hongō Church adopted a new name that in a sense signaled the broadened nature of the organization's horizons beyond the church itself. It chose to call itself the "Tokyo Fujinkai," or "Tokyo Women's Group," and its membership surpassed forty members by the summer of 1901.[33] That June the Tokyo Fujinkai pledged "to promote knowledge, elevate morality, and obtain the harmonious development of women" and to "fully devote themselves to the vocation of women, young and old, in the family and in society."[34] In contrast to the group's previous iteration, however, women including Tokyo Women's Higher Normal School teacher Yasui Tetsu and Tōyō Eiwa Women's School teacher Ōe (Miyajima) Sumi (1875–1948) were more frequently diversifying the gender profile of speakers in the last decade of the Meiji period.[35] By including the term "harmonious" in their statement of purpose, they made clear that the group claimed no ambitions to disrupt the social order in or beyond the church. However, the statement also depicts an organization turning much greater attention to the relationship between their congregation and Japanese society at large and also to the role of women in carrying out that relationship. While a new beginning, these changes also echoed one set of outward-looking initiatives that the group had undertaken in the mid-1890s.

The Hongō *fujinkai* had launched a separate group to train women to apply the Christian moral mandate of caring for others to medical care. In 1894, the group solicited the help of Takata Kōan (1861–1945), founding physician at the

Western-style Internal Medicine Clinic in Kanda's Surugadai neighborhood, to establish a new program at Hongō. With the church member Takata as the instructor, the Hongō *fujinkai* opened the Nursing Arts Study Group (Kangohō Gakushūkai). This body drew on the new surge of interest in both volunteer and professional nursing stoked by the Japanese Red Cross Society (JCRS) and its nurse training center in Tokyo, as well as other institutions.[36] Founded in 1887, that organization and its hospital in fact built on late Tokugawa precedents in humane and compassionate healing, such as the Juntendō medical school, established in 1843, and the Hakuaisha (Society for Universal Compassion), established in 1877.[37] Bolstered by the effectiveness and positive international reputation of the JRCS, by the end of the 1890s nursing had come into its own as both a new, respectable women's profession and a worthy voluntary pursuit in Japan.[38] It was in this context that students of nursing and other women in Tokyo joined the Kangohō Gakushūkai. The informal school aimed to equip students with essential everyday nursing knowledge. Women from age fifteen with basic education were eligible to attend the six-month sessions for a very nominal fee of ten sen, and the meetings took place weekly on Sunday afternoons in the Hongō Church building.[39] In 1895, attendees for weekly classes averaged fifty-five women.[40] Following the Hongō Fire of 1898 and the destruction of the church, the meetings continued in temporary spaces until the group moved into the new Hongō Church edifice in 1901.

At that time, Hongō's Tokyo Fujinkai was "prospering" and seeking advice about what new religious enterprise they could undertake.[41] The group eventually adopted the proposal of Murakami Kōta, one of the group's few male members. In 1901 the *fujinkai* established a Believer Women's Nurse Group (Dōshi Kangofukai) that would remain highly active until the mid-1910s.[42] Building on the momentum of the nursing study group, this organization began with the "intention of doing something necessary for the world."[43] Referring to a lack of trained nurses as well as what they perceived as the impersonal, cold treatment of the sick, members aimed to "answer, to a small extent, the requests of these days."[44] More broadly, the Dōshi Kangofukai formed in response to a continuing public health crisis in Meiji Japan. They were keenly aware that the nation's health care system prioritized the separation of the healthy from the ill and of the healthier elites from the poorer ill. While most hospitals in turn-of-the-twentieth-century Japan were infectious isolation hospitals, there did exist a few ordinary hospitals that administered better care. However, their cost was typically prohibitive, perpetuating the poor health of the lower classes in general and the urban lower classes in particular.[45] By 1900, however, a few Western-trained Japanese physicians were increasingly aligning themselves with the ideas of physician and politician Nagayo Sensai (1838–1902), who strongly advocated improving public health and hygiene.[46]

In their effort to address these issues, the Believer Women's Nurse Group enlisted the help of Western-trained physicians who were active participants in the larger public health movement in Japan. Obstetrician Kinoshita Seichū (1869–1952), internist Takata Kōan (1861–1945), and other doctors advised the church-based group as they worked to "implement the nursing arts and dispatch nurses."[47] The members resolved to act with "politeness [and] generosity," to give care "without the intention to profit," and to "wholly demonstrate the seriousness becoming of a nurse." In addition, their aims belied a clear interest in filling perceived lacunae in Japan's health care system related to public health. While practicing the art of nursing, the women resolved to be "at ease even with the afflicted," an attitude that, they implied, was not nourished by the existing medical establishment.

Members, however, could develop this stance by "paying attention to the spiritual cultivation" of themselves and their patients. Beyond general nursing demands, they also committed themselves to complying with all requests for "massage" as well.[48] Western massage, introduced to the country by Japanese army doctors, had become a popular, new form of treatment in the Meiji era, replacing the traditional Japanese massage art of *anma*.[49] The *dōshi kangofukai* had evidently become so convinced of its effectiveness that they included it in their mission statement. The group's insistence on massage and not-for-profit, compassionate care echoed wider calls and efforts by physicians and philanthropists in Japan to reshape the nature of medical care. It also provides evidence of the diffusion of this novel health care paradigm from elite, Western-trained Japanese physicians to women seekers of medical knowledge beyond official channels for nursing education. So while the Red Cross trained the members of the Ladies Volunteer Nursing Association (Jizen Kangofukai), physicians and nurses at Hongō Church's *dōshi kangofukai* provided a brand of training and nurse visits all its own.[50]

Tokyo Protestant churches' *fujinkai* were also closely tied to Christian women's voluntary organizations. Leading *fujinkai* members at major churches in the capital were also actively involved in the YWCA and the WCTU. Church *fujinkai* members with close relations to the pastors of large Japanese Protestant churches in Tokyo were often devoted Japan YWCA members. Ebina Miya (1862–1952) and Kozaki Chiyo (1863–1939), the wives of the pastors of Hongō and Reinanzaka, respectively, belonged to the organization and contributed to its organ *Joshi seinenkai* [Young Women's World].[51] The daughter of Fujimichō pastor Uemura Masahisa was another case in point. Uemura Tamaki (1890–1982) returned to the Fujimichō *fujinkai* just after graduating from Wellesley College in 1915. She also involved herself in the YWCA in 1915 and spoke at the summer conference.[52] The links between church *fujinkai* at the YWCA, however, went well beyond such figures. Kawai Michi (1877–1953) of Fujimichō Church's *fujinkai* became national secretary of the Japan YWCA.[53] Fellow Fujimichō Church *fujinkai* member Ōe Sumi was a long-term member of the Japan YWCA and acted as a member of the organization's Central Committee in the Taishō period.[54] And at Hongō, *fujinkai* members and fellow educators Okonogi Matsuko and Yasui Tetsu (1870–1945) were contributing authors for *Joshi seinenkai* as well.[55] While local YWCA chapters were hosted primarily by Christian schools, church *fujinkai* members clearly also promoted the organization at church. Yasui, for instance, publicized YWCA events such as their summer conference in 1909, in *Shinjokai,* the Hongō Church women's journal she edited.[56] The same periodical also publicized WCTU events.[57]

Japanese Protestant church *fujinkai* were especially instrumental in developing Japan's first voluntary women's national organization, the Japan WCTU. From 1886, this organization's members quested to reform private and public behavior through campaigns against licensed prostitution, concubinage, and the exclusion of women from National Diet audiences and political gatherings more generally. For most of the Meiji period, the WCTU was the primary advocate for women's rights, legal protection, education, and improved social status in Japan. From the first visit of World WCTU envoy Mary Leavitt (1830–1912) to Japan in 1886, the relationship between Protestant church *fujinkai* and the Japan WCTU was both visible and strong. Along with local women's groups and girls' schools, churches were one of the spaces that hosted Leavitt during her trip.[58] The connection continued throughout the Meiji and Taishō periods, leading scholars to characterize the WCTU as primarily a reformist Japanese churchwomen's movement.[59] Alongside foreign missionaries and Protestant girls' school students, the churchwomen were an important element in WCTU activities, as Elizabeth Dorn Lublin has noted.[60]

Protestant church *fujinkai* were in fact an integral building block for both the local WCTU chapters and the national organization. Under the auspices of churchwomen's groups, the *reihaidō* and meeting rooms of Tokyo's Protestant churches became formative spaces for this association of women reformers working diligently for the moral and social improvement of their nation. From the first meetings that gave birth to the Tokyo WCTU, Japan's first chapter, the church constituted a principal gathering space for the organization. Soon after her arrival in June, Leavitt made speeches to promote the WCTU and recruit members on 2, 5, and 9 July 1886 in a building identified by WCTU historian

Azuma Moriya as "naka-roku-banchō Kōgisho."[61] This meeting facility was in fact the nascent Banchō Church. That building and other Protestant churches in Tokyo would continue to play an important role in hosting WCTU events.

Throughout the Meiji and Taishō periods, the interior spaces of Protestant churches constituted the primary meeting places for the monthly local chapter and annual national meetings of the Japan WCTU across the country. Meetings often took place in conjunction with the specific churches' *fujinkai,* and many individual women's names appear on the membership lists of both the Japan WCTU and Protestant churches' *fujinkai.*[62] Beginning in the late 1880s, the large annual WCTU meetings *(sōkai)* for making major decisions and announcements drew hundreds of members inside the *reihaidō* of Protestant churches that housed local chapters. Notably, Reinanzaka hosted the inaugural meeting for the Japan WCTU in 1893, the new national organization that would include the older Tokyo WCTU.[63] That same year, Banchō also hosted a series of *ensetukai* organized for and by the Japan WCTU.[64] Between 1886 and 1923, the organization's annual meeting took place in Tokyo fifteen times, and the events took place either in the *reihaidō* of one of these churches or in university auditoriums.[65] Reinanzaka Church again hosted the Japan WCTU general meeting in 1921 as Reinanzaka *fujinkai* member Kozaki Chiyo (1863–1939), wife of pastor Kozaki Hiromichi, was rewarded for her continued service to the organization since the early 1890s with the national presidency.[66]

During Japan's second modern international conflict, church *fujinkai* and the gathering spaces of the church played an integral role in one particular national WCTU project surrounding wartime mobilization. In cooperation with the state, the Japan WCTU made a valuable contribution to efforts on the home front by overseeing the assembly and collection of *imonbukuro* (comfort bags) from all over Japan.[67] These bags, sent to men on the front lines during the Russo-Japanese War, were filled with "socks, gloves, needles, thread, buttons, writing paper, pencils, dried plums, temperance leaflets, and Christian tracts," among other items.[68] In Tokyo, WCTU president Yajima Kajiko used a space in Joshi Gakuin, the elite Christian girls' higher school that she ran in the Banchō neighborhood, for the assembly of *imonbukuro.* However, church classrooms and meeting rooms also served as central spaces for the *imonbukuro* project. Members of the Reinanzaka and Banchō *fujinkai* who were affiliated with the WCTU and other national women's organizations met at Reinanzaka to coordinate and assemble comfort bags in 1905.[69] As part of a related initiative, these two *fujinkai* also made hundreds of *senninbari* for those church members, or members' relatives, who were in the armed forces.[70] These "thousand-stitch belts" carried hundreds of individual stitches or knots made by friends and relatives and were thought to bring luck to the soldiers. In addition to the alleged good fortune, these belts also brought to the soldiers the thoughts and prayers of those closest to them and extended the hands of these particular Tokyo Fujinkai all the way to the Liaodong Peninsula, often through the War Department, which shipped large bundles of WCTU *imonbukuro* for free.[71] This category of activity proved to be one of the few government-endorsed public roles for Japanese women seeking political integration in a system that purposefully excluded them.[72]

While church *fujinkai* were participants within Japanese military imperialism, it was still their endeavors in social reform and improvement that most characterized their contributions to Japanese society. The development of *fujinkai* at Tokyo's largest Protestant churches took place within and drew on larger movements aimed at improving the living conditions, morale, and morality of Japanese in an uncertain age of unprecedented urbanization and industrialization. For instance, the late Meiji period saw the introduction and growth of the settlement house movement in urban Tokyo—a movement led largely by Japanese Protestants affiliated with the capital's most popular congregations. While the role of individual Japanese Protestants has been discussed by scholars, it is also important to acknowledge that church *fujinkai* as organizations also played an active role in this movement. The Reinanzaka *fujinkai,* for instance, transformed the Protestant church into a space for actual social reform. In 1900, in coordination with the WCTU's Sex Industry Reform Department (Fūzoku Kyōfū-Bu), the group opened the Fūzoku Mamori Gakkō (School to Protect Young Girls from Prostitution) within Reinanzaka's facilities. Through this program, the *fujinkai* aimed to rescue girls from prostitution and to train *fujinkai* members and others in the neighboring community to assist at-risk young women through financial, informational, and moral intervention.[73]

The Reinanzaka Church women's group was also significantly involved in a wider social movement prioritizing the welfare of underprivileged urban Japanese children. Church *fujinkai,* including those that admitted male members, worked well within dominant Meiji constructions of womanhood that most readily condoned women's interventions in the public sphere that corresponded to accepted gender roles. In the Meiji period, women's public contributions were largely grounded in "traditional feminine responsibilities" related to nurturing and home management.[74] At Reinanzaka, the *fujinkai* was strongly connected with the Family School (Katei Gakkō), an institution founded and led by Reinanzaka member and former pastor Tomeoka Kōsuke.[75] The school was appropriately established in the Sugamo neighborhood, where Japan's first modern European-style prison opened in 1895.[76] Tomeoka founded the private reformatory with the aim of offering delinquent minors between the ages of eight and sixteen the love and discipline characteristic of an ideal Protestant Christian home.[77] To support the work at the Family School, the women gave a fixed monthly contribution that they determined together at group meetings.[78] In those monthly meetings, they also discussed and organized regular visits to the school.[79] Eventually the *fujinkai* of Reinanzaka sought to involve themselves more directly in educating young children.

In 1917, the Reinanzaka *fujinkai* made use of the church space to realize their social ideals for children. After acting as the strongest proponents for the inclusion of a kindergarten space in the new church, the group then established and administered Reinanzaka Kindergarten.[80] The *fujinkai* appointed their own members to run the school, including the principal, Kozaki Chiyo, and at least two of the institution's first teachers: the poet Asano Haruko; and Terao Kikuko, wife of the Tokyo Astronomical Observatory's director, Terao Hisashi.[81] While it was a private, tuition-based school, the *fujinkai* still found ways to maintain their commitment to more underprivileged students. For instance, the Reinanzaka kindergarteners brought in grain, fruit, and vegetables in November, and the Reinanzaka *fujinkai* collected and distributed these goods to the pioneering public Futaba Kindergarten.[82] Beyond their importance on a regular basis, the spaces of Reinanzaka Church also proved important when an unparalleled natural disaster struck the capital.

On 1 September 1923, the Great Kantō Earthquake devastated Tokyo to an extent it would not see again until the city's destruction during World War II. At the forefront of community relief efforts in Akasaka Ward was the Reinanzaka *fujinkai*. The group organized the conversion of the mostly intact church building's Sunday school and kindergarten rooms into shelter and relief stations for the Reinanzaka and Azabu neighborhood residents and posted a sign that read, "Anyone in need, come take refuge."[83] Members of the community heeded the invitation, and during that difficult first week, more than one hundred people stayed in the church facility. As the city began to live again and people moved out, some fifty families remained sheltering there in early October. The *fujinkai* also served boiled potable water to neighborhood residents during the citywide water shortage of early September.[84] The work of this single church-based group on this single occasion points to the strong and significant connections between the Protestant church and the local community in Tokyo.

Fujinkai, often Japanese Protestant churches' oldest groups, were also the groups that most actively and concretely addressed social issues in Japan. Although these groups did not launch a frontal assault on the male dominance or gender inequality pervasive within their churches or in Japan in general, their work was highly significant. These women engaged with local and national questions, trends, and movements, participating in a larger effort to expand women's presence in the public sphere. Protestant churches' physical and discursive spaces legitimated and to some extent protected women in their more public roles as activists and organizers. *Fujinkai* members also led women's reform organizations such as the WCTU and YWCA and established trailblazing new educational institutions, such as Futaba Kindergarten and Tokyo Woman's Christian University, among other achievements.[85]

Yet the women of Tokyo's largest Japanese Protestant churches have been largely overlooked. Churchgoing young Japanese men have attracted much more attention from scholars and local church historians, as have the male-led church *seinenkai* (youth groups) to which so many of them belonged. In a society that systematically placed the most emphasis on the achievements of men, it is unsurprising that *seinenkai,* and the legacies of their better-known male leaders, have occupied a larger place in the historical record than church *fujinkai.* Furthermore, church *seinenkai* in Tokyo were directly affiliated with the Japan Kirisutokyō Seinenkai, or YMCA—an organization led by Japanese Christian men primarily for Japanese men. Leading Japanese Protestant men figure prominently in scholarship extending from the 1970s that demonstrates the noteworthy intellectual and social influence of the Japan YMCA.[86] In particular, research on Japanese YMCA leaders in Korea and Manchuria and on the reception of Korean students by the Japan YMCA continues to make this one of the most interesting lines of academic inquiry regarding Christianity in the Japanese empire.[87] Adding to the notoriety of this national organization, and the church *seinenkai* members who were its leaders in imperial Japan and afterward, were the well-publicized and well-attended events that took place in the Tokyo YMCA Hall (Kirisutokyō Seinenkaikan) in Kanda. Built in 1894, this site regularly hosted the largest gatherings of Protestants in Tokyo.[88] However, in order to grasp the scope of Protestantism's engagement with society and the movement's impact on modern Japan, it is essential to also consider the activism of Japanese women working together in *fujinkai.* In many cases, women at church also helped foster *seinenkai* through fundraising and emphasizing the need for new buildings with more auxiliary gathering spaces.

Seinenkai in Tokyo Protestant Churches

The growth and popularity of the YMCA was directly related to the tremendous increase in adolescents and university-age students or *seinen* (youth) attending church in turn-of-the-century Tokyo. Their numbers and their activism within the church were so salient that they in fact came to characterize those institutions in the eyes of many. Tokyo Imperial University professor of psychology Matsumoto Akatarō (1865–1943), a Hongō member from his student days, recalled, like many others, that the church was "often called the student church."[89] Similarly, the youth were one of the constituencies most associated with Reinanzaka Church in the Meiji and Taishō periods, along with its distinguished elder members.[90] There, pastor Kozaki continued to nurture the interest in the intellectual and spiritual development of young Japanese men and women that had led him, Uemura Masahisa, and Tokyo University preparatory schoolteacher Kanda Naibu (1857–1923) to establish the Tokyo YMCA in 1880.[91]

And from the start of his ministry, Ichibanchō pastor Uemura Masahisa had also focused on youth, whose energy, innocence, and earnestness he loved.[92] The pastor appreciated the youth because they stood in stark contrast to the older Japanese, "who oppose[d] changing old customs" and would consequently "rot along with the cedar wood of the back gate."[93] These efforts were paying off by 1903, when his church's yearly Christmas youth gathering drew seventy-nine young men and women.[94] At nearby Banchō Church, the elite middle-aged and elderly attendees gave the church its reputation. Pastor Tsunajima recalled that by his arrival in 1897 the church had already become known as the capital's *kizoku* (aristocrat) church and as a church with members whose means, positions, and status allowed them to wear *furisode* (long-sleeved kimonos).[95] However, dozens of students from the capital's higher schools and universities were also among Banchō's attendees. Throughout the last decade of the Meiji period, Tsunajima regularly targeted them—the so-called anguished youth (*hanmon seinen*)—with sermons about the potential and hope of youth.[96]

Youth greatly preoccupied Protestant pastors and came to emblematize the social space of the church in imperial Japan. The bright students gave the church a "youthful, energetic, and cerebral atmosphere," a scholar aptly notes about Hongō at the turn of the twentieth century.[97] In fact, while church *seinenkai* have rarely been mentioned as such, decades of scholarship have highlighted the involvement of young Japanese men and women with Protestant congregations. Biographies of the famous children's author Iwaya Sazanami (1870–1933) describe his participation at Banchō Church as a teenager.[98] Before she became Japan's first woman professional reporter, Hani Motoko (1873–1957) joined Ichibanchō Church.[99] In 1907, a year after that congregation moved and adopted the name Fujimichō Church, future prime minister Katayama Tetsu (1887–1978) became a member there.[100] The youth who have received the most attention, however, were the attendees of Hongō Church. Labor organizer Suzuki Bunji (1885–1946) became active at the church in his student days at Tokyo Imperial

University.[101] He had followed in the footsteps of fellow Sendai native Yoshino Sakuzō (1878–1933), whose lifelong association with Hongō began when he too studied at the top imperial university.[102] Yoshino's participation at Hongō figured prominently and in explicit ways, in his career as a legal scholar and liberal reformist thinker, attracting continued attention from historians.[103] These disparate pieces only begin to shed light on youth participation in Protestant churches in the capital. The *seinenkai* brought youth together for spiritual, social, and intellectual exchange, and studying these church-based youth groups illuminates further how young Japanese youth interacted at church in Tokyo. Analyzing these groups offers a window into the cultivation and deployment of the youthful energy within the Protestant churches.

The establishment of *seinenkai* in Tokyo's leading congregations took place in two waves, separated by disagreements and events that in the end served to galvanize the Protestant movement in general and youth groups in particular. Around 1890, the first church youth groups in the capital appeared, and these *seinenkai* prospered during the early 1890s.[104] Ichibanchō Church's *seinenkai* had already established itself and come into its own by 1890, and it began to organize sermons as well as social activities.[105] A youth group at Banchō was established in January 1893 with thirty members.[106] Although the pastors of Hongō and Reinanzaka successfully attracted young Japanese men and women in those years, *seinenkai* were not formed at these churches during this first phase. From approximately 1893, however, Tokyo's fastest-growing Protestant congregations stagnated or shrank.[107] Reinanzaka, with 259 members in 1891, counted on average only 60 attendees in 1893, and Banchō recorded similar numbers.[108] The situation was most dire during the Sino-Japanese War (1894 and 1895), when the Kumiai (Congregationalist) churches, the denomination of Hongō, Reinanzaka, and Banchō, lost nearly two thousand members and growth screeched to a halt.[109]

To blame, in part, were disagreements among Japanese pastors and between Japanese pastors and missionaries over the new Liberal Theology, which contradicted the literal biblical interpretations of traditional Protestantism.[110] Complicating matters were Christianity's association with a hypocritical, racist Western other[111] and loud criticisms of Christianity as "foreign" and "unpatriotic."[112] These dynamics also led several Japanese pastors to seek institutional independence from Western missionaries, gaining administrative and financial control but weakening their churches' resources in the short term.[113] However, the crisis in leadership discussed earlier was just as pivotal as these other factors. From pastor Kanamori Michitomo's (1857–1945) resignation from Banchō and apostasy, to Yokoi's departure from Hongō for the United States, to

Kozaki's acceptance of the presidency of Dōshisha in 1892, major churches were literally left leaderless. And then the Hongō Fire of 1898 ravaged the grandiose 1891 Hongō Church building.

However, between 1897 and 1898, returning, remaining, and new Japanese Protestant leaders rebuilt the capital's leading congregations. Galvanized by the difficult years of the mid-decade, they developed churches that combined independence, progressive thought, and practical morality while also valorizing Japanese national identity. In this context, a second stage in the establishment of *seinenkai* occurred. The revival of congregations such as Hongō, Reinanzaka, and Banchō ushered in a new wave of youth participation around the turn of the century, spawning new and larger *seinenkai.* With the return of Kozaki to Reinanzaka and the efforts of the elder *fujinkai,* the church's youth established a *seinenkai* in the late spring of 1899.[114] The group had more than twenty members by March 1900.[115] The recently founded *seinenkai* at Reinanzaka's satellite congregation, Banchō Church, was active by early 1903.[116] The new century also brought continued vigor to the youth group at Ichibanchō Church with the launching of the *seinenkai*'s youth evangelism campaign in 1901.[117] During those same years Hongō Church cemented its reputation as a church for students and young adults with the establishment of its dynamic church-based youth group.

On Saturday, 20 October 1900, a handful of young men held a ceremony to formally establish the new Hongō *seinenkai.* There had been no formal Hongō youth group before. And as pastor Ebina Danjō recalled, even the older organizations like the women's group and elders' group at Hongō had all but ceased to exist two years before, following the Hongō Fire.[118] However, meeting in the Ikizaka Evangelical Church of the Evangelical Lutheran mission, the new youth association was born.[119] Calling itself the Meidōkai (Bright Path Society), the group resolved to "mutually cultivate" themselves and to "be good friends to the youth in the decayed atmosphere of the capital."[120] The group gathered on Saturdays and hosted speeches and Bible lectures from its first meetings. After the completion of the new Hongō building in 1901, the group met in the church and only continued to grow. By 1902 it included eighty-four members.[121] In an effort to clarify the objectives of the Meidōkai, leaders issued a mission statement that December.[122] The group aimed to foster "solidarity between fellow young believers" and to strive for the goal of "improving one another's character, spreading ideas . . . [and] constantly improving one another's faith." And finally, they resolved "to shine the bright light of Christianity among the fellow youth of our surroundings."[123]

As their objectives demonstrate, the new youth group had much in common with the church's burgeoning *fujinkai.* Like Hongō's Tokyo Fujinkai, the

Meidōkai targeted the youth in their neighborhoods within the capital. The group also resembled the women's group in that it highlighted the immoral atmosphere of Tokyo and members' moral imperative to improve it through Christianity. For both, the elevation of moral standards and behavior was intimately connected with spiritual and intellectual cultivation. The Meidōkai was, like the *fujinkai,* also committed to promoting knowledge and disseminating ideas aimed at refining the character of its members by hosting speakers to address religious and secular topics. In those same years, the Hongō Meidōkai hosted talks by several of the same men so often invited by the Tokyo Fujinkai, in addition to prominent figures like Shimada Saburō, Abe Isoo, and Nitobe Inazō.[124] Drawing crowds of up to seven hundred to the Hongō Church, the group often chose to host their lectures and speeches in other, larger venues increasingly available to them. The largest and most commonly used alternative venue was the Kanda YMCA Hall, which had seating for five hundred.[125] Thus, the church represented only one of several gathering spaces the Meidōkai used to host major events. However, the regular meetings of the organization typically occurred at Hongō Church's Ikizaka building after its completion in 1901, and during such meetings, some group events occurring outside the church were planned. The regular use of the church was therefore yet another commonality between the church youth group and the *fujinkai.*

Church youth groups like that at Hongō occasionally responded to the consequences of modernization and to local and national crises in ways that again echoed the activism of the church *fujinkai.* In June 1890, for instance, the Ichibanchō Church *seinenkai* joined with students of Meiji Girls' School to establish the Poor Aid and Charity Association.[126] They sought to address the problems facing the working poor, a problem that continued to preoccupy churchgoing Japanese youth. Responding to the poverty of factory workers and their families, the Hongō *seinenkai* (formerly the Meidōkai) led a fundraising campaign in 1915.[127] The members visited families in the industrial Honjo Ward, one of the city's most productive areas, and one of its poorest, to distribute the funds.[128]

Like Tokyo's factory zones, Japan's poorest regions also suffered in the midst of the country's prosperity. Just as Japan concluded its first victory over a Western nation in September 1905, a crop failure began to take a heavy toll on the Tōhoku region, where subsistence farming had been replaced by cash-crop agriculture. A fatal combination of cold, wet, and overcast weather in August and hot, dry weather in September left as little as 12 percent of the rice crop harvestable in the worst-hit prefectures. Unemployment abounded, and estimates of 1 million starving people circulated in US newspapers.[129] Missionaries and, later, Christian organizations in Japan took a leading role in gathering food and funds for the victims, while significant government and private assistance in the US and Japan took longer to materialize. Aware of the continued shortages and cold conditions still plaguing the region in early 1907, the Reinanzaka *seinenkai* that February organized a drive to collect money and goods for the starving people. Among Joshi Gakuin students and fifty-eight other individuals, the group oversaw the collection of "185 articles of clothing, 450 socks, 305 satin leggings, 216 miscellaneous articles" as well as a small sum of "10 yen and 60 sen." After spending 2 yen and 60 sen to pack and ship the items, they deposited the rest with the Tōhōku Poor Crop Relief Committee of the Tokyo YMCA's Evangelical Alliance.[130] Again, in 1910, when historically heavy rains carried the Arakawa River over its dikes and caused flooding in most of downtown Tokyo, the Reinanzaka *seinenkai* made an effort to respond. Braving the scorching heat of late August, members went from door to door collecting money for the flood victims.[131] Such efforts point to further lines of commonality running between church *seinenkai* and church *fujinkai*.

Despite these shared characteristics, church youth groups differed significantly from women's groups in their social engagement beyond the church. In the Meiji and Taishō periods, Tokyo church *seinenkai* were primarily focused on spiritual and intellectual development and on discussing rather than participating in social activism. Nihonbashi Church *seinenkai*'s speech events surrounding the Ashio copper mine pollution problem were more of an exception than the norm. The group hosted those *enzetsukai* in collaboration with the Ashio Copper Mine Aid Women's Association, whose founders, WCTU leaders Yajima Kajiko and Ushioda Chiseko (1844–1903), spoke in late 1900 and early 1901.[132] However, among Tokyo's largest Protestant churches, the explicit emphasis on carrying out social reform and activism found in church *fujinkai* was not as present in *seinenkai*. So while many of the same social and political questions interested both groups, church youth groups were less explicitly focused on taking direct action. Rather, church-based youth groups in the capital specialized in hosting speeches and lectures and promoting discussion of important religious and secular issues of the day.

Hongō's *seinenkai*, the largest and most active church *seinenkai* in Tokyo, illustrates this predominant emphasis on cultivating knowledge and discussion. The *enzetsukai* of the Meidōkai were one of the organization's two most defining characteristics. In these events pastors, members, and clergy and lay invitees spoke on issues ranging from intellectual and social trends in the West to the fate of Japanese colonial subjects to moral reform to concrete social problems in urban Japan. These and many other themes ran through speeches like those analyzed in the preceding chapter, and at Hongō it was the church youth group that principally planned and hosted such speeches. The Meidōkai as an institution became the leader in cultivating a vibrant, well-informed, reform-minded discursive space in the church and in the auxiliary spaces where they held large events. While its members did undertake relief and charity work on occasion, these activities were exceedingly rare. Rather, the group was true to its charter, which contained no mandate for such activism but did commit the members to the pursuit of "intellectual enlightenment." However, the group was deeply committed to engaging verbally with the currents and dilemmas of the capital, the empire, and the world.

Beyond the spoken word, the teenagers and young adults of Hongō Church also used the printed word to comment on and interpret the ideas and events of the day. In July 1900, several of the men who founded the Meidōkai that October created *Shinjin* (New Man), a new monthly periodical published by the church.[133] From its first issue, the journal came to constitute the other defining characteristic of the youth at Hongō. Until the journal's last run in January 1926, this publication embodied the questioning, critical spirit of the church's youth.[134] The Tokyo Imperial University students on the editorial staff included the managing editors Mizawa Tadasu (1878–1942), Oyama Tōsuke (1879–1919), Yoshino Sakuzō (1878–1933), and assistant editor Uchigasaki Sakusaburō (1877–1947).[135] They announced *Shinjin* as a nondenominational endeavor and committed themselves to working to "elucidate the principles of religious morality and discuss issues of education, philosophy, and art." Furthermore, the journal was intended to enhance "the moral education of young men and women" and, among other objectives, to "present beautiful literature" to readers.[136] Under the guidance of editor-in-chief Ebina Danjō, the young men created a church organ that would become one of the leading Christian intellectual journals in early twentieth-century Japan.

In this, Ebina and his editors joined the larger Japanese Christian publishing field that his fellow pastors Uemura and Kozaki had initiated twenty years before. The two pastors had launched the journal *Rikugo zasshi* (Cosmos) to improve morality and promote Christianity in 1880, and it quickly became a well-respected intellectual publication.[137] Since 1890, Kozaki and Uemura had also sat atop the two most widely circulated Christian weeklies, the *Kirisutokyō shimbun* (Christian Newspaper) and *Fukuin shinpō* (Gospel News), respectively, as editors.[138] In 1890 Uemura had also begun publishing the biweekly social thought journal *Nihon hyōron* (Japan Review).[139] Consciously invoking the new century, the Japanese Protestant editors of *Shinjin* also added their new journal to that field in 1900. The journal published between five hundred and six hundred copies each month, although its reach clearly extended more broadly than those numbers would indicate.[140] This blossoming extended within Christianity beyond Protestantism as well. John Ono, the country's first ordained Russian Orthodox priest, started a journal in the late 1870s that dealt with religion as well as education, literature, and morality.[141] And between 1892 and 1907 the Russian Orthodox Church published a pioneering women's journal called *Uranishiki* (Inner Brocade). Edited by evangelist Yamada Toyohiko (1875–1945), this monthly periodical included articles on many secular topics, including the position of women in Meiji Japan.[142] In 1905, Roman Catholic missionaries and Japanese students added their own publication to the growing world of Christian media. The small monthly journal *Shin Risō*, which ran for over two years, brought Catholic theology and social thought to bear on contemporary topics and current events.[143] It was into this vibrant milieu that Shinjin was born.

While each *Shinjin* issue included a weekly sermon by Ebina Danjō or another Hongō pastor and many essays on Christianity, the journal was a truly broad intellectual endeavor. Essays on religion and philosophy were among the most common. Reaching beyond Christianity, authors often dealt with topics like Zen Buddhism and the relationship between Christianity and Buddhism. From positions of mutual distrust and complete dissensus, adherents of Buddhism and Christianity came increasingly into dialogue during the final years of the Meiji period.[144] Both groups were deeply engaged in observing one another and increasingly seeking intellectual and spiritual common ground. Such efforts only intensified as the state expanded its authority over belief.[145] *Shinjin* became a site for Christians to explore Buddhism from a religious as well as a philosophical perspective. In fact, religious philosophy featured prominently in the journal as well: articles appeared on themes such as the ethical activism philosophy of Rudolph Christoph Eucken (1846–1926).[146] Ebina and other authors also frequently discussed the role of Christianity in cultivating a strong, ethical "character" *(jinkaku)*.[147] And essayists discussed the religious implications of leading German philosophers Johann Gottlieb Fichte, Johann Gottfried von Herder, and Georg Wilhelm Friedrich Hegel.[148]

Among the ideas that most interested *Shinjin* authors were those directly related to current events in the Japanese and international context. The birth of the Japanese labor movement, the Russo-Japanese War (1904–1905), the annexation of Korea (1910), the Great Treason Incident (1911), the death of Emperor Meiji (1912), the suicide of General Nogi Maresuke (1849–1912) and his wife Shizuko (1859–1912), World War I, and other major events of the early twentieth century were the subjects of journal essays. Accordingly, authors often wrote on the related ideologies of patriotism, racism, pacifism, imperialism, democracy, and socialism.[149] And contributors from various disciplinary backgrounds addressed these issues. The animal biologist Yatsu Naohide (1877–1947), for instance, wrote a critique of *Nihon jinshu kaizō* (Japan Racial Improvement), a recently published work by Unno Yukinari (1879–1954) on eugenics. From a scientific and Christian moral standpoint, Yatsu highlighted what he saw as flaws in Unno's work and expressed concern about the growing eugenics movement in Japan.[150] Articles and transcribed speeches on these themes repeatedly examined the ideological foundations of modern society in Japan and beyond from a Christian perspective. In other words, this religious thought journal became considerably political and in fact was subject to more than one punitive publication ban from the Home Ministry's censorship department.[151]

The journal, despite its small circulation, maintained a relatively high visibility among members of the educated elite—a visibility further facilitated by Meidōkai members, who moved throughout Japan after graduation. Japan scholars with an interest in modern religion, philosophy, or history have been particularly interested in the publication's content and its connections with key ideas and movements for social change in Japan. Among the authors and editors were young men who would become highly influential as writers and activists. Popular democracy theorist Yoshino Sakuzō, Japan Socialist Party founder Abe Isoo, his fellow Diet member Uchigasaki Sakusaburō, journalist and Diet member Oyama Tōsuke, and pioneering labor organizer Suzuki Bunji all edited or wrote for *Shinjin*. And these *Shinjin* staff members became educators and mentors for young men at top institutions of higher education in the capital, again assuring the journal's continued visibility. Yoshino taught at Tokyo Imperial University, and Abe, Oyama, and Uchigasaki taught at Waseda University.

Yet it is essential to view the journal, with its small circulation and readership, as part of, and contributing to, the larger social space taking shape in Tokyo's leading Protestant churches. The narrow focus on *Shinjin* has had the tendency to emphasize the intellectual life of a few Protestant Japanese young men associated with the male-edited, (primarily) male-written journal published by the male-led *seinenkai* affiliated with the male-oriented YMCA. The church's social space also expanded through the efforts of women, the dynamism of the *fujinkai* and *seinenkai enzetsukai,* and the concrete efforts within and beyond the church to effect social change. All of these elements were part of the picture at Hongō and played an important role in the church's development, but the same was true of other Protestant congregations in Tokyo that lacked a publication like *Shinjin.* Examining church-based groups is one strategy for recovering the histories of youth beyond *Shinjin* and of the activities of youth at Reinanzaka, Fujimichō, and Banchō. And considering the capital's largest Protestant churches together can enhance our understanding of the social space cultivated at church and its impact on Japan.

In conjunction with a larger trend toward lay participation in Buddhism and Christianity in Japan, churches offered a path for youth and women in the educated elite to take part in the public sphere. Despite many aspects in common with lay Buddhist temple-based organizations, church-based *fujinkai* and *seinenkai* in imperial-era Tokyo were distinguished by their engagement with local and national "real-world" problems and their emphasis on the category of modernity. In addition, rather than constituting a small, marginal population on the fringe of their religious institution, these groups represented a central and sizable part of their congregations and the larger Protestant religious movement. From the 1890s, such lay participation defined Protestantism in Japan, and the church space played an increasingly important role in facilitating its development.

Women's groups were the first church-based organizations in the capital, and they gave women new opportunities for leadership and public speaking. As the *fujinkai* developed, they grew larger, featured more women speakers, and moved from the private space of the home into the arguably public space of the church building. Through the church, women connected to one another and to the leading national women's Christian reform organization, the WCTU. Women used these connections to bring international, national, and local issues into the church and often organized concrete responses to problems beyond the church. From the few remaining records, it is clear that women's groups created subsidiary organizations to address social problems, and some of these developed into actual institutions for reform or education. The *fujinkai* were also the arm of the church extending out into the community, from supporting Christian-initiated endeavors to providing relief in times of crisis.

While church-based *seinenkai* were also engaged in fundraising and relief work in moments of severe disaster, they primarily used words to engage with the world around them. The student members devoted most of their energy to speech meetings and to spiritual and intellectual pursuits, with the hope that improving themselves and helping others to cultivate better morality would lead to real change. In some cases, church *seinenkai* acted as planning sites and incubators for larger gatherings and movements taking place outside the church. At Hongō, where students made up by far the largest portion of the membership, the *seinenkai* was particularly active.[152] The Meidōkai and the journal associated with it, *Shinjin*, promoted the objectives of studying and spreading moral education and other fields of knowledge. In the early twentieth century, *Shinjin* became a well-known fixture in the landscape of Japanese Christian intellectual journalism. As with the women of church *fujinkai,* the church could also act as a pathway to society for *seinenkai* members, especially young men, and the life trajectories of *Shinjin*'s founding editors provide a case in point. Several among the first editorial board members went on to demonstrate the connection between morality and activism in their careers as educators, politicians, journalists, and union organizers. As this chapter has demonstrated, however, there were many lanes through the church to society for women as well as youth participating in the social space of Tokyo's largest churches in the Meiji and early Taishō eras.

Protestant churches in the capital were relatively successful in imperial Japan, in contrast to the status and negative connotations that had entirely dominated the image of Christianity less than a generation before. This success depended on those churches' ability to attract members of Japan's educated elite, make Christianity relevant to them, and provide concrete ways to link the knowledge and ideals that circulated in Protestant social space with the world outside. The regular meetings, speeches, and other events that women's and youth groups organized were a key aspect of that strategy, and the pastors of the capital's largest congregations encouraged these groups. In conjunction with the Sunday sermons, these activities constituted the social space of the Protestant church. They were a central and defining element of the Protestant church experience in imperial Japan, and they left an indelible mark on attendees, who in turn left their mark on Japan.

CHAPTER SEVEN

From the Church into Society

Its detractors persistently characterized Protestant Christianity as un-Japanese and irreconcilable with Japanese identity. However, the popularity of Protestantism among the educated elite and the visibility of its ideals in various efforts to improve society defied such simple critiques. For a religion so incompatible with the Japanese national community, how ironic that the Protestant movement offered thousands of Japanese just that: community. Central to this development was the social space of the church. As members of church-based groups, churchgoers attended regular meetings, participated in activities, and listened to lay and ordained speakers address key religious and secular issues. Even more numerous were the people who attended the Sunday sermon, Sunday school, and other elements in the life of the church. Most of them belonged to Protestant churches as members. This recognition of belonging was so important that hundreds of those in Tokyo's largest churches maintained their membership in—and their financial contributions to—the congregation after moving far away in Japan and even abroad. And in some cases, Japanese individuals like Tokutomi Sohō who were merely passers-through or occasional attendees developed "somewhat of a connection" with congregations in the capital.[1] Belonging at church, therefore, was not dependent or synonymous with belonging to the church, and the limits of that belonging were broad.

The physical space of the church building was deeply implicated in fostering community. Reinanzaka, Banchō, Hongō, and Fujimichō Churches grew to accommodate the growth of their congregations. From figures in the low single digits in the early 1880s, these congregations grew to several hundred, and Fujimichō eventually surpassed one thousand members. When counted along with the hundreds of nonmember attendees, the size of church congregations was even higher. And these church buildings brought them all together. Beyond the question of size, these church bodies were relatively large ideologically as well. Most attendees came from similar socioeconomic backgrounds, but they held an array of views on political ideologies and key, divisive social issues. Advocates of capitalism or democracy sat next to proponents of radical socialism. Attendees with differing perspectives on questions ranging from nationalism and empire to gender roles coexisted and frequently interacted within these congregations. Among them was also a mixture of Japanese nonbelievers, lifelong believers, and those who fell in between. So the defining common element of community in the capital's largest congregations was not necessarily religious conviction or spirituality either. Rather, attendees shared the physical space of the church and the social spaces that took shape inside.

Participating in the community within Tokyo's largest Protestant churches also presented Japanese churchgoers with new opportunities to engage with the greater Japanese community beyond the church. The discursive space and the various forms of collaboration that took shape at church equipped attendees with new social ideals that were relevant to their hopes and concerns about Japanese society. The same social space also encouraged the development of greater social awareness and brought important, timely issues from the larger Japanese social context into the church. Finally, churches fostered among Japanese women and men the creation and mobilization of networks aimed at social change. These aspects of the church experience helped attract Japanese to the church but also affected many Japanese on a significant, personal level.

The experiences that churchgoers had within the church often left a lasting impression on their lives and in turn on their engagement with the world beyond the church. Particularly literate and expressive, the attendees of Tokyo's leading congregations spoke and wrote about participation at church in speeches, published diaries, memoirs, and autobiographical articles and books. Beyond these, fellow attendees and pastors also shed light on the experiences of other churchgoers. Sources often highlight a role in attendees' spiritual or intellectual development and in their cultivation of interpersonal relationships. In several cases, however, the convictions, perspectives, and relationships that attendees formed within the church had broader repercussions in the secular world. Japanese churchgoers made significant contributions to the public sphere in realms such as education, journalism, politics, social work, and even business. The new, influential Christian worldviews and social outlooks running through these efforts were nourished in a number of other environments, including Christian schools. However, the social spaces of the church were especially formative, and for many churchgoers there was an explicit link between their endeavors in broader Japanese society and the discourse and interactions inside the church.

Defining and Relativizing "Large" Protestant Churches in Tokyo

From small beginnings between the late 1870s and the mid-1880s, Reinanzaka, Fujimichō, Banchō, and Hongō developed along roughly similar lines in the 1880s, 1890s and early 1900s and blossomed into large congregations. With only ten members at its founding in 1879, Reinanzaka recorded 466 members at its peak in 1908. Kozaki Hiromichi still drew a mixed audience of 445 to Reinanzaka on Sundays in 1923, on the eve of the Great Kantō Earthquake.[2] At Hongō, Ebina Danjō's Sunday sermons drew 672 listeners into the church's *reihaidō* in 1909, a notable increase from the 30 men and women who founded the congregation in 1886.[3] The figure was also well above the 237 listeners at his increasingly rare sermons in May 1919, on the eve of his departure to take up the presidency of Dōshisha.[4] Banchō Church, the smallest of these congregations, grew from 30 members at its founding in 1886 to 312 members in 1905.[5] In 1919, attendance figures for church events at Banchō reached almost 400.[6] Like these three churches of the Congregational denomination, the capital's largest Presbyterian church, Fujimichō Church, also began small in 1886, with a congregation of 50 members—a critical mass composed of those already familiar with Uemura. By the end of the Meiji period on, however, Fujimichō had outpaced its fellow churches in Tokyo. The church had 1,055 members in 1912 and 1,775 in 1923.[7]

It was less their absolute sizes than their relative, contextualized sizes that distinguished the congregations of Reinanzaka, Banchō, Hongō, and Fujimichō. In comparison with the megachurches of the late nineteenth century like Charles Spurgeon's Metropolitan Tabernacle in London, they were objectively small.[8] Even in Japan, the congregations of Kobe Church, Okayama Church, Osaka's Tenma Church and Osaka Church, Kyoto's Shijō Church, and Imabari Church in Ehime Prefecture at times equaled or surpassed in size those of their Congregational counterparts in Tokyo.[9] However, Tokyo was the undeniable center of Protestantism in Japan, with three of Japan's largest Congregational churches and the country's largest Presbyterian church.[10] These four congregations were the largest among Tokyo's Protestant churches, which numbered 125 in the final year of the Meiji period.[11] And Fujimichō Church in Tokyo stood as "the great citadel" of Presbyterianism—the largest Protestant denomination in imperial Japan before World War I.[12] Similarly, the Congregational churches, Hongō, Reinanzaka, and Banchō, were consistently among the largest in the capital. Charles Eby's 1891 Central Tabernacle had seating for six hundred. Yet, lacking a pastor like Uemura or Ebina, the impressive church failed to attract many students and often stood largely empty.[13] By contrast, these Japanese-led churches were often full, their growth requiring new and larger buildings in the Meiji and early Taishō periods. For the most part, however, leading congregations in the capital did not compete among themselves, often lending and renting spaces to one another and occasionally encouraging members to transfer between them.

The four Tokyo Protestant churches at the center of this study were also significantly large in relation to the religious gathering spaces of their primary competitors. Buddhism combated its marginalization amid the rise of state Shinto and the growth of Christianity by evangelizing.[14] There was no refuting the clear preponderance of Buddhism in Meiji and Taishō Japan or the minuscule size of the Protestant Christian population. But these congregations were large and dynamic enough to attract the attention, and even envy, of Buddhist clerics and intellectuals in Tokyo. One Buddhist leader reportedly lamented to Kozaki that Buddhism's most dynamic speakers, "no matter how eloquent the preacher, could not bring as many people out" or attract attendees as regularly as Protestant pastors did.[15] Kozaki recalled Kuroda Shindō (1855–1916) telling him that although True Pure Land priest Chikazumi Jōkan (1870–1941) preached successfully in Tokyo, he drew crowds that "seldom exceeded one hundred."[16] In fact, Chikazumi himself complained of an absence of dynamism and attractiveness for Buddhism in Tokyo in the early 1900s. In his view, the fault lay not only in the quality of the sermons but also in the fact that there was "no hall to which Buddhists can affiliate themselves in the capital."[17] It was in no small part to remedy this lack that the priest established the Kyūdō Kaikan in 1915 as an innovative Buddhist religious space designed to facilitate regular lay participation.[18]

One defining indication of Protestant churches' success in the capital that was at least equally important as congregation size to the religion's position vis-à-vis Buddhism was its demographic makeup. The physical and social spaces of these churches worked together to draw in women and men of Japan's new educated elite. Most belonged to the "new professional bureaucratic middle classes," in which membership had "everything to do with educational accomplishment."[19] A few churchgoers had their origins among the old court and warrior elite but still relied on education to achieve rank and influence in the new Japan. The former daimyo of Kishiwada, Viscount Okabe Nagamoto (1855–1925), attended Keio University and Cambridge University before he acceded to posts including vice minister of foreign affairs, Tokyo governor, minister of justice, and Privy Council member. And he was a lifelong member of Banchō Church.[20] It was more typical, however, that Japanese Protestant church attendees rose from less illustrious backgrounds to become university students and then professors, lawyers, judges, journalists, economists, entrepreneurs, government bureaucrats, and other such occupations in Tokyo. Protestant churches in fact had a well-known reputation for attracting the cosmopolitan, ambitious members of this class. Recognizing the popularity of Christianity and church attendance among this demographic, Buddhist institutions turned unprecedented attention to it as well. The Higashi Honganji headquarters underwrote and offered significant support to Chikazumi's observational voyage to the United States. They then sponsored his subsequent ministry to students of Tokyo Imperial University and Tokyo First Higher School and his establishment of the Kyūdō Gakusha (Way-Seekers' School) and, later, the Kyūdō Kaikan.[21] Meanwhile, hundreds of students at the nation's top institutions of higher education and professionals in fields such as law, elected and nonelected government, education, journalism, and medicine continued to gather in Protestant churches. So despite their small size, these leading Tokyo congregations boasted a concentration of social capital, credentials, ambitions, connections, and knowledge unparalleled within other religious gathering spaces in Japan.

Members of this educated elite were drawn to one of Tokyo's largest Japanese Protestant churches through an interplay of factors such as physical proximity, the influence of teachers, classmates, and friends, and an interest in pastors sparked by public appearances and print media. Yet despite the differences in their paths into these churches, attendees found some common, appealing features. One of the most attractive was these churches' ability to host discourse that challenged or complicated state-sanctioned ideological orthodoxy. Church represented one of very few spaces in imperial Japan open to gatherings of individuals envisioning dramatic, progressive social and political transformations. So while a variety of differing opinions flourished alongside one another and not every sermon or speech or meeting was about reconfiguring Japanese society, the theme was both common and welcome. This environment could be alluring to the most idealistic and driven members of the "second generation of Meiji youth."[22] They had come of age during the Meiji transition, and their youth was "dominated by a sense of nation *[kokkakan]* rather than a sense of self *[kojinkan]*."[23] At the same time, the open discursive space of the Protestant church held appeal for many of the "agonized youth" *(hanmon seinen)* of the so-called third generation of Meiji youth as well.[24] These young Japanese men and women, born in the 1880s and 1890s, were characterized by their social concerns, modern curiosity, internationally informed perspectives, and awareness of the "individual."[25] Constituents from both groups seeking to think and speak about more progressive and more egalitarian futures for Japan often found their way to church on their paths to liberal political thought and activism.

Taking the Tokyo Protestant Church Experience outside the Church

Such was the case with perhaps the most often studied Japanese Protestant layman, but also with others for whom the important role of church attendance has been less examined. Just as he reached the age of "vitality and vigor when one searches for ideals and tries to make independent decisions," Tokyo Imperial University student Yoshino Sakuzō began attending Hongō Church.[26] What he found at Hongō responded to these needs and objectives, and through his experiences and interactions at church Yoshino developed and elaborated on a religiously motivated, socially concerned activism. As Yoshino frequently acknowledged, Ebina Danjō's sermons and writings instilled in him values such as Christian humanism, universal brotherhood, and the worth of the individual and demonstrated the legitimacy of social criticism from a religious perspective.[27] As Jung-sun Han has remarked, Yoshino attributed to Ebina a central role in his intellectual development. In particular, Ebina's "sermons every Sunday" left not only a religious but a foundational impact on how Yoshino thought about scientific and historical analysis.[28] Ebina's emphasis on the concept of *jinkaku* (character), in particular, became a fundamental element in Yoshino's political perspective.[29] Responsible for transcribing Ebina's sermons in *Shinjin,* Yoshino was well positioned to familiarize himself with their content and meaning.[30] However, through frequent speeches by laypersons and pastors hosted by the Meidōkai and Tokyo Fujinkai at Hongō, Yoshino also heard and made speeches that advocated social awareness, activism, and reform.[31] These kinds of effects extended to his role as an editor of *Shinjin* from its inaugural issue. In reviewing content and contributed articles, he practiced articulating social and political commentary and promoting the application of Christian social ideals to secular problems.[32]

From 1913, as a professor of politics at Tokyo Imperial University, Yoshino could draw on this extensive set of church experiences, along with both education and life experiences acquired abroad in China, the US, Germany, and England, to address Japan's tumultuous social situation. He successfully rethought the sociopolitical bases for Japan and propagated a new vision for the nation that was grounded in Christian social ideals fostered within the church. Yoshino transformed his Christian social ideals into legitimated political realities by reconceptualizing the responsibility of the Japanese intellectual to the broader Japanese society. Contrary to the tendency of most prewar academics in Japan to communicate their ideas to other academics, he envisioned for scholars a public role that involved educating the Japanese public through mass print media.[33] Beginning with the establishment of the University Extension Society and its semimonthly magazine *Kokumin kōdan* (People's Lectern) in 1915, Yoshino brought the intellectual resources of some of Japan's top institutions to bear on the social problems that had accompanied Japan's modernization.

In the pages of this periodical, Yoshino first gave form to the theory of *minponshugi* (literally "democracy based on the people") that, through its elaboration in more widely circulated progressive magazines such as *Chūō kōron*, would become one of the most popular and controversial arguments for parliamentary government in pre–World War II Japan.[34] He argued for a form of democracy in which the popularly elected government would function through and for the benefit of the people whose rights of speech, religion, press, and assembly were to be protected by that government, while keeping both the Meiji Constitution and the political sanctity of the emperor wholly untouched.[35] The appearance of Yoshino's concept in 1916 helped mark the beginning of the political mood known as "Taishō Democracy," and his eventual censure and resignation in 1924 roughly corresponded to the end of the liberal atmosphere that had prevailed just before.[36] By taking this discussion of democracy out of limited academic circles and into publications with wider readerships, Yoshino established an example and a tradition of the mass dissemination of information and opinions by scholars that outlived his own academic career.

Yoshino's students at Tokyo Imperial University carried on his legacy of broadened sociopolitical discussion as the editors and contributors of *Daigaku hyōron* [University Review]. Under Yoshino's supervision, the review included articles on emergent social and political issues, including but not limited to democracy, by liberal professors.[37] In 1917, these efforts gave birth to a student-run and student-written journal titled *Democracy* (later renamed *Senku* [Pioneer]) that became the organ of the Tokyo Imperial University *shinjinkai*. This group was built around Yoshino and committed itself to a sweeping program of sociopolitical reform, from creating and running a settlement house to fighting for universal suffrage, with clear roots in conceptions of Yoshino's Christian humanism.[38] Among their number were Akamatsu Katsumaro, the political activist and founder of the Shakai Minshūtō (Socialist People's Party);[39] labor activist and journalist Miyazaki Ryūsuke (1892–1971);[40] and labor leader and politician Asō Hisashi (1891–1940).[41] Japan's first socialist prime minister, Katayama Tetsu (1887–1978), has also written much about the influence of Yoshino on his views of society and humanity.[42] Yoshino encouraged these students to publish their thoughts for the benefit of society, and in the long run many of them continued writing and acting on behalf of their fellow countrymen. His own writings and the objectives of his students' activism and perspective, as young men and afterward, evince a specific set of Christian ideals that in part had their roots in the discursive space that Yoshino encountered at Hongō.

Yoshino attended Hongō with many others whose church experiences there had an impact on other political thinkers and activists as well. Prolific socialist author and journalist Ishikawa Sanshirō (1876–1956) began attending Hongō near the end of his studies at Tokyo Hōgakuin (the forerunner of Chūō University) in 1902 and was baptized that March by Ebina.[43] The following year he began coediting the *Heimin shimbun* (Commoners' Newspaper) with socialist-anarchist Kōtoku Shūsui, but he also continued attending sermons without fail.[44] Ebina's messages contained much of interest for Ishikawa, who incorporated them into his core beliefs and motivations for social reform. Looking back on his life, Ishikawa wrote, "I learned to devote my life to social justice. I was inspired to give my entire being enthusiastically to mankind. This spirit of devotion I learned from Ebina's teachings about Christ."[45] Although Ishikawa's brand of Christianity changed as his sociopolitical ideas developed over time, he kept his attention centered on the betterment of the plight of humanity.[46] By importing and translating ideas and narratives by anarcho-communist thinker Peter Kropotkin (1842–1921), naturalist author Émile Zola (1840–1902), and other Western authors, by chronicling Japanese socialism, and by advocating his own version of anarcho-syndicalism, Ishikawa worked throughout his life for social justice and major social change.[47]

Just as Ishikawa's attendance at Hongō became less frequent following the close of the Russo-Japanese War, a student with a great passion for the underprivileged and dedication to reforming Japan joined the church. In 1906, Suzuki Bunji (1885–1946) arrived in the capital after graduating from the Second Higher School in Sendai and enrolled in Tokyo Imperial University. At the church, Suzuki took over the part-time paid position recently held by his senior classmate from Sendai, Yoshino. As the transcriber for the pastor's sermons, Suzuki took detailed notes each Sunday, gaining new perspectives and understanding in the process. This job was, however, more than just a means of procuring food and shelter for Suzuki, and it revealed to the young Imperial University student the way he should live.[48] It should come as no surprise, then, that in retrospect, as he reflected on the origins of his social activism, he noted the importance of virtues that pastor Ebina frequently espoused. Suzuki explained, for instance, that his "basic motive arose from my position of

Christian humanitarianism," a position strongly present in Ebina's sermons.[49] Soon he, like his friend and mentor Yoshino, also became a contributor to *Shinjin*. Like Ishikawa, Suzuki's views on religion and society eventually took him away from Hongō. In Suzuki's case, he embraced Unitarianism and used the mission's Unity Hall to establish the Yūaikai (Friendship Society), Japan's first labor union, in 1912. From the early Taishō period through the early 1940s, Suzuki worked and succeeded at transforming the Japanese labor movement into a political force capable of achieving concrete results for the working class. His Yūaikai paved the way for the true mass labor unionism of the 1920s. Suzuki also lent his support and energy to the Shakai Minshutō as a founding member of the central executive committee in 1925 that successfully lobbied with Yoshino and others for universal manhood suffrage.[50]

While these names associated with Hongō are among those Japanese best-known for combining Christianity with social activism and reform, they were far from alone. Among the few thousands of women and men who attended Reinanzaka, Banchō, Fujimichō, and Hongō Churches between the 1880s and the early 1920s, many drew on experiences and connections made at church in impactful efforts to apply Protestant social ideals to real social problems. A brief examination of a dozen such figures who worked in a range of distinctly modern professions and who left substantial indications of the role of church attendance in their lives can serve to illustrate the nature of this process. Judge Mitsui Hisaji (b. 1875), a member of Reinanzaka Church from 1902, felt strongly that faith and action were connected. In addition to visiting believers in their homes, Mitsui put his convictions in action in the church as a Sunday school teacher, and from around 1907 as its director.[51] In the public sphere, he established Japan's first court for juvenile delinquents, the Tokyo Juvenile Court, in 1918. As the court's first judge, Mitsui prioritized rehabilitation and care over punishment, evincing a sense of justice informed by Christian morality and of reform based on Protestant humanitarian ideals.[52] He was described in one publication as a man whose "whole soul is taken up in the effort to reclaim these delinquent children before they develop into thorough-going criminals."[53] And churchgoers at Banchō evinced strong commitments to social reform as well. In 1896, when Katayama Sen (1859–1933) returned from his studies in the US at Grinnell, Andover Theological Seminary, and Yale School of Divinity as an avid Christian socialist, it was Banchō Church that he and his wife Fude joined.[54] And it was during his seven-year membership at Banchō that Katayama founded the Social Problems Study Group (1896);[55] Tokyo's first settlement house, Kingsley Hall (1897);[56] the Socialism Study Group (1898); and the exceedingly short-lived Socialist Democratic Party (1901). Katayama participated actively at

Banchō and drew on his connections there, becoming a trustee and Sunday school director, and occasionally he gave lectures on socialism there.[57] As his new congregation welcomed its new pastor Tsunajima Kakichi and celebrated its ten-year anniversary in December 1896, Katayama was one of the two chairmen for the event.[58]

Ichibanchō Church and its successor Fujimichō Church proved, like Banchō and Hongō, welcoming for leftist thinkers. Katayama frequented the church in the early twentieth century but was not a member. In Katayama's efforts to establish a night school for laborers and a kindergarten for workers' children, Ichibanchō's pastor Uemura showed himself to be a like-minded and enthusiastic contributor.[59] Admittedly, these stances did not make Uemura an advocate of confrontational activism. Uemura at times discouraged Katayama and many others from taking direct action and radical positions. Katayama even recalled the pastor saying, "Our church doesn't need people wearing workmen's coats *[happi]*."[60] By the turn of the century, however, the pastor had created a church that nonetheless welcomed the working class. As Katayama noted, Ichibanchō was filled with "clerks [and] shop and company employees" who were keenly attuned to the workers movement.[61] Since the 1890s, Uemura had been committed to solving social problems and was therefore interested in the ideas and endeavors of socialists.[62]

This affinity in part explains the attraction of the congregation for young, aspiring socialists and progressives. In 1907, the Tokyo Imperial University student destined to become Japan's first socialist prime minister joined Uemura's church in its new Fujimichō building.[63] Katayama Tetsu admired the "great figure" and "great pastor" who was so "brimming with vigor."[64] Like so many students, he was drawn to Uemura as one who "expressed his opinion boldly and candidly . . . not only on the religion question but also on philosophy [and] politics" and addressed issues from "the social perspective, human perspective, and world perspective."[65] It was also around this time that the increasingly liberal journalist Tagawa Daikichirō, a member of Banchō since his baptism there in 1891 by Kozaki, found that the progressive atmosphere of Fujimichō Church corresponded better to his worldview.

That is not to say that Banchō was of little significance in the life of Tagawa, however. His experiences at church during his fourteen years as a member of Banchō were formative and played an important role in his efforts to connect religious ideals and social activism. During those years, Tagawa gained recognition as a journalist, participated in the Social Problems Study Group, and was elected to the Imperial Diet. As a Tokyo Senmon Gakkō student, Tagawa first attended Banchō Church at the invitation of Fuchizawa Noe (1850–1936), a woman whose self-supported study trip to the United States in the 1880s garnered considerable attention in Japan. However, it was the kind intervention of "the mother of [his] faith," Vice Minister of Justice Miyoshi Taizō (1845–1908), that truly integrated Tagawa into the congregation. Miyoshi made an effort to get to know the young new attendee, and Tagawa noticed.

Over the years, Tagawa came to admire Miyoshi for his faith and his conscientiousness, watching him very closely at church. The future Supreme Court justice sat in the same seat on Sundays, almost never missing services and prayer group. The less disciplined Tagawa was impressed by Miyoshi's ability to stay focused, abstaining from "moving his body, changing his orientation, [or] lowering his head."[66] Tagawa's comments point to the importance that church held for Miyoshi, who "listened attentively to the sermon" and sat in the same seat in the front row each week.[67] The vice minister of justice, who "never missed [church] in the morning or the evening" and never "appeared even slightly bored" to Tagawa, clearly cared deeply about attending church.[68] Miyoshi demonstrated his commitment to the Ichibanchō Church as the Sunday school director in the 1890s.[69] He also underscored the importance of "fellowship" at the church in a speech in September 1906. In the midst of the Russo-Japanese War, he had fallen away from the congregation on account of the preponderance of a type of religion that he perceived to be "form only."[70] "Unable to set aside the strong feelings" connecting him to the church, however, Miyoshi returned that year to request forgiveness and acceptance back into church membership. Incontrovertibly, then, Tagawa's observations of his mentor as a committed attendee at Ichibanchō aligned well with the significance that Miyoshi himself assigned the church in his life. After stepping down from the Supreme Court, Miyoshi spent the last decade of his life working for Christian social ideals. He served in the upper house of the Imperial Diet, defended liberal activists and thinkers as an attorney, and acted as an adviser and supporter for the city of Tokyo's Yōiku-in, a welfare center dedicated to the sick and needy.

What might appear to be simple observations, however, held a larger meaning for Tagawa. He deeply respected Miyoshi precisely because he demonstrated such "bearing," often comparing his own bearing at church years later to that of Miyoshi.[71] A member of a generation particularly searching for role models and guidance, Tagawa was "happy . . . and grateful" to have such a friend.[72] Clearly Miyoshi had followed through on a precept that he had once shared with Tagawa. He believed that "one must interact with young people . . . and make friends with the people of the 20th century," and as Tagawa developed, so too did he. From his efforts to increase constitutional literacy among youth in the early twentieth century to his position as director of the Tokyo YMCA to his accession to the presidency of Meiji Gakuin University in 1925, Tagawa focused tremendous energy on working with young Japanese.[73]

In 1904, Tagawa joined Ichibanchō Church.[74] In the person of Uemura, Tagawa found another person to admire at church. He considered the pastor's devotion and self-sacrifice commendable.[75] Now as a public figure himself, however, Tagawa also appreciated Uemura's position as a vocal leader. In sharp contrast to the quiet and still judge Miyoshi, Uemura was ready to "declare his beliefs without hesitation."[76] Tagawa counted Uemura among the "pioneer Christian warriors" fighting continuously to make religion relevant to society.[77] By the time Tagawa joined Ichibanchō, the church had hundreds of members interested in implementing the Christian social gospel, and he made lasting, impactful connections with some of them. The congregation's sole non-Japanese member, Caroline MacDonald (1874–1931), became not only a fellow church elder but also a close friend of Tagawa at Fujimichō. Just before MacDonald's untimely death from a fatal illness, Tagawa visited and explained that even among Japanese he had never had such a good friend.[78] Their collaboration on MacDonald's settlement house project resulted in 1924 in the creation of the Shinrinkan (Neighborhood House), a space for the poorer working classes in Tokyo modeled on Jane Addams's Hull House. By the mid-1920s, the settlement house had become the most important institution for the education of social workers, postincarceration reform of criminals and juvenile delinquents, and service to prisoners' wives and children in Tokyo.[79] Also in the realm of crime and punishment, Tagawa was dedicated to shedding light on the problems inherent in the Japanese prison system and seeking reform. His connections with MacDonald, here again, were instrumental. She organized and hosted a meeting between prison warden Arima Shirosuke (1864–1934) and Tagawa in 1919 about social problems in general and furthering the humanization of prisoner care.[80]

Arima, Tagawa, and MacDonald also all provided prefaces to the autobiographical prison memoir of Tōkichi Ishii (d. 1918) and facilitated its publication. The book, *A Gentleman in Prison,* tells the story of a hardened criminal awaiting execution whose conversion to Christianity has given him new strength and peace. But the true value of the work lay in its ability to shed light on the potential for repentance and reform in prisoners. Already a hallmark of "the Christian Warden" Arima and of Tagawa and MacDonald, this reform-centered approach found some vindication in the work. For Tagawa, whose early interest in socialism had developed into close ties to the American Federation of Labor and the newly founded International Labor Organization, the story also highlighted the underlying social problems that nourished crime. Tagawa knew more than most politicians and journalists about incarceration because he had spent three months in prison in 1918. He had been arrested for the crime of *lèse-majesté* following the publication of an article criticizing statesman Yamagata Aritomo and the elitist, nondemocratic functions of the *genrō* (elder statesmen). It was in no small part this experience that led Tagawa to prioritize prison reform after his release, a project he discussed with his first and most frequent visitor during his incarceration, Caroline MacDonald.[81]

MacDonald's relationship with members of Fujimichō Church were instrumental in other ways as well. Uzawa Fusaaki (1872–1955) had worked with MacDonald and Tagawa to establish the Shinrinkan and held the position of chairman. Originally a missionary sent by the World YWCA, MacDonald worked among and through church members at Fujimichō Church for this organization as well. As she strove to transfer the Japan YWCA leadership into Japanese hands in 1912, she and many others considered dynamic and well-traveled Bryn Mawr graduate Kawai Michi (1877–1953), also a member of Fujimichō, to be the best choice. MacDonald relied not only on her personal persuasive capacities, however, but also on those of the church's pastor Uemura Masahisa to convince Kawai to accept a salaried position as the national secretary of the organization, which she did in 1912.[82] Under Kawai's leadership, the YWCA spread throughout Japan and, with it, initiatives ranging from hygiene and exercise to comfort and morale work for soldiers to programs for the promotion of women's education.[83] This very public position helped prepare Kawai for her later career as an internationalist and as a representative from Japanese Christian institutions to the US.

The church also left a deep impression on the two career paths of Kawai's fellow Fujimichō member Hani Motoko. As a student of Meiji Girls' School in 1890, the young woman who would become Japan's first female journalist was caught up in a stream of girl students who were attracted to Ichibanchō Church by the Sunday sermons of Uemura Masahisa. Although looking back in later life, she reckoned that she "seemed to have understood very little," Hani also recalled that she was "spellbound by the Rev. Uemura's impassioned sermons."[84] Even after her baptism that year, Hani was full of questions and uncertainties about Christianity.[85] However, the sermons deeply moved Hani.[86] Furthermore, the content of those confusing but inspiring sermons added to the understanding of the Christian social mandate that she acquired at Iwamoto Yoshiharu's Meiji Girls' School. And her profession of faith served as more of a declaration of her commitment to "live by the Christian moral code" than of religious conviction.[87]

That conviction did eventually come, however, and both her social and spiritual perspectives manifested themselves in her work in journalism and later in higher education. In the 1890s, Hani struggled to realize her ambition to become a journalist in spite of the repeated gender-based refusals she received. Her decision to carry "a statement among my application papers explaining why, as a woman, I wished to be a copy editor" was surely her own.[88] It is worth noting, however, that it echoed the perspective of the pastor of the church she attended for decades. In his sermons and administrative decisions at Ichibanchō and later Fujimichō, Uemura demonstrated a belief in women's abilities to work and hold leadership positions beyond the home that corresponded well with those of Hani.[89] She procured her first position in journalism with the *Hōchi shimbun* in 1897 and in 1903 launched her own journal, *Katei no tomo* (Family's Friend). The journal, renamed *Fujin no tomo* (Woman's Friend) in 1908, focused on women's daily life and issues such as marriage and education, but also dealt with women's liberation, employment, and emotions.[90] Through it she offered a widely popular guide for those in, or striving to achieve, middle-class lifestyles.[91] The publication was also "an organ for the spread of various international and Christian doctrines."[92] In particular, her perspective aligned well with Uemura's emphasis on women and family, on the one hand, and the improvement of women's place in society, on the other.[93] In 1921, she and her husband Yoshikazu founded Jiyū Gakuen, a girls' school that emphasized freedom of thought and freedom to learn the values of hard work, along with a synthesis of Christian and Confucian ideals. In this institution as well, there were traces of Uemura's denunciations of blind nationalistic chauvinism, patriotic obedience, and unquestioning conformity. While the assertion of certain American Christians that "it was because of Uemura that Mrs. Motoko Hani started her revolutionary Freedom School for girls" certainly exaggerates the pastor's influence and minimizes Hani's independent inspiration and motivation, Uemura clearly did impact her and her school.[94] Neither the teachers nor the state were the most important educators at Jiyū Gakuen; instead, Hani explained that there was "only one unchanging teacher. This is Christ."[95] Although there were periods during which she did not attend Fujimichō and she eventually embraced the Nonchurch Movement of Uchimura Kanzō, this church's influence on Hani was lasting and significant. The connection was again confirmed at the end of her life, when her family invited Fujimichō pastor Miyoshi Tsutomu (1878–1975) to say a prayer at her funeral.[96]

The experiences at church of the founder of Japan's second private women's university, Tokyo Woman's Christian University, herself an editor as well, also proved transformative and impactful. Yasui Tetsu, who "originally hated

Christianity," returned from studying at Cambridge University's Hughes Hall with a profoundly different perspective.[97] With a Japanese Christian friend, Yasui began attending Hongō Church in 1900. She chose the church in particular because it "had no connection with foreign missions," a clear reference to her negative experience with condescending Western missionaries in Japan and abroad.[98] From her baptism there in 1900 by pastor Ebina until her death in 1945, Yasui was an active member of the congregation and of the church's Tokyo Fujinkai and *kangofukai*.[99] In 1909, after more time abroad in Europe and Thailand, Yasui became a founding editor of Hongō Church's women's periodical, *Shinjokai* (New Women's World). Aimed at young women and the adults who raised and educated them, the publication sought to act as a guide to modern moral and spiritual development. While dozens of women wrote pieces, Yasui's imprint on the periodical as its editor until 1917 and its most frequent contributor is unmistakable. The overall message of her articles was that women were responsible for knowing themselves, cultivating strong morality, and leading purposeful lives. Although far from a radical feminist, Yasui repeatedly encouraged women to seek "true education"—one that taught women how to think rather than simply to fulfill their duties—and to use it to exercise agency in their lives.[100]

Beyond the two thousand readers of *Shinjokai* and those who read her various other articles for secular publications, Yasui influenced many young women as an educator. Before 1918, she spent most of her teaching career in Japan as a psychology teacher at Tokyo Women's Normal School, with short stays at Iwate Prefecture Normal School, the Peeresses' School (Gakushuin), and Tsuda Umeko's English School. In 1918, Yasui cofounded Tokyo Woman's Christian University on the ideals of Protestant Christianity and "true education" that she had developed over the years. Yasui, as dean and then as president—and Japan's first woman university president at that—in 1925 led an institution devoted to Christianity-based moral education, high ideals, and "independent study to foster creative intellectual ability."[101] The curriculum that she largely designed and implemented with her collaborators Nitobe Inazō (1862–1933) and American Presbyterian missionary August Karl Reischauer (1879–1971) was one of liberal education. Required courses ranged from ethics and English and math to Bible studies, psychology, physical education, and literary criticism.[102] These courses reflect Yasui's conviction that women deserved and were capable of education equal to that of men.[103]

Running through Yasui's journalistic and educational endeavors are religious and social ideals that she developed at church. One scholar, lamenting the fact that the most authoritative biography of Yasui hardly mentions Ebina, wrote that to understand Yasui, it is imperative to think about Ebina's influence on her.[104] He therefore argued that one "can infer" that, like Yoshino, Yasui absorbed the ideas of her pastor.[105] In fact, however, Yasui herself left some indication of the importance of Ebina and the Hongō congregation in her life. Looking back while she was in her sixties, she wrote that "my faith became strong through the pastors' sermons."[106] Yasui recalled with fondness working with Ebina on *Shinjokai* at church and at the pastor's home. Through their interactions inside as well as outside the church, she gradually developed a "closeness" with Ebina that allowed her to live a "life full of hope, gratitude, and vigor."[107] At Ebina's funeral in 1933, Yasui recalled that she had been "flooded with emotion" at her baptism by Ebina. In her eulogizing words, she then committed herself to continuing to "follow in his footsteps" and renewing the "serious thoughts and strong resolutions" that she held at that time.[108] In the meantime, Yasui had carried Ebina's emphasis on developing character *(jinkaku)* into her professional life. As a dormitory dean and a professor, Yasui "wanted to raise girls of noble character."[109] The congregation as a whole, however, was also an integral element in her life. Beyond its pastor, she wrote that "Hongō Church made a deep spiritual impression on me, and it is an unforgettable . . . place."[110] That place, for her, was characterized by "the overflowing energy and affection" of the church's members.[111]

Among those members to whom Yasui was closest was the educator who brought her to Hongō Church in 1900 in the first place. Noguchi Yuka (1866–1950), a lifelong friend of Yasui from their days teaching at Iwate Prefecture Normal School in Morioka, was another member of Hongō Church who translated Protestantism's social messages into social action. While Yasui, Hani, and Kawai, who founded Keisen School for Young Women (forerunner to Keisen University), focused their efforts on higher education for women, Noguchi was most interested in the educational development of young Japanese children. She and her Christian colleague Morishima Mine (1868–1936) were struck by the glaring disparities in wealth and childcare between the poor street children they saw each day on the way to work and the children of the nobility at the Peers' School (Gakushūin), where they taught.[112] Drawing on a network of Japanese and Western church attendees that she had cultivated by attending social gatherings at Hongō and Banchō, the educator set out to realize a new social vision for underprivileged Japanese preschool-age children. "Something had to be done, and this thought became stronger. So one day the two of us told the missionary Miss Denton who always frequented Banchō Church of this feeling and asked her for help. She was sympathetic, and we decided to hold a charity concert in order to raise funds."[113] In addition to missionary and teacher Florence Denton

(1857–1947), the aforementioned Banchō member Miyoshi Taizō was one of the project's most outspoken supporters and biggest financial backers in its early stages.[114]

The result of their efforts was Japan's first public kindergarten, Futaba Yōchien, established in 1900.[115] With the cooperation of dozens of supporters, Noguchi and Morishima were able to stop working at the Peers' Girls' School kindergarten, devote their entire attention to Futaba, and make it into a neighborhood success.[116] By 1923, the institution had grown to include a home for single mothers and their children and a physician-staffed night dispensary for the working class and their children.[117] The kindergarten was so effective that it caught the eye of administrators in the Home Ministry, who began making annual grants to the two women for Futaba. By the 1910s, the institution had helped to legitimize day care as a response to problems relating to poverty. It would ultimately also demonstrate the utility to the state of free education and health care for underprivileged children.[118]

The fate of the family in modern Japan preoccupied not only women churchgoers like Noguchi and Hani but also men. Ishikawa Takeyoshi (1887–1961) drew from his church experience and church-based social interactions to help shape debates over the definition of the New Woman in Japan. A native of Oita Prefecture in Kyūshū, Ishikawa came to the capital as an adolescent and then worked at the Dōbunkan, a reputed publisher of works on European language and culture. As a teen he was drawn to Hongō Church, like so many other young men and women in Tokyo, through Ebina's reputation and eloquence. Ishikawa quickly became active in the church's Meidōkai, and in 1907 he was baptized by Ebina.[119] His participation in the events surrounding Hongō's Tokyo Fujinkai, in particular, exerted a major formative influence on the construction of his social outlook and objectives. In 1936, while referring to the environment surrounding the women's group in particular, he recalled: "Separated far from my family, living a sad life, what gave me the one thread of warm support was the friendly mood of this church. [It] awakened in me the desire to work for the sake of the Japanese family, and through the church I came to know . . . the preciousness of the family."[120] Through his interactions within Hongō's Tokyo Fujinkai, he came to believe that "purifying the family [was] the handiest way to purify Japan," and he took appropriate measures to realize this goal.[121]

Ishikawa attributed in large part his high regard for domesticity and the role of the Japanese housewife to his church experience at Hongō, and he increasingly propagated these priorities to female audiences through his positions in the publishing world. Between 1908 and the late 1920s, Ishikawa progressed from journalist to editor to, as one scholar has dubbed him, the "king of mass-circulation women's magazines."[122] His career began with a short, successful tenure as a writer and later as editor for fledgling women's magazine *Fujokai* (Women's World), 1910–1950, and a brief post as editor of friend and mentor Hani Motoko's *Fujin no tomo*.

Clearly inspired by Hani and driven by his own ideas on the family and the household, Ishikawa organized a study group on home economics in 1915 and began editing and publishing *Shufu no tomo* (Housewife's Friend), Japan's first modern magazine specifically for housewives, in 1917.[123] Viewing the improvement of the Japanese family as his Christian responsibility and duty to Japan, he set out to equip women with the knowledge that he deemed necessary for the management of the household.[124] In doing so, Ishikawa reinforced conceptualizations, shared by many of his fellow male and female *fujinkai* members, of the home as women's proper place, while aiming to offer women tools to educate and empower themselves within that sphere.[125] Ishikawa's *Shufu no tomo* became and remains Japan's best-selling women's magazine, and from the early Shōwa period, his views on the home, the wife, and magazine marketing and management had come to dominate an entire segment of the publishing industry.

Although students, intellectuals, and activists represented the majority of attendees and members at Hongō, there were in fact many others who, like Ishikawa, belonged to the world of business. In 1905, the membership included 168 students and 49 businesspersons.[126] The church offered Japanese businessmen the space and opportunity to reflect on the relationship of their companies to Christian social ideals, but also to establish connections between socially aware Christian business owners. Akimoto Naohisa (b. 1863) founded and ran Sekai Kōtsūsha, a successful publishing company in Tokyo. While he and his wife Mitsu worked fervently for the church, his work for social education with fellow member and businessman Kobayashi Tomijirō (1852–1910) was particularly noteworthy.[127] As the young editors of *Shinjin* and Ebina completed the first issue of the journal, their fundraising fell far short of the printing costs. It was Akimoto who underwrote the first issues, after which point subscriptions allowed the journal to continue.[128] Araki Masayumi (1854–1917), the owner of a lacquerware business in the capital, also worked to spread Christian belief and ideas into the greater Japanese society.[129] From 1910 until 1916, Hongō member Araki was the director of the YMCA. Like Akimoto, he worked with Kobayashi, establishing the Kanda-kai, a Christian businessmen's club, in 1909.[130] The association aimed to develop business ethics and promote the exchange of knowledge.

The figure connecting these two, Kobayashi Tomijirō, was widely known in Japan for his efforts to improve society in accordance with Christian ideals. Originally involved in his family's sake business in Saitama, he would eventually become a leading advocate for temperance as a path to moral and social reform.[131] After a series of failures and a depression that nearly led him to suicide, Kobayashi began attending Kobe's Tamon Church and converted to Christianity in 1888. In 1891 he landed in Tokyo, where he founded Lion Corporation, a soap and toothpaste manufacturing company through which he sought to work for the benefit of people and society. The company's website today continues to make reference to this fundamental mission.[132] With his enterprise and his wealth, Kobayashi launched initiatives aimed at helping the working classes. In addition to the Kanda-kai, which focused on business leaders, he also established the Kobayashi night school in 1901 to provide workers with general education and instruction in sewing.[133] As teachers, he hired young recent graduates of Christian schools like the future actress Kurihara Gyokuyō (1883–1922), and he brought in lecturers like labor organizer Suzuki Bunji who could impart Christian social ideals to the workers.[134] He also created a temperance society for his employees.[135] In addition, Kobayashi was a generous philanthropist, giving money to causes in Japan and abroad. The YMCA, of which he briefly served as director, was but one of the many recipients of funds.[136] Through his connections with pastors and other Christians in the Kansai region, Kobayashi also gave funds and time to the development of Okayama Orphanage.[137] This pioneering institution had some twelve hundred children and two hundred staff in 1906 and included a "Lion Hall," highlighting the benefactor's use of his company as a tool for addressing social problems.[138]

Efforts like these and his impact on many individuals go a long way toward explaining why thousands of men and women from all over Japan gathered for his funeral in 1910 in Tokyo. The sizable procession began at the Lion headquarters and ended in the YMCA Hall, where dozens of dignitaries, associates, and friends spoke to the crowd.[139] Among the speakers was Ebina Danjō who, as pastor and friend, was especially close to Kobayashi. His memorial sermon for the Hongō member underscored his strong relationship with, and importance to, the church since he had become a member in 1891.[140] The support of Kobayashi had been particularly crucial during the difficult years when the church reestablished itself with Ebina at the helm in 1897 and then lost its building in the Hongō Fire of 1898.[141] Giving of his time and money, Kobayashi remained a pillar of the church. As one church member at the time put it, "Ebina spiritually built Hongō Church and Kobayashi physically built Hongō Church."[142] So as the city mourned that December day in 1910, the devastation of the church and its pastor was particularly evident.

Just as he clearly meant a great deal to Ebina and the greater membership of Hongō, the church also had a significant impact on Kobayashi Tomijirō and his well-known efforts to better society. Lectures and sermons on the Bible at church inspired him to become a Christian, and they continued to influence him throughout his life.[143] So when Ebina recalled that Kobayashi "saw everything from a Christian perspective," that vantage point was consistently and deeply informed by the discourse that Kobayashi encountered through his unfailing church attendance.[144] Throughout the 1890s, Kobayashi listened in particular to sermons that promoted the so-called New (or Liberal) Theology. This theology, which viewed the Bible as a human, context-embedded historical and cultural product, "cut to pieces" the obstacles impeding the entrepreneur's faith. Through the near dissolution and then the rebirth of Hongō Church, he maintained his dedication to the church. Then, according to Ebina, Kobayashi's "religious life made a great turn because of what was happening at Hongō Church."[145] While surely the member's personal devotional life was of the utmost importance, Ebina here asserted that the social space of Hongō was also pivotal. At that time in particular, the atmosphere at the church was defined by Ebina's sermons and the speech meetings and lectures of the Tokyo Fujinkai and Meidōkai. It was then that Kobayashi "started a new religious life in society."[146] This new life was devoted to applying progressive Protestant ideals to the real social problems surrounding him through his financial and administrative involvement with his company's night school and temperance organization, the Kanda-kai, the YMCA, and orphanages in Okayama, Tokyo, Yokohama, Kyoto, Osaka, Kobe, and other cities.[147] He also drew on connections made at church to carry out his philanthropy.

Thousands of Japanese men and women found their way into Protestant churches in the late nineteenth and early twentieth centuries. Japanese church attendees in that period shared a great deal. They primarily belonged to the educated elite, and many of them became associated with leading churches in the capital while they were students. Many of them were determined to propagate Protestant ideals in Japanese society as editors, authors, and teachers. This same impulse drove church attendees to establish and support institutions and organizations that explicitly aimed to realize those ideals in concrete ways, from the first free kindergarten to schools and universities to orphanages to labor unions.

The lines of commonality, however, should not lead to the mischaracterization of Japanese Protestant church attendees as a monolithic body. Kobayashi, who had not pursued higher education and who joined the church when he was nearly thirty years of age, is a case in point. The lives of the various working-class members of Fujimichō in the late Meiji period, too, differed from those of the young members of the educated elite with whom they attended church. And as their diverse initiatives demonstrate, even among the social influencers and reformers examined in this chapter, there were considerable differences of perspective on issues such as socialism and the rights and responsibilities of women. Only by acknowledging this relative diversity can we truly assess these spaces' ability to host a social space of broad appeal and to foster community.

Church experiences were deeply meaningful and transformative for many churchgoers in Meiji and Taishō Japan. At Fujimichō, Hongō, Banchō, and Reinanzaka, attendees recalled the important roles that pastors' sermons played in their spiritual, intellectual, and moral development. However, this chapter has shown that impactful experiences at church went far beyond the sermon. From giving and listening to lectures to writing and reading articles for *Shinjin* or *Shinjokai,* attendees actively participated in the exchange of information and ideas. In addition to the discursive space of the church, the social interactions proved to be consequential. Close relationships with pastors and with fellow attendees developed through formal and informal types of social gatherings and simply through conversations. Protestant churches fostered not only friendship but also collaborations and synergies among attendees.

Through its impacts on attendees, the social space of Protestant churches came to have a significant impact on Japanese society. In Tokyo, men and women carried the ideals that appeared again and again in sermons, speeches, and lectures at their churches into the public sphere. They taught, spoke, and wrote for secular audiences, bringing concepts like *minponshugi* and "true education" to the greater Japanese public. They explicitly inscribed the social messages absorbed at church in the new institutions and organizations that they founded. A publication like *Shufu no tomo,* which came to play a dominant role in constructions of womanhood in modern Japan, embodied the particular vision of women and the family that its founder developed at church. Applying this approach, even a corporation became an implement of progressivist social change. At the same time, attendees engaged in direct political action as politicians and activists brought the church experience with them as well. Christian humanism and other key concepts that saturated the discursive space of Tokyo's largest Protestant churches became fundamental elements in more radical reform efforts of labor organizers and leftist activists, as well as many others not treated in this work.

Even a list of all the attendees of just Tokyo's largest Protestant churches would extend well beyond the few names discussed here. The foregoing has focused on Japanese churchgoers whose experiences at church contributed to their involvement in movements and efforts to improve society. Dozens of other churchgoers made noteworthy contributions to Japan but are not examined here:

figures like renowned naturalist author Kunikida Doppo (1871–1908) and seminal English literature scholar Saitō Takeshi (1887–1982), who acknowledge that Uemura's sermons had a strong influence on their literary understanding, are beyond the scope of the chapter.[148] And even within this narrow ambit, the chapter is still far from comprehensive. Instead, the analysis presented here suggests the broader contours of the relationship between the experience of Protestant church attendance in imperial Japan and the application of Christian ideals in the wider society.

Connections between Protestant church attendees and the broader public sphere in Japan also of course originated in churches besides these four congregations and beyond the capital. For instance, Nihonbashi Church, founded and led by Presbyterian pastor Kitahara Yoshimichi (1846–1894) in 1879, was a particularly active congregation during the Meiji period. Members in the late 1880s included young authors Hoshino Tenchi (1862–1950) and Hirata Tokuboku (1873–1943), whose acquaintance at church formed the basis for their collaboration in a literary circle. In 1893 the group launched *Bungakkai* (Literary World), a pioneering and widely influential literary magazine that ran until 1898.[149] And as mentioned earlier, in 1901 and 1902 the church's *seinenkai* hosted events aiming to publicize the injustices surrounding the Ashio Copper Mine and raise awareness and funds.[150] Down in Shinagawa, poet and novelist Shimazaki Tōson (1872–1943) was briefly a member of Presbyterian Takanawa (Ōimachi) Church, where Kimura Kumaji was pastor. Despite leaving the church after approximately five years, Shimazaki maintained a close relationship with Kumaji and benefited from his mentorship.[151] In large part through them, the young man acquired a teaching position at Meiji Girls' School; an assistant editor position on that school principal's journal, *Jogaku zasshi;* and the acquaintance of lifelong friend and mentor Kitamura Tōkoku.[152] As many scholars have noted, Unity Hall of the Japan Unitarian Association in Mita was another Protestant gathering space with long-standing ties to intellectual and social movements. Attendees such as Katayama Sen, Murai Tomoyoshi (1861–1944), and Kōtoku Shūsui developed their ideas on socialism and cultivated deep intellectual and activist ties through meetings and lectures in the building's library and lecture hall.[153] Much less examined are the hundreds of churches in major metropolitan areas in northern Japan and central and southwestern Japan. However, the potential for such a study is suggested by even a brief look at events taking place in Osaka's Naniwa Church. The church's *seinenkai* organized fundraising drives to alleviate suffering like that caused by the 1896 Sanriku earthquake in the Tōhoku region.[154] And between 1910 and 1923 regular *seinenkai* and *fujinkai enzetsukai* featured prominent Christian figures such as journalist Katō Naoshi (1873–1952), educator Naruse Jinzō, social reformer Hayashi Utako (1865–1946), and Italian literary scholar Oga Hisayoshi (1865–1937).[155] As a result of various factors, from Western missionaries' control over location, establishment, and construction to issues with turnover in Japanese leadership, none of these church congregations had as many direct, impactful links to movements to rethink and change Japanese society as the Fujimichō, Reinanzaka, Banchō, and Hongō Churches. However, these small additional plot points do demonstrate that these four churches were indeed part of a much larger phenomenon. Japanese women and men utilized the physical and social spaces of Japanese Protestant churches to develop ideas and networks throughout Japan that significantly affected the country again and again. From the late 1880s until the 1920s, church space was central to the association of Protestantism in word and deed, with social movements aimed at addressing the promises and problems of Japanese modernity.

Epilogue

Just before noon on the first day of September in 1923, the Great Kantō Earthquake shook and ripped its way through Tokyo and the neighboring areas. The vibrations and the subsequent fire took more than one hundred thousand lives in the space of only three days.[1] Exacerbating the catastrophe's toll on Tokyo residents was the damage it did to their built spaces. The buildings where Japanese lived, studied, and worked collapsed and burned in the country's worst modern natural disaster to date. This included the destruction of over three hundred thousand homes, which left 1.38 million inhabitants displaced.[2] In addition, the buildings of major institutions central to Japanese lives in Tokyo perished. The cataclysm demolished 80 percent of the capital's business district and destroyed the headquarters of 121 major banks, resulting in an even more dire economic situation for survivors.[3] Another development that compounded the suffering of residents was the loss of so many of their religious gathering spaces. The earthquake decimated 633 Buddhist temples, 151 Shinto shrines, and 202 Christian churches.[4] Among them were the edifices of three of Tokyo's four largest Protestant congregations: the Fujimichō, Hongō, and Banchō Churches. Reinanzaka somehow miraculously survived, and as mentioned earlier, its building served as a shelter in the immediate aftermath of the earthquake.

The devastation the Great Kantō Earthquake caused to these three buildings in fact served to concretize a change already underway within and around the capital's most popular churches. Although these churches would all be rebuilt between 1926 and 1929 and would again host vibrant social spaces with ties to those congregations' pasts, the earthquake punctuated the gradual ending of an era. In terms of leadership, the early 1920s saw a changing of the guard among these churches' influential pastors. After having recently reduced his preaching duties, Ebina left Hongō Church to become president of Dōshisha in Kyoto in 1920. He was succeeded as pastor by Noguchi Matsuhiko (pastor, 1920–1925) who was in turn succeeded by Nukaga Shikanosuke (pastor, 1925–1941). Ebina returned as honorary pastor in 1929. At Reinanzaka the same period brought similar changes. In 1922, Kozaki passed the position of Reinanzaka head pastor on to his son Michio, who would remain pastor until 1961. After stepping down, Kozaki Hiromichi occupied himself increasingly with international Christian engagements such as the World Evangelism Conference and World Sunday School Association. As for Uemura, from the days following the earthquake until his death in 1925, he never fully recovered from the shock of the disaster. After his death, debate over his successor resulted in a split in the congregation and departure of over one hundred Fujimichō members for pastor Takakura Tokutarō's (1885–1934) new Shinanomachi Church. Meanwhile, the slightly smaller congregation at Fujimichō continued under the brief leadership of Minami Renpei, who passed away in 1926, and then Miyoshi Tsutomu (1878–1975), who held that position until 1948. Banchō Church pastor Tsunajima Kakichi, on the other hand, carried on his role as pastor until his retirement in 1931. So of the pastors who established and led Tokyo's largest congregations in the Meiji period, only Tsunajima remained as those churches began figuratively and literally to rebuild after 1925.

The new buildings and new pastors belonged to a new era in the relationship between Protestant religious gathering space and the Japanese state. To begin with, the church ceased to benefit from the relative freedom with which its special status had endowed it in the Meiji period. The aura of Westernization and modernity that surrounded much church space had not been impenetrable during the Meiji era, and cracks within it appeared at moments of heightened nationalistic fervor. Following the promulgation of the Imperial Rescript in 1891 and during Japan's wars with China and with Russia, the anger of Japanese non-Christians was sometimes directed at these Western-style buildings. However, during the Hibiya Riot in early September 1905, when enraged mobs burned thirteen Tokyo churches to the ground, the nature of the fissure in Christian space's protective aura was especially portentous.[5] Following Japan's victory over Russia and signing of an indemnity-free Treaty of Portsmouth, rioters in the capital specifically targeted Western-style buildings whose functions were associated with Westernization, modernity, and authority. They destroyed modern Western-style brick buildings including the Home Minister's Residence in Hibiya, two police stations, and nearly three-quarters of the police boxes. They also attacked streetcars, whose price had risen by 33 percent after a newly imposed and unpopular transportation tax.[6] The decision to include churches among these Western-style, modern edifices is indicative of their special status but also of the liabilities that came with such associations. And like these sites, the riots signaled an erosion of that status.

The erosion was only partial, however, and Protestant churches in particular continued to function as a privileged social and physical space. One test of this status had come in the wake of the High Treason Incident of 1911. Convicted on highly circumstantial and inconclusive evidence of plotting to assassinate Emperor Meiji, physician Oishi Seinosuke (1867–1911) was executed along with ten others. At the request of the deceased's family, Uemura held a memorial service for the Christian socialist physician at Fujimichō Church. In doing so, the pastor disobeyed an injunction forbidding funerals for High Treason Incident defendants and showed considerable courage.[7] Although opposed to pastors becoming activists, he worried about authoritarianism and supported Christian lay social activists who challenged it.[8] However, this undertaking by Uemura and Fujimichō member Uzawa Fusaaki, Oishi's lawyer, also betrays a strong confidence in the soundness of the real and imagined walls of the church. That confidence was well founded, apparently: the few plainclothes policemen who came to monitor the event were forced to wait outside.[9]

By the mid-1920s, however, the walls of Tokyo's leading Protestant churches were much less secure. Churches, like the religious gathering spaces of other religions, were increasingly subject to new scrutiny in the Taishō period. The eyes and ears of the Home Ministry's Special Higher Police (Tokkō), established in 1911, and other thought-policing bodies multiplied and became more invasive. They penetrated the walls of universities, businesses, meeting halls, homes, and even churches.[10] In 1925, their powers expanded with the passage of the Public Security Peace Preservation Law, a law clearly intended to provide the government with the mandate and tools to suppress and punish political dissidents. The law was intentionally vague on what an effort aiming at "altering the *kokutai*" would look like, but much clearer on the penalties for contravention. The maximum penalty was ten years in prison, but an imperial decree amended the law to also include a maximum penalty of death.[11] In that context, the discursive spaces, organizational activities, and concerted actions in which Protestant church attendees engaged there were much less safe than they had been in earlier decades. Yet by the 1920s, censors and agents investigating disruptive groups and ideologies at Protestant churches would have had much more fruitful searches elsewhere.

While the government's networks of surveillance gained new means and the prerogative to access the social spaces inside Protestant churches, the reality was that most mainstream Protestant leaders had no intention of making such measures necessary. Christianity had become thoroughly Japanese but also significantly less threatening for the government.[12] By the 1920s, Protestant churches decreasingly hosted discourse that aimed to dramatically reimagine Japan or activities with the objective of radical social change. Furthermore, they offered less and less room for pastors and attendees to oppose or even question the state.

This process began at the tail end of the Meiji period but coexisted and shared attention with the realization of so many of the projects rooted in ideals, experiences, and networks developed within Protestant churches. New colleges, magazines, settlement houses, labor unions, political theories, and other elements contributed to the broader flourishing of so-called Taishō Democracy even as mainstream organized Christianity and the state grew closer.

Meanwhile, many leftists decried the contradictions inherent in espousing progressive, egalitarian Protestant ideals while cooperating with a government that largely disparaged those values. This was a civilian government elected by only 2 percent of the male population and composed primarily of the members drawn from the hereditary elite.[13] Furthermore, the government had close ties to major industries and the military, both of which exploited the Japanese proletariat and the colonized East Asian subaltern. Several prominent Christian socialists were especially disappointed that Protestantism had lost its critical perspective on Japanese society and the government that presided over it. While some abandoned Christianity altogether, a few of these figures left the capital's largest Protestant congregations and became Unitarians. They availed themselves of the movement's Unity Hall in Mita to continue discussing socialism and social problems until the end of the American Unitarian Association mission to Japan in 1921.[14]

Part of what so many intellectuals and activists found particularly disheartening was that Protestant Christianity ceased to stand at a critical distance from the state and the state's objectives for the people of Japan. The national identity and destiny of Japan, and Protestant Christianity's compatibility with both, preoccupied Protestant leaders like the pastors of Tokyo's largest congregations throughout the Meiji period. However, the years following Japan's victory over Russia in the Russo-Japanese War in 1905 saw Christianity and the ideals and actions of Japanese imperialism become much more than compatible.[15] Japanese Roman Catholics demonstrated their loyalty to the Japanese imperial project by providing support for soldiers and their families during the war, and Japanese Russian Orthodox church members sent three thousand comfort bags to Japanese prisoners of war in Russia. However, it was Protestantism that most emphatically embraced this connection.[16] Many of Protestantism's loudest voices argued that Christianity enshrined important Japanese virtues, that Japan's military accomplishments and imperial expansion were the work of God, and that Japanese Christians were meant to lead the liberating *mission civilisatrice* in Asia.[17] This was especially true of the Kumiai (Congregationalist) denomination but also characterized many Presbyterian and Methodist leaders and others. Such perspectives would have been unremarkable in a Western Christian context. The westward expansion and Amerindian expropriation of the nineteenth century was often explained in terms of a destiny manifested to Americans by God.[18] Similarly, pastors and priests in Europe strove to convince the public that World War I was a holy war and that God was on their side.[19] Such claims in Meiji Japan were part of a campaign to demonstrate to the people of that country, and their government, that Christianity and modern imperial Japan could mutually embody one another.

Efforts like these helped to convince the Meiji government that indeed Christians could fully assume their Japanese identity—an identity that according to imperial edicts and policies as well as government ideologues necessarily encompassed an explicit willingness to serve the state. After officially recognizing Christianity as a legal religion in 1899, the government offered the religious movement opportunities to fulfill this obligation. The most symbolically significant of these was the Conference of the Three Religions organized by the Home Ministry in February 1912. Its purpose, in the words of Home Minister Hara Takashi, was to solicit the help of religious leaders to "promote sound spiritual progress parallel to the material development of the nation and to improve the social condition of the people."[20] The conference attendees consisted of seven Christian leaders, including one delegate each from the Congregational, Presbyterian, and Methodist denominations, along with fifty-one Buddhist leaders and thirteen Shinto leaders.[21] While there was apparently a general enthusiasm among religious leaders in the days leading up to the event, the response from Christian denominations was quick and thoroughly optimistic.[22] They hoped to work with the government to help the Japanese people. Yet the event, entirely organized by the government and attended by three members of the cabinet, clearly served the government's new project "to enlist religion into ideological service."[23] By participating, leading Christians and their Buddhist and sect Shinto counterparts overtly embraced the Meiji government's "subjectified grammar of religion" that aimed to neutralize religion's ability to challenge or subvert the state—a state that had bolstered its legitimacy and cultivated civil obedience through religion.[24]

The Three Religions Conference marked the application of the so-called emperor system ideology to the world of religion, as Dohi Akio and several others have written.[25] Dohi succinctly describes a process in which the government publicly bestowed recognition on religious groups and organizations like those of Christianity, and in return those groups advocated "assisting the imperial will."[26] This same process was at work in 1908 when Tenrikyō received official recognition as the last of the thirteen Shinto sects.[27] In fact, the government effectively mobilized this strategy well outside the realm of religion. The increased recognition that women's groups received in imperial Japan after 1930 in exchange for their promotion of ideals and campaigns that suited the needs of the state was a case in point.[28] Another aspect of the emperor system at work in the conference and in religionists' wholehearted support of it was "moral suasion" *(kyōka)*.[29] Officials and ideologues in the service of the state had ceaselessly emphasized the importance of revering the imperial institution, its government, and the Japanese national polity. This occurred through a bombardment of information on proper behavior and thought that left most Japanese citizens acting and thinking in ways acceptable to the state. Japanese Protestant leaders were, like all Japanese, immersed in various forms of moral suasion, and most actively embraced the state. It is important to note, however, that far more than most Japanese, Protestant pastors had had to fight for inclusion and recognition by the state and grasped the opportunity to demonstrate their belonging within the "Shinto secular" with particular fervor.[30]

Japan's expansionism afforded Protestant leaders an ideal context in which to prove their consonance with the Japanese imperial project as well as their usefulness and loyalty to Japan. This was a privilege that Roman Catholicism sought during the Russo-Japanese War but was denied.[31] In particular, Congregationalist pastors and missionaries deeply involved themselves in Japan's empire. From 1903, when the denomination's leadership launched the initiative to establish churches for Japanese in Korea onward, Congregationalists focused significant energy and manpower on that country. It was especially in the context of Korean annexation, however, that pastors sought to make Christianity a tool to soften the impact of colonization, ease the process of assimilation, and hasten the spiritual salvation of that country's people.[32] Although not as central a figure as his protégé, Kobe Church pastor Watase Tsunekichi (or Tsuneyoshi) (1867–1944), Hongō's Ebina Danjō thoroughly implicated himself in the evangelization of Korea.[33] He had argued that Korea would benefit immensely from Japanese intervention, even before the Russo-Japanese War, when Korea became a Japanese protectorate.[34] In 1910 and again in 1911, Ebina traveled to Seoul and other places in Korea to promote the growth of the new Japanese congregationalist mission to that country.

On his second trip, Ebina went as chairman of the Korean missionary activity expansion fund and met with Japanese governor-general Terauchi Masatake (1852–1919) and high-ranking Japanese officials. Back in Japan, he had also secured donations for the Congregationalist mission in Korea from prominent figures such as elder statesmen and entrepreneurs as well as from the office of the governor-general.[35] By 1918, Japanese Congregationalism counted 149 churches in Korea with more than thirteen thousand Korean members. Notably, government funding and the protection of the Japanese police gave their mission an unusual advantage.[36] The following year, however, the March First movement for independence led to a sharp decline in Korean membership in their churches. Surprisingly, a Japanese Congregationalist missionary acted as an informant on Koreans involved in the anti-Japanese May Fourth movement in Shanghai that year as well.[37] Of course, Protestants were not alone in mobilizing religion to facilitate empire. The efforts of Takeda Hanshi (1863–1911) and the Sōtō Zen sect to control but also reinvigorate a largely moribund Korean Buddhism presented parallels.[38] Yet aspects of the Japanese Congregationalist mission's activities, from explicitly championing assimilation to aligning their work with the colonial government and engaging in espionage, make it stand out.

While there were important exceptions to Japanese support and participation in imperial expansion and to the Conference of the Three Religions, Japanese Protestantism largely supported the state at home and abroad. Congregationalist pastor Kashiwagi Gien and Nonchurch Movement founder Uchimura Kanzō were pastors who opposed imperialism and blind obedience to the emperor system.[39] Yet they represented the minority position on topics related to the political situation in Meiji and Taishō Japan. Most Christian leaders drew near to the state, and the actions of pastors like Watase and Ebina speak for themselves. Even beyond the Congregationalist denomination, Protestants in general stood with and not against the state, and this only increased during the 1930s.

In the postwar period, this topic has greatly occupied individual believers and the religious institutions to which they belong. The United Church of Christ in Japan (Nihon Kirisuto Kyōdan; UCCJ), an extant body created from the state-led amalgamation of most of Japan's Presbyterian, Reformed, Methodist, and Congregationalist churches into a single religious body in the 1940s, has struggled with the legacy of collaboration and complacency of Protestant churches vis-à-vis the state in imperial Japan. In 1967 the UCCJ issued a "Confession of Wartime Responsibility."[40] They sought "the forgiveness of the peoples of all nations, particularly in Asia" for having "approved of and supported that war and encouraged prayers for victory."[41] The grounds for this apology can easily be extended back to the period when the Conference of the Three Religions and the Congregational mission to Korea ultimately prioritized the well-being of the nation over the religious, moral, and even political freedom of individuals in Japan and its broader empire. Understandably, such expressions of guilt and regret have colored how Christians, Christian institutions, and even scholars characterize the Protestant movement in imperial Japan. Scholars have written to "indict the behavior and beliefs" of Protestants who supported empire and the state and have praised those Japanese Protestant "exemplars of Christian living" who resisted and opposed the forces of militarism, imperialism, and ethnic nationalism.[42]

However, this perspective, entirely refracted through the lens of postwar knowledge, is inherently teleological and can hide important insights. First, Japanese Protestant pastors sought to assert their Japaneseness both in defense against criticisms of un-Japaneseness and in order to identify with their Japanese members and compatriots. Furthermore, they aimed to fully overcome the barriers separating Christianity from Japanese society. From this vantage point, they were in many ways successful in meeting their objectives. It is even possible to view their collaboration with the state as the ultimate recognition of that success. Rather than Japanese using an imported Western Protestant Christianity to view and change Japan, they were proudly and unequivocally Japanese pastors who developed distinct forms of Protestant belief and ideals that were well suited to their Japanese cultural and ideological environment. Second, the dominant perspective on the development of Japanese Protestantism tends to oversimplify the beliefs and ideals of pastors and other leaders. The imposition of this type of ex post facto historical judgment on Meiji- and Taishō-era Japanese Protestants tends to define them largely by what they failed to do and how they failed to see. Examining Protestantism in Japan at the level of the church space, however, yields a more complex picture.

A number of diverse viewpoints and ideological stances contended in the space of the capital's largest Protestant churches. From just after the turn of the century, Protestant leaders in Tokyo increasingly cooperating with the state or, in rare cases like that of Uemura, quietly opposed and avoided engagement with the state. Pastors like Ebina committed themselves and their institutions to participating in Japan's empire. Yet during those same years the church hosted a discursive space that promoted many ideals that complicated, redefined, or contradicted important aspects of the emperor system ideology. Pastors emphasized the importance of belonging to and serving the nation-state, but often tempered such directives with reflections that relativized and contextualized Japanese identity and the Japanese past. Furthermore, these pastors' sermons advocated humanitarianism, brotherhood, individual responsibility and agency, and a sensitivity to the social problems of modern Japan—all values that refuted prevalent motifs of emperor-centered collectivism. The church also hosted speeches and lectures by lay speakers on scientific and literary topics, as well as more contentious themes like the woman question and even socialism. So at a time when the state claimed the exclusive right to dictate the ultimate social purposes of religion, attendees and pastors were actively thinking about and discussing the relationship between Protestant Christianity and society. Churchgoers also used the church space to organize and implement projects that filled roles prescribed or encouraged by the state, but attendees far exceeded these limits. *Seinenkai* and *fujinkai* engaged with the currents and dilemmas of the capital, the empire, and the world through publications and efforts in relief work, education, and social reform.

Like the perspectives expressed and activities undertaken at Hongō, Reinanzaka, Banchō, and Fujimichō, participants in those churches' social spaces were not all the same. Among them were not only conservative but also moderate and more radical thinkers. The congregations of these churches were filled with women and men with ages ranging from adolescence to senescence who interpreted their shared Protestant mandate to improve society in different ways. When the political beliefs of attendees clashed too violently with those of these churches' decreasingly oppositional pastors, they moved on. However, their experiences in the space of the church and the networks they built there often proved fundamentally important to their development as individuals and to their contributions to the greater Japanese society. In other cases, long-term and lifelong members mobilized ideals and networks cultivated in the social space of the capital's leading churches to make noteworthy impacts on modern Japan. They included the public intellectuals, activists, social reformers journalists, college professors, politicians, and businessmen studied here and thousands more. Japanese-led urban Protestant churches hosted or facilitated the creation of Japan's first labor union, first modern magazine for housewives, first public kindergarten, and second university for women, and the Taishō era's foremost theory of popular constitutional democracy. In addition, these churches' social spaces were instrumental in the formation of networks for social reform in domains such as the prison system, the settlement movement, the temperance movement, the movement against licensed prostitution, and the YWCA. In the late Meiji period and the subsequent era of Taishō Democracy, Japanese-led Protestant churches consistently nurtured the socially aware discourse and social activism at work within these and many other social movements.

Japan scholars have pointed repeatedly to a connection between Protestant Christianity and significant social, intellectual, cultural, and political developments in modern Japan. For decades, scholarship on topics tangentially related to Protestant Christianity has made mention of this connection. They have ranged broadly from studies on Tokyo First Higher School and Tokyo Imperial University students to juvenile delinquency to neighborhood political organization and participation to the women's movement and beyond. To anchor this aspect of their research, many of these scholars have relied on the sizable literature on Japanese Protestantism in which this connection has received the most attention. Historians, sociologists, and theologians in Japan, the United States, and Canada have argued convincingly that Japanese Protestants were indeed influential in the making of modern Japan. They have also shown that Christian ideals and social networks were particularly important in some well-known figures' contributions to Japanese society.

Despite all this work, however, our existing understanding of the relationship between Protestant Christianity and Japanese society in imperial Japan requires reconsideration—a task that scholars are clearly still motivated to undertake, given the continued work on this topic. In particular, recent research in two areas has revealed the inadequacy of the current narrative. First, scholars now agree that Meiji officials strove to confine religion, aside from select key dereligionized elements of emperor-centered Shinto, to the "private" sphere and to limit its ability to reach and influence secular society.[43] Many works on Japanese Protestantism, particularly those focusing on mission schools, Christian voluntary organizations, and Christian periodicals, have again and again highlighted the outsize presence of that religious movement in the public sphere. But questions of how the Japanese Protestant movement facilitated networks and opportunities for mobilizing Protestant ideals in the public sphere in the context of 1894 and 1900 laws restricting freedoms of the press and public, political assembly and efforts like Directive 12 to remove religion from education have persisted. Second, scholarship over the past decade has described and analyzed the efforts of reform-minded and progressive Buddhist clergy and laymen to connect the religion with both Western modernity and the people and problems of greater Japanese society.[44] Yet, relative to the much larger Japanese Buddhist population, Japanese Protestants were disproportionately overrepresented in modern intellectual, social, and political endeavors. Our knowledge on Protestant Christianity in Japan falls short in offering explanations for this as well. The foregoing chapters have mobilized a new framework for investigating the history of the Japanese Protestant movement in order to build a narrative capable of accounting for these developments.

This work has asked and responded to new questions about the position of urban space and architectural space in the development of Japanese Protestant Christianity in the capital, focusing on the buildings most explicitly conceptualized and utilized to connect the religion with Japanese secular society. Physical space was clearly central to the religious movement's ability to reach and impact society through the social spaces that took shape within church buildings. Pastors' purposeful use of specific types of urban space in the capital near the nation's top students and leaders in education, government, and business placed their congregations in propitious locations. By 1887, all of the capital's largest Protestant congregations had established long-term sites in the Yamanote, where they built and rebuilt a distinct form of Japanese religious gathering space. Their churches were privileged, hybrid, built spaces: they benefited from the special, protected status of Christian space and its associability with the West. Yet their Japanese leaders, attendees, funds, and architects increasingly endowed these spaces with Japanese meaning as well. The four churches in this study possessed eye-catching exteriors and functionally designed but impressive interiors that could bring Japanese religious seekers together in new and meaningful ways.

In examining Protestant Christianity, the categories of location and built space are also useful because they provide a novel perspective through which to understand the status of the physical and social space of the religion in the larger religious landscape of imperial Japan. Shinto and Buddhist institutions and dynamic Japanese New Religions placed an ambiguous emphasis on the capital, and older centers in the greater Kinki region largely maintained their predominance. Meanwhile, new Buddhist and Shinto institutions that aimed to transform these religions' presence and influence in Tokyo suffered from a lack of strong institutional support, and Tenrikyō's base there faltered as government surveillance increased in the 1890s. By contrast, Protestantism embraced the potential of the capital and unequivocally claimed it as the center of the religious movement. Operating as largely or entirely autonomous, they were able to operate with minimal constraints and directives from larger religious organizational bodies.

Leading Protestant congregations used this relative freedom and the privileged, hybrid nature of church space when they built and rebuilt churches in the capital. The churches examined here had small, informal gathering spaces, *reihaidō,* and *shūkaidō* in which pastors and laypersons spoke and churchgoers regularly interacted. These stood in contrast to other Japanese religious spaces, the vast majority of which were dedicated to formal ritual, ceremony, and instruction—religious activities that upheld the state's *subjectification* of religion's relationship with society. Both sect and so-called State Shinto spaces had little choice, as they were largely subject to the prerogatives of the government from the first years of the Meiji period. The state exerted its power over Shinto by imposing a new ranking system, granting and withholding funding for shrines as they suited its ends, and closing nearly half the shrines in Japan in the early twentieth century. Arguably, state control over Buddhist spaces was considerably weaker. However, as it struggled to recover from its economic and administrative disenfranchisement and from anti-Buddhist persecution in the early Meiji period and to redefine itself in the new modern Japanese context, Buddhist space largely obeyed traditional and uncontestable spatial logic. In addition, the Meiji government did find ways to insinuate its authority over Buddhist space as well. From the expropriation of Zōjō-ji for the Great Teaching Academy to the refusal to refund repairs at Matsuo-ji, the state made clear that it still held considerable power over the fate of Buddhist religious gathering spaces.

It was only in the last years of the Meiji period that new religious spaces that were both centrally located among the target population and equipped with more interactive spaces took shape. From officials working to develop and strengthen State Shinto to religious leaders like Chikazumi Jōkan, new ways of thinking about religious space in the modern context led to buildings that were radical departures from what came before. Chikazumi Jōkan's Kyūdō Kaikan stands as a reminder of his use of urban and built space to attract members of the educated elite and make Buddhism relevant and impactful for them.

Ultimately, these were the same goals with relation to Christianity that drove pastors of Hongō, Banchō, Reinanzaka, and Fujimichō from the late 1870s. The lively social spaces that came to characterize Japanese Protestant congregations in the Meiji and Taishō eras were deeply connected to the urban and physical spaces of their church buildings. Members of the educated elite often attended Protestant churches that had been strategically located in the neighborhoods where they worked, studied, or resided. Inside, churches included multifunctional spaces that could host social gatherings of various sizes and with varying objectives. The *reihaidō* was well suited for the pastoral and lay *enzetsukai* and *kōenkai* that came to characterize Protestantism in imperial Japan, and they grew larger as church memberships rose. From the early 1890s, these church buildings increasingly included auxiliary spaces for smaller, less formal gatherings. In addition to Sunday school, prayer meetings, and Bible study, activities that lie beyond the scope of this book, churches' classrooms and meeting rooms were the site of smaller gatherings such as the regular meetings of church-based groups. For each of these elements of the social space, the aura of Westernization and modernity and the legacy of protection under the treaty port system were crucial. They served to enhance church buildings' ability to host discourse and gatherings whose themes, messages, and objectives that at times challenged the ideological orthodoxy of imperial Japan. They were also the site of interactions that led to the formation of networks aimed at improving society, even in a period when these churches' founding pastors leaned more toward the emperor system or away from active resistance to the state. The study of these churches can begin to answer long-standing questions about the relationship between

Protestant Christianity and movements for social change in modern Japan. It was largely through dynamic social spaces in well-placed, new, built spaces like Tokyo's leading Japanese Protestant churches that the religion reached and influenced the lives of Japanese women and men whose ideas and actions left such an indelible mark on Japan.

Notes

(Re)Introducing Christianity in Modern Japan

1. Tokutomi Iichirō, "Jūnen shukuga" [10th anniversary celebration], *Shinjin* 9, no. 1 (January 1908): 18.

2. For instance, on Japan's first labor union, see Stephen S. Large, *The Rise of Labor in Japan: The Yūaikai, 1912–1919* (Tokyo: Sophia University Press, 1972); on *Jogaku zasshi* [Women's education magazine] and its founding editor, Iwamoto Yoshiharu, see Rebecca L. Copeland, *Lost Leaves: Women Writers of Meiji Japan* (Honolulu: University of Hawai'i Press, 2000), chap. 1; on Noguchi Yuka's Futaba Yochien (kindergarten), see Kathleen Uno, *Passages to Modernity: Motherhood, Childhood, and Social Reform in Early Twentieth-Century Japan* (Honolulu: University of Hawai'i Press, 1999), chap. 3; and on Yoshino Sakuzō's democratic thought, see Peter Duus, "Yoshino Sakuzo: The Christian as Political Critic," *Journal of Japanese Studies* 4, no. 2 (1978): 301–326.

3. Otis Cary, *A History of Christianity in Japan*, vol. 1: *Roman Catholic and Greek Orthodox Missions* (New York: Fleming H. Revell, 1909), 337.

4. Ibid., 1:355.

5. Ibid., 1:414.

6. This process is described well in Robin Cohen, "Creolization and Cultural Globalization: The Soft Sounds of Fugitive Power," *Globalizations* 4, no. 3 (2007): 369–384.

7. For an early work that described and analyzed this historical moment and its ties to Christianity, see Matsuo Takayoshi, *Taishō demokurashi no kenkyū* [A study on "Taishō democracy"] (Tokyo: Aoki shoten, 1966).

8. Helen Ballhatchet estimates that in 1912, of the 189,000 Christians in Japan, 90,000 were Protestants. Helen Ballhatchet, "The Modern Missionary Movement in Japan: Roman Catholic, Protestant, Orthodox," in *Handbook of Christianity in Japan*, ed. Mark Mullins (Leiden: Brill, 2003), 57. And recently Kevin Doak has reminded scholars that Catholics had already come to outnumber Protestants by 1900. However, regarding their location and social impact, he notes that Japanese Catholics were densely concentrated in Nagasaki and were poorly educated and more rural, making for a sharp contrast with the Protestant population. Kevin Doak, ed., *Xavier's Legacies: Catholicism in Modern Japanese Culture* (Vancouver: University of British Columbia Press, 2012), 13.

9. Dohi Akio, "Sankyōkaidō: Seiji, kyōiku, shūkyō to no kanren ni oite 1" [The Conference of the Three Religions: In reference to politics, education, and religion 1], *Kirisutokyō shakai mondai kenkyū*, no. 11 (March 1967): 90–115; and Dohi Akio, "Sankyōkaidō: Seiji, kyōiku, shūkyō to no kanren ni oite 2" [The Conference of the Three Religions: In reference to politics, education, and religion 2], *Kirisutokyō shakai mondai kenkyū*, nos. 14–15 (March 1969):

72–93; George Heber Jones, "An Official Conference on Religion in Japan," *Journal of Race Development* 3, no. 2 (October 1912): 228.

10. Elizabeth Dorn Lublin, *Reforming Japan: The Women's Christian Temperance Union in the Meiji Period* (Vancouver: University of British Columbia Press, 2010), chap. 6. See also Nakamoto Kahoru, "1930 nendai Tokyo YWCA *Watashidomo no ie* ni okeru shakai jigyō to kyōiku katsudō no tenkai" [The development of social work and educational activities in the 1930s Tokyo YWCA *Our House*], *Tōyō Daigaku daigakuin kiyō*, no. 47 (2010): 424.

11. See Emily Anderson, *Christianity and Imperialism in Modern Japan: Empire for God* (London: Bloomsbury, 2014); Takayoshi Matsuo, "The Japanese Protestants in Korea, Part One: The Missionary Activities of the Japanese Congregational Church in Korea," trans. S. Takiguchi, *Modern Asian Studies* 13, no. 4 (1979): 401–429; and Takayoshi Matsuo, "The Japanese Protestants in Korea, Part Two: The 1st March Movement and the Japanese Protestants," trans. S. Takiguchi, *Modern Asian Studies* 13, no. 4 (1979): 581–615.

12. Andrew Gordon, *A Modern History of Japan from Tokugawa Times to the Present* (New York: Oxford University Press, 2014), 108.

13. Yamaguchi Teruomi, *Meiji kokka to shūkyō* [The Meiji state and religion] (Tokyo: Tokyo Daigaku Shuppankai, 1999), chap. 1; and Michel Mohr, *Buddhism, Unitarianism, and the Meiji Competition for Universality* (Cambridge, MA: Harvard University Asia Center, 2014), chap. 4.

14. James Mark Shields, *Against Harmony: Progressive and Radical Buddhism in Modern Japan* (New York: Oxford University Press, 2017), 17, 101.

15. Judith Snodgrass, *Presenting Japan to the West: Orientalism, Occidentalism, and the Columbian Exposition* (Chapel Hill: University of North Carolina Press, 2003), 127.

16. Shields, *Against Harmony*, chap. 2.

17. Trent Maxey, *The "Greatest Problem": Religion and State Formation in Meiji Japan* (Cambridge, MA: Harvard University Asia Center, 2014), 13. See also Jason Ananda Josephson, *The Invention of Religion in Japan* (Chicago: University of Chicago Press, 2012).

18. Shields, *Against Harmony*, 17.

19. For instances of such synopses of Hongō Church see Irwin Scheiner, *Christian Converts and Social Protest in Meiji Japan* (Berkeley: University of California Press, 1970); and Jung-Sun N. Han, *An Imperial Path to Modernity: Yoshino Sakuzō and a New Liberal Order in East Asia, 1905–1937* (Cambridge, MA: Harvard University Asia Center, 2012).

20. For instance, see Jon Thares Davidann, *A World of Crisis and Progress: The American YMCA in Japan 1890–1930* (Bethlehem, PA: Lehigh University Press, 1998); and Noriko Kawamura Ishii, *American Women Missionaries at Kobe College, 1873–1909* (New York: Routledge, 2004).

21. Morioka Kiyomi, *Chihō no shōtoshi ni okeru Kirisutokyō kyōkai no keisei: Kōzuke Annaka Kyōkai no kōzō bunseki* [The formation of a Christian church in a countryside village: A structural analysis of Kōzuke Annaka Church] (Tokyo: Nihon Kirisuto Kyōdan Senkyō Kenkyūsho, 1959).

22. Morioka Kiyomi, *Meiji Kirisutokyokai keisei no shakaishi* [The social history of formation of the Meiji Christian Church] (Tokyo: University of Tokyo Press, 2005), sec. 2, chap. 1.

23. Emily Anderson, *Christianity and Imperialism*.

24. Mark Mullins, *Christianity Made in Japan: A Study of Indigenous Movements* (Honolulu: University of Hawai'i Press, 1998), 55. For the two most authoritative accounts of the life, thought, and impact of Uchimura, see Suzuki Norihisa, *Uchimura Kanzō* (Tokyo:

Iwanami shoten, 1983); and John F. Howes, *Uchimura Kanzō: Japan's Modern Prophet, 1861–1930* (Vancouver: University of British Columbia Press, 2005).

25. Uchimura Kanzō, *Uchimura Kanzō zenshū* [The collected works of Uchimura Kanzō], vol. 31 (Tokyo: Iwanami shoten, 1981–1984), 132.

26. John F. Howes, "Christian Prophecy in Japan: Uchimura Kanzō," *Japanese Journal of Religious Studies* 34, no. 1 (2007): 133; William H. H. Norman, "Kanzō Uchimura: Founder of the Non-church Movement," *Contemporary Religions in Japan* 5, no. 1 (March 1964): 35–36; Howes, *Uchimura Kanzō*, 200.

27. Miura Hiroshi, "The Biblical Research Method of Uchimura Kanzō," in *Living for Jesus: The Social and Theological Thought of Uchimura Kanzō*, ed. Shibuya Hiroshi and Chiba Shin (Grand Rapids, MI: Eerdmans, 2013), 115.

28. Gwendolyn Wright, "Cultural History: Europeans, Americans, and the Meanings of Space," *Journal of the Society of Architectural Historians* 64, no. 4 (2005): 436–440.

29. Daniel V. Botsman, *Punishment and Power in the Making of Modern Japan* (Princeton, NJ: Princeton University Press, 2005).

30. See Jordan Sand, *House and Home in Modern Japan: Architecture, Domestic Space, and Bourgeois Culture, 1880–1930* (Cambridge, MA: Harvard University Press, 2003).

31. Motoi Yasuhirō, "Dōshisha Shingakkan no hensen: From Classroom No. 30 to Clarke Memorial Hall of Theology," *Kirisutokyō shigaku* 70, no. 1 (June 2008): 1–22.

32. Rikkyō University Professor Tōya Tetsushi's chapter on Fujimichō Church is simply a condensed summary of the church-funded institutional history of Fujimichō Church that he also wrote and is entirely descriptive. It does appear in a scholarly publication with a broader audience, however, and therefore deserves mention as a scholarly work as well. Tōya Tetsushi, "Fujimichō Kyōkai shishō" [Extract from Fujimichō Church history], in *Nihon purotesutanto shi no shomondai* [Various issues in Japanese Protestant history], ed. Nihon purotesutanto shikenkyūkai (Tokyo: Yuzankaku, 1983), 283–316.

33. Morioka, *Meiji Kirsutokyōkai keisei*, 126, 133.

34. Mohr, *Buddhism, Unitarianism, and the Meiji Competition for Universality*, 31–33.

35. Mary Louise Pratt, *Imperial Eyes: Travel Writing and Transculturation* (New York: Routledge, 1992), 8; Michael Auslin, *Negotiating with Imperialism: The Unequal Treaties and the Culture of Japanese Diplomacy* (Cambridge, MA: Harvard University Press, 2009); Joseph M. Henning, *Outposts of Civilization: Race, Religion, and the Formative Years of American-Japanese Relations* (New York: New York University Press, 2000); and James E. Hoare, *Japan Treaty Ports and Foreign Settlements: The Uninvited Guests, 1858–1899* (Folkestone, UK: Japan Library, 1994).

36. Jinnai Hidenobu, *Tokyo: A Spatial Anthropology*, trans. Kimiko Nishimura (Berkeley: University of California Press, 1995); Edward Seidensticker, *Low City, High City, Tokyo from Edo to the Earthquake: How the Shogun's Ancient Capital Became a Great Modern City, 1867–1923* (Cambridge, MA: Harvard University Press, 1991).

37. Henri Lefebvre, *The Production of Space*, trans. Donald Nicholson-Smith (Malden, MA: Blackwell, 1991), 404.

38. Ibid.

39. See Auslin, *Negotiating with Imperialism*, 34. Here he draws attention to the "protection of Japanese space," as a high priority for the new Meiji regime.

40. Charles R. Boxer, *The Christian Century in Japan 1549–1650* (Berkeley: University of California Press, 1967), chaps. 7 and 8.

41. Ibid.

42. Kiri Paramore, *Ideology and Christianity in Japan* (Abingdon, UK: Routledge, 2009), chaps. 3, 4, and 5.

43. Nam-lin Hur, *Death and Social Order in Tokugawa Japan: Buddhism, Anti-Christianity, and the Danka System* (Cambridge, MA: Harvard University Asia Center, 2007); see also Paramore, *Ideology and Christianity in Japan*, chap. 3.

44. Auslin, *Negotiating with Imperialism*, 34.

45. Treaty of Amity and Commerce between the United States and Japan, 1858, Article 8.

46. F. G. Notehelfer, *Japan through American Eyes: The Journal of Francis Hall 1859–1866* (Princeton, NJ: Princeton University Press, 1993), 24.

47. Although the treaties opened the ports of Niigata (1868) and Hakodate (1859) to foreign trade as well, neither of these attracted a sufficient number of Westerners to warrant the establishment of foreign settlement zones. James E. Hoare provides single-digit foreign resident population numbers at these sites. See Hoare, *Japan's Treaty Ports*.

48. Lane Earns, "The Foreign Settlement in Nagasaki, 1859–1869," *The Historian* 56, no. 3 (1994): 488.

49. Otis Cary, *A History of Christianity in Japan*, vol. 2 (New York: Fleming H. Revell, 1909), 278–280.

50. Ibid., 2:278, 281.

51. Ibid., 2:490. See also William Elliot Griffis, *Guido Verbeck of Japan: A Citizen of No Country. A Life Story of Foundation Work Inaugurated by Guido Fridolin Verbeck* (London: Oliphant, Anderson, and Ferrier, 1901), 124–125.

52. Chushichi Tsuzuki, *The Pursuit of Power in Modern Japan 1825–1995* (Oxford: Oxford University Press, 2000), 64. For more names see Benjamin Duke, *The History of Modern Japanese Education: Constructing the National School: Constructing the National School System, 1872–1890* (New Brunswick, NJ: Rutgers University Press, 1999), 44.

53. A. Hamish Ion, *American Missionaries, Christian Oyatoi, and Japan, 1859–73* (Vancouver: University of British Columbia Press, 2009), 50.

54. Ibid., 37. See also Richard Smethurst, *From Foot Soldier to Finance Minister: Takahashi Korekiyo, Japan's Keynes* (Cambridge, MA: Harvard University Asia Center, 2007), 45–46.

55. Kōbe shimbun bunka seikatsu bu, ed., *Hito moyuru shirarezaru kindai Hyōgo no senkakushatachi* [A single sprout: The unknown pioneers of modern Hyōgo] (Kobe: Kōbe shimbun sōgō shuppan sentā, 2001), 104–105. See also Tanaka Tomoko, "Meiji shoki no Kobe to senkyō i Beri: Iryō wo meguru chiiki no rikigaku" [The missionary medical doctor Berry in Kobe: The regional dynamics of medical work in the early Meiji era], *KSMK* 52 (December 2003): 58–81.

56. Numbers cited in different sources range from thirty to sixty. See, for instance, Samuel Mossman, *New Japan, the Land of the Rising Sun: Its Annals during the Past Twenty Years, Recording the Remarkable Progress of the Japanese in Western Civilization* (London: John Murray, 1873), 144; and Rutherford Alcock, *The Capital of the Tycoon*, vol. 2 (London: Longman, Green, Longman, Roberts, and Green, 1863), 431.

57. Thomas Burkman, "The Urakami Incidents and the Struggle for Religious Toleration," *Japanese Journal of Religious Studies* 1, nos. 2–3 (June–September 1974): 155; and Ion, *American Missionaries, Christian Oyatoi*, 108.

58. Ion, *American Missionaries, Christian Oyatoi*, 115–116; Cary, *A History of Christianity in Japan*, 1:316, 328, 332–333; Hur, *Death and Social Order*, 341.

59. Cary, *A History of Christianity in Japan,* 2:66.

60. Griffis, *Guido Verbeck of Japan,* 182–184.

61. Ibid., 264, quoting a letter from Guido Verbeck (22 February 1873).

62. Burkman, "The Urakami Incidents," 153.

63. Frederick G. Notehelfer, *American Samurai: Captain L. L. Janes and Japan* (Princeton, NJ: Princeton University Press, 1985), 103.

64. A. Hamish Ion, "Edward Warren Clark and Early Meiji Japan: A Case Study of Cultural Contact," *Modern Asian Studies* 11, no. 4 (1977), 557–572; see also Cary, *A History of Christianity in Japan,* 2:74.

65. Notehelfer, *American Samurai,* 182.

66. In talks with the United States, officials nevertheless mentioned religious freedom as a prerequisite for treaty renegotiation. See John Breen, "'Earnest Desires': The Iwakura Embassy and Meiji Religious Policy," *Japan Forum* 10, no. 2 (1998): 155; and John Breen, "Beyond the Prohibition: Christianity in Restoration Japan," in *Japan and Christianity: Impacts and Responses,* ed. John Breen and Mark Williams (London: Macmillan, 1996), 90.

67. Hur, *Death and Social Order,* 348.

68. Helen Hardacre, "Creating State Shinto: The Great Promulgation Campaign and the New Religions," *Journal of Japanese Studies* 12, no. 1 (1986): 42. See also Allan G. Grapard, "Japan's Ignored Cultural Revolution: The Separation of Shinto and Buddhist Divinities in Meiji (shinbutsu bunri) and a Case Study: Tonomine," *History of Religions* 23, no. 3 (February 1984): 240–265; and James Ketelaar, *Of Heretics and Martyrs in Meiji Japan: Buddhism and Its Persecution* (Princeton, NJ: Princeton University Press, 1990), chap. 2.

69. Hur, *Death and Social Order,* 374. See also Martin Collcutt, "Buddhism: The Threat of Eradication," in *Japan in Transition: From Tokugawa to Meiji,* ed. Marius B. Jansen and Gilbert Rozman (Princeton, NJ: Princeton University Press, 1986), 143–167.

70. Hur, *Death and Social Order,* 346.

71. Cary, *A History of Christianity in Japan,* 1:336, 352. It was precisely in remedy of this situation that the Roman Catholic bishop of Tokyo Pierre-Marie Osouf (1829–1906) solicited the Society of Mary (La Société de Marie) to open colleges in Japan. The group established the prestigious Marianist schools Gyōsei Gakuin (1888) in Tokyo, Kaisai Gakuin in Nagasaki (1891), Meisei Gakuin in Osaka (1898), and St. Joseph's School in Yokohama (1901). See ibid., 358; and Joseph Leonard van Hecken, *The Catholic Church in Japan since 1859* (Tokyo: Herder Agency, 1963), 159–160.

72. A. Hamish Ion, *The Cross and the Rising Sun,* vol. 1: *The Canadian Missionary Movement in the Japanese Empire, 1872–1931* (Toronto: Wilfrid Laurier University Press, 1990), 65, 117.

73. Ballhatchet, "The Modern Missionary Movement in Japan," 44.

74. Kohiyama Rui, "Kirisutokyō ni motodzuku kindai Nihon no joshi kyōiku saikō" [A reconsideration of modern women's education grounded in Christianity], in *Kindai Nihon no Kirisutokyō to joshi kyōiku* [Modern Christianity and women's education], ed. Kirisutokyō shigakkai (Tokyo: Kyōbunkan, 2016), 11.

75. For instance, see Ishii, *American Women Missionaries.* It is worth noting that the predecessor of Joshi Gakuin, Sakurai Girls' School (est. 1876), was a Japanese-funded endeavor founded in cooperation with the Presbyterian mission. See Margaret Ernestine Burton, *The Education of Women in Japan* (London: Fleming H. Revell, 1914), 41.

76. For some works that shed light on how this occurred, see Aoyama Nao, *Yasui Tetsu den* [Biography of Yasui Tetsu] (Tokyo: Iwanami shoten, 1949); Ishii, *American Women Missionaries;* Tanaka Tomoko, *Kindai Nihon kōtō kyōiku taisei no reimei: Kosakusuru chiki to kuni to Kirisutokyōkai* [The dawn of the Modern Japanese high school education system: The intersection of region, country, and the Christian world] (Kyoto: Shibunkaku shuppan, 2012); and Barbara Rose, *Tsuda Umeko and Women's Education in Japan* (New Haven, CT: Yale University Press, 1992).

77. See Cary, *A History of Christianity in Japan,* vol. 1, chap. 6.

78. Cary, *A History of Christianity in Japan,* 1:342–343.

79. See J. Nelson Jennings, *Theology in Japan: Takakura Tokutaro, 1885–1934* (New York: University Press of America, 2005), 89. He summarizes well the conclusions that pioneering sociologist Sumiya Mikio made in his "Chūsan kaikyū to Kirisutokyō" [The middle class and Christianity], *Fukuin to sekai* 9, no. 6 (June 1954): 23–28.

80. David Ambaras, "Social Knowledge, Cultural Capital, and the New Middle Class in Japan, 1895–1912," *Journal of Japanese Studies* 24, no. 1 (Winter 1998): 1, 8.

81. See Steve Bruce, *Politics and Religion* (Malden, MA: Blackwell, 2003), chap. 5; and David Levine and Daniel Stoll, "Empowerment and Power in Latin America," in *Transnational Religion and Fading States,* ed. Susanne Hoeber Rudolph and James Piscatori (Boulder, CO: Westview, 1997), 63–103.

82. See Notehelfer, *American Samurai;* Scheiner, *Christian Converts and Social Protest;* Helen Ballhatchet, "Confucianism and Christianity in Meiji Japan: The Case of Kozaki Hiromichi," *Journal of the Royal Asiatic Society* 1, no. 2 (1988): 349–369; John F. Howes, "Japanese Christians and American Missionaries," in *Changing Japanese Attitudes towards Modernization,* ed. Marius Jansen (Princeton, NJ: Princeton University Press, 1965), 337–368; Dohi Akio, *Nihon Purotesutanto Kirisutokyō shi* [A history of Japanese Protestant Christianity] (Tokyo: Shinkyō Shuppansha, 1980).

83. See Scheiner, *Christian Converts and Social Protest;* Ōuchi Saburō, *Nihon Kirisutokyō shi* [History of Japanese Christianity] (Tokyo: Nihon Kirisuto Kyōdan Shuppan kyoku, 1970); Takeda Kiyoko, *Uemura Masahisa: Sono shisōteki kōsatsu* [Uemura Masahisa: An ideological inquiry] (Tokyo: Kyōbunkan, 2001); Kudō Eiichi, *Meiji-ki no Kirisutokyō: Nihon Purotesutanto shiwa* [Meiji-era Christianity: Historical tales of Japanese Protestants] (Tokyo: Kyōbunkan, 1979).

84. Allan G. Grapard, *The Protocol of the Gods: A Study of the Kasuga Cult in Japanese History* (Berkeley: University of California Press, 1992), 256.

85. Courtney J. Campbell, "Space, Place and Scale: Human Geography and Spatial History in *Past and Present,*" *Past and Present* 238, no. 1 (May 2018): 23.

86. Nam-Lin Hur, *Prayer and Play in Late Tokugawa Japan: Asakusa Sensōji and Edo Society* (Cambridge, MA: Harvard University Asia Center, 2000), chap. 3.

87. Sarah Thal, *Rearranging the Landscape of the Gods: The Politics of a Plgrimmage Site in Japan, 1573–1912* (Chicago: University of Chicago Press, 2005), 209.

88. Thomas F. Gierlyn, "A Space for Place in Sociology," *Annual Review of Sociology* 26 (2000): 465.

89. See Michel de Certeau, *The Practice of Everyday Life,* trans. Steven Rendall (Berkeley: University of California Press, 1984), 96–97; and Lefebvre, *The Production of Space,* chap. 3.

90. See Henry D. Smith II, "Tokyo as an Idea: An Exploration of Japanese Urban Thought until 1945," *Journal of Japanese Studies* 4, no. 1 (Winter 1978): 53–55. On the phenomenon of

tokainetsu (city fever), see Carol Gluck, *Japan's Modern Myths: Ideology in the Late Meiji Period* (Princeton, NJ: Princeton University Press, 1985), 159.

91. Sophia Psarra treats such meaning as the "semantic meanings of buildings and places, and the contribution of architecture to the expression of social and cultural messages . . . but also the ordering of spaces and social relationships." See Sophia Psarra, *Architecture and Narrative: The Formation of Space and Cultural Meaning* (New York: Routledge, 2009), 2.

92. Sand, *House and Home in Modern Japan*, 4.

93. Peter Berger, *The Desecularization of the World* (Grand Rapids, MI: Eerdmans, 1999).

94. Nancy Fraser, "Rethinking the Public Sphere: A Contribution to the Critique of Actually Existing Democracy," *Social Text*, nos. 25–26 (1990): 57.

95. Jürgen Habermas, *The Structural Transformation of the Public Sphere: An Inquiry into a Category of Bourgeois Society*, trans. Thomas Burger (1978; repr., Cambridge, MA: MIT Press, 1989), 30; Jürgen Habermas, Sara Lennox, and Frank Lennox, "The Public Sphere: An Encyclopedia Article," *New German Critique* 1, no. 3 (1974): 49.

96. See Maxey, *The "Greatest Problem"*; Hur, *Death and Social Order;* Hardacre, "Creating State Shinto"; Ketelaar, *Of Heretics and Martyrs.*

97. See Sharon H. Nolte and Sally Ann Hastings, "The Meiji State's Policy toward Women," in *Recreating Japanese Women, 1600–1945*, ed. Gail Lee Bernstein (Berkeley: University of California Press, 1991), 154–155; and James L. Huffman, *Creating a Public: People and Press in Meiji Japan* (Honolulu: University of Hawai'i Press, 1997), 76–77, for succinct overviews.

98. Massimiliano Tomasi, "Oratory in Meiji and Taishō Japan: Public Speaking and the Formation of a New Written Language," *Monumenta Nipponica* 71, no. 1 (Spring 2002): 44.

99. Maxey, *The "Greatest Problem,"* 136.

100. Barbara Ambros, *Women in Japanese Religions* (New York: New York University Press, 2015), 129.

101. Shields, *Against Harmony*, 41. He finds support for this interpretation in Janine Tasca Sawada, *Practical Pursuits: Religion, Politics, and Personal Cultivation in Nineteenth-Century Japan* (Honolulu: University of Hawai'i Press, 2004), 6.

102. Richard Jaffe, "The Buddhist Cleric as Japanese Subject: Buddhism and the Household Registration System," in *New Directions in the Study of Meiji Japan*, ed. Helen Hardacre and Adam L. Kern (Leiden: Brill, 1997), 529. See also Maxey, *The "Greatest Problem,"* 113.

103. Maxey, *The "Greatest Problem,"* 136.

104. Stephen S. Large, "Buddhism, Socialism, and Protest in Prewar Japan: The Career of Seno'o Girō," *Modern Asian Studies* 21, no. 1 (1987): 154. On Uchiyama, see Brian Daizen Victoria, *Zen at War* (Lanham, MD: Rowman & Littlefield, 2006), chap. 3. On Takagi and Uchiyama, see Shields, *Against Harmony*, chap. 4.

105. Annaka Church pastor Kashiwagi Gien, a particularly outspoken social and political critic, expressed his views often in his church's newspaper, earning fines on more than one occasion. However, the state never directly intervened in his church or sought to silence him at the pulpit. On his indictment and fine in 1909, see Emily Anderson, "Containing Voices in the Wilderness: Censorship and Religious Dissent in the Japanese Countryside," *Church History* 83, no. 2 (June 2014): 398–421.

106. One such example will receive attention in the epilogue. See A. Hamish Ion, "The Cross under an Imperial Sun," in *Handbook of Christianity in Japan*, ed. Mark Mullins (Leiden: Brill, 2003), 73; Margaret Prang, *A Heart at Leisure from Itself: Caroline MacDonald of Japan* (Vancouver: University of British Columbia Press, 1995), 79; and Morinaga

Eisaburō, *"Rokutei" Ōishi Seinosuke* [The particular Ōishi Seinosuke] (Tokyo: Iwanami shoten, 1977), 329.

107. Gluck, *Japan's Modern Myths,* 135.

108. Josephson, *The Invention of Religion in Japan,* 133–134.

109. Mara Patessio, "The Creation of Public Spaces by Women in the Early Meiji Period and the Tokyo Fujin Kyōfūkai," *International Journal of Asian Studies* 3, no. 2 (2006): 156.

110. Nolte and Hastings, "The Meiji State's Policy toward Women," 154; Marnie Anderson, "Women and Political Life in Early Meiji Japan: The Case of the Okayama Joshi Konshinkai (Okayama Women's Friendship Society)," *U.S.-Japan Women's Journal,* no. 44 (2013): 47. For a broader treatment of these trends and their context, see Marnie Anderson, *A Place in Public: Women's Rights in Meiji Japan* (Cambridge, MA: Harvard University Asia Center, 2010), chap. 4.

111. Irokawa Daikichi, *The Culture of the Meiji Period,* ed. and trans. Marius B. Jansen (Princeton, NJ: Princeton University Press, 1985), 202; and Yoshitake Oka, "Generational Conflict after the Russo-Japanese War," trans. J. Victor Koschman, in *Conflict in Modern Japanese History: The Neglected Tradition,* ed. Tetsuo Najita and J. Victor Koschman (Princeton, NJ: Princeton University Press, 1982), 209.

Chapter One: Placing Japanese Protestant Churches in Tokyo

1. Takashi Fujitani, *Splendid Monarchy: Power and Pageantry in Imperial Japan* (Berkeley: University of California Press, 1996), chap. 2.

2. Ibid., 37.

3. The first Roman Catholic bishop, Bernard Petitjean, moved the residence of the Apostolic Vicariate of Japan from Yokohama to Nagasaki—his original mission site—in 1866. In 1880, he moved the seat of his new bishopric, the Apostolic Vicariate of Southern Japan, from Osaka to Nagasaki. And between 1890 and 1891, Nagasaki was confirmed as the center of Roman Catholicism in Japan. In addition to continuing as the seat of the southern vicariate, the city became the site of the single seminary in Japan for the most qualified Japanese novitiates and the first national Roman Catholic synod. Cary, *A History of Christianity in Japan,* 1:341, 352, 355.

4. A. Hamish Ion, *The Cross and the Rising Sun,* vol. 2: *The British Protestant Missionary Movement in Japan, Korea, and Taiwan, 1865–1945* (Toronto: Wilfrid Laurier University Press, 1993), 43.

5. William E. Deal, *Handbook to Life in Medieval and Early Modern Japan* (New York: Oxford University Press, 2006), 329–332. On the Tōkaido that carried so many of these new arrivals, see Stephen Addiss and Marilyn Stokstad, eds., *Tōkaidō, on the Road: Pilgrimage, Travel, and Culture* (Lawrence: University of Kansas Press, 1982).

6. Gilbert Rozman, "Edo's Importance in the Changing Tokugawa Society," *Journal of Japanese Studies* 1, no. 1 (Autumn 1974): 93–94.

7. Henry D. Smith II, "The Edo-Tokyo Transition: In Search of Common Ground," in *Japan in Transition from Tokugawa to Meiji,* ed. Marius Jansen and Gilbert Rozman (Princeton, NJ: Princeton University Press, 1986), 347, 350.

8. Henry D. Smith, "Tokyo as an Idea," 53–55.

9. Fujimori Terunobu, *Kindai Nihon no yōfū kenchiku: Kaika hen* [Western architecture of modern Japan: Civilization volume] (Tokyo: Chikuma shobō, 2017), 41.

10. On the heavy flow of newcomers into Meiji-era Tokyo, see Hiroshi Ohbuchi, "Demographic Transition in the Process of Japanese Industrialization," in *Japanese Industrialization and Its Social Consequences,* ed. Hugh T. Patrick (Berkeley: University of California Press, 1976), 329–362.

11. Ambaras, "Social Knowledge, Cultural Capital," 1.

12. Gluck, *Japan's Modern Myths,* 159.

13. Maxey, *The "Greatest Problem,"* 40.

14. Hardacre, "Creating State Shinto," 42; Maxey, *The "Greatest Problem,"* 40.

15. Hardacre, "Creating State Shinto," 47; Helen Hardacre, *Shinto: A History* (New York: Oxford University Press, 2017), 376–377.

16. Hardacre, *Shinto,* 377.

17. Nobutaka Inoue and Mark Teeuwen, "The Formation of Sect Shinto in Modernizing Japan," *Japanese Journal of Religious Studies* 29, nos. 3–4 (Fall 2002): 422.

18. Hardacre, *Shinto: A History,* 383.

19. Hans Martin Krämer, *Shimaji Mokurai and the Reconception of Religion and the Secular in Modern Japan* (Honolulu: University of Hawaiʻi Press, 2015), 14.

20. Maxey, *The "Greatest Problem,"* chap. 3.

21. Sōda Ichirō, "Tokyo no Tenrikyō" [Tokyo's Tenrikyō], *Glocal Tenri* (March 2015): 3.

22. Ibid.

23. Roy Tetsuo Forbes, "Schism, Orthodoxy and Heresy in the History of Tenrikyo: Three Case Studies" (MA thesis, University of Hawaiʻi Manoa, 2005), 79–80.

24. Ibid., 77.

25. Hardacre, "Creating State Shinto," 47.

26. Maxey, *The "Greatest Problem,"* 136.

27. The successful battle by the Ōtani leadership of Higashi Honganji to move the new and increasingly popular Shinshū University from Tokyo in 1911 to Kyoto offered evidence of the continued prioritization of this base. It later became Ōtani University. See Jeff Schroeder, "After Kiyozawa: A Study of Shin Buddhist Modernization, 1890–1956" (PhD diss., Duke University, 2015), 200.

28. Forbes, "Schism, Orthodoxy and Heresy," 77–80.

29. Ion, *The Cross and Rising Sun,* 2:43.

30. Yuasa Yōzō, *Nobiyuku kyōkai* [The growing church] (Tokyo: Kyōbunkan, 1941), 9–15.

31. Ibid.

32. *Dai Nihon Teikoku Naimusho tōkei hōkoku* [Statistical report of the Home Ministry of the Great Empire of Japan], vol. 16 (Tokyo: Naimushō, 1900), 343–344.

33. Ibid.

34. Ibid. The recent work of geographer Oda Masayasu also highlights the continued predominance of Tokyo and the growth of Protestant church numbers in the Kansai region from 1899 to 1939. Oda Masayasu, "Senzen-ki ni okeru Nihon no Kirisutokyō bunpo to chiikikubun" [Distribution of Christianity and the division of the region in prewar Japan], *Komazawa chiri,* no. 53 (2017): 27.

35. *Dai Nihon Teikoku Naimusho tōkei hōkoku* 28 (1912): 287.

36. Oda, "Senzen-ki ni okeru Nihon no Kirisutokyō bunpo to chiikikubun," 27.

37. See, for instance, Scheiner, *Christian Converts and Social Protest,* 28, 34.

38. Seidensticker, *Low City, High City,* 36–37.

39. Ion, *American Missionaries, Christian Oyatoi,* chap. 7.

40. Robert A. Rosenstone, *Mirror in the Shrine: American Encounters with Meiji Japan* (Cambridge, MA: Harvard University Press, 1988), 130.

41. Amamiya Eiichi, *Wakaki Uemura Masahisa* [Young Uemura Masahisa] (Tokyo: Shinkyō shuppan, 2007), 170.

42. Oshikawa Masayoshi traveled to Sendai in Miyagi Prefecture. Yamamoto Hideteru went to minister in distant Kōchi, and Miura Tooru and Tomekawa Ichiro both went on to found churches in Kagoshima and other areas in Kyushu. See Saba Wataru, *Uemura Masahisa to sono jidai* [Uemura Masahisa and his times], vol. 3 (Tokyo: Kyōbunkan, 1941–1942).

43. Motoi, "Doshisha Shingakkan no hensen," 2.

44. Notehelfer, *American Samurai,* chaps. 7–9.

45. Ibuka became primarily an educator. Tamura Naoomi resigned as pastor of his Ginza Independent Church and traveled to the United States, where he attended Auburn Seminary. Emily Anderson, "Tamura Naoomi's 'The Japanese Bride': Christianity, Nationalism, and Family in Meiji Japan," *Japanese Journal of Religious Studies* 34, no. 1 (2007): 209.

46. Saba Wataru, *Uemura Masahisa to sono jidai,* vol. 1 (Tokyo: Kyōbunkan, 1941–1942), 657–659.

47. Amamiya, *Wakaki Uemura Masahisa,* 172.

48. Ibid.

49. Kyōgoku Junichirō, *Uemura Masahisa: Sono hito to shisō* [Uemura Masahisa: The man and his thought] (Tokyo: Shinkyō shuppan, 1966), 33–34.

50. Ibid., 19, 33.

51. Amamiya, *Wakaki Uemura Masahisa,* 134.

52. Uemura Masahisa, "Fukuzawa sensei shi jiji kogoto gūhyō," *Rikugo zasshi* 13 (25 November 1881): 41.

53. Amamiya, *Wakaki Uemura Masahisa,* 133.

54. Yuasa, *Nobiyuku kyōkai,* 25.

55. *Annual Report of the American Board of Commissioners for Foreign Missions,* vol. 101 (Boston: Congregational House, 1911), 173. For a list of postings, see Jerome Davis, "Letter to NG Clark July 21, 1879, Hiyezan," reel 329, American Board of Commissioners for Foreign Missions Archives, 1810–1961 (ABC 1-91), Houghton Library, Harvard University.

56. Cary, *A History of Christianity in Japan,* 2:139.

57. Yuasa, *Nobiyuku kyōkai,* 25.

58. Ibid.

59. Kozaki Hiromichi, *70-nen no kaikō* [Reminiscences of 70 years] (Tokyo: Keiseisha, 1927), 36.

60. Yuasa, *Nobiyuku kyōkai,* 27.

61. Ibid.

62. Ballhatchet, "Confucianism and Christianity in Meiji Japan," 356.

63. Notehelfer, *American Samurai,* 187.

64. Ebina Danjō, *Kirisutokyō gairon mikankō* [Unfinished draft of an introduction to Christianity] (Tokyo: Ebina Ichio, 1937), 62–63.

65. Yuasa, *Nobiyuku kyōkai,* 26.

66. Kozaki, *70-nen,* 37.

67. Ibid.

68. *Shichi ichi zappō,* no. 52 (December 26, 1879): 3. The Gunyōsha was established in 1879 among Dōshisha graduates dedicated to practicing and spreading Christianity. Hara Makoto,

Reinanzaka Kyōkai no shinkō no ishizue [The cornerstone of Reinanzaka Church's faith] (Tokyo: Nihon Kirisutokyōdan Reinanzaka Kyōkai, 2015), 42–45.

69. Yuasa, *Nobiyuku kyōkai*, 26.

70. Kozaki, *70-nen*, 38.

71. Ibid. On the organization see *Meiroku Zasshi: Journal of the Japanese Enlightenment*, trans. William Reynolds Braisted (Cambridge, MA: Harvard University Press, 1976).

72. Kozaki, *70-nen*, 38.

73. Ibid.

74. Ibid.

75. Ibid., 55.

76. Nihon Kumiai Hongō Kirisutokyōkai, *Hongō Kirisutokyōkai sōritsu 50-nen shi* [The fifty-year history of the establishment of Hongō Church] (Tokyo: Nihon Kumiai Hongō Kirisutokyōkai, 1936), 81.

77. Iwai Fumio, *Ebina Danjō* (Tokyo: Nihon Kirisutokyōdan Shuppankyoku, 1973), 108.

78. Ebina Danjō, "Sōritsu jidai no Hongō kyōkai," in Nihon Kumiai Hongō Kirisutokyōkai, *Hongō Kirisutokyōkai sōritsu 50-nen shi*, 81.

79. Nihon Kumiai Hongō Kirisutokyōkai, *Hongō Kirisutokyōkai sōritsu 50-nen shi*, 83.

80. This, not the year 1891 mentioned by Jung-Sun N. Han and others, is the correct date for the founding of Hongō Church. Han, *An Imperial Path to Modernity*, 48.

81. Ibid., 84; Watase Tsunekichi, *Ebina Danjō sensei* [Reverend Ebina Danjō] (Tokyo: Ryūginsha, 1938), 178.

82. Nihon Kumiai Hongō Kirisutokyōkai, *Hongō Kirisutokyōkai sōritsu 50-nen shi*, 84.

83. Matsuoka Hachirō, "Yoshino Sakuzō to Kirisutokyō no eikyō 4" [Yoshino Sakuzō and the influence of Christianity, 4], *Tōyō hōgaku* 37, no. 2 (January 1994): 45.

84. Nihon Kirisutokyō Rekishi Daijiten Henshū Iinkai, ed., *Nihon Kirisutokyō rekishi daijiten* [Historical dictionary of Japanese Christianity] (Tokyo: Kyōbunkan, 1988), 1463. See also Sugii Mutsurō, *Kumamoto bando kenkyū* [Study of the Kumamoto band] (Kyoto: Doshisha Daigaku Jinbun kagaku kenkyūjo, 1965).

85. *Our Day: A Record and Review of Current Reform* 4 (July–December 1889): 392.

86. Yokoi Tokio, "Letter to Rev. J. D. Davis, Rev. D. W. Learned, Rev. M. L. Gordon, Dr. J. C. Berry," Tokyo, December 12, 1888, reel 346, ABC 16.4.1 v. 2. Mission to Japan, 1871–1880, Houghton Library, Harvard University.

87. Ibid.

88. Ibid. These men were the leaders of the Japan Mission of the American Board of Commissioners for Foreign Missions.

89. First Higher School was an elite preparatory high school for students seeking admission to the Imperial University, and First Middle School was the associated middle school.

90. See Nakamura Kennosuke, *Senkyōshi Nikolai to Meiji Nihon* [Missionary Nikolai and Meiji Japan] (Tokyo: Iwanami shoten, 1996); and Ion, *The Cross and the Rising Sun*, 1:100.

91. Shields, *Against Harmony*, 33–34.

92. Sōda, "Tokyo no Tenrikyō," 3.

93. Gluck, *Japan's Modern Myths*, 139; Maxey, *The "Greatest Problem,"* 160; Hardacre, "Creating State Shinto," 51.

94. Shimazono Susumu, "State Shinto in the Lives of the People: The Establishment of Emperor Worship, Modern Nationalism, and Shrine Shinto in Late Meiji," *Japanese Journal of Religious Studies* 36, no. 1 (2009): 109.

95. Ibid., 116.

96. Note that this is the congregation later renamed Fujimichō Church.

97. *Directory of the Living Non-graduates of Yale University: Issue of 1914* (New Haven, CT: Tuttle, Morehouse & Taylor, 1914), 71.

98. *Ebina Danjō shuki* [Note by Ebina Danjō], reproduced in Iwai Fumio, *Ebina Danjō,* 141.

99. Ii Kiyoshi and Fugami Seizō, eds., *Reinanzaka Kyōkai 100-nen shi* (Tokyo: Kirisutokyōdan Reinanzaka Kyōkai, 1979), 156.

100. In the early twentieth century, Kanamori again embraced his Christian convictions and became a prominent evangelist and reformer with the Salvation Army. See Paul Kanamori, *Kanamori's Life-Story Told by Himself: How the Higher Criticism Wrecked a Japanese Christian—and How He Came Back* (Philadelphia: Sunday School Times Co., 1921).

101. Tenrikyo Overseas Mission Department, *A Historical Sketch of Tenrikyo,* translation of *Oyasama Nensai to Tomoni* (Tenri: Tenri Doyusha, 1990), 10.

102. Forbes, "Schism, Orthodoxy and Heresy," 84–91.

103. Ibid., 100–101.

104. Shimazono, "State Shinto in the Lives of the People," 117.

105. Yoshinaga Shin'ichi, "Theosophy and Buddhist Reformers in the Middle of the Meiji Period: An Introduction," *Japanese Religions* 34, no. 2 (2009): 121.

106. Shields, *Against Harmony,* 5; Ōtani Eiichi, "The Movement Called 'New Buddhism' in Meiji Japan," in *Modern Buddhism in Japan,* ed. Hayashi Makoto, Ōtani Eiichi, and Paul L. Swanson (Nagoya: Nanzan, 2014), 72.

107. Shields, *Against Harmony,* chap. 2.

108. See Ōtani, "The Movement Called 'New Buddhism,'" 52–84; and Yoshinaga, "Theosophy and Buddhist Reformers," 122.

109. See Garrett Washington, "Fighting Brick with Brick: Chikazumi Jōkan and Buddhism's Response to the Christian Spatial Menace in Japan," *Cross-Currents: East Asian History and Culture Review E-Journal,* no. 6 (March 2013): 95–120.

110. Kozaki Hiromichi, *The Autobiography of a Japanese Pastor: Reminiscences of Seventy Years,* trans. Kozaki Nariaki (Tokyo: Kyōbunkan, 1933), 152.

111. Ibid., 64–65.

112. Watase, *Ebina Danjō sensei,* 227.

113. Iwai Fumio, *Ebina Danjō,* 140.

114. Watase, *Ebina Danjō sensei,* 230, citing Ebina Danjō, "Kōbe Kyōkai ai kyōdai onchū" [For the beloved brothers and sisters of Kobe Church] (2 May 1897).

115. Ibid.

116. Iwai Fumio, *Ebina Danjō,* 140, citing "Ebina Danjō shuki" [Note from Ebina Danjō].

117. Jinnai Hidenobu, *Tokyo: A Spatial Anthropology,* trans. Kimiko Nishimura (Berkeley: University of California Press, 1995), 86.

118. Ibid., 88.

119. Ibid., 83.

120. Ibid., 82.

121. For an introduction to this concept, see Maki Fumihiko, *Miegakure suru no toshi: Edo kara Tokyo e* [The seen and unseen city: From Edo to Tokyo] (Tokyo: Kagoshima Shuppankai, 1980).

122. John Nelson, "Social Memory as Ritual Practice: Commemorating Spirits of the Military Dead at Yasukuni Shinto Shrine," *Journal of Asian Studies* 62, no. 2 (May 2003): 447. See also Tsubouchi Yuzō, *Yasukuni* (Tokyo: Shinchōsha, 1999), 42, 49–50.

123. An 1878 map already shows this lane, complete with the iconic cedar trees. See Yasuda Torao, *15 ku 6 gun Tokyo kubun zenzu* [Complete map of the 15 wards and 6 prefectures] (Tokyo: Tsunajima Kamekichi, 1878).

124. Nelson, "Social Memory as Ritual Practice," 447.

125. See André Sorensen, *The Making of Urban Japan: Cities and Planning from Edo to the Twenty-First Century* (London: Routledge, 2002), chap. 2; and Carola Hein, "Shaping Tokyo: Land Development and Planning Practice in the Early Modern Japanese Metropolis," *Journal of Urban History* 36, no. 4 (2010): 447–484.

126. Nelson, "Social Memory as Ritual Practice," 447.

127. Henry D. Smith, "The Edo-Tokyo Transition," 370–371.

128. Ogino Ginko graduated in 1879, for instance.

129. See *Tōkyō joshi kōtō shihan gakkō* [Tokyo Women's Higher Normal School] (Tokyo: Daiichi Shobō, 1981); and Ann M. Harrington, "Women and Higher Education in the Japanese Empire (1895–1945)," *Journal of Asian History* 21, no. 2 (1987): 169–186.

130. Saba, *Uemura Masahisa to sono jidai,* 3:48. (This term refers to students who received lodging in exchange for housework.)

131. *Acts and Proceedings of the General Synod of the Reformed Church in America* (New York: Board of Publication of the Reformed Church, 1884), 89.

132. Doron Cohen, *The Japanese Translations of the Hebrew Bible: History, Inventory and Analysis* (Leiden: Brill, 2013), 53. See also Akiyama Shigeo, *Meiji jinbutsu shūi monogatari: Kirisutokyō no ichi keifu* [A collection of tales of Meiji figures: A genealogy of Christianity] (Tokyo: Kirisutokyō shuppan, 1982), 243–275.

133. Addison Soltau, "Uemura Masahisa (1857–1925): First Generation Pastor, Christian Leader and Instinctive Proponent of Indigenized Christianity in Japan 1982" (DD diss., Concordia Seminary, 1982), 75; Aoyoshi Katsuhisa, *Uemura Masahisa den* [The biography of Uemura Masahisa] (Tokyo: Kyōbunkan, 1935), 60–61, 129; *Fifty-Second Annual Report of the Board of Foreign Missions of the Reformed Church in America and Twenty-Seventh of Separate Action with the Treasurer's Tabular and Summary Report of Receipts, for the Year Ending April 30th, 1884* (New York: Board of Foreign Missions Press, 1884), 89.

134. Tōya Tetsushi, ed., *Fujimichō 80-nen shi* (Tokyo: Kirisutokyōdan Fujimichō Kyōkai, 1978), 6; Saba, *Uemura Masahisa to sono jidai,* 3:85.

135. Jinnai, *Tokyo,* 40.

136. Ibid., 45.

137. Nihon rekishi gakkai, ed., *Meiji isshin shinjinmei jiten* [Meiji Restoration new biographical dictionary] (Tokyo: Yoshikawa kyōbunkan, 1981), 815; Gluck, *Japan's Modern Myths,* 80. Hijikata was a member of the Privy Council. See Donald Keene, *Emperor Meiji and His World, 1852–1912* (New York: Columbia University Press, 2002), 482. The placement information comes from Kanazawa Ryōta, *Shinsen Tokyo zenzu* [Newly compiled complete map of Tokyo] (Tokyo: Okura Yasugoro, 1892).

138. Susan Burns, "Bodies and Borders: Syphilis, Prostitution, and the Nation in Japan, 1860–1890," *US-Japan Women's Journal English Supplement* 15 (1998): 17. Iwasa also helped design the new Japanese medical system in 1869. Shizu Sakai, "History of Medical Care at Inpatient Facilities in Japan," *Journal of the Medical Association of Japan* 54, no. 6 (November/

December 2011): 354. In 1874 Iwasa was chief physician at the newly created, if short-lived, Tokyo Prefectural Hospital.

139. Kanazawa, *Shinsen Tokyo zenzu.*

140. Andō Rikinosuke, *Tokyo-shi zenzu* [Complete map of Tokyo City] (Tokyo: Andō Rikinosuke, 1905).

141. Margaret Mehl, *Private Academies of Chinese Learning in Meiji Japan: The Decline and Transformation of the Kangaku juku* (Copenhagen: Nordic Institute of Asian Studies, 2003), 71–72.

142. *Historical Sketches of the Missions under the Care of the Board of Foreign Missions of the Presbyterian Church* (Philadelphia: Woman's Foreign Missionary Society of the Presbyterian Church, 1891), 112. Note that the school later moved to Kami Ni-banchō, still within blocks of Ichibanchō Church. See Andō, *Tokyo-shi zenzu.* The school was also renamed Joshi Gakuin in 1893 after a merger with Graham Seminary. At the turn of the century, the school had some two hundred students. Edward Marx, *Leonie Gilmour: When East Weds West* (Lexington, KY: Botchan Books, 2013), 195. See Andō, *Tokyo-shi zenzu.*

143. Fujita Yoshimi, "'Meiji jogakkō wo oboegaki: Meiji-ki Roman-shugi to Kirisutokyō" [Remembering Meiji Girls' School: Romanticism and Christianity], *Risshō Daigaku bungakubu ronsō* 71 (1981): 27.

144. Rumi Yasutake, *Transnational Women's Activism: The United States, Japan, and Japanese Immigrant Communities in California, 1859–1920* (New York: New York University Press, 2004), 43.

145. Copeland, *Lost Leaves,* 250. See also Yasutake, *Transnational Women's Activism,* 43.

146. Yoshinori Fujii, *Iwamoto Yoshiharu: Seigi to ai ni ikite* [Iwamoto Yoshiharu: Living by righteousness and love] (Tokyo: Asahi shuppansha, 2005).

147. Saba, *Uemura Masahisa to sono jidai,* 3:84.

148. Tōya, *Fujimichō 80-nen shi,* 7.

149. Fujimichō Kyōkai 100-nen Shiryō Iinkai, ed., *Fujimichō Kyōkai 100-nen shi: Bunshū, nenpyō* [The 100-year history of Fujimichō Church: anthology, chronology] (Tokyo: Nihon Kirisutokyōdan, 1987), 5. This is a reproduction of Uemura Masahisa, "Fujimichō kyōkai sōritsu 30 nen" [Fujimichō Church at 30 years] (n.p., 1917).

150. Cary, *A History of Christianity in Japan,* 2:142.

151. Hardacre, "Creating State Shinto," 44.

152. The campaign was carried out by the new Meiji government's Department of Divinity or Rites *(jingikan),* which was demoted to the Ministry of Divinity (Jingishō) in 1871 and again to an office within the Ministry of Education in 1872. See Hardacre, *Shintō and the State,* 36; Ketelaar, *Of Heretics and Martyrs,* 95–96.

153. See Paramore, *Ideology and Christianity in Japan,* chap. 6.

154. Hardacre, "Creating State Shinto," 42. See also Grapard, "Japan's Ignored Cultural Revolution"; and Ketelaar, *Of Heretics and Martyrs,* chap. 2.

155. Notto Thelle, *Buddhism and Christianity in Japan: From Conflict to Dialogue, 1854–1899* (Honolulu: University of Hawai'i Press, 1987), 91.

156. Ibid., 93.

157. On the foundation of Shin-sakana-chō Church, see Yuasa, *Nobiyuku kyōkai,* 27–32.

158. Ii and Fugami, *Reinanzaka Kyōkai 100-nen shi,* 53–54. The Gakunōsha was both an important center for agricultural learning and a hub for Christian students and instructors including Uchimura Kanzō (1861–1930) in Tokyo during the mid-Meiji period. For more on

the school and its founder, see Takasaki Sōji, *Tsuda Sen hyōden: Mō hitotsu no kindaika wo mezashita hito* [Critical biography of Tsuda Sen: Another person who sought modernization] (Urayasu, Japan: Sōfūkan, 2008); and Miyakoda Toyosaburō, *Tsuda Sen: Meiji no Kirisutosha* [Tsuda Sen: Meiji Christian] (Tokyo: Miyakoda Toyosaburō, 1972).

159. Tristan R. Grunow, "Paving Power: Western Urban Planning and Imperial Space from the Streets of Meiji Tokyo to Colonial Seoul," *Journal of Urban History* 42, no. 3 (May 2016): 507.

160. Donald Ritchie, *Tokyo: A View of the City* (London: Reaktion Books, 1999), 126.

161. See Nihon Kirisutokyōdan Ginza Kyōkai, *Ginza Kyōkai 90-nen shi* [The 90-year history of Ginza Church] (Tokyo: Nihon Kirisutokyōdan Ginza Kyōkai, 1981); and Tamura Naoomi, *Shinkō 50-nen shi* [Fifty years of faith] (1924; repr., Tokyo: Nihon Tosho Sentā, 2003).

162. For more on Tsukiji College, see E. Rothesay Miller, *Sketch of the North Japan Mission* (New York: Board of Foreign Missions, Reformed Church of America, 1901), 47. On Rokuban Girls' School, see Ion, *American Missionaries, Christian Oyatoi,* 198. On Kaigan Girls' School, see Elizabeth Eder, *Constructing Opportunity: American Women Educators in Early Meiji Japan* (London: Lexington Books, 2003), 104.

163. Ii and Fugami, *Reinanzaka Kyōkai 100-nen shi,* 55.

164. Ii and Fugami, *Reinanzaka Kyōkai 100-nen shi,* 54. See also Yuasa, *Nobiyuku kyōkai,* 46–49.

165. Kozaki, *Autobiography of a Japanese Pastor,* 77.

166. Ii and Fugami, *Reinanzaka Kyōkai 100-nen shi,* 59.

167. Yuasa, *Nobiyuku kyōkai,* 80.

168. Kozaki, *Autobiography of a Japanese Pastor,* 281.

169. On Ikeda Kensai, see Ikeda bunsho kenkyūkai, ed., *Tōdai igakubu shodai sōri Ikeda Kensai: Ikeda bunsho no kenkyū* [First president of Tokyo University medical department: A study of Ikeda's writings] (Tokyo: Shibunkaku shuppan, 2006); on Tanaka Fujimaro, see Nishii Toyosaku, *Shishaku Tanaka Fujimaro Den* [Biography of Viscount Fujimaro Tanaka] (Tokyo: Kōsaijuku, 1934).

170. On Ōki Takatō, see Henry D. Smith, "The Edo-Tokyo Transition," 355–356. For more on the Genrōin, the senate of Japan before the creation of the Diet, see Junji Banno, *The Establishment of the Japanese Constitutional System,* trans. J. A. A. Stockwin (London: Routledge, 1992).

171. Ōkura zaibatsu kenkyū, ed., *Ōkura zaibatsu no kenkyū* [Study of Ōkura Industrial Group] (Tokyo: Chikafuji shuppansha, 1982).

172. On Kuroda Kiyotaka see Keene, *Emperor Meiji and His World,* 415.

173. See Kenneth Colegrove, "The Japanese Privy Council," *American Political Science Review* 25, no. 4 (November 1931): 881–905.

174. Itō Kiyoshi, *Banchō Kyōkai 100-nen shi* (Tokyo: Nihon Kirisutokyōdan Banchō Kyōkai, 1986), 25.

175. He lived in Kaminibanchō. See *Yearbook of the Young Men's Christian Associations of North America* (New York: YMCA International Committee, 1899), 149.

176. K. R. Iseki, ed., *Who's Who Hakushi in Great Japan,* vol. 3 (Tokyo: Hattensha, 1926), 21–22.

177. Okabe Nagamoto, another Reinanzaka member who established the new congregation, who left to become vice minister of the Japanese legation in London between 1886 and 1889. Ion, *American Missionaries, Christian Oyatoi,* 134.

178. See Tomita Hiroyuki and Kami Shōichirō, eds., *Nihon Kirisuto kyōjidō bungaku zenshū* [Complete works of Christian juvenile literature] (Tokyo: Kyōbunkan, 1984), 119.

179. See Ebina's recollections in Nihon Kumiai Hongō Kirisutokyōkai, *Hongō Kirisutokyōkai sōritsu 50-nen shi*, 82.

180. Ibid., 85.

181. Yumichō Hongō Kyōkai, *Yumichō Hongō Kyōkai 100-nen shi*, 23.

182. Harper Coates, "A Cry for Help," *Japan Weekly Mail*, 2 April 1898, 348.

183. Nihon Kumiai Hongō Kirisutokyōkai, *Hongō Kirisutokyōkai sōritsu 50-nen shi*, 91–92.

184. Takahashi Mikio, *Hongōkan no hanseiki* [The half-century of the Hongōkan] (Tokyo: Takahashi Mikio, 2007), 3.

185. Karasawa Buyasu, *Saisei gakusha haikō no rekishi* [History of the closing of the Saisei Gakusha], *Nihon Ishigaku zasshi* 40, no. 3 (September 1994): 293–304.

186. See Ebina's recollections in Nihon Kumiai Hongō Kirisutokyōkai, *Hongō Kirisutokyōkai sōritsu 50-nen shi*, 83.

187. Ebina Danjō, "Sōgyō jidai no Hongō Kyōkai" [The founding days of Hongō Church], in Nihon Kumiai Hongō Kirisutokyōkai, *Hongō Kirisutokyōkai sōritsu 50-nen shi*, 83.

188. Shiba Ryōtarō, *Hongō kaiwai* (Tokyo: Asahi Shimbunsha, 2005), 22–23.

189. Ion, *The Cross and the Rising Sun*, 1:100.

190. On Chikazumi and these sites, see Washington, "Fighting Brick with Brick."

191. Maxey, *The "Greatest Problem,"* 3.

192. Daniel Clarence Holtom, "The Political Philosophy of Modern Shintō: A Study of the State Religion of Japan" (PhD diss., University of Chicago, 1922), 280.

193. Nelson, "Social Memory as Ritual Practice," 450.

194. Kaigun Kyōiku Honbu, *Kaigun dokuhon* [Navy manual] (Tokyo: Kaigun Kyōiku Honbu, 1905), 39–40.

195. Cyril Powles, "Yasukuni Jinja Hōan: Religion and Politics in Contemporary Japan," *Pacific Affairs* 49, no. 3 (Autumn 1976): 497.

196. Minor L. Rogers and Ann T. Rogers, "The Honganji: Guardian of the State (1868–1945)," *Japanese Journal of Religious Studies* 17, no. 1 (March 1990): 7–9.

Chapter Two: Building the Japanese Protestant Church in Tokyo

1. Nelson, "Social Memory as Ritual Practice."

2. For photos of Gorin Kyōkaidō, see Misawa Hiroaki, *Ooinaru isan: Nagasaki no kyōkai* [A great heritage: The churches of Nagasaki] (Tokyo: Chi Shobō, 2000). On Ōno Kyōkaidō see "Shinshitei no bunkazai" [Newly designated cultural assets], *Gekkan Bunkazai* [Cultural assets monthly], no. 538 (July 2008): 12–41. Both churches also figure in Nagasaki Bunkensha, eds., *Nagasaki Yūgaku 2: Nagasaki/Amakusa no kyōkai to junreichi kanzen gaido* [Nagasaki Study-Travel 2: Complete Guide to the Churches and Pilgrimage Sites of Nagasaki-Amakusa] (Nagasaki: Nagasaki Bunkensha, 2005).

3. On Oura Church in particular, see Dallas Finn, *Meiji Revisited: The Sites of Victorian Japan* (New York: Weatherhill, 1995), 12–13.

4. See Nihon Kirisuto Shin Sakae Kyōkai 60-nen shi Iinkai, ed., *Nippon Kirisuto Shin Sakae Kyokai 60-nen shi* [Sixty-year history of the Shin Sakae Church] (Tokyo: Nihon Kirisuto Shin Sakae Kyokai, 1933).

5. Yuasa, *Nobiyuku kyōkai,* 10–12.

6. Cary, *A History of Christianity in Japan,* 1:365–366.

7. *Christian Movement in Japan* 2 (1904): 197.

8. Cary, *A History of Christianity in Japan,* 1:419.

9. Ibid., 1:422. See also statistics in "The Christian Movement in Japan," no. 6, Tokyo 1908.

10. Gülsüm Baydar, "The Cultural Burden of Architecture," *Journal of Architectural Education* 57, no. 4 (May 2004): 21.

11. Homi Bhabha, *The Location of Culture* (London: Routledge, 1994), 50.

12. *American Board of Commissioners for Foreign Missions Annual Report* 96, June 1906, 168.

13. Dohi Akio, *Nihon Purotesutanto kyōkai no seiritsu to tenkai* [The establishment and development of the Japanese Protestant Church] (Tokyo: Nihon Kirisutokyōdan shuppan kyoku, 1975), 109–110. See also Ion, *American Missionaries, Christian Oyatoi,* 268; and Ernest W. Clement, *A Short History of Japan* (Chicago: University of Chicago Press, 1915), 117.

14. See Dohi, *Nihon Purotesutanto kyōkai no seiritsu,* 110.

15. Jon Thares Davidann, "The American YMCA in Meiji Japan: God's World Gone Awry," *Journal of World History* 6, no. 1 (Spring 1995): 124.

16. Jennings, *Theology in Japan,* 93.

17. "Missions in Japan, 1905," in *Presbyterian Board of Foreign Missions Relating to Japan and Korea,* 1900–1914 (Cleveland, 1917), 207–208. The number of churches in 1903 was seventy-five (ibid., 213).

18. Charlotte B. Deforest, *Evolution of a Missionary* (New York: Fleming H. Revell, 1914), 65.

19. *American Board of Commissioners for Foreign Missions Annual Report* 96, June 1906, 168 (my emphasis).

20. See Pettee, *A Chapter of Mission History in Modern Japan,* 68. These churches were distinct from the American Board mission-sponsored churches and the use of the name "Kumiai" was made conditional on Japanese-only funding in 1906. *American Board of Commissioners for Foreign Missions Annual Report* 96 (June 1906): 168.

21. E. Rothesay Miller, *Sketch of the North Japan Mission,* 24.

22. Ibid.

23. Wilbert R. Shenk, "Rufus Anderson and Henry Venn: A Special Relationship?," *International Bulletin of Missionary Research* 5, no. 4 (October 1981): 168–172.

24. William L. Sachs, "'Self-Support': The Episcopal Mission and Nationalism in Japan," *Church History* 58, no. 4 (December 1989): 497, citing McKim to John Wood, 5 September 1902, JR, Box 43.

25. Proceedings of the General Conference of Protestant Missionaries in Japan (Tokyo, 1901), 52.

26. Sachs, "'Self-Support,'" 489, 499.

27. Ion, *The Cross and the Rising Sun,* 2:128.

28. Dohi, *Nihon Purotesutanto kyōkai no seiritsu,* 110–111.

29. On the functional and theological considerations of church architecture, see Keith L. Sprunger, "Church Architecture and Worship in a Dutch Context," *Church History* 66, no. 1 (March 1997): 36–53; and Gwen W. Steege, "'The 'Book of Plans' and the Early Romanesque

Revival in the United States: A Study in Architectural Patronage," *Journal of the Society of Architectural Historians* 46, no. 3 (September 1987): 215–227.

30. Sand, *House and Home in Modern Japan,* 13.

31. Ibid., 267–268.

32. Shunichi Watanabe, "Metropolitanism as a Way of Life: The Case of Tokyo, 1868–1930," in *Metropolis 1890–1940,* ed. Anthony Sutcliffe (London: Mansell, 1984), 409–418.

33. Sorensen, *The Making of Urban Japan,* 70–71.

34. Ibid., 66.

35. Ibid., 68–69.

36. Ibid., 70.

37. Shunichi Watanabe, "Metropolitanism as a Way of Life," 418.

38. Sand, *House and Home in Modern Japan,* 271.

39. Hein, "Shaping Tokyo," 461. In fact, Hein interestingly highlights that the introduction of broader thoroughfares on top of the old Edo grid reduced plot size and forced buildings upward. Ibid., 457. On the persistence of the Edo layout in modern Tokyo, see Jinnai, *Tokyo.*

40. Ketelaar, *Of Heretics and Martyrs,* chap. 2. This process began as early as 1860 in some areas.

41. Ibid.

42. John Breen, "Ideologues, Bureaucrats, and Priests: On 'Shinto' and 'Buddhism' in Early Meiji Japan," in *Shinto in History: Ways of the Kami,* ed. John Breen and Mark Teeuwen (Honolulu: University of Hawai'i Press, 2000), 230.

43. Cherie Wendelken, "The Tectonics of Japanese Style: Architect and Carpenter in the Late Meiji Period," *Art Journal* 55, no. 3 (Fall 1996): 34. The measure, largely formulated by architect and scholar Itō Chūta (1867–1954), was clearly meant to protect and preserve Japan's cultural heritage, and yet it also took authority away from Japanese traditional religious spaces in very concrete ways.

44. Nelson, "Social Memory as Ritual Practice," 450.

45. Thal, *Rearranging the Landscape of the Gods,* 278–285.

46. Wilbur Fridell, "A Fresh Look at State Shinto," *Journal of the American Academy of Religion* 44, no. 3 (1976): 548.

47. On *Jinja gappei,* see Irokawa, *The Culture of the Meiji Period,* 286; and Wilbur Fridell, *Japanese Shrine Mergers, 1906–1912* (Tokyo: Sophia University Press, 1973).

48. Hardacre, *Shinto: A History,* 416. On the role of local shrines in the "Thrift and Diligence Campaign" of 1908, see Fridell, *Japanese Shrine Mergers,* 46.

49. Fridell, *Japanese Shrine Mergers,* 46.

50. Hardacre, *Shinto: A History,* 417. On the melancholy and feelings of helplessness of villagers at the loss of local shrines, see Fridell, *Japanese Shrine Mergers,* 82.

51. Hardacre, *Shinto: A History,* 412.

52. Ibid., 416.

53. On the Home Ministry's restrictive conditions qualifying *minsha* to receive ceremonial offerings, see Fridell, *Japanese Shrine Mergers,* 13.

54. Treaty of Amity and Commerce between the United States and Japan, 1858, Article 8.

55. The Great Kantō Earthquake in 1923 and the firebombing of Tokyo in 1945 destroyed many of the documents that could have shed light on transactional details of building and lot purchases for these pastors' churches.

56. Ion, *American Missionaries, Christian Oyatai,* 48. Presbyterian missionary David Thompson (1835–1915) in fact complained of the protection that he and his church received from English, French, and German soldiers. As the Hibiya Riots made clear, however, even this status did not make churches immune to all attacks. Emily Anderson, *Christianity and Imperialism,* 90–91.

57. Kozaki, *Autobiography of a Japanese Pastor,* 53–54.

58. Yuasa, *Nobiyuku kyōkai,* 46–49.

59. *Kirisutokyō shimbun,* no. 140 (1 April 1886): 8.

60. Ii and Fugami, *Reinanzaka Kyōkai 100-nen shi,* 106, paraphrasing *Reinanzaka Kyōkai kiroku* [Record of Reinanzaka Church].

61. Ii and Fugami, *Reinanzaka Kyōkai 100-nen shi,* 106–107.

62. American Board of Commissioners for Foreign Missions, *Annual Report of the American Board for Commissioners of Foreign Missions* (Boston: Board Congregation House, 1891), xxiv. See also "Jerome Davis to Rev. N. G. Clark Kioto June 16, 1879," ABC 16.4.1 v. 2, Mission to Japan, 1871–1880, Reel 329, American Board of Commissioners for Foreign Missions Archives, 1810–1961 (ABC 1-91), Houghton Library, Harvard University.

63. Ii and Fugami, *Reinanzaka Kyōkai 100-nen shi,* 106–107. This might have been American Presbyterian missionary J. P. Porter, who worked in Kanagawa and was responsible for helping found Muromachi Church in Kyoto.

64. Yuasa, *Nobiyuku kyōkai,* 83.

65. Ii and Fugami, *Reinanzaka Kyōkai 100-nen shi,* 106.

66. Morris Low, "Promoting Scientific and Technological Change in Tokyo, 1870–1930: Museums, Industrial Exhibitions, and the City," in *Urban Modernity: Cultural Innovation in the Second Industrial Revolution,* ed. Miriam Levin, Sophie Forgan, Martina Hessler, Robert H. Kargon, and Morris Low (Cambridge, MA: MIT Press, 210), 224. Although this style is also referred to as pseudo-Western *(giyōfū)* architecture, the concept of hybridity and compromise is more accurate than that of failed imitation in describing most of these buildings in the context of the current book.

67. Heino Engel, *Measure and Construction of the Japanese House* (Tokyo: Charles Tuttle, 1985), 88.

68. See Kiryū-shi kyōiku iinkai, *Kiryū Meijikan jūyōbunkazai kyū-Gunma-ken eiseijo* [Kiryū Meijikan: Important cultural property, the Old Gunma Prefecture Public Health Bureau] (Kiryū: Kiryū-shi kyōiku iinkai, 1986).

69. Tōya, *Fujimichō 80-nen shi,* 34–35.

70. Saba Wataru, *Uemura Masahisa to sono jidai,* vol. 3 (Tokyo: Kyōbunkan, 1941–1942), 83.

71. Uemura Masahisa, "A Brief Autobiography of Uemura Masahisa," in Aoyoshi Katsuhisa, *Uemura Masahisa den* [The biography of Uemura Masahisa] (Tokyo: Kyōbunkan, 1935), 508.

72. Rev. D. C. Greene, DD, "Church News from Tokyo," *Christian Union* (2 April 1892): 654.

73. Ibid.

74. Itō Kiyoshi, *Banchō Kyōkai 100-nen shi,* 38.

75. Ibid.

76. Greene, "Church News from Tokyo," 654.

77. Yumichō Hongō Kyōkai, *Yumichō Hongō Kyōkai 100-nen shi,* 22.

78. Ebina Danjō, "Sōritsu jidai no Hongō kyōkai," in Nihon Kumiai Hongō Kirisutokyōkai, *Hongō Kirisutokyōkai sōritsu 50-nen shi*, 85.

79. Ibid., 23.

80. *Kirisutokyō shimbun*, no. 304 (22 May 1889): 11.

81. *Hongō Kirisutokyō Kaidō (Takekawa-chō Kaidō)* [Hongō Christian Church (The Takekawa-neighborhood Church)] (Tokyo: Shūeisha, 1891).

82. See, for instance, Dōshisha Sōritsu 100-shūnen Kinen Shashinshū Henshū Iinkai, ed., *Dōshisha: Sono 100 nen no ayumi* [Doshisha: Its 100-year path] (Kyoto: Dōshisha, 1975).

83. Yumichō Hongō Kyōkai, *Yumichō Hongō Kyōkai 100-nen shi*, 25. For a recent biography of Tatsuno, see Azama Hideki, *Tōkyō-eki no kenchiku-ka Tatsuno Kingo den* [Biography of the architect of Tokyo Station, Tatsuno Kingo] (Tokyo: Kōdansha, 2009).

84. Sand, *House and Home in Modern Japan*, 112. See also Jonathan Reynolds, "Teaching Architectural History in Japan: Building a Context for Contemporary Practice," *Journal of the Society of Architectural Historians* 61, no. 4 (December 2002): 531; and Christine Manzano Visita, "Japanese Cultural Transition: Meiji Architecture and the Effect of Cross-Cultural Exchange with the West," *The Forum: Cal Poly's Journal of History* 1, no. 1 (2009): 34.

85. See Watanabe Toshio, "Josiah Conder's Rokumeikan: Architecture and National Representation in Meiji Japan," *Art Journal* 55, no. 3 (Fall 1996): 21–27.

86. See *Hongō Kirisuto kyōkaidō*. For more on Ishii, see Muramatsu Teijirō, *Nihon kindai kenchiku shi no-to: Saiyō kan wo tateta hitobito* [Notes on the history of modern Japanese architecture: The people who built Western buildings] (Tokyo: Sekai Shoin, 1965).

87. Alice Y. Tseng, "Styling Japan: The Case of Josiah Condor and the Museum at Ueno, Tokyo," *The Journal of the Society of Architectural Historians* 63, no. 4 (December 2004): 481.

88. On these architectural styles, see Megan Aldrich, *Gothic Revival* (London: Phaidon, 1994); Phoebe B. Stanton, *The Gothic Revival and American Church Architecture: An Episode in Taste, 1840–1856* (Baltimore: Johns Hopkins University Press, 1968); and Marcus Whiffen, *American Architecture since 1780: A Guide to the Styles* (Cambridge, MA: MIT Press, 1992).

89. Yumichō Hongō Kyōkai, *Yumichō Hongō Kyōkai 100-nen shi*, 25. This rough estimate is based on Daniel C. Greene's assertion that one yen was equivalent to three-quarters of a US dollar in 1892. See Greene, "Church News from Tokyo," 654.

90. Yumichō Hongō Kyōkai, *Yumichō Hongō Kyōkai 100-nen shi*, 60. This devasting fire occurred on 23 March 1898. See "Hongō no taika" [Hongō's Great Fire], in *Tokyo no shōbō 100 nen no ayumi—Meiji gōki* [One hundred years of Tokyo firefighting—the late Meiji period] (Tokyo: Tokyo Shōbōchō, 1980), 89–90.

91. The 1901 Ikizaka building would in turn be leveled by the Great Kantō Earthquake of 1923. In the aftermath of that disaster, Hongō Church member and architect Nakamura Mamoru (1890–1933) designed a new, impressive building that is still in use today.

92. *Shinjin* 2, no. 3 (1 October 1901): 42.

93. Mimatsu Shunpei, *Uemura sensei no omoide* [Recollections of Dr. Uemura] (Tokyo: Arupasha, 1935), 94, 98.

94. See Saba, *Uemura Masahisa to sono jidai*, 3:153. See also *Fukuin shimpō*, no. 564 (19 April 1906): 12.

95. *Japan Daily Mail*, 28 April 1906, 436.

96. Mimatsu, *Uemura sensei no omoide*, 98–99. The author, a disciple of Uemura, refers to this family only as "Mr. Y" and "Mrs. Y."

97. Ibid., 103.

98. Soltau, "Uemura Masahisa," 76.

99. Kozaki, *Autobiography of a Japanese Pastor,* 268.

100. *Reinanzaka kyōhō,* 30 August 1908, 1–2.

101. Ibid.

102. On C. H. Spurgeon, see W. Y. Fullerton. *Charles Haddon Spurgeon: A Biography* (New York: Hodder and Stoughton, 1919), chap. 7.

103. Kozaki, *Autobiography of a Japanese Pastor,* 390.

104. Ii and Fugami, *Reinanzaka Kyōkai 100-nen shi,* 231, citing "Arata-na dekita shi-nai saikō tō [The capital's newly completed, tallest tower]," *Tokyo Yūkan shimbun,* May 25, 1917.

105. Ryan K. Smith, "The Cross: Church Symbol and Contest in Nineteenth-Century America," *Church History* 70, no. 4 (December 2001): 713.

106. Ii and Fugami, *Reinanzaka Kyōkai 100-nen shi,* 235.

107. On Czech glassware, see Andy McConnell, *Miller's 20th-Century Glass* (London: Miller's Buying Guides, 2006). On Moser Glass, see Gary Baldwin, *Moser Glass: The Klabin Collection* (New York: Healing Wisdom Publications, 2006), chap. 1.

108. Kozaki, *Autobiography of a Japanese Pastor,* 268.

109. Ii and Fugami, *Reinanzaka Kyōkai 100-nen shi,* 230.

110. Yuasa, *Nobiyuku kyōkai,* 222. It is not clear whether Kozaki is referring to the renowned chemist Charles James (1880–1928), of the University of New Hampshire, who could have reasonably known Nakaseko or had acquaintances in common with Yale alumni Nakaseko, or someone else.

111. Ii and Fugami, *Reinanzaka Kyōkai 100-nen shi,* 230.

112. Nelson, "Social Memory as Ritual Practice," 450.

113. Yumichō Hongō Kyōkai, *Yumichō Hongō Kyōkai 100-nen shi,* 798.

114. Ibid., 61.

115. Suzuki Kōhei, "Nichi-yō gakkō no omoide" [Memories of Sunday school], in Hongō Kirisutokyōkai, *Hongō Kyōkai sōritsu 50-nen shi,* 206.

116. Hiroshi Watanabe, *The Architecture of Tokyo: An Architectural History in 571 Individual Presentations* (Stuttgart: Edition Axel Menges, 2001), 79.

117. Botond Bognar, *Contemporary Japanese Architecture* (New York: Van Nostrand Reinhold, 1985), 13.

118. Ibid.

119. Hirai Yuka, "Shōgai 'atarashii kenchiku' wo tsukuri tsutzuketa kenchiku-ka Sone Tatsuzō" [Life, the architect who continued building 'new architecture' Sone Tatsuzō], *Inax Report,* no. 167 (July 2006): 14.

120. Saba, *Uemura Masahisa to sono jidai 3,* 156. The same date appears in Hirai, "Shōgai 'atarashii kenchiku,'" 14.

121. Washington, "Fighting Brick with Brick."

122. Ienaga Saburō, "Japan's Modernization and Buddhism," *Contemporary Religions in Japanese Religions* 6, no. 1 (1965): 11.

123. The Japanese terms for meeting hall and sanctuary are often used almost interchangeably in primary sources on Japanese Protestant Christianity, in contrast to the denomination-specific differences apparent in the names given to these spaces in the United States. See Yumichō Hongō Kyōkai, *Yumichō Hongō Kyōkai 100-nen shi,* 20, 21, 256, for examples of both terms for the same space in this congregation's church buildings.

124. L. Michael White, *Building God's House in the Roman World* (Baltimore: Johns Hopkins University Press, 1990).

125. Kozaki, *Autobiography of a Japanese Pastor*, 77.

126. Greene in *Christian Union*, 2 April 1892, 654.

127. *Shinjin* 2, no. 4 (1 November 1901): 44; Tōya, *Fujimichō 80-nen shi*, 10–11.

128. Ii and Fugami, *Reinanzaka Kyōkai 100-nen shi*, 227, citing "Aratana dekita shinai no saikō tō."

129. Ii and Fugami, *Reinanzaka Kyōkai 100-nen shi*, 113.

130. Yumichō Hongō, *Hongō Kyōkai 100-nen shi*, 60.

131. Tōya, *Fujimichō 80-nen shi*, 35, quoting from *Kyōkai tsūshin* (February 1899).

132. Saba, *Uemura Masahisa to sono jidai*, 3:155.

133. Several large gathering spaces have also been added such as the Sanshūden (Assembly Hall). For information on the original buildings, see Yasukuni Jinja, *Yasukuni Jinja ichiran: Bekkaku kanpei* (Tokyo: Yasukuni Jinja, 1911); and Yasukuni Jinja Shamusho, *Yasukuni jinja* (Tokyo: Yasukuni Jinja Shamusho, 1976). See also Nelson, "Social Memory as Ritual Practice," 449. For an overview of Kanda Myōjin's buildings and their history, see Kanda Myōjin shikō kankōkai, *Kanda Myōjin shikō* (Tokyo: Kanda Myōjin Shikō Kankōkai, 1992).

134. On the physical history of the temple, see Isaka Michiko, *Zōjōji kyūkeidai chiku rekishi-teki kenzōbutsu nado chōsa hōkokusho* [Historical study and report on the buildings in the district of the former Zōjōji Precincts] (Tokyo: Keidai kenkyū Jimu kyoku, 2003).

135. Shigenaga Yoshihide, ed., *Meiji Jingū gozōei kinen shashinchō* [Commemorative photo album of the construction of Meiji Shrine] (Tokyo: Yoshida shoten, 1920).

136. See "Dai Nihon Tōkyō Shiba San'enzan Zōjōji kyōnai zenzu" (1901) at https://ja.m.wikipedia.org/wiki/ファイル:増上寺_(絵葉書00)_大日本東京芝三縁山増上寺境内全図.jpg (accessed 26 May 2020); "Shiba kōen no zu," in *Tokyo annai 2* [Tokyo guide 2], ed. Shiyakusho shishi hensan kakari (Tokyo: Shōkadō, 1907), 35.

137. Meiji Shrine's Kinenkan and the Zōjōji Kaikan are two examples of this development.

138. On the revolution in American church architecture that took place in the late nineteenth century, see Jeanne Halgren Kilde, *When Church Became Theatre: The Transformation of Evangelical Architecture and Worship in Nineteenth-Century America* (Oxford: Oxford University Press, 2002).

139. Ernest Best, *Christian Faith and Cultural Crisis: The Japanese Case* (Leiden: Brill, 1966), 144.

140. Tōya, *Fujimichō 80-nen shi*, 35, quoting from *Kyōkai tsūshin* (February 1899); and Mimatsu, *Uemura sensei no omoide*, 98.

141. *Shinjin* 2, no. 4 (November 1901): 43.

142. Aihara Ichirōsuke, "Omoidadzuru koto to hitobito" [Remembering things and people], in Hongō Kirisutokyōkai, *Hongō Kyōkai sōritsu 50-nen*, 190.

143. *Reinanzaka kyōhō*, 30 August 1908, 1–2.

144. Ebina, "Sōgyō no jidai," in Hongō Kirisutokyōkai, *Hongō Kyōkai sōritsu 50-nen*, 33.

145. Suzuki Kōhei, "Nichi-yō gakkō no omoide" [Memories of Sunday school], in Hongō Kirisutokyōkai, *Hongō Kyōkai sōritsu 50-nen*, 206.

146. Ibid.

147. Ibid.

148. Hongō Kirisutokyōkai, *Hongō Kyōkai sōritsu 50-nen*, 39.

149. Ii and Fugami, *Reinanzaka Kyōkai 100-nen shi,* 235.

150. Ii and Fugami, *Reinanzaka Kyōkai 100-nen shi,* 235, citing "Aratana dekita shinai no saikō tō." Reinanzaka, like all of the other churches studied here, lacked any adjacent outdoor space until the addition of a kindergarten playground in the early 1930s.

Chapter Three: Preaching Self and World in the Capital

1. Massimiliano Tomasi, "Oratory in Meiji and Taishō Japan: Public Speaking and the Formation of a New Written Language," *Monumenta Nipponica* 71, no. 1 (Spring 2002): 44.

2. Ibid., 52.

3. Huffman, *Creating a Public,* 76–77; Matsuo Takayoshi, "The Development of Democracy in Japan—Taishō Democracy: Its Flowering and Breakdown," *Developing Economies* 4, no. 4 (December 1966): 617.

4. Sheldon Garon, *Molding Japanese Minds: The State in Everyday Life* (Princeton, NJ: Princeton University Press, 1997), 118–119; Sharon H. Nolte and Sally Ann Hastings, "The Meiji State's Policy toward Women," in *Recreating Japanese Women, 1600–1945,* ed. Gail Lee Bernstein (Berkeley: University of California Press, 1991), 154–155.

5. Matsuo, "The Development of Democracy," 617.

6. Hardacre, "Creating State Shinto"; Hardacre, *Shinto and the State,* 42–48.

7. Ketelaar, *Of Heretics and Martyrs,* 123.

8. Ibid., 92.

9. Jaffe, "The Buddhist Cleric as Japanese Subject," 529.

10. Maxey, *The "Greatest Problem,"* 189.

11. Hardacre, *Shinto and the State,* 37.

12. Shields, *Against Harmony,* 134. On Chikazumi see Iwata Fumiaki, *Kindai Bukkyō to seinen: Chikazumi Jōkan to sono jidai* [Modern Buddhism and youth: Chikazumi Jōkan and his times] (Tokyo: Iwanami shoten, 2014).

13. Shields, *Against Harmony,* 134.

14. Ibid., 286.

15. Emily Anderson, *Christianity and Imperialism,* 14.

16. Ibid., 214. See also Emily Anderson, "Containing Voices in the Wilderness." Cyril H. Powles highlights the fact that Kashiwagi was never arrested: see "Pacifism in Japan: 1918–1945," in *Challenge to Mars: Essays on Pacifism from 1918 to 1945,* ed. Peter Brock and Thomas Paul Socknat (Toronto: University of Toronto Press, 1999), 434.

17. For an insightful characterization of this confusion, see Kenneth Pyle, *The New Generation in Meiji Japan: Problems of Cultural Identity, 1885–1895* (Stanford, CA: Stanford University Press, 1969), 118, 119.

18. On these ideals in the thought of leading Enlightenment philosophers, see Louis Dupré, *The Enlightenment and the Intellectual Foundations of Modern Culture* (New Haven, CT: Yale University Press, 2004), chaps. 4 and 5.

19. Hiratsuka Raichō, *In the Beginning, When Woman Was the Sun: The Autobiography of a Japanese Feminist,* trans. Teruko Craig (New York: Columbia University Press, 2006), 77.

20. Ōsugi Sakai, *The Autobiography of Ōsugi Sakae,* trans. Byron K. Marshall (Berkeley: University of California Press, 1992), 185.

21. Ibid.

22. Yoshino Sakuzō, "Shakaishugi to Kirisutokyō," *Shinjin* 6, no. 9 (September 1905): 32.

23. Jennings, *Theology in Japan,* 43. Here Jennings is drawing from one of Takakura Tokutarō's earliest biographers. See Oshio Tsutomu, "Takakura sensei no deatta hitobito," *Fukuin to sekai* 3, no. 2 (1954): 37.

24. Hani Motoko, *Hansei wo kataru* [Half my life] (1955; repr., Tokyo: Nihon Tosho Senta, 1997), 60. For a translated abridged version of this work, see Hani Motoko, "Stories of My Life," trans. Chieko Irie Mulhern, in *Heroic with Grace: Legendary Women of Japan,* ed. Chieko Irie Mulhern (New York: M. E. Sharpe, 1991), 236–264. Mulhern's translation of Hani's phrase "hikitsukerarete kiite ita" appears on 250.

25. Wasaki Kotarō, "Kindai Nihon ni Okeru 'hanmon seinen' no saikentō: 1900 nendai ni okeru seinen no henyō katei" [Reexamining "anguished youth" in modern Japan: The transformative process of youth in the 1900s], *Nihon no kyōiku shigaku: Kyōiku shigakkai kiyō* 55 (2012): 19–31.

26. Itō Kiyoshi, *Banchō Kyōkai 100-nen shi,* 55.

27. Takeda Kiyoko, *"Rikugo zasshi," Shisō* 462 (December 1962): 109–120; Kishimoto, *Japanese Religion in the Meiji Era,* 225, 294; Scheiner, *Christian Converts and Social Protest,* 108. See also Dōshisha Daigaku Jinbunkagaku Kenkyūsho, ed., *"Rikugō zasshi" no kenkyū* [Study of *Rikugo zasshi*] (Tokyo: Kyōbunkan, 1984); and Yosuke Nirei, "Toward a Modern Belief: Modernist Protestantism and Problems of National Religion in Meiji Japan," *Japanese Journal of Religious Studies* 34, no. 1 (2007): 151–175. Although originally a Buddhist monthly journal, *Chūō kōron* became one of the nation's leading secular literary magazines during the late Meiji period. See *Chūō kōron sha 70-nen shi* (Tokyo: Chūō Kōronsha, 1955). The translation "The Nation's Friend" is the one employed by the journal's founding editor, Tokutomi Sohō, as the English subtitle in the inaugural issue. See *Kokumin no tomo* 1, no. 1 (February 1887): 1. On Christian authorship and ideals in the *Mainichi shimbun,* see Huffman, *Creating a Public,* 255, 258, 295.

28. For instance, Aasulv Lande makes reference to Uemura Masahisa's 1898 sermon "Kirisutokyō no bushidō." See Aasulv Lande, *Meiji Protestantism in History and Historiography: A Comparative Study of Japanese and Western Interpretation of Early Protestantism in Japan* (New York: Lang, 1989), 78. Banchō's very popular pastor Tsunajima Kakichi has seldom been mentioned, let alone studied by scholars. The exception is Emily Anderson, who mentions him and a sermon he gave in colonial Korea in Anderson, *Christianity and Imperialism,* 144–145.

29. Scheiner, *Christian Converts and Social Protest,* 108. See also Sumiya Mikio, *Kindai Nihon no keisei to kirisutokyō* [Christianity and the development of modern Japan] (Tokyo: Shinkyō Shuppansha, 1950), chap. 2.

30. For instance, Reinanzaka's morning service took place at 10 a.m., and another sermon was given at 7 p.m. in 1916. *Reinanzaka kyōhō,* no. 2 (4 June 1916): 2. And Hongō member Ishikawa Takeyoshi (1887–1961) recalled the popularity of evening sermons at his church during his youth. Hongō Kirisutokyōkai, *Hongō Kyōkai sōritsu 50-nen,* 229.

31. Mark Garner, "Preaching as a Communicative Event: A Discourse Analysis of Sermons by Robert Rollock (1555–1599)," *Renaissance and Reformation Review* 9, no. 1 (2007): 46.

32. See E. P. Bettinghaus and M. J. Cody, *Persuasive Communication* (New York: Holt, Rinehart & Winston, 1987).

33. Braj Mohan, "A Demonstration of the Discourse Dissection Model (DDM) with an Analysis of F. D. Roosevelt's 'Pearl Harbour' Address to the Nation," *SKASE Journal of Theoretical Linguistics* 3 (2016): 63.

34. Garner, "Preaching as a Communicative Event," 53.

35. Yoshinare Akiko, *Ebina Danjō no seiji shisō* [The political thought of Ebina Danjō], 12–13, 17–18.

36. Sekioka, "Ebina Danjō ni okeru sekaishugi to Nihonshugi," 28.

37. Shuma Iwai, "Japanese Christianity in the Meiji Era: An Analysis of Ebina Danjo's Perspective on Shintoistic Christianity," *Transformation: An International Journal of Holistic Mission Studies* 25, no. 4 (October 2008), 198.

38. Jennings, *Theology in Japan,* 106–108. For a discussion of the arrival of New Theology in Japan, see Suzuki Norihisa, *Meiji shūkyō shichō no kenkyū* (Tokyo: Tokyo Daigaku Shuppankai, 1979), 27–47. For solid overviews of New Theology in Meiji Japan, see Saba, *Uemura Masahisa to sono jidai,* 5:200–205; Robert S. Schwantes, "Christianity versus Science: A Conflict of Ideas in Meiji Japan," *Far Eastern Quarterly* 12, no. 2 (February 1953): 123–132; and Nirei, "Toward a Modern Belief."

39. Nirei, "Toward a Modern Belief," 155.

40. This point is well articulated in Jennings, *Theology in Japan,* 108.

41. See Sekioka, "Ebina Danjō ni okeru sekaishugi to Nihonshugi," 42. Here he supplements his own insightful analysis with words from pastor Yuasa Yōzō's *Waga kuni ni okeru 3 dai kirisutokyō shisōka* (Tokyo: Keiseisha, 1942), 49.

42. Takenaka Masao, "Kozaki Hiromichi ni okeru kokka shisō no tenkai: Meiji zenhanki wo chūshin ni" [Development of thought on the nation by Kozaki in the early Meiji period], in *Kumamoto Bando Kenkyū Nihon Purotesutantizumu no ichigenryū to tenkai* [Studies on the Kumamoto Band: A stream of Japanese Protestantism and its development], ed. Doshisha Daigaku Jimbun kagaku (Tokyo: Misuzu Shobō, 1966), 261. See also Dohi Akio, "Jukyō yori Kirisutokyō he no michi" [A way from Confucianism to Christianity], in *Dōshisha no shisōka tachi: Gekan* [Thinkers of the Doshisha: 2nd volume], ed. Wada Yōichi (Kyoto: Dōshisha Daigaku seikyō Shuppanbu, 1973), 33.

43. Scheiner, *Christian Converts and Social Protest,* 70.

44. Imanaka Kanshi, "Yokoi Shonan no Jitsugaku to Yōgaku" [Yokoi Shonan's Jitsugaku and Western studies], *Kirisutokyo Shakai Mondai Kenkyu,* no. 4 (March 1961): 8–23.

45. Dohi Akio, "Jukyō yori Kirisutokyō he no michi" [A way from Confucianism to Christianity], in Wada, *Dōshisha no shisōka tachi: Gekan,* 86–87. See also Shuma Iwai, "Japanese Christianity in the Meiji Era," 122.

46. Scheiner, *Christian Converts and Social Protest,* 92.

47. John Pierson, *Tokutomi Sohō 1863–1957: A Journalist for Modern Japan* (Princeton, NJ: Princeton University Press, 1980), 57–58.

48. Ibid., 62.

49. Scheiner, *Christian Converts and Social Protest,* 190.

50. Davidann, *A World of Crisis and Progress,* 56.

51. Imanaka Kanshi, "Kozaki Hiromichi no *Seikyō shinron* ni tsuite" [On Kozaki Hiromichi's *New essay on the relationship of politics and religion*], *Kirisutokyō Shakai Mondai Kenkyū* 30 (1982): 4.

52. See Kumano Yoshitaka, *Nihon Kirisutokyō shingaku shisōshi* [History of Japanese Christian theological thought] (Tokyo: Shinkyō Shuppansha, 1968), 210–214, on historicization; and Dohi Akio, "The First Generation: Christian Leaders in the First Period," in Furuya, *A History of Japanese Theology,* 31, on Kozaki's arguments against biblical infallibility.

53. Dohi, "The First Generation," 31.

54. Ibid., 32.
55. Ballhatchet, "Confucianism and Christianity in Meiji Japan," 356.
56. Dohi, "The First Generation," 32–33.
57. Ballhatchet, "Confucianism and Christianity in Meiji Japan," 358.
58. These sermon titles appear in the following four issues: *Reinanzaka kyōhō,* no. 13 (January 1902): 2; *Reinanzaka kyōhō,* no. 16 (August 1902): 2; *Reinanzaka kyōhō,* no. 17 (April 1903): 2; *Reinanzaka kyōhō,* no. 21 (December 1903): 1.
59. Kozaki, *Kozaki Hiromichi zenshū,* 5:1–6.
60. Ibid.
61. Ibid., 5:6.
62. Ibid., 5:308.
63. Ballhatchet, "Confucianism and Christianity in Meiji Japan," 358.
64. Jennings, *Theology in Japan,* 107.
65. Soltau, "Uemura Masahisa," 59–60.
66. Morioka Kiyomi, "Meiji zenki ni okeru shizoku to Kirisutokyō," *Shukutoku Daigaku shakaigakubu kenkyū kiyō* 38 (2004): 137; Saba, *Uemura Masahisa to sono jidai,* 1:687.
67. Byong-il Choi, *Kindai Nihon no kaikaku-ha Kirisutokyō: Uemura Masahisa to Takakura Tokutarō no shisōshi-teki kenkyū* [Reformed Christianity in modern Japan: Intellectual history study of Uemura Masahisa and Takakura Tokutarō] (Fukuoka: Hanashōin, 2007), 30. For reference to his famous code, one of several sources of so-called *bushidō,* see Henry Leach, "The Heart of Things," *Chambers's Journal,* no. 6 (December 1906–November 1907): 194.
68. Soltau, "Uemura Masahisa," 30.
69. Dohi, *Nihon Purotesutanto Kirisutokyōkai shi,* 184; citing Kyōgoku, *Uemura Masahisa,* 16–19; Uemura, *Uemura Masahisa zenshū,* 8:298–299.
70. Dohi, *Nihon Purotesutanto Kirisutokyōkai shi,* 184.
71. Scheiner, *Christian Converts and Social Protest,* 27.
72. Soltau, "Uemura Masahisa," 49.
73. Ibid., 69; Uemura, *Uemura Masahisa zenshū,* 5:569.
74. Scheiner, *Christian Converts and Social Protest,* 238.
75. Ibid., 113.
76. Ibid., 113.
77. Ibid., 240, 232, 233.
78. Soltau, "Uemura Masahisa," 83–85.
79. Thomas John Hastings, *Practical Theology and the One Body of Christ: Toward a Mission-Ecumenical Model* (Grand Rapids, MI: Eerdmans, 2007), 71.
80. Soltau, "Uemura Masahisa," 103.
81. Dohi, *Nihon Purotesutanto Kirisutokyōkai shi;* Ernest Best, "Christian Faith and Cultural Crisis: The Japanese Case," *Journal of Religion* 41, no. 1 (January 1961): 26; and Nirei, "Toward a Modern Belief," 164.
82. Scheiner, *Christian Converts and Social Protest,* 239, 244; Charles Germany, *Protestant Theologies in Modern Japan* (Tokyo: International Institute for the Study of Religions Press, 1965), 18.
83. Uemura, *Uemura Masahisa zenshū,* 1:185.
84. Ibid., 1:142, 1:572, 3:103.
85. Ibid., 1:167.

86. Anesaki Masaharu, *History of Japanese Religion, with Special Reference to the Social and Moral Life of the Nation* (London: Kegan Paul, Trench, Trubner and Co., 1930); Takeda Kiyoko, "Japanese Christianity: Between Orthodoxy and Heterodoxy," in *Authority and the Individual in Japan: Citizen Protest in Historical Perspective*, ed. J. Victor Koschmann (Tokyo: University of Tokyo Press, 1978); Unuma Hiroko, *Kindai Nihon no kirisutokyō shisōkatachi* [Modern Japan's Christian intellectuals] (Tokyo: Nihon Kirisuto Kyōdan, 1989); and Nirei, "Toward a Modern Belief," 161–162.

87. Davidann, *A World of Crisis and Progress*, 78. Here he is summarizing Ōhata Kiyoshi and Ikado Fujio's conclusions in Kishimoto, *Japanese Religion in the Meiji Era*, 275.

88. Richard Drummond, *A History of Christianity in Japan* (Grand Rapids, MI: Eerdmans, 1971), 212; Dohi Akio, "Christianity and Politics in the Taishō Period of Democracy, Part 1," *Journal of Japanese Religions* 5, no. 4 (April 1969): 22–23; and Takenaka Masao, *Reconciliation and Renewal in Japan* (New York: Student Volunteer Movement for Christian Missions and Friendship Press, 1957), 70. For a good English-language summary of Uemura's stance, see Jennings, *Theology in Japan*, 87–88.

89. On Niijima's emphasis on students' responsibility to be leaders in reforming Japan, see Scheiner, *Christian Converts and Social Protest*, 180–181.

90. Eric Hobsbawm and Terrence Ranger, eds., *The Invention of Tradition* (Cambridge: Cambridge University Press, 1983), 1. On the construction of a national past in the late Tokugawa era (1600–1868), see Susan L. Burns, *Before the Nation: Kokugaku and the Imagining of Continuity in Early Modern Japan* (Durham, NC: Duke University Press, 2003). For the creation and popularization of a Japanese imperial past in the Meiji period, see Fujitani, *Splendid Monarchy*.

91. These quotes come from Gluck, *Japan's Modern Myths*, 121.

92. See the translation in *The Japan Yearbook* (Tokyo: Japan Yearbook Office, 1911), 496, as cited in Holtom, "The Political Philosophy of Modern Shintō," 41.

93. Gluck, *Japan's Modern Myths*, 146.

94. Kozaki Hiromichi, *Kozaki Hiromichi zenshū*, vol. 5 (Tokyo: Nihon Tosho senta-, 2000), 32.

95. Uemura, *Uemura Masahisa zenshū*, 1:134.

96. Ebina Danjō, "Shin bushidō" [New bushidō], *Shinjin* 3, no. 10 (October 1902): 2–10; reprinted in Ebina, *Ebina Danjō no sekkyōshū* [The collected sermons of Ebina Danjō] (Tokyo: Shinkyō shuppansha, 1973), 85.

97. Ebina Danjō, "Ima wa kitō toki nari" [Now is the time for prayer], *Shinjin* 6, no. 10 (October 1905): 12.

98. Davidann, *A World of Crisis and Progress*, 63.

99. Ebina, "Ima wa kitō toki nari."

100. Kozaki, *Kozaki Hiromichi zenshū*, 5:240.

101. Uemura Masahisa, quoted in *Reformed Church Review* 4, no. 9 (April 1905): 266.

102. Various scholars have treated the connections between Christianity and Confucianism that Kozaki sketched. See Scheiner, *Christian Converts and Social Protest*; Notehelfer, *American Samurai*; Ballhatchet, "Confucianism and Christianity in Meiji Japan," 349–369; Lande, *Meiji Protestantism in History and Historiography*, 46; Ebisawa Arimichi and Ōuchi Saburō, *Nihon Kirisutokyō shi* [History of Japanese Christianity] (Tokyo: Nihon Kirisuto Kyōdan Shuppan kyoku, 1970); and Dohi, "Christianity and Politics in the Taishō Period of Democracy, Part 1," 1–25.

103. De Bary, Gluck, and Tiedemann, *Sources of Japanese Tradition,* 672.

104. Andrew Gordon, *A Modern History of Japan,* 64–66.

105. On the Freedom and People's Rights movement, see Irokawa Daikichi, "Freedom and the Concept of People's Rights," in *Modern Japan: An Interpretive Anthology,* ed. Irwin Scheiner (New York: Macmillan, 1974). On Ashio, see F. G. Notehelfer, "Between Tradition and Modernity: Labor and the Ashio Copper Mine," *Monumenta Nipponica* 39, no. 1 (Spring 1984): 11–24; and Nimura Kazuo, *The Ashio Riot of 1907: A Social History of Mining in Japan* (Durham, NC: Duke University Press, 2000). On the Rice Riots, see Michael Lewis, *Rioters and Citizens: Mass Protest in Imperial Japan* (Berkeley: University of California Press, 1990).

106. Peter Duus, "Yoshino Sakuzō: The Christian as Political Critic," *Journal of Japanese Studies* 4, no. 2 (Summer 1978): 301.

107. Dohi Akio, "Christianity and Politics in the Taishō Period of Democracy, Part 2," *Japanese Religions* 7, no. 3 (July 1972): 52. Here Dohi cites Yoshino Sakuzō, "Shakashugi to kirisutokyō," *Shinjin* 20, no. 7 (July 1919). However, the correct citation for the quote is Yoshino Sakuzō, "Demokurashii to Kirisutokyō," *Shinjin* 20, no. 3 (March 1919): 8.

108. Kozaki, *Kozaki Hiromichi zenshū,* 5:348.

109. Ibid., 5:348–349.

110. Ibid., 5:30.

111. Ebina, "Kunshi kuni no igi" [The meaning of a virtuous country], *Shinjin* 4, no. 2 (February 1903): 18.

112. Emily Anderson, *Christianity and Imperialism,* 120.

113. Tsunajima Kakichi, *Gyakkyō no fukuin* [The gospel of adversity] (Tokyo: Keiseisha, 1924), 133.

114. Ibid., 133, 124.

115. Uemura, *Uemura Masahisa zenshū,* 1:450.

116. Kozaki, *Kozaki Hiromichi zenshū,* 5:141.

117. Ebina Danjō, "Joshi no tomo" [Women's friend], *Shinjokai* 5, no. 12 (December 1913), reprinted in Ebina, *Ebina Danjō sekkyōshū,* 182.

118. Uemura, *Uemura Masahisa zenshū,* 1:174.

119. Ibid.

120. Matsuo, "The Japanese Protestants in Korea, Part One," 408–409.

121. Ibid., 412. Michael Isaac Shapiro, "Christian Culture and Military Rule: Assimilation and Its Limits during the First Decade of Japan's Colonial Rule in Korea, 1910–19" (PhD diss., University of California Berkeley, 2010), 5.

122. Matsuo, "The Japanese Protestants in Korea, Part One," 414.

123. Shapiro, "Christian Culture and Military Rule," 53.

124. Jung-Sun N. Han, *An Imperial Path to Modernity,* 51, quoting from Ebina Danjō, "Nihon Minzoku no bōchō to kyōkaryoku," *Shinjin* 5, no. 2 (February 1904): 2–3.

125. Ebina Danjō, "Yūkoku no shijō" [Patriotic feeling], *Shinjin* 13, no. 12 (December 1912): 10.

126. Emily Anderson, *Christianity and Imperialism,* 111.

127. Ibid., 145.

128. Gluck, *Japan's Modern Myths,* 133. Here she is summarizing "Shūkyō to kyōiku no kansei ni tsuite: Inoue Tetsujirō-shi no danwa," *Kyōiku jiron* (1892).

129. William G. Beasley, *The Meiji Restoration* (Stanford, CA: Stanford University Press, 1972), 385–386.

130. Howell, *Geographies of Identity in Nineteenth-Century Japan,* 83–85, 89. For a volume dedicated entirely to the Eta Emancipation Edict of 1871, Proclamation 61 of the Council of State, see Harada Tomohiko and Uesugi Satoru, eds., *"Kaihōrei" no seiritsu* [Establishment of the Emancipation Edict] (Tokyo: San'ichi Shobo, 1984); George De Vos and Hiroshi Wagatsuma, eds., *Japan's Invisible Race: Caste in Culture and Personality* (Berkeley: University of California Press, 1966), 34.

131. Gluck, *Japan's Modern Myths,* 182, quoting Yanagita Kunio, *Kokyō shichijūnen* (Tokyo: Asahi Shinbunsha, 1974), 119–120.

132. Kozaki, *Kozaki Hiromichi zenshū,* 5:349.

133. Ibid.

134. For specific reference to such lectures and their rural counterparts, see Gluck, *Japan's Modern Myths,* 248.

135. Kozaki, *Kozaki Hiromichi zenshū,* 5:348.

136. Ibid., 5:347.

137. Ibid., 5:349.

138. Ebina, "Kunshi kuni no igi."

139. Ebina Danjō, "Kirisutokyō to demokurashii" [Christianity and democracy], *Shinjin* 21, no. 6 (June 1920): 15, 16. It is worth noting that this stance differed from Ebina's earlier writings around the Russo-Japanese War on the need for Koreans to depend culturally and politically on a superior country, embodied in the term *Jidai shugi* (事大主義). See Shapiro, "Christian Culture and Military Rule," 68–70.

140. Kozaki, *Kozaki Hiromichi zenshū,* 5:350.

141. Uemura, *Uemura Masahisa zenshū,* 1:174. Here it is unclear whether Uemura was referring to aboriginal Taiwanese or Chinese in Taiwan.

142. Tsunajima, *Gyakkyō no fukuin,* 125–126.

143. Ibid., 141.

144. Kozaki, *Kozaki Hiromichi zenshū,* 5:142–143.

145. Ebina, "Ima wa kitō toki nari."

146. Kozaki, *Kozaki Hiromichi zenshū,* 5:215.

147. Sharon Sievers, *Flowers in Salt: The Beginnings of Feminist Consciousness in Modern Japan* (Stanford, CA: Stanford University Press, 1983), 10; and Nolte and Hastings, "The Meiji State's Policy toward Women," 153.

148. Nolte and Hastings, "The Meiji State's Policy toward Women," 155–156.

149. See Mori Arinori, "Saishōron 1–5" [On wives and concubines], *Meiroku zasshi,* nos. 8, 11, 15, 20, 27 (1874). On the foundation and content of *Meiroku zasshi,* a journal published by a handful of men interested in popularizing Western concepts and ideals, see William Braisted, trans. and ed., *Meiroku Zasshi: Journal of the Japanese Enlightenment* (Cambridge, MA: Harvard University Press, 1976). In particular, see his translation of Mori's article "Saishōron 3" [On wives and concubines 3], *Meiroku zasshi,* no. 15 (November 1874): 1–2, on 189–191. For a summary of the *Meiroku zasshi* authors' views on women, see Sievers, *Flowers in Salt,* 16–25; and Mikiso Hane, "Fukuzawa Yukichi and Women's Rights," in *Japan and Transition: Thought and Action in the Meiji Era, 1868–1912,* ed. Hilary Conroy, Sandra T. W. Davis, and Wayne Patterson (Canbury, NJ: Associated University Presses, 1984), 96–112.

150. Sievers, *Flowers in Salt,* 30, 33–44.

151. Ibid., 45.

152. Nolte and Hastings, "The Meiji State's Policy toward Women," 156.

153. On the role of local custom in some areas of pre-Meiji Japanese male-female relations, see Harald Fuess, *Divorce in Japan: Family, Gender, and the State, 1600–2000* (Stanford, CA: Stanford University Press, 2004), 74–75, 116–117. On the specific class-based restrictions that applied to women with samurai status, see Nolte and Hastings, "The Meiji State's Policy toward Women," 153; and Patessio, "The Creation of Public Spaces," 166.

154. Hayashida Kazuhiro, "Development of Election Law in Japan," *Journal of Law and Politics* (of Kyūshū University Law Society) 34, no. 1 (1967): 4. This article also provides a concise overview of the suffrage system's evolution.

155. Nolte and Hastings, "The Meiji State's Policy toward Women," 154–155; and Vera Mackie, *Creating Socialist Women in Japan: Gender, Labour, and Activism, 1900–1937* (Cambridge: Cambridge University Press, 1997).

156. On the unequal grounds for divorce in Edo and Meiji Japan and other major stipulations of the Meiji Civil Code of 1898, see Fuess, *Divorce in Japan,* 77, 109, 117; and Sievers, *Flowers in Salt,* 111.

157. Nolte and Hastings, "The Meiji State's Policy toward Women," 154.

158. Patessio, "The Creation of Public Spaces," 166.

159. Nolte and Hastings, "The Meiji State's Policy toward Women," 153, 158.

160. Ibid., 156.

161. Ebina, "Joshi no tomo," reprinted in *Ebina Danjō sekkyōshū,* 183.

162. Kozaki, *Kozaki Hiromichi zenshū,* 5:95.

163. On the new position of the head of household, see Fuess, *Divorce in Japan,* 109; and Sievers, *Flowers in Salt,* 111.

164. Kozaki, *Kozaki Hiromichi zenshū,* 5:95.

165. Uemura, *Uemura Masahisa zenshū,* 1:100. See also Helen Ballhatchet, "Christianity and Gender Relationships in Japan: Case Studies of Marriage and Divorce in Early Meiji Protestant Circles," *Japanese Journal of Religious Studies* 34, no. 1 (2007): 187. Here she draws similar conclusions based on a book of his titled *Seikyō shinron* [Confucianism and Christianity].

166. By using the term "moral teacher" *(dōtoku no sensei)* instead of the literal and commonly used translation "judges" *(shishi),* Uemura made a word choice that places specific emphasis on the moral rectitude and influence of these biblical figures.

167. Uemura, *Uemura Masahisa zenshū,* 1:101.

168. Ibid., 1:107.

169. Ebina, "Shin bushidō," reprinted in Ebina, *Ebina Danjō sekkyōshū,* 83.

170. Kozaki, *Kozaki Hiromichi zenshū,* 5:348.

171. Uemura, *Uemura Masahisa zenshū,* 3:103.

172. Ann Sherif, *Mirror: The Fiction and Essays of Kōda Aya* (Honolulu: University of Hawai'i Press, 1999), 8. This conclusion is based on a description given in Drummond, *A History of Christianity in Japan,* 219. See also Ballhatchet, "Christianity and Gender Relationships in Japan," 183.

173. Tsunajima, *Gyakkyō no fukuin,* 121.

174. Ebina, "Joshi no tomo," reprinted in *Ebina Danjō sekkyōshū,* 187. Ebina was clearly making reference to Mill's *The Subjection of Women,* first translated into Japanese in 1878. Daisuke Arie, "Lost in Translation: How Japan's Intellectuals Translated *On Liberty* (1859) and Utilitarian Writings in the Meiji Era and After," *Yokohama Journal of Social Sciences* 14, no. 6 (February 2010): 669. See John Stuart Mill, *The Subjection of Women* (New York: D. Appleton and Co., 1869). In Japanese, see John Stuart Mill, *Fujin no fukujū,* trans. Kataguchi Tairirō

(Tokyo: Shūeikaku, 1923). For Fukuzawa's thoughts on this work by Mill, see his *Gakumon no susume* in Fukuzawa Yukichi, *Fukuzawa zenshū* [Collected works of Fukuzawa Yukichi] (Tokyo: Jiji Shimpōsha, 1925–1926).

175. Ebina, "Joshi no tomo," reprinted in *Ebina Danjō sekkyōshū,* 182.

176. On Tamura and his observations in the US and the response of the Japanese Protestant pastorate, see Emily Anderson, "Tamura Naoomi's *The Japanese Bride,*" 211.

177. Uemura, *Uemura Masahisa zenshū,* 1:174.

178. Kozaki, *Kozaki Hiromichi zenshū,* 5:113.

179. Ibid., 5:112.

180. Ibid., 5:110.

181. Ebina Danjō, "Shūkyō to dōtoku" [Religion and morality], *Shinjin* 1, no. 8 (February 1901): 12.

182. Ebina, "Kunshi kuni no igi."

183. Uemura, *Uemura Masahisa zenshū,* 2:572.

184. Duus, "Yoshino Sakuzō," 314, citing Ebina Danjō, "Shinkyōku no shakaiteki chii," *Shinjin* 6, no. 9 (September 1905): 1–6.

185. Ebina, "Shūkyō to dōtoku," 12.

186. Tsunajima, *Gyakkō no fukuin,* 9–11.

187. Ibid.

188. Ibid.

189. Ibid.

190. Uemura, *Uemura Masahisa zenshū,* 1:64.

191. Ibid., 1:134.

192. Ebina Danjō, "Katei no Kirisuto" [Christ of the family], *Shinjokai* 8, no. 3 (March 1916); reprinted in Ebina Danjō, *Ebina Danjō* (Tokyo: Nihon Kirisutokyōdan Shuppan kyoku, 2003), 174.

193. The initial charity organization has since evolved into the National Crittenton Foundation, administering Florence Crittenton Homes throughout the United States. See Katherine G. Aiken, *Harnessing the Power of Motherhood: The National Florence Crittenton Mission, 1883–1925* (Knoxville: University of Tennessee Press, 1998).

194. Tsunajima, *Gyakkō no fukuin,* 174. Tsunajima translated the term "fallen women" as *rinraku no onna.*

195. Uemura in fact refers to Washington's "devotion." See Uemura, *Uemura Masahisa zenshū,* 1:33. Although this passage comes from Exodus 20:12 in the Old Testament, which can also be found in the Pentateuch of the Judaic Torah, imperatives to honor and or obey one's parents also appear in Mark 7:10, Luke 18:20, Colossians 3:20, and various other places in the Christian New Testament. In the New Testament, the emphasis on honoring one's parents due to one's obligations under the law is enhanced by the emphasis on love, strongly emphasized by Christ and his disciples, as the root of such actions. See Peter Balla, *The Child-Parent Relationship in the New Testament and Its Environment* (Tübingen: Mohr Siebeck, 2003), chaps. 4, 5, and 6.

196. Uemura, *Uemura Masahisa zenshū,* 1:33.

197. Ibid., 1:16.

198. Shields, *Against Harmony,* chaps. 1 and 2.

199. Chikazumi Jōkan, *Shinkō Mondai* [The problem of faith] (Tokyo: Bunmeidō, 1904), esp. 139–145.

Chapter Four: Preaching the National Imaginary

1. On the nation-state as the predominant social form produced by the conditions of modernity, see Anthony Giddens, *Modernity and Self-Identity: Self and Society in the Late Modern Age* (Stanford, CA: Stanford University Press, 1991), 15.

2. On the nation as an imagined political community see Benedict Anderson, *Imagined Communities: Reflections on the Origin and Spread of Nationalism* (London: Verso, 1991), 6–7.

3. For brief summaries of government efforts to foster nationalism among Japanese citizens, see Gordon, *A Modern History of Japan*, 111–113; Gluck, *Japan's Modern Myths*, 102; and Takashi Fujitani, *Splendid Monarchy: Power and Pageantry in Modern Japan* (Berkeley: University of California Press, 1998), 42–65.

4. Gluck, *Japan's Modern Myths*, 10. Gluck has employed the term *minkan* (popular) to distinguish these individuals from ideologues directly affiliated (officially and unofficially) with the national government.

5. For these examples and others, see Tomasi, "Oratory in Meiji and Taishō Japan"; Peter Duus, *Party Rivalry and Political Change in Taishō Japan* (Cambridge, MA: Harvard University Press, 1968); and Pyle, *The New Generation in Meiji Japan*.

6. R. Ellwood, *Tenrikyō: A Pilgrimage Faith* (Tenri: Tenrikyō University, 1982), 105.

7. See Thelle, *Buddhism and Christianity in Japan*, chaps. 7–9.

8. Christopher Ives, *Imperial Way Zen: Ichikawa Hakugen's Critique and Lingering Questions for Buddhist Ethics* (Honolulu: University of Hawai'i Press, 2009), 19.

9. James E. Ketelaar, "*Kaikyōron:* Buddhism Confronts Modernity," *Zen Buddhism Today* 12 (1996): 31.

10. Kiyozawa Manshi, *Kiyozawa Manshi zenshū* [The collected works of Kiyozawa Manshi] (Tokyo: Iwanami shoten, 2002–2003), 6:79; Jacques Fasan, "Religion and Ethics in the Thought of Kiyozawa Manshi," in *Pure Lands in Asian Texts and Contexts: An Anthology*, ed. Georgia T. Halkias and Richard K. Payne (Honolulu: University of Hawai'i Press, 2019), 56.

11. Edwin Lee, "Nichiren and Nationalism: The Religious Patriotism of Tanaka Chigaku," *Monumenta Nipponica* 30, no. 1 (1975): 22–23.

12. Ibid., 34.

13. Tsukada Osamu, *Tennōseika no Kirisutokyō: Nihon no Seikōkokai no tatakai to kunan* [Emperor-system Christianity: The battle and hardship of the Japan Episcopal Church] (Tokyo: Shinkyō Shuppansha, 1981), 230.

14. Gluck, *Japan's Modern Myths*, 154; Davidann, *A World of Crisis and Progress*, 159.

15. Takahashi Masao, "Uemura Masahisa no 'Warera mizukara no kyōkai' to Meiji seifu" [Uemura Masahisa's "Our personal church" and the Meiji government], in *Nihon Purotesutanto shi no shosō* [Various aspects of Protestant Christian history], ed. Takahashi Masao (Saitama: Seigakuin Daigaku Shuppansha, 1995), 206, citing Uemura Masahisa, "Kirisutokyō no aikokushin" [The patriotism of Christianity], *Fukuin shinpō* (November 1906).

16. Takahashi Masao, *Nihon Purotesutanto shi*, 206.

17. Prasenjit Duara, *Rescuing History from the Nation: Questioning Narratives of Modern China* (Chicago: University of Chicago Press, 1997), 8.

18. Josephson, *The Invention of Religion in Japan*, 133–134.

19. Duara, *Rescuing History from the Nation*, 8. For an introduction to Duara's neologism "nation-view," see ibid., 10.

20. Lande, *Meiji Protestantism in History and Historiography*, 92.

21. Gluck, *Japan's Modern Myths*, 135.

22. See Shuma Iwai, "Japanese Christianity in the Meiji Era"; Wada Yōichi, ed., *Dōshisha no shisōkatachi* (Kyoto: Dōshisha Daigaku Seikyō shuppanbu, 1965–1973); and Dōshisha Daigaku Jinbun Kagaku Kenkyūjo, ed., *Kumamoto bando kenkyū: Nihon Purotesutantoisumu, genryū to kaiten* (Tokyo: Misuzu Shogo, 1965). Other works on Ebina's nationalism include Imanaka Kanshi, "Ebina Danjō to sono shisō," *Kirisutokyō shakai mondai kenkyū* 23 (March 1975): 1–27; Kuniyasu Take, "Ebina Danjō no sensō ron," *Kirisutokyō shakai mondai kenkyū* 23 (March 1975): 44–82; and Sekioka Kazushige, "Ebina Danjō ni okeru sekaishugi to Nihonshugi," *Kirisutokyō shakai mondai kenkyū* 44 (December 1995): 26–48.

23. Tsunajima Kakichi, *Gyakkyō no fukuin* (Tokyo: Keiseisha, 1924), 7–8.

24. Ibid.

25. Ibid., 121. Given the details provided in this quote, it is reasonable to infer that this sermon dates from 1916 or 1917.

26. Ibid., 122.

27. See Judg. 7 RSV.

28. On this incident, see Naoko Shimazu, *Japanese Society at War: Death, Memory and the Russo-Japanese War* (Cambridge: Cambridge University Press, 2009), 123–124, 202–203.

29. Tsunajima, *Gyakkyō no fukuin*, 106.

30. Ibid., 105.

31. Ibid., 107, 109.

32. Ibid., 110, 111.

33. For an illustration of the means by which samurai learned to practice self-cultivation, see Marleen Kassel, *Tokugawa Confucian Education: The Kangien Academy of Hirose Tanso, 1782–1856* (Albany: State University of New York Press, 1996). On the inculcation of loyalty and filial piety in Japanese students during the Meiji period, see Wilbur M. Fridell, "Government Ethics Textbooks in Late Meiji Japan," *Journal of Asian Studies* 29, no. 4 (August 1970): 823–833.

34. Emily Anderson, *Christianity and Imperialism*, 145.

35. J. Nelson Jennings, *Theology in Japan: Takakura Tokutaro, 1885–1934* (New York: University Press of America, 2005), 126.

36. See Walter A. Skya, *Japan's Holy War: The Ideology of Radical Shinto Ultranationalism* (Durham, NC: Duke University Press, 2009); and Richard H. Minear, *Japanese Tradition and Western Law: Emperor, State, and Law in the Thought of Hozumi Yatsuka* (Cambridge, MA: Harvard University Press, 1970).

37. Uemura Masahisa, *Uemura Masahisa zenshū*, vol. 1 (Tokyo: Uemura Zenshū Kankōkai, 1931–1934), 169.

38. Ibid.

39. Ibid., 1:170.

40. See Jennings, *Theology in Japan;* and Takenaka, *Reconciliation and Renewal in Japan.*

41. For the original text of this epic poem, see Johann Wolfgang von Goethe, *Hermann and Dorothea*, trans. Ellen Frothingham, in *The Harvard Classics*, vol. 19, part 4 (New York: P. F. Collier & Son, 1909–1914).

42. Uemura, *Uemura Masahisa zenshū*, 1:170.

43. Ibid., 1:174.

44. Leo T. S. Ching, *Becoming Japanese: Colonial Taiwan and the Politics of Identity Formation* (Berkeley: University of California Press, 2001), 137–143.

45. Uemura, *Uemura Masahisa zenshū,* 1:174.

46. Ibid., 1:172.

47. On the pervasiveness of the "love suicide" in turn-of-the-century Japan, see the stories of famous Meiji author and pulse-taker Higuchi Ichiyō. See Timothy J. Van Compernolle, *The Uses of Memory: The Critique of Modernity in the Fiction of Higuchi Ichiyō* (Cambridge, MA: Harvard University Asia Center, 2006).

48. On the popularity of *bushidō* and *bushidō*-related heroes in the Meiji period, see Cyril H. Powles, "Bushidō: Its Admirers and Its Critics," in *Nitobe Inazō: Japan's Bridge across the Pacific,* ed. John F. Howes (Boulder, CO: Westview, 1995), 107–118; John Tucker, "Tokugawa Intellectual History and Prewar Ideology: The Case of Inoue Tetsujirō, Yamaga Sokō, and the Forty-Seven Rōnin," *Sino-Japanese Studies* 14 (2002): 35–70; and G. Cameron Hurst III, "Honor, and Loyality: The Bushidō Ideal," *Philosophy East and West* 40, no. 4 (October 1990): 511–527.

49. Oleg Benesch, *Inventing the Way of the Samurai: Nationalism, Internationalism, and Bushido in Modern Japan* (New York: Oxford University Press, 2014).

50. Tucker, "Tokugawa Intellectual History and Prewar Ideology," 3. In particular, see Inoue Tetsujirō, *Bushidō sōsho,* 3 vols. (Tokyo: Hakubunkan, 1906–1909).

51. Daidōji Yūzan, *Budō Shoshinshū,* ed. Tetsushi Furukawa (1720; repr., Tokyo: Iwanami shoten, 1943), 161.

52. Uemura, *Uemura Masahisa zenshū,* 1:189.

53. Ibid.

54. Ibid., 1:185, 192.

55. Ibid., 1:191. "Fujimichō," the name of the neighborhood in which the school and Fujimichō Church were located, refers to the fact that the neighborhood looks out on Mount Fuji, making this particular song a logical choice.

56. Ibid., 1:192.

57. See Sandra T. W. Davis, "Treaty Revision," in *Japan in Transition: Thought and Action in the Meiji Era, 1868–1912,* ed. Hilary Conroy, Sandra T. W. Davis, and Wayne Patterson (London: Associated University Presses, 1984), 151–173.

58. See Nitobe Inazō, *Bushido: The Soul of Japan* (Philadelphia: Leeds and Biddle Co., 1900). See also Hurst, "Honor, and Loyality," 511–514.

59. Uemura, *Uemura Masahisa zenshū,* 1:185.

60. Jennings, *Theology in Japan,* 121.

61. Uemura, *Uemura Masahisa zenshū,* 1:194.

62. Ibid.

63. Ozaki Yukio, *The Autobiography of Ozaki Yukio: The Struggle for Constitutional Government in Japan,* trans. Fujiko Hara, ed. Marius Jansen (Princeton, NJ: Princeton University Press, 2001), 136.

64. Uemura, *Uemura Masahisa zenshū,* 1:195.

65. Ibid.

66. Ibid., 1:197.

67. Dohi, "Christianity and Politics in the Taishō Period of Democracy, Part 1," 1–24.

68. See Paramore, *Ideology and Christianity in Japan,* chap. 6.

69. For the standard historical account of this incident, see Ōzawa Saburō, *Uchimura Kanzō fukei jiken* [The Uchimura Kanzō lèse-majesté incident] (Tokyo: Shinkyō Shuppansha, 1961); Suzuki Norihisa, *Uchimura Kanzō to sono jidai: Shiga Shigetaka to no hikaku* [Uchimura

Kanzō and his times: A comparison with Shiga Shigetaka] (Tokyo: Nihon Kirisuto Kyōdan Shuppan kyoku, 1975), 137; and Saba Wataru, *Uemura Masahisa to sono jidai,* vol. 5 (Tokyo: Kyōbunkan, 1941–1942), 766–770. In English, see John F. Howes, *Uchimura Kanzō,* 72–75; Gluck, *Japan's Modern Myths,* 132; Thelle, *Buddhism and Christianity in Japan,* 121–125.

70. Gluck, *Japan's Modern Myths,* 128.

71. Inoue Tetsujirō, *Kyōiku to shūkyō no shōtotsu* [The clash of education and religion] (Tokyo: Tetsugakushoin, 1893). For a thorough analysis of the anti-Christian ramifications of this text, see Paramore, *Ideology and Christianity in Japan,* 148–150; and Seki Kōsaku, *Inoue hakase to kirisutokyōto* [Dr. Inoue and Christianity] (Tokyo: Tetsugakushoin, 1893).

72. Gluck, *Japan's Modern Myths,* 133. See also Inoue Tetsujirō, *Kyōiku to shūkyō no shōtotsu,* quoted in Seki Kōsaku, *Inoue Hakase to Kirisutokyōtō* [Dr. Inoue and Christianity], vol. 1 (Tokyo: Testugaku Shoin, 1896), 70–71.

73. Thelle, *Buddhism and Christianity in Japan,* 124. Thelle is referring to a particular article in *Reichikai zasshi.*

74. Kozaki, *Kozaki Hiromichi zenshū,* 5:14.

75. Charles E. Neu, *An Uncertain Friendship: Theodore Roosevelt and Japan, 1906–1909* (Cambridge, MA: Harvard University Press, 1967).

76. Roger Daniels, *The Politics of Prejudice: The Anti-Japanese Movement in California and the Struggle for Japanese Exclusion* (Berkeley: University of California Press, 1999).

77. Kozaki, *Kozaki Hiromichi zenshū,* 5:15.

78. Notehelfer, *American Samurai,* 137, 139–140.

79. Gluck, *Japan's Modern Myths,* 129–130; Inoue Tetsujirō, *Chokugo engi* (1891), in *Kyōiku chokugo kanpatsu kankei shiryōshū* [Collection of materials related to the promulgation of the imperial rescript on education], vol. 3 (Tokyo: Kokumin seishin bunka kenkyūjo, 1939), 230–231.

80. Kozaki, *Kozaki Hiromichi zenshū,* 238.

81. Gluck, *Japan's Modern Myths,* 217; and Yamaji Aizan, "Meiji taitei oyobi sono jidai," *Kokumin zasshi* 3, no. 16 (15 August 1912).

82. Gluck, *Japan's Modern Myths,* 219.

83. Ibid.

84. Kozaki, *Kozaki Hiromichi zenshū,* 213.

85. Ibid., 230.

86. Ibid., 231.

87. Ibid., 232–233.

88. Empire Day was a national holiday, created in 1872 and then positioned on 11 February beginning in 1873. This holiday was a celebration of Japan's founding emperor, Jimmu, and the unbroken line of emperors who have succeeded him up to the present. Officially abolished by the Supreme Commander of Allied Powers after World War II, the holiday continued and was reborn, with fewer associations with the emperor, as National Foundation Day (Kenkoku kinen no hi). See Hardacre, *Shintō and the State,* 101–103.

89. Richard J. Samuels, *Rich Country, Strong Army: National Security and the Technological Transformation of Japan* (Ithaca, NY: Cornell University Press, 1994), 34–37. For a concise explanation of the "Rich Country, Strong Army" concept, see Beasley, *The Meiji Restoration,* 210.

90. Kozaki, *Kozaki Hiromichi zenshū,* 207.

91. Ibid., 208.

92. Ibid., 237.
93. Ibid.
94. Ibid., 238.
95. Ebina Danjō, "Gojin no shūyō" [Our cultivation], *Shinjin* 1, no. 7 (February 1901): 7.
96. Ibid., 7.
97. Ibid., 8.
98. Skya, *Japan's Holy War,* 56. Here he has translated this phrase from Hozumi Yatsuka, *Kokumin kyōiku: Aikokushin* [National education: Patriotism] (Tokyo: Yuhikaku, 1897), 16.
99. Ebina, "Gojin no shūyō," 9.
100. Ibid.
101. Ebina Danjō, "Sensō no bi" [The beauty of war], *Shinjin* 5, no. 8 (August 1904): 22.
102. For examples of this term's use, see Maekawa Shinjirō, *Zetsudai naru jinkaku* (Tokyo: Seikokai shuppansha, 1929); and Saiga Hiroyoshi, *Saigō nanshūoū: Daijinkan no ikan* (Tokyo: Shizendō shoten, 1919).
103. On *Yamato damashii* and its wartime popularity, see Gluck, *Japan's Modern Myths,* 136.
104. On Saigō see Charles S. Yates, "Saigo Takamori in the Emergence of Meiji Japan," *Modern Asian Studies* 28, no. 3 (July 1994): 449–474. It is worth noting that Saiga Hiroyoshi, author of one of the few works with *daijinkaku* in its title, used this term to praise Saigō Takamori, just as Ebina did.
105. Ebina, "Sensō no bi," 22. For background on the origins and importance of the shrine, see Nelson, "Social Memory as Ritual Practice."
106. Ebina, "Sensō no bi," 17. Here Ebina refers to the incident written of in the *Heike Monogatari* in which Nasu no Yoichi shot down a red fan, thought to be a trap, hoisted up on a Taira vessel by a lady of the court. See the story in Helen Craig McCollough, *The Tale of the Heike* (Stanford, CA: Stanford University Press, 1988), 367–369.
107. Ebina, "Sensō no bi," 20.
108. Ibid., 21.
109. Ibid.
110. Ibid., 20, 22.
111. Ebina, "Gojin no shūyō," 10. Here Ebina is referring to Hideyoshi's ultimately unsuccessful attempts to invade China through Korea in 1592 and 1598. See Mary Elizabeth Berry, *Hideyoshi* (Cambridge, MA: Harvard University Press, 1982).
112. Ebina, "Gojin no shūyō," 10.
113. Ebina Danjō, "Shinbushidō" [The new way of the warrior], *Shinjin* 2, no. 10 (1 May 1902): 12.
114. Ibid.
115. For an overview of Japanese colonization, see Ramon H. Myers and Mark R. Peattie, eds., *The Japanese Colonial Empire, 1895–1945* (Princeton, NJ: Princeton University Press, 1984).
116. Thomas F. Millard, "Japanese Immigration into Korea," *Annals of the American Academy of Political and Social Science* 34, no. 2 (September 1909): 185.
117. Myers and Peattie, *The Japanese Colonial Empire,* 89.
118. Ebina, "Shinbushidō," 12.
119. See Michael Adas, *Machines as the Measure of Men: Science, Technology, and Ideologies of Western Dominance* (Ithaca, NY: Cornell University Press, 1989), 210–221.

120. Ebina, "Shinbushidō," 12, reprinted in Ebina, *Ebina Danjō no sekkyōshū,* 86.

121. For the translated text of the Imperial Rescript, see Gluck, *Japan's Modern Myths,* 121.

122. Ebina, "Shinbushidō," 12, reprinted in Ebina, *Ebina Danjō no sekkyōshū,* 86.

123. Ebina, "Shinbushidō," 12.

124. Ebina, "Ima wa kitō toki nari," 14.

125. Ebina, "Shinbushidō," 12.

126. Ebina, "Kirisutokyō to demokurashii," 22.

127. Gluck, *Japan's Modern Myths,* 130.

128. On the explicit links between national education and *bushidō,* as manifested in documents such as the 1890 Imperial Rescript on Education and the Bōshin Rescript of 1908, see Yushi Ito, *Yamaji Aizan and His Time: Nationalism and Debating Japanese History* (Folkestone, UK: Global Oriental, 2007), 426.

Chapter Five: The Lay Lectern—Discourse beyond Religion at Church

1. Snodgrass, *Presenting Japan,* chap. 8, citing the manifesto "Bankoku shūkyō dai kai gi ni tsuie kaku shū kyōkai ni nozomu" [A request to All Sects Council concerning the World's Parliament of Religions], *Shūkyō* (5 April 1893): 294–299.

2. Shields, *Against Harmony,* 41, 157–162. Sawada does note that for those Confucian officials, the society was as much about Zen as it was about poetry, reflection, and calligraphy.

3. Snodgrass, *Presenting Japan,* 126.

4. Ibid., 250; Shields, *Against Harmony,* 45.

5. On faith conversations and faith confessions published in *Kyūdō journal,* see Iwata Fumiaki, *Kindai Bukkyō to seinen: Chikazumi Jōkan to sono jidai* [Modern Buddhism and youth: Chikazumi Jōkan and his times] (Tokyo: Iwanami shoten, 2014), 59–64; see also Ōmi Toshihiro, *Kindai Bukkyō no naka no Shinshū: Chikazumi Jōkan to kyūdōsha tachi* [Shin in the midst of modern Buddhism: Chikazumi Jōkan and seekers of the way] (Kyoto: Hōzōkan, 2014), 95–96.

6. Uesugi Bunshū, "Bukkyō no sensōron" [Buddhism's perspective on war], *Kyūdō* 1, no. 5 (May 1904): 21–23.

7. Sawada, *Practical Pursuits,* 145.

8. Hiroshi Watanabe, *The Architecture of Tokyo,* 62. In the Taishō period, Osaka Central Assembly Hall hosted lectures by religionists like Nichirenist proselytizer Tanaka Chigaku on politically and socially relevant topics. See chapter 4; see also Lee, "Nichiren and Nationalism," 22–23.

9. *Reinanzaka kyōhō,* no. 9 (7 July 1901): 1.

10. *Fukuin Shimpo,* no. 157 (1 July 1898): 14.

11. *Kirisutokyō shimbun,* no. 489 (9 December 1892): 3.

12. Ibid.

13. *Hongō Kyokai geppō,* no. 5 (10 June 1919): 4.

14. Ōta Takeko diary (unpublished), as transcribed in Saba, *Uemura Masahisa to sono jidai,* 3:102.

15. Amherst College, *Amherst College Alumni Address List* (Amherst, MA: Amherst College, 1904), 43; *Kirisutokyō shimbun,* no. 342 (14 February 1890): 2.

16. Ibid. Also mentioned in *Jogaku zasshi* 201 (22 February 1890): 27.

17. *Kirisutokyō shimbun,* no. 360 (20 June 1890): 3.

18. *Kirisutokyō shimbun,* no. 431 (30 October 1891): 3.

19. On Shimada, see Takahashi Masao, *Shimada Saburō den* [The biography of Shimada Saburō] (Tokyo: Mahoroba shobō, 1988).

20. On Shimada at Ichibanchō, see Takahashi Masao, *Meiji no Kirisutokyō* [Meiji Christianity] (Tokyo: Yoshikawa Kyōbunkan, 2003), 129.

21. *Kirisutokyō shimbun,* no. 489 (9 December 1892): 3.

22. See Clara A. Whitney, *Clara's Diary: An American Girl in Japan,* ed. William Steele and Tamiko Ichimata (Tokyo: Kodansha International, 1979), 206–207. See also Edwin Taylor Iglehart, ed., *The Christian Movement in the Japanese Empire including Korea and Formosa: A Year Book for 1919,* 17th annual issue (Tokyo: Kyōbunkan, 1919), 275–277.

23. Huffman, *Creating a Public,* 87.

24. Thomas R. H. Havens, *Nishi Amane and Modern Japanese Thought* (Princeton, NJ: Princeton University Press, 1970), 166.

25. Davidann, *A World of Crisis and Progress,* 64.

26. Notehelfer, *American Samurai,* 234.

27. *Kirisutokyō shimbun,* no. 519 (7 July 1893): 2.

28. Helen Ballhatchet, "The Religion of the West versus the Science of the West: The Evolution Controversy in Late Nineteenth Century Japan," in *Japan and Christianity: Impacts and Responses,* ed. John Breen and Mark Williams (New York: St. Martin's, 1996), 107–121.

29. Ballhatchet, "The Religion of the West," 116–117.

30. See *Kirisutokyō shimbun,* no. 436 (4 December 1891): 3; *Kirisutokyō shimbun,* no. 437 (11 December 1891): 3; *Kirisutokyō shimbun,* no. 438 (18 December 1891): 3; *Kirisutokyō shimbun,* no. 436 (4 December 1891): 3; *Kirisutokyō shimbun,* no. 444 (29 January 1892): 3; *Kirisutokyō shimbun,* no. 451 (18 March 1892): 2; *Kirisutokyō shimbun,* no. 453 (1 April 1892): 2. The texts of some of these lectures have been transcribed in Yokoi Tokio, *Hongō kaidō gakujutsu kōen* (Tokyo: Keiseisha, 1892). The second series is mentioned in several places, including Hongō Kyōkai, *Hongō 100-nen shi,* 233–234; Yamauchi Haruko, *Asakawa Kan'ichi ron: Sono gakumon keisei to jissen* [Kan'ichi Asakawa: His development as an academic practitioner] (Tokyo: Waseda Daigaku shuppanbu, 2009), 73; and Mizuno Hirota, "Meiji-ki yōmeigaku kenkyū no bokkō: Inoue Tetsujirō *Nihon Yōmeigaku-ha no tetsugaku*" [The sudden rise of Yōmei studies in the Meiji period: Inoue Tetsujiro *The Philosophy of the Japan Yōmei studies school*], *Shisōshi kenkyū* 24 (December 2017): 75.

31. This number is the attendance figure for the 12 December *kōenkai. Kirisutokyō shimbun,* no. 438 (3 December 1891): 3.

32. *Kirisutokyō shimbun,* no. 437 (11 December 1891): 3; *Kirisutokyō shimbun,* no. 438 (18 December 1891): 3.

33. On Dr. Kitazato Shibasaburō, see Yamauchi, *Asakawa Kan'ichi ron,* 71–73.

34. On Tokutomi Sohō's relationships with young Kozaki, Yokoi, and Ebina at Captain Leroy Lansing Janes's Kumamoto School for Western Studies, see Notehelfer, *American Samurai,* chap. 9; Pierson, *Tokutomi Sohō,* chap. 2; and Scheiner, *Christian Converts and Social Protest,* 80.

35. Pierson, *Tokutomi Sohō,* 394.

36. On Yoshida Shōin, see Harry D. Harootunian, *Toward Restoration: The Growth of Political Consciousness in Tokugawa, Japan* (Berkeley: University of California Press, 1970), chap. 4.

37. *Kirisutokyō shimbun,* no. 451 (18 March 1892): 2; and *Kirisutokyō shimbun,* no. 452 (25 March 1892): 3. Scholar Yamauchi Haruko dates this talk to 19 March 1893, but the actual date appears to have been 19 March 1892.

38. Murakami Senjō, "Bukkyō no ni dai ganmoku" [Buddhism's two great main points], in *Hongō Kaidō gakujutsu kōen,* ed. Yokoi Tokio [Hongō Church Science Lectures] (Tokyo: Keiseisha, 1892), 61.

39. Ibid., 63.

40. Shields, *Against Harmony,* 75; Paramore, *Ideology and Christianity in Japan,* 133.

41. Walter Dening, "Confucian Philosophy in Japan: Reviews of Dr. Inoue Tetsujirō's Three Volumes on This Philosophy," *Transactions of the Asiatic Society of Japan* 36 (1908): 102; see also Snodgrass, *Presenting Japan,* 140.

42. Inoue Tetsujirō, *Kyōiku to shūkyō no shōtotsu.* For more on this text see Emily Anderson, *Christianity and Imperialism,* 39; and Paramore, *Ideology and Christianity in Japan,* 148–153.

43. Inoue Tetsujirō, "Ōyōmei no gaku wo ronzu" [Discussing the study of Ōyōmei], in Yokoi, *Hongō Kaidō gakujutsu kōen,* 46.

44. Ibid., 47.

45. Ibid., 59.

46. Ibid., 56.

47. Ermanno Bencivenga, "Knowledge vs. Belief," *Philosophical Forum* 30, no. 1 (March 1999): 3–11.

48. Ion, *American Missionaries, Christian Oyatoi,* 272; Jennings, *Theology in Japan,* 105.

49. *Kirisutokyō shimbun,* no. 537 (10 November 1893): 2.

50. *Kirisutokyō shimbun,* no. 580 (7 September 1894): 2.

51. *Kirisutokyō shimbun,* no. 189 (26 October 1894): 13.

52. *Kirisutokyō shimbun,* no. 982 (20 June 1902): 19.

53. *Kirisutokyō shimbun,* no. 983 (27 June 1902): 18. On the Fukushima Incident, in which Sugiyama participated as an adolescent, see Roger M. Bowen, *Rebellion and Democracy in Meiji Japan* (Berkeley: University of California Press, 1980), chap. 1, 325–326.

54. See https://kotobank.jp/word/寺尾新-1093040 (accessed 26 May 2020).

55. *Reinanzaka kyōhō,* no. 18 (April–June 1903): 3.

56. Chushichi Tsuzuki, "Kōtoku, Ōsugi, and Japanese Anarchism," *Hitotsubashi Journal of Social Studies* 3, no. 1 (3) (March 1966): 32.

57. Hyman Kublin, "The Origins of Japanese Socialist Tradition," *Journal of Politics* 14, no. 2 (May 1952): 261.

58. See George M. Beckmann and Genji Okubo, *The Japanese Communist Party 1922–1945* (Stanford, CA: Stanford University Press, 1969), 3; and Mackie, *Creating Socialist Women,* 47; and Vera Mackie, *Feminism in Modern Japan: Citizenship, Embodiment and Sexuality* (Cambridge: Cambridge University Press, 2002), 232, 258.

59. Kublin, "The Origins of Japanese Socialist Tradition," 262. This was Unity Hall in Mita, established by Clay MacCauley in 1894. For more on MacCauley and the intellectual climate of Unity Hall, see Mohr, *Buddhism, Unitarianism, and the Meiji Competition for Universality,* 27–32.

60. On the change from a reading group to an association in 1900, see Mackie, *Creating Socialist Women,* 230. See also Matsuda Shigeo, ed., *Abe Isoo nenpyō, chosaku mokuroku* [Abe Isoo chronology, works index] (Kurashiki: Matsuda Shigeo, 2002), 8.

61. *Reinanzaka kyōhō,* no. 19 (July–September 1903): 1.

62. *Reinanzaka kyōhō,* no. 25 (December 1904): 2.
63. Matsuda, "Abe Isoo nenpyō," 7.
64. Ōsugi, *The Autobiography of Ōsugi Sakae,* 122.
65. Ibid.
66. Kublin, "The Origins of Japanese Socialist Tradition," 262.
67. Dohi, *Nihon Purotesutanto Kirisutokyō shi,* 204.
68. F. G. Notehelfer, *Kōtoku Shūsui: Portrait of a Japanese Radical* (New York: Cambridge University Press, 1971), 62.
69. Emily Anderson, *Christianity and Imperialism,* 82.
70. Yasuo Furuya, ed. and trans., *A History of Theology in Japan* (Grand Rapids, MI: Eerdmans, 1997), 50.
71. Cyril H. Powles, "Abe Isoo: The Utility Man," in *Pacifism in Japan: The Christian and Socialist Tradition,* ed. Nobuya Bamba and John F. Howes (Vancouver: University of British Columbia Press, 1978), 146.
72. Ibid.
73. On Katayama's membership at Banchō, see Sally A. Hastings, *Neighborhood and Nation in Tokyo, 1905–1937* (Pittsburgh: University of Pittsburgh Press, 1995), 24.
74. Tōya, *Fujimichō hachijūnen shi,* 27.
75. *Reinanzaka kyōhō,* no. 19 (July–September 1903): 3.
76. On Noguchi, see Norimasa Morita, "Yone Noguchi (1875–1947)," in *Britain and Japan: Biographical Portraits,* vol. 8, ed. Hugh Cortazzi (Folkestone, UK: Global Oriental, 2013), 415. See also Hori Madoka, *"Nijū kokuseki shijin" Noguchi Yonejirō* ["Dual citizen poet" Noguchi Yonejirō] (Nagoya: Nagoya Daigaku shuppankai, 2012).
77. See Norimasa Morita, "Yone Noguchi."
78. *Reinanzaka kyōhō,* no. 14 (June–July 1909): 12.
79. *Reinanzaka kyōhō,* no. 24 (18 February 1911): 5.
80. *Kirisutokyō shimbun,* no. 1433 (2 March 1911): 9.
81. Ibid.
82. *Reinanzaka kyōhō,* 15 June 1923, 3.
83. Ōsugi, *The Autobiography of Ōsugi Sakae,* 121.
84. Ibid., 122.
85. Hiratsuka, *In the Beginning,* 77.
86. Sievers, *Flowers in Salt,* 169.
87. For what remains one of the most frequently used collections of documents related to the *fujin mondai* in prewar Japan, see Ichikawa Fusae, Maruoka Hideo, Akamatsu Ryōko, Mitsui Tametomo, Yuzawa Yasuhiko, Ichibangase Yasuko, and Yamaguchi Miyoko, eds., *Nihon Fujin Mondai Shiryō Shūsei,* 10 vols. (Tokyo: Domesu Shuppan, 1977–1981). For an introduction to late Meiji and Taishō phases of the *fujin mondai* debates, see Sharon H. Nolte, *Liberalism in Modern Japan: Ishibashi Tanzan and His Teachers, 1905–1960* (Berkeley: University of California Press, 1987), chap. 3.
88. Sievers, *Flowers in Salt,* chap. 2.
89. Ibid. See also Marnie S. Anderson, "Kishida Toshiko and the Rise of the Female Speaker in Meiji Japan," *U.S.-Japan Women's Journal,* nos. 30/31 (2006): 36.
90. On Okayama, see Marnie S. Anderson, *A Place in Public;* and Mara Patessio, *Women and Public Life in Early Meiji Japan: The Development of the Feminist Movement* (Ann Arbor: University of Michigan Press, 2011). On the WCTU, see Lublin, *Reforming Japan.*

91. Mackie, *Feminism in Modern Japan,* 32.

92. *Reinanzaka kyōhō,* no. 18 (April–June 1903): 3.

93. On Iwaya's church attendance and participation, see Kuwabara Saburō, ed., *Iwaya Sazanami nikki honkoku to kenkyū: Ji Meiji nijūnen shi Meiji nijū nana nen* (Tokyo: Keiō Gijuku Daigaku Shuppansha, 1998); and Kinya Katsuo, *Iwaya Sazanami: Otogi sakka he no michi* (Tokyo: Keiō Gijuku Daigaku Shuppan sha, 2000).

94. *Kirisutokyō shimbun,* no. 1162 (7 December 1905): 4.

95. *Kirisutokyō shimbun,* no. 1029 (14 May 1903): 4. His talk was about the popular author Higuchi Ichiyō.

96. *Kirisutokyō shimbun,* no. 1162 (7 December 1905): 4.

97. Ibid.

98. *Reinanzaka kyōhō,* no. 3 (June 1908): 2.

99. Ibid.

100. *Reinanzaka kyōhō,* no. 23 (December 1910): 2–3.

101. Dina Lowy, "Nora and the 'New Woman': Visions of Gender and Modernity in Early Twentieth-Century Japan," *U.S.-Japan Women's Journal,* no. 26 (2004): 76.

102. On the founding of the journal, see Dina Lowy, *The Japanese "New Woman": Images of Gender and Modernity* (New Brunswick, NJ: Rutgers University Press, 2007); Sievers, *Flowers in Salt;* Hiroko Tomida, *Hiratsuka Raichō and Early Japanese Feminism* (Leiden: Brill, 2004); and Jan Bardsley, *The Bluestockings of Japan: New Woman Essays and Fiction from Seitō, 1911–1916* (Ann Arbor: University of Michigan Press, 2007).

103. Lowy, "Nora and the 'New Woman,'" 75.

104. Ibid.

105. For a detailed discussion of the play and its implications, see Lowy, *The Japanese "New Woman,"* chap. 2.

106. Yoshino Sakuzō, "Seikoku fujin no zatsugo" [Some words on Chinese women], *Shinjokai* 1, no. 1 (April 1909): 7–9.

107. Yuan also held the position of viceroy of Zhili and minister of Beiyan. See Jerome Chen, *Yuan Shih-k'ai, 1859–1916: Brutus Assumes the Purple* (Stanford, CA: Stanford University Press, 1961).

108. Yoshino, "Seikoku fujin," 8.

109. Ibid.

110. Patessio, "The Creation of Public Spaces," 156.

111. See Rumi Yasutake, "Men, Women, and Temperance in Meiji Japan: Engendering WCTU Activism from a Transnational Perspective," *Japanese Journal of American Studies* 17 (2006): 101.

112. On the future General Hibiki's membership at Ichibanchō Church, see Prang, *A Heart at Leisure from Itself,* 157.

113. *Fukuin shimpō,* no. 155 (17 June 1898): 12–13.

114. *Reinanzaka kyōhō,* no. 23 (December 1910): 2. On Mitani Tamiko's role at Joshi Gakuin, see "Mitani Tamiko" hensan iinkai, ed., *Mitani Tamiko* (Tokyo: Joshi Gakuin, 1991). See also https://www.joshigakuin.ed.jp/school/deveropment/ (accessed 26 May 2020).

115. Garrett L. Washington, "Christianity and 'True Education': Yasui Tetsu's Contribution to Women's Education in Imperial Japan," in *Christianity and the Modern Woman in East Asia Christianity and the Modern Woman in East Asia,* ed. Garrett L. Washington (Leiden: Brill, 2018), 144.

116. Yasui Tetsu, "Gendai fujin no shūyō" [Modern women's cultivation], *Shinjokai* 1, no. 1 (1 April 1909): 3.

117. Ibid.

118. Ibid.

119. Ninomiya Teiko, "Tōraku no seikatsu" [Fully happy life], *Shinjokai* 3, no. 9 (1 September 1911): 10–14. For mention of Ninomiya, see Prang, *A Heart at Leisure from Itself*, 94.

120. Okonogi Matsuko, "Fujin no katsuki" [Women's energy], *Shinjokai* 3, no. 7 (1 July 1911): 12–14. On Okonogi's study abroad, teaching career, and married name "Tsuji," see Sally A. Hastings, "Traveling to Learn, Learning to Lead: Japanese Women as American College Students, 1900–1941," in *Modern Girls on the Go: Gender, Mobility, and Labor in Japan*, ed. Alisa Freedman, Laura Miller, and Christine R. Yano (Stanford, CA: Stanford University Press, 2013), 197, 266.

121. Okonogi, "Fujin no katsuki," 12.

122. Ibid., 13.

123. Ibid., 12.

124. Ibid.

125. On the accessibility of teaching as an occupation for women in imperial Japan, see, for instance, Nolte, "Liberalism in Modern Japan," 93.

126. Okonogi, "Fujin no katsuki," 13.

127. Washington, "Christianity and 'True Education,'" 148, 150–151.

128. *Kirisutokyō shimbun*, no. 1463 (28 September 1911): 10. On Hirooka's participation in the Osaka YWCA, see Prang, *A Heart at Leisure from Itself*, 84, 88.

129. *Kirisutokyō shimbun*, no. 1463 (28 September 1911): 10.

130. On the Tokyo YMCA Hall, see Nihon Kirisutokyō Rekishi Daijiten Henshū Iinkai, eds., *Nihon Kirisutokyō shi nenpyō: Purotesutanto no bubun* [Japan Christian historical chronology: Protestant section] (Tokyo: Kyōbunkan, 1988), 47. On the Japan YWCA Hall, see Nakamoto Kahoru, "Joshi seinenkyōiku kikai to shite no YWCA no teichaku katei: 1920 nendai no Nihon YWCA to Tokyo YWCA no ugoki wo chūshin to shite" [The establishment process of the YWCA as a young women's education organization: Focusing on the development of the Japan YWCA and Tokyo YWCA of the 1920s], *Tōyō Daigaku daigakuin kiyō*, no. 48 (2011): 409.

131. *Reinanzaka kyōhō*, no. 2 (April 1923): 4.

132. *Kirisutokyō sekai*, no. 1546 (8 May 1913): 9.

133. *Kirisutokyō sekai*, no. 1721 (28 September 1916): 10.

134. *Hongō Kyōkai geppō*, no. 14 (10 March 1920): 4.

Chapter Six: Church-Based Groups and Activism in the Church

1. It is worth noting that Roman Catholic missionary Father Claudius Ferrand (1868–1930) launched several initiatives to encourage participation and community among young Japanese Catholics in Tokyo, including an eighty-member Catholic student club that met monthly. See Cary, *A History of Christianity in Japan*, 1:364.

2. See Thelle, *Buddhism and Christianity;* and Jiryu Mark Rutschman-Byler, *Soto Zen in Meiji Japan: Life and Times of Nishiari Bokusan* (PhD diss., University of California Berkeley, 2014), 17.

3. Ikeda Eishun, “Teaching Assemblies and Lay Societies in the Formation of Modern Sectarian Buddhism,” *Japanese Journal of Religious Studies* 25, nos. 1/2 (Spring 1998): 29.

4. Jessica Starling, “Neither Nun nor Laywoman: The Good Wives and Wise Mothers of Jōdo Shinshū Temples,” *Japanese Journal of Religious Studies* 40, no. 2 (Summer 2013): 284.

5. Ibid.

6. Ibid., 285–295.

7. Ketelaar, *Of Heretics and Martyrs,* 132–133.

8. See Robert Sharf, “The Zen of Japanese Nationalism,” in *Curators of the Buddha: The Study of Buddhism under Colonialism,* ed. Donald S. Lopez Jr. (Chicago: University of Chicago Press, 1995), 141; and Mark L. Blum, *Cultivating Spirituality: A Shin Buddhist Anthology* (Albany: State University of New York Press, 2011), 30–31.

9. Marnie S. Anderson, “Women and Political Life in Early Meiji Japan,” 47.

10. Nolte and Hastings, “The Meiji State’s Policy toward Women,” 154; Sheldon Garon, “Women’s Groups and the Japanese State Contending Approaches to Political Integration, 1890–1945,” *Journal of Japanese Studies* 19, no. 1 (1993): 10.

11. *Annual Report of the American Board of Commissioners for Foreign Missions,* vol. 81 (Boston: Stanley and Usher, 1891), 79.

12. *Fukuin shūhō* 37 (21 November 1890): 11–15.

13. *Annual Report of the American Board of Commissioners for Foreign Missions,* 81:79.

14. Yōzō, *Nobiyuku kyōkai,* 187.

15. Ibid.

16. *Fukuin shimpō,* no. 246 (14 March 1900): 12.

17. *Kirisutokyō shimbun,* no. 612 (29 March 1895): 3.

18. Marnie S. Anderson, *A Place in Public,* 11. On Western-style formal dances held at the Rokumeikan, see Sally A. Hastings, “A Dinner Party Is Not a Revolution: Space, Gender, and Hierarchy in Meiji Japan,” *U.S.-Japan Women’s Journal (English Supplement),* no. 18 (2000): 107–132.

19. Yuasa, *Nobiyuku kyōkai,* 188.

20. Kozaki Hiromichi, *Reminiscences of Seventy Years: The Autobiography of a Japanese Pastor,* trans. Kozaki Nariaki (Tokyo: Kyōbunkan, 1933), 168.

21. Yuasa, *Nobiyuku kyōkai,* 186.

22. Kozaki, *Autobiography of a Japanese Pastor,* 168.

23. *Reinanzaka kyōhō,* no. 10 (23 August 1901): 4.

24. Ibid.

25. Ibid.

26. Tōya, *Fujimichō hachijūnen shi,* 14; and Nihon purotesutanto shikenkyūkai, *Nihon purotesutanto shi no shomondai,* 290.

27. *Fukuin shimpō,* no. 156 (24 June 1898): 14. While Tokutomi Sohō’s speech is reproduced in *Fukuin shimpō,* Hibiki Yoneko’s speech was not.

28. *Kirisutokyō shimbun,* no. 754 (1 January 1898): 7.

29. Hongō Kirisuto Kyōkai, *Hongō Kyōkai sōritsu 50 nen,* 39.

30. Kelly H. Chong, *Deliverance and Submission: Evangelical Women and the Negotiation of Patriarchy in South Korea* (Cambridge, MA: Harvard University Asia Center, 2008), 117.

31. Hastings and Nolte, “The Meiji State’s Policy toward Women,” 153.

32. *Kirisutokyō shimbun,* no. 754 (1 January 1898): 7.

33. Ibid.

34. *Shinjin* 2, no. 11 (June 1901): 34.

35. Yumichō Hongō Kyōkai, *Yumichō Hongō Kyōkai 100-nen shi,* 361–364.

36. Kamemiya Michiko, *Nihon Sekijūjisha to kangofu* [The Japanese Red Cross Society and nursing] (Tokyo: Domesu shuppan, 1983).

37. Sho Konishi, "The Emergence of an International Humanitarian Organization in Japan: The Tokugawa Origins of the Japanese Red Cross," *American Historical Review* 119, no. 4 (October 2014): 1129–1153.

38. Dōyōkai rekishibukai, "Nihon Sekijūjisha kangofuyōseijo, sono 3: Nissei sensō to Nichi seki kangofu" [The history of nursing in Japan, vol. 3: Chinese-Japanese War and the Red Cross nurses], *Kangofu zasshi* 36, no. 1 (January 1972): 74–80.

39. Yumichō Hongō Kyōkai, *Yumichō Hongō Kyōkai 100-nen shi,* 364.

40. *Kirisutokyō shimbun,* no. 623 (5 July 1895): 3–4.

41. Murakami Kōta, "Bokyōkai toshite no Hongō Kyōkai" [Hongō Church as my mother church], in Hongō Kirisuto Kyōkai, *Hongō Kyōkai sōritsu 50 nen,* 153.

42. Ibid.

43. *Shinjin* 3, no. 8 (August 1902): 36.

44. Ibid.

45. Garrett L. Washington, "St. Luke's Hospital and the Modernisation of Japan, 1874–1928," *Health and History* 15, no. 2 (December 2013): 10.

46. Susan L. Burns, "Constructing the National Body: Public Health and the Nation in Nineteenth-Century Japan," in *Nation Work: Asian Elites and National Identities,* ed. Timothy Brook and Andre Schmid (Ann Arbor: University of Michigan Press, 2000), 17–49.

47. *Shinjin* 3, no. 8 (August 1902): 36.

48. Ibid.

49. On the introduction of Western massage in Japan and its role in displacing *anma,* see Wakuda Tetsuji, "Kindai Nihon ni okeru massaaji iryō no dōnyū" [First introduction of massage treatment in modern Japan], *Nihon ishigaku zasshi* 49, no. 2 (July 2003): 263–276.

50. Eiko Shinotsuka, "Japanese Care Assistants in Hospitals, 1918–1988," in *Japanese Women at Work,* ed. Janet Hunter (New York: Routledge, 1993), 155.

51. See, for instance, Ebina Miya's article in *Joshi seinenkai* 12, no. 11 (1 December 1915): 12–16; and Kozaki Chiyo's article in *Joshi seinenkai* 6, no. 9 (15 October 1909): 3–5.

52. *Joshi Seinenkai* 12, no. 9 (1 September 1915): 64–65.

53. On Kawai at Fujimichō and in the YWCA, see Kimura Keiko, *Kawai Michi no shōgai: Hikari ni ayunda hito* [Kawai Michi's life: A person walking in the light] (Tokyo: Iwanami shoten, 2002).

54. For more on Ōe, see Ōhama Tetsuya, *Ōe Sumi sensei* [Professor Ōe Sumi] (Tokyo: Tokyo Kaseigakuin Kōinkai, 1978).

55. *Joshi seinenkai* 8, no. 6 (1 June 1911): 1–3.

56. *Shinjokai* 1, no. 4 (1 June 1909): 40.

57. For instance, see *Shinjokai* 1, no. 6 (1 September 1909): 40; and *Shinjokai* 4, no. 8 (1 September 1912): 25–28.

58. Patessio, "The Creation of Public Spaces," 155–182.

59. Rumi Yasutake, "Men, Women, and Temperance in Meiji Japan," 99; Lublin, *Reforming Japan,* 165.

60. See Lublin, *Reforming Japan,* chap. 6.

61. Azuma Moriya, *Nihon Kirisutokyō Fujin Kyōfukai 50-nen shi* [Fifty-year history of Japan Women's Christian Temperance Union] (Tokyo: Nihon Kirisutokyō Fujin Kyōfukai, 1936), 35.

62. Ibid., 360. Some churches with less active *fujinkai* held the meeting in conjunction with their *seinenkai* instead.

63. Ibid., 93.

64. *Kirisutokyō shimbun,* no. 517 (23 June 1893): 10; *Kirisutokyō shimbun,* no. 540 (1 December 1893): 11.

65. Azuma, *Nihon Kirisutokyō Fujin Kyōfukai 50-nen shi,* 1011.

66. Ibid., 391.

67. Lublin, *Reforming Japan,* 165–166; Rumi Yasutake, *Transnational Women's Activism,* 95–98.

68. Lublin, *Reforming Japan,* 165–166.

69. Tōya, *Fujimichō 80-nen shi,* 63.

70. Ibid.

71. Lublin, *Reforming Japan,* 166.

72. Garon, "Women's Groups and the Japanese State," 14–15.

73. Azuma, *Nihon Kirisutokyō Fujin Kyōfukai 50-nen shi,* 69.

74. Nolte and Hastings, "The Meiji State's Policy toward Women," 161; Margaret Mehl, "Women Educators and the Confucian Tradition in Meiji Japan (1868–1912): Miwada Masako and Atomi Kakei," *Women's History Review* 10, no. 4 (2001): 596.

75. Ambaras, "Social Knowledge, Cultural Capital," 15.

76. Botsman, *Punishment and Power,* 198.

77. Ambaras, "Social Knowledge, Cultural Capital," 28. See also *Fukuin shimpō,* no. 230 (33 November 1889): 15.

78. *Reinanzaka kyōhō,* no. 5 (10 March 1901): 6.

79. *Fukuin shimpō,* no. 537 (12 October 1905): 12; Ii and Fugami, *Reinanzaka Kyōkai 100-nen shi,* 277.

80. Kozaki, *Autobiography of a Japanese Pastor,* 270–271.

81. Ii and Fugami, *Reinanzaka Kyōkai 100-nen shi,* 269.

82. Kozaki, *Autobiography of a Japanese Pastor,* 270–271.

83. Ibid., 324–327.

84. Ibid. They apparently stored water in the church's baptismal tank.

85. On Kawai Michi at Fujimichō see Kimura Keiko, *Kawai Michi no shōgai;* on Noguchi Yuka at Hongō, see Kaide Sumiko, *Noguchi Yuka no shōgai* [The life of Noguchi Yuka] (Tokyo: Kirisuto shimbunsha, 1974).

86. For instance, see Davidann, *A World of Crisis and Progress;* and Takahashi Matsuo, *Meiji no Kirisutokyō* (Tokyo: Yoshikawa kyōbunkan, 2003).

87. See Matsuo, "The Japanese Protestants in Korea, Part One"; Matsuo, "The Japanese Protestants in Korea, Part Two"; Emily Anderson, *Christianity and Imperialism;* Dolf-Alexander Neuhaus, "Assimilating Korea: Japanese Protestants, 'East Asian Christianity' and the Education of Koreans in Japan, 1905–1920," *Paedagogica Historica* 52, no. 6 (2016): 614–628; and Shapiro, "Christian Culture and Military Rule."

88. Ochiai Norio, "Tokyo Kirisutokyō seinenkai" [Tokyo YMCA], in *Kirisutokyō rekishi daijiten hensūhū iinkai,* ed. Nihon Kirisutokyō rekishi daijiten [Japanese Christian historical dictionary] (Tokyo: Kyōbunkan, 1988), 488.

89. Hongō Kirisutokyōkai, *Hongō 50-nen,* 116.

90. Yuasa, *Nobiyuku kyōkai,* 185.

91. Kozaki, *Autobiography of a Japanese Pastor,* 61–62; Ion, *The Cross and the Rising Sun,* 1:89.

92. Tōya, *Fujimichō hachijūnen shi,* 42, citing Ogawa Junjirō, "Fujimichō kyōkai oboegaki" [Fujimichō Church notes], and Saba, *Uemura Masahisa to sono jidai,* vol. 5.

93. Kyōgoku Junichirō, *Uemura Masahisa,* 33–34, citing Uemura, *Uemura Masahisa zenshū,* 3:361.

94. Nihon Purotesutanto shikenkyūkai, *Nihon Purotesutanto shi no sho,* 290, citing *Fujimichō kyōkai kiroku.*

95. *Banchō kyōhō* (14 March 1930). Before the Meiji Restoration in 1868, the term *furisode* typically referred to members of the warrior class. During the Meiji era, the term came to be applied to members of the titled nobility (often of samurai origin or with ties to the imperial court). By the later prewar period, however, the term acquired associations with women's traditional clothing. For a great story that illustrates the Edo-period use of *furisode,* see the short story "Furisodé" in Lafcadio Hearn, *In Ghostly Japan* (Boston: Little, Brown, and Co., 1899), 5–8.

96. Gail Lee Bernstein, *Japanese Marxist: A Portrait of Kawakami Hajime, 1879–1946* (Cambridge, MA: Harvard University Press, 1976), 29.

97. Emily Anderson, *Christianity and Imperialism,* 68.

98. On Iwaya's church attendance and participation see Kuwabara, *Iwaya Sazanami nikki;* and Kinya, *Iwaya Sazanami.*

99. Hani, *Hansei wo kataru,* 50. See also Mulhern, *Heroic with Grace,* chap. 8.

100. Prang, *A Heart at Leisure from Itself,* 283.

101. Byron K. Marshall, *Academic Freedom and the Japanese Imperial University, 1868–1939* (Berkeley: University of California Press, 1992), 94–95.

102. Duus, "Yoshino Sakuzō," 308–309.

103. For instance, see Yosuke Nirei, "Globalism and Liberal Expansionism in Meiji Protestant Discourse," *Social Science Japan Journal* 15, no. 1 (2012): 75–92; Han, *An Imperial Path to Modernity,* chap. 2; and Emily Anderson, *Christianity and Imperialism,* 72.

104. The first *seinenkai* in Tokyo churches appeared in the late 1880s. The youth of Nihonbashi Church established the Nihonbashi *kurabu* (club) in 1889, for instance. See Kirisutokyō Dōshinkai, ed., "Seinen kyodai wo tsugu" [Telling of young brothers and sisters], 4, http://nakano-psc.org/wp-content/uploads/2019/09/e48b727c4657f14bc6a3a8683d752bff.pdf (accessed 20 May 2020).

105. *Fukuin shūhō,* no. 9 (1 May 1890): 3; Tōya, *Fujimichō 80-nen shi,* 98.

106. *Kirisutokyō shimbun,* no. 505 (31 March 1893): 2.

107. Best, *Christian Faith and Cultural Crisis,* 144.

108. Yuasa, *Nobiyuku kyōkai,* 118.

109. Schwantes, "Christianity versus Science," 131. There were more than seventy congregations in 1895. See Pettee, *A Chapter of Mission History in Modern Japan,* 178. However, these losses were most acute in major urban areas.

110. Ibid., 149–150; Suzuki Norihisa, *Meiji shūkyō shichō no kenkyū;* Dohi, *Nihon Purotesutanto Kirisutokyō shi,* 172; Hiroko Unuma, *Shiryō ni yoru Nihon Kirisutokyōshi* [Christianity history according to the documents] (Ageo, Japan: Seigakuin Daigaku Shuppankai, 1992), 35–36, 139–140. For a wider discussion on the arrival and impact of

Unitarianism and Liberal Theology, see Mohr, *Buddhism, Unitarianism, and the Meiji Competition for Universality;* Nirei, "Toward a Modern Belief"; and Ballhatchet, "The Religion of the West," 107–121. For an introduction to the content and repercussions of Liberal Theology, see Jennings, *Theology in Japan,* 110–115; and Davidann, *A World of Crisis and Progress,* 56.

111. Ōhama Tetsuya, *Meiji Kirisutokyō kyōkai shi no kenkyū* [A study of the Meiji Christian church] (Tokyo: Yoshikawa Kōbunkan, 1979), 295–330. For a brief summary of Ōhama's insights, see Ballhatchet, "The Modern Missionary Movement in Japan," 47.

112. In particular, Imperial University professor Inoue Tetsujirō stood out as Christianity's strongest critic. For instance, see Paramore, *Ideology and Christianity in Japan,* chap. 6.

113. Davidann, *A World of Crisis and Progress,* chap. 3.

114. *Fukuin shimpō,* no. 211 (14 July 1899): 13.

115. *Fukuin shimpō,* no. 246 (14 March 1900): 12.

116. *Fukuin shimpō,* no. 399 (19 February 1903): 14.

117. Saba, *Uemura Masahisa to sono jidai,* 3:97.

118. Hongō Kirisutokyōkai, *Hongō Kyōkai sōritsu 50-nen,* 33.

119. Ibid.

120. *Shinjin* 1, no. 5 (1 December 1900): 27.

121. Ōta Masao, "Hongō Kyōkai no hitobito," in *Shinjin, Shinjokai no kenkyū: 20 seiki shodai Kirisutokyō ja-narizumu* [Study of *Shinjin, Shinjokai*: Early 20th-century Christian journalism], ed. Doshisha Daigaku Jinbun Kagaku Kenkyūsho (Kyoto: Jinbun shoin, 1999), 211.

122. Yumichō Hongō Kyōkai, *Yumichō Hongō Kyōkai 100-nen shi,* 340.

123. Meidōkai iin, "Meidōkai kōryō [Meidōkai mission statement]," *Shinjin* 1, no. 5 (1 December 1900): 27.

124. Yumichō Hongō Kyōkai, *Yumichō Hongō Kyōkai 100-nen shi,* 335–337.

125. Clemens Büttner and Stefan Weinzierl, "The Acoustics of Early Concert Venues in Japan," *Deutsche Gesellschaft für Akustik* (2010): 629.

126. *Fukuin shūhō,* no. 15 (20 June 1890): 3; Tōya, *Fujimichō 80-nen shi,* 98.

127. Yumichō Hongō Kyōkai, *Yumichō Hongō Kyōkai 100-nen shi,* 75.

128. Ibid.

129. M. William Steele, "The Great Northern Famine of 1905–1906: Two Sides of International Aid," *Asian Cultural Studies* 39 (March 2013): 2.

130. *Reinanzaka kyōhō,* no. 1 (January 1907): 3.

131. *Reinanzaka kyōhō,* no. 21 (September 1910): 4.

132. Kudō Eiichi, "Ashio kōdoku jiken ni okeru Ushioda Chiseko: Kirisutokyō no mondai wo chūshin to shite" [Chiseko Ushioda and her Christian faith in the Ashio mine pollution case], *Mita gakkai zasshi* 75, no. 3 (June 1982): 3–16.

133. Ōta Masao, "Hongō kyōkai no hitobito," 209.

134. Takenaka Masao, "*Shinjin* ni okeru shūkyō shisō" [Religious thought in *Shinjin*], in Dōshisha, *Shinjin, Shinjokai no kenkyū,* 45.

135. *Shinjin* 1, no. 5 (December 1900): 1.

136. *Shinjin* 1, no. 1 (July 1900): 1.

137. Ion, *The Cross and Rising Sun,* 1:89; Notehelfer, *American Samurai,* 234.

138. Kozaki, *Autobiography of a Japanese Pastor,* 90; Jennings, *Theology in Japan,* 125.

139. Morioka, "Meiji zen-ki ni okeru shizoku to Kirisutokyō," 139. See also Tomi Suzuki, *Narrating the Self: Fictions of Japanese Modernity* (Stanford, CA: Stanford University Press, 1996), 201.

140. Yumichō Hongō Kyōkai, *Yumichō Hongō Kyōkai 100-nen shi,* 279.

141. Cary, *A History of Christianity in Japan,* 1:409.

142. *Japan Weekly Mail,* 11 November 1899, 495. See also Cary, *A History of Christianity in Japan,* 1:421.

143. Yamanashi Atsushi, "20-seki shodai ni okeru tenkanki no Nihon Katorikku kyōkai: Pa-ri senkyōkai to Nihonjin Katorikkusha no kankei wo chūshin ni" [The Catholic Church of Japan in the age of transition at the beginning of the twentieth century: The relationship between the Paris Foreign Missions Society and Japanese Catholics], *Nihon kenkyū* (2011): 221–304. See also Cary, *A History of Christianity in Japan,* 1:365.

144. See Thelle, *Buddhism and Christianity in Japan;* and Mohr, *Buddhism, Unitarianism, and the Meiji Competition for Universality.*

145. Mohr, *Buddhism, Unitarianism, and the Meiji Competition for Universality,* chap. 4.

146. Mizutani Makoto, "*Shinjin* to doitsu shūkyō tetsugaku" [*Shinjin* and German religious philosophy], in Dōshisha, *Shinjin, Shinjokai no kenkyū,* 64–66, 70.

147. Takenaka Masao, "*Shinjin* ni okeru shūkyō shisō," 47.

148. For instance, see Emily Anderson, *Christianity and Imperialism,* 69; Ōta Masao, "Yoshino Sakuzō to Kirisutokyō" [Yoshino Sakuzō and Christianity], in Dōshisha, *Shinjin, Shinjokai no kenkyū,* 290.

149. Yumichō Hongō Kyōkai, *Yumichō Hongō Kyōkai 100-nen shi,* 277–278.

150. Kobayashi Naomasa, "*Shinjin* ni okeru shizen kagakusha, Yatsu Naohide" [Natural scientist Yatsu Naohide in *Shinjin*], in Dōshisha, *Shinjin, Shinjokai no kenkyū,* 313.

151. Dōshisha, *Shinjin, Shinjokai no kenkyū,* 24.

152. Statistically speaking, the young attendees far outnumbered their elders. Of the 250 Hongō members who lived in Tokyo in 1905, only 40 of them had families in the capital. Only 49 of them were aged over thirty-nine, and only 29 were aged between twenty-nine and thirty-eight. By contrast, there were 147 young men and women who were between nineteen and twenty-eight years old. "Meiji 37 nen do genzai kaiin no gaikan" [Overview of current members for Meiji 37], *Shinjin* 6, no. 11 (November 1905): 59–60.

Chapter Seven: From the Church into Society

1. Tokutomi "Jūnen shukuga," 18.

2. *Reinanzaka kyōhō,* no. 3 (15 May 1913): 2.

3. Yumichō Hongō Kyōkai, *Yumichō Hongō Kyōkai 100-nen shi,* 64.

4. *Hongō Kyokai geppō,* no. 2 (10 March 1919): 3.

5. These figures appear in *Kirisutokyō sekai,* no. 1087 (30 June 1904): 5; and *Kirisutokyō sekai,* no. 1089 (14 July 1904): 5.

6. Itō Kiyoshi, *Banchō Kyōkai 100-nen shi,* 92.

7. Tōya, "Fujimchō kyōkai-shi shō," 299, 302.

8. David E. Eagle, "Historicizing the Megachurch," *Journal of Social History* 48, no. 3 (1 March 2015): 594.

9. See "Kumiai kyōkai genkyō ippan Meiji 38 nen jūnen gatsu matsu no chōsa," reprinted in Itō Kiyoshi, *Banchō Kyōkai 100-nen shi,* 68.

10. See figures in Shiono Kazuo, *Nihon Kumiai Kirisuto kyōkai shi kenkyū josetu* (Tokyo: Shinkyō Shuppansha, 1995), 343, 365, 367.

11. *Dai Nihon Teikoku Naimusho tōkei hōkoku* [Statistical report of the Home Ministry of the Great Empire of Japan], vol. 28 (1912), 287.

12. Drummond, *A History of Christianity in Japan,* 210.

13. Ion, *The Cross and the Rising Sun,* 1:100.

14. See Winston Davis, *Japanese Religion and Society: Paradigms of Structure and Change* (Albany: State University of New York Press, 1992), chap. 5.

15. Kozaki, *Reminiscences of Seventy Years,* 216.

16. Ibid.

17. Chikazumi, *Shinkō mondai,* 195.

18. Washington, "Fighting Brick with Brick," 101–102.

19. See Peter Duus, "Liberal Intellectuals and Social Conflict in Taishō Japan," in *Conflict in Modern Japanese History,* ed. Tetsuo Najita and J. Victor Koschmann (Princeton, NJ: Princeton University Press, 1982), 421.

20. On the life of Okabe, see Ogawa Masamichi, *Hyōden Okabe Nagamoto—Meiji wo ikita saigō no hanshu* [Critical biography: Okabe Nagamoto—The last feudal lord who lived in Meiji] (Tokyo: Keiō Gijuku Daigaku Shuppankai, 2006). On his membership at Banchō, see Samuel John Umbreit, "The Japanese Response to the Christian Appeal," *Christian Movement in Japan, Korea, and Formosa* 19 (1921): 71.

21. Chikazumi, *Shinkō mondai,* 190.

22. Irokawa, *The Culture of the Meiji Period,* 202.

23. See Oka, "Generational Conflict after the Russo-Japanese War," 209.

24. The term *hanmon seinen* was frequently used to encapsulate the shock and confusion that awaited the generations of youth who had been born during or just after the Meiji Restoration. Bernstein, *Japanese Marxist,* 29.

25. Oka, "Generational Conflict after the Russo-Japanese War," 208.

26. Duus, "Yoshino Sakuzō," 303, citing Yoshino Sakuzō, "Gakusei hikaku mondai" [Student comparison problem], *Shinjin* 6, no. 3 (March 1905).

27. On Ebina's influence on Yoshino, see Dohi, "Christianity and Politics," 42; Duus, "Yoshino Sakuzō," 309, 313–314; Ion, *The Cross and the Rising Sun,* 1:10; and Takayoshi Matsuo, "Profile of the Asian Minded Man VII," 289.

28. Han, *An Imperial Path to Modernity,* 42.

29. Ōtsuka Noyuri, "Yasui Tetsu—Joshi kōtō kyōiku no kaitakusha" [Yasui Tetsu: Pioneer in women's higher education], in *Purotesutanto Jinbutsushi—Kindai Nihon no Bunka Keisei* [History of Protestant figures: The formation of modern Japanese culture], ed. Kirisutokyō Bunka Gakkai (Tokyo: Yorudansha, 1990), 404.

30. Uchigasaki Sakusaburō, "Hongō Kyōkai jidai no omoide" [Recollections from the period of Hongō Church], in Hongō Kirisutokyōkai, *Hongō Kyōkai sōritsu 50-nen,* 162.

31. See Duus, "Yoshino Sakuzō," 314. Han, *An Imperial Path to Modernity,* 51, notes that a speech by Shimada Saburō on Japanese imperial mandate in Korea in February 1905 was important in helping Yoshino to form his concept of liberal imperialism.

32. Yumichō Hongō Kyōkai, *Yumichō Hongō Kyōkai 100-nen shi,* 697; Matsuo, *Taishō demokurashi no kenkyū,* 170–176.

33. Henry D. Smith II, *Japan's First Student Radicals* (Cambridge, MA: Harvard University Press, 1972), 32.

34. Ibid., 35.

35. Bernard S. Silberman, "The Political Theory and Program of Yoshino Sakuzō," *Journal of Modern History* 31, no. 4 (December 1959): 310–324.

36. Peter Duus and John Whitney Hall, eds., *Cambridge History of Japan* (Cambridge: Cambridge University Press, 1988), 6:673–680.

37. Sheldon Garon, *The State and Labor in Modern Japan* (Berkeley: University of California Press, 1987), 36.

38. Henry D. Smith, *Japan's First Student Radicals,* 37, 52–57.

39. Large, "Buddhism and Political Renovation in Prewar Japan," 33–66; and Louis Frédéric, *Japan Encyclopedia,* trans. Käthe Roth (Cambridge, MA: Harvard University Press, 2002), 17.

40. See Sally Ann Hastings, "Urban Voters," in *Shōwa Japan: Political, Economic, and Social History, 1926–1989,* ed. Stephen S. Large (New York: Routledge, 1998), 105–133.

41. Stephen S. Large, "Nishio Suehiro and the Japanese Social Democratic Movement, 1920–1940," *Journal of Asian Studies* 36, no. 1 (November 1976): 37–56.

42. Katayama Tetsu, *Kaikō to tenbō* [Prospect and retrospect] (Tokyo: Fukumura Shuppan Kabushiki Kaisha, 1967), chap. 4.

43. Ōta Masao, "Ishikawa Sanshirō, Hongō kyōkai to heiminsha" [Ishikawa Sanshirō, Hongō Church and the *Heiminsha*], *Shoki shakaishugi kenkyū* 18 (2005): 61–62.

44. Ibid., 64.

45. Ishikawa Sanshirō, *Ishikawa Sanshirō chosakushū,* vol. 8 (Tokyo: Seishisha, 1977), 63.

46. Isao Tsujino, "Ishikawa Sanshirō," *Kirisutokyō shakai mondai kenkyū* [The study of Christianity and social problems] 23 (March 1975): 83–115.

47. On Ishikawa's development as an activist, see Hyman Kublin, "The Japanese Socialists and the Russo-Japanese War," *Journal of Modern History* 22, no. 4 (December 1950): 329; and George Elison, "Kōtoku Shūsui: The Change in Thought," *Monumenta Nipponica* 22, nos. 3/4 (1967): 437–467.

48. Matsuo, *Taishō demokurashi no kenkyū,* 142.

49. Large, *The Rise of Labor in Japan,* 12. See also Suzuki Bunji, *Rōdō undō nijūnen* [Twenty years of the labor movement] (Tokyo: Sōdōmei 50-nen shi Kankō Iinkai, 1966), 46–71.

50. Ion, *The Cross and the Rising Sun,* 1:10. On Suzuki's role in labor initiatives and his political impact, see Stephen S. Large, "The Japanese Labor Movement, 1912–1919: Suzuki Bunji and the Yuaikai," *Journal of Asian Studies* 29, no. 3 (1970): 559–579; and Garon, *The State and Labor,* 106–110.

51. See *Reinanzaka kyōhō,* no. 1 (25 February 1907): 3. Although the church's name is not mentioned, this role is mentioned in David Ambaras, *Bad Youth: Juvenile Delinquency and the Politics of Everyday Life in Modern Japan* (Berkeley: University of California Press, 2006), 107.

52. Ii and Fugami, *Reinanzaka Kyōkai 100-nen shi,* 266.

53. Caroline MacDonald, "Juvenile Delinquency and Its Aftermath," *Christian Movement in Japan, Korea, and Formosa* 19 (1921): 134.

54. Itō Kiyoshi, *Banchō Kyōkai 100-nen shi,* 46; Hastings, *Neighborhood and Nation in Tokyo,* 24.

55. Tsuzuki, "Kōtoko Shūsui, Ōsugi Sakae, and Japanese Anarchism," 32.

56. George Claeys, ed., *Encyclopedia of Nineteenth-Century Thought* (New York: Routledge, 2005), 341. For the most thorough discussion of Kingsley Hall in English, see

Hyman Kublin, *Asian Revolutionary: The Life of Katayama Sen* (Princeton, NJ: Princeton University Press, 1964), chap. 7.

57. Itō Kiyoshi, *Banchō Kyōkai 100-nen shi,* 50.

58. Ibid.

59. Mimatsu, *Uemura sensei no omoide,* 254.

60. Katayama Sen, *Jiden* [Autobiography] (Tokyo: Risōsha, 1949), 239.

61. Ibid.

62. Ibid., 255.

63. Tōya, *Fujimichō 80-nen shi,* 27.

64. Katayama Tetsu, *Waga shi waga tomo* [Our teachers our friends] (Tokyo: Sōnessha, 1948), 27.

65. Ibid.

66. Saba, *Uemura Masahisa to sono jidai,* 5:863.

67. Ibid.

68. Ibid., 5:859, 863; Tagawa Daikichirō, "Miyoshi-shi no koto-domo" [About Mr. Miyoshi], *Fukuin shinpō,* no. 688 (3 September 1908): 2.

69. Saba, *Uemura Masahisa to sono jidai,* 5:867.

70. Ibid., 866.

71. Ibid., 863.

72. Tagawa, "Miyoshi-shi no koto-domo," 2.

73. Endō Kōichi, "Tagawa Daikichirō no seiji shisō" [The political thought of Tagawa Daikichiro], *Meiji Gakuin Daigaku shakai gaku—shakai fukushi gaku kenkyū,* no. 138 (16 March 2012): 1–62; and Seki Naoki, "Tagawa Daikichirō no shimin kyōikuron to sono jissen: Toshi shakai kyōiku no paionia" [Tagawa Daikichi's concept and practice of civic education: A pioneer of urban social education], *Bunsei bulletin* 12 (2000): 71–80.

74. Itō Kiyoshi, *Banchō Kyōkai 100-nen shi,* 48.

75. Saba, *Uemura Masahisa to sono jidai,* 5:157. Here Saba includes the speech Tagawa gave at the dedication of the new Fujimichō Church building. The speech is mentioned in *Fukuin shinpō,* no. 564 (19 April 1906): 12.

76. Ibid.

77. Ibid.

78. Prang, *A Heart at Leisure from Itself,* 270.

79. Gerald H. Anderson, ed., *Biographical Dictionary of Christian Missions* (New York: Macmillan Reference, 1998), 420; and Prang, *A Heart at Leisure from Itself,* chap. 10.

80. Prang, *A Heart at Leisure from Itself,* 153.

81. Ibid., 151–152.

82. Ibid., 87.

83. On Kawai's life and service to the Japan YWCA, see Kimura Keiko, *Kawai Michi no shōgai.*

84. See Mulhern, *Heroic with Grace,* 250, where the author translates the text from Hani Motoko's autobiography, *Hansei wo kataru,* 60.

85. Ibid.

86. Uniya Michiyo, "Hani Motoko: Sono oitachi to shisō keisei" [Hani Motoko: Her development and intellectual formation], *Seikatsu Gakuin Tanki Daigako kiyō* 3 (25 March 1980): 99; and Fukada Mikio, "Shisō to shinkō no setten: Hani Motoko no kyōikuron" [The

connection of thought and faith: Educational philosophy of Motoko Hani], *Kirisutokyō kenkyū* 38, nos. 1–2 (February 1974): 180–198.

87. Mulhern, *Heroic with Grace,* 251, translating Hani, *Hansei wo kataru,* 64.

88. Ibid., 255, translating Hani, *Hansei wo kataru,* 72.

89. Sherif, *Mirror,* 8. This conclusion is based on a description given in Drummond, *A History of Christianity in Japan,* 219. See also Ballhatchet, "Christianity and Gender Relationships in Japan," 183.

90. Mulhern, *Heroic with Grace,* 229.

91. Ambaras, *Bad Youth,* 82.

92. Charles W. Iglehart, ed., *The Japan Christian Year Book* (Tokyo: Kyōbunkan, 1939), 132–133.

93. Uemura, *Uemura Masahisa zenshū,* 3:103.

94. Marianna Nugent Prichard and Norman Young Prichard, *Ten against the Storm* (New York: Friendship Press, [1957]), 93.

95. Ōtsuka Noyuri, "Yasui Tetsu," 424, citing Yasui Tetsu, *Choshakushū,* 18:40.

96. Ōtsuka, "Yasui Tetsu," 424.

97. Yasui Tetsuko, "Waga Shinkō no Keireki" [The personal history of my faith], *Shinjin* 18, no. 6 (June 1917): 82.

98. Yasui Tetsu, "Hongō Kyōkai to watashi" [Hongō Church and I], in Hongō Kirisutokyōkai, *Hongō Kyōkai sōritsu 50-nen,* 155.

99. See Yasui Tetsu, "Fujinkai ni nozomu" [Hopes for the women's group], *Shinjokai* 5, no. 6 (June 1913): 2–5; and Aoyama Nao, *Yasui Tetsu to Tokyo Joshi Daigaku* [Yasui Tetsu and Tokyo Women's Christian University] (Tokyo: Keiō Tsūshin, 1982), 79.

100. Yasui Tetsu, "Makoto ni kyōiku aru Fujin" [Truly educated women], *Shinjokai* 1, no. 9 (December 1909): 2.

101. Yasui Tetsu, "Kyōiku no hōshin" [Educational objectives], *Gakkyūkai* 1 (1922): 3.

102. Ibid.

103. Takamizawa Junko, "Yasui Tetsu (1870–1945)," in *Gojin no senseitachi,* ed. Nihon Kirisutokyōdan (Tokyo: Nihon Kirisutokyōdan Shuppanbu, 1960), 62.

104. Ōtsuka, "Yasui Tetsu," 404.

105. Ibid., 405.

106. Yasui, "Hongō Kyōkai to watashi," 155.

107. Ibid.

108. Aoyama, *Yasui Tetsu to Tokyo Joshi Daigaku,* 79.

109. Ibid., 80.

110. Yasui, "Hongō Kyōkai to watashi," 157.

111. Ibid., 155.

112. Uno, *Passages to Modernity,* 54. Here Uno is drawing from Noguchi's diary entry as transcribed in Kanzaki Kiyoshi, *Gendai Nihon no fujin den* (Tokyo: Sangaku Shōbo, 1940), 59.

113. Kaide, *Noguchi Yuka no shōgai,* 40–42.

114. Ibid., 41.

115. Uno, *Passages to Modernity,* chap. 3.

116. Kaide, *Noguchi Yuka no shōgai,* 42. See also Sally A. Hastings, *Neighborhood and Nation in Tokyo,* 24. Mary Florence Denton was a missionary with the American Board of Commissioners for Foreign Missions. She taught English and biblical literature at Dōshisha but was temporarily employed at Kōran Girls' School in Tokyo during Dōshisha's

administrative disputes over foreign involvement around 1899. See Edward T. James, Janet Wilson James, and Paul S. Boyer, eds., *Notable American Women, 1607–1950: A Biographical Dictionary,* vol. 2 (Cambridge, MA: Radcliffe College, 1971), 465–466.

117. See Nakanishi Kazuko, "Futaba Yōchien kara Futaba ikuen he no ayumi ni kansuru—kōsatsu: Yōgo to kyōiku wo awasemotsu boiku to netowa-ku tsukuri no mosaku" [Searching to construct a network for infant care and education: A study of the process of construction from Futaba Kindergarten to Futaba Nursery School], *Japanese Journal of the Historical Studies of Early Childhood Education and Care* 4 (2009): 29–46.

118. Uno, *Passages to Modernity,* 72–73, 89–92.

119. Nihon Kirisutokyō Rekishi Daijiten Henshū Iinkai, ed., *Nihon Kirisutokyō rekishi daijiten,* 103. For more on Ishikawa's church involvement, see Ishikawa Takeyoshi, *Shinkō zatsugo* [Some words about faith] (Tokyo: Shufu no Tomo sha, 1959); and Ishikawa Takeyoshi, *Fuun kara kōun he* [From misfortune to fortune] (Tokyo: Shufu no tomo sha, 1926).

120. See Ishikawa Takeyoshi, "Watashi no kyūdō jidai," in Hongō Kirisutokyōkai, *Hongō Kyōkai sōritsu 50-nen,* 229–231.

121. Ibid.

122. Sarah Frederick, *Turning Pages: Reading and Writing Women's Magazines in Interwar Japan* (Honolulu: University of Hawai'i Press, 2006), 87.

123. On the origins of *Shufu no tomo* see Barbara Sato, "An Alternate Informant: Middle Class Women and Mass Magazines in 1920s Japan," in *Being Modern in Japan: Culture and Society in Japan from the 1910s to the 1930s,* ed. Elise K. Tipton and John Clark (Honolulu: University of Hawai'i Press, 2000), 137–153.

124. Sato, "An Alternate Informant," 141.

125. Frederick, *Turning Pages,* 84–86.

126. Sadaie Osamu, "*Shinjin, Shinjokai* wo sasaeta Hongō Kyōkai no jigyōka Shinto" [The businessmen believers who supported *Shinjin, Shinjokai*], in Doshisha Daigaku Jinbunkagaku Kenkyūjo, *Shinjin, Shinjokai no kenkyū,* 401.

127. Ibid., 405.

128. Katō Naoshi, *Kobayashi Tomijirō den* [The biography of Kobayashi Tomijirō] (Tokyo: Keiseisha, 1911), 70.

129. Sadaie, "*Shinjin, Shinjokai,*" 416.

130. Ibid.

131. Ebina Danjō, "Jo" [Foreword], in Katō, *Kobayashi Tomijirō den,* 10.

132. "The Heart of Lion's Sustainability," https://www.lion.co.jp/en/csr/story/about/ (accessed 26 May 2020).

133. *Herald of Gospel Liberty* (30 April 1908): 21.

134. Minegishi Hideo, "Kindai Nihon Kirisutokyō shakai kōken ron: Kobayashi Tomijiro, Kurosawa Torizō, Morinagawa Taichirō" [Modern Japan Christian social contributions: Kobayashi Tomijiro, Kurosawa Torizō, Morinagawa Taichirō], *Ōkurayama ronshū* (25 March 2017): 137.

135. *Herald of Gospel Liberty* (30 April 1908): 21.

136. Sadaie, "*Shinjin, Shinjokai,*" 410.

137. Minegishi, "Kindai Nihon Kirisutokyō shakai," 136–137.

138. Ibid., 137. For an outstanding analysis of the institution, see Tanya Sue Maus, "Ishii Juji, the Okayama Orphanage, and the Chausubaru Settlement: A Vision of Child Relief

through Communal Labor and a Sustainable Local Economy, 1887–1926" (PhD diss., University of Chicago, 2007).

139. Bunkachō, "Bunka isan on-rain Cultural Heritage online" http://bunka.nii.ac.jp/heritages/detail/224516 (accessed 26 May 2020). Film of the cortège and ceremony has survived. And in 2011 the Agency of Cultural Affairs declared the recording an Important Cultural Property for capturing the faces and social customs of mourners and the bustling city of Tokyo in the background.

140. Ebina Danjō, "Ebina Danjō no tsuitō sekkyō" [Ebina Danjō's memorial sermon], in Katō, *Kobayashi Tomijirō den,* 176–191.

141. Katō, *Kobayashi Tomijirō den,* 68.

142. Ibid., 69.

143. Ebina, "Jo," in Katō, *Kobayashi Tomijirō den,* 8.

144. Ibid.

145. Ibid., 9.

146. Ibid.

147. Yumichō Hongō Kyōkai, *Yumichō Hongō Kyōkai 100-nen shi,* 403–404.

148. Terazono Tsukasa, "Uemura Masahisa to Kunikida Doppo," *Kokugo to Kokubungaku,* no. 351 (July 1953): 37–44; and Saitō Takeshi, *Omoide no hitobito* [The people of my recollections] (Tokyo: Shinkyō shuppansha, 1965), 227–228.

149. Shimazaki Tōson, *Chikuma River Sketches,* trans. William E. Naff (Honolulu: University of Hawai'i Press, 1991), 127.

150. Kudō, "Ashio kōdoku jiken ni okeru Ushioda Chiseko," *Mita gakkai zasshi* 75, no. 3 (June 1982): 3–16.

151. Joseph Roggendorf, "Shimazaki Tōson: A Maker of the Modern Japanese Novel," *Monumenta Nipponica* 7, nos. 1/2 (1951): 43; Rene Andersson, "Burakumin and Shimazaki Toson's Hakai: Images of Discrimination in Modern Japanese Literature" (PhD diss., Lund University, 2000), 59–60.

152. P. A. George, *Enlightenment of Women and Social Change* (New Delhi: Northern Book Center, 2006), 35. On Kitamura's own relationship with Sukiyabashi (later Ginza) Presbyterian Church and its pastor, Tamura Naoomi, see Kasahara Yoshitaka, "Kitamura Tōkoku no shinkō" [Kitamura Tōkoku's faith], in *Nihon no kindaika to Kirisutokyō* [Japanese modernization and Christianity], ed. Dōshisha Daigaku Jinbunken kenkyūjo and Kirisutokyō shakai mondai kenkyūkai (Kyoto: Doshisha Daigaku Jinbunken, 1973), 177–178.

153. Mohr, *Buddhism, Unitarianism, and the Meiji Competition for Universality,* 111–112; Hastings, *Neighborhood and Nation in Tokyo,* 132; Kublin, "The Origins of the Japanese Socialist Tradition," 262.

154. Arano Kōtarō, ed., *Naniwa Kirisutokyōkai ryakushi* [A brief history of Naniwa Church] (Osaka: Naniwa Kirisutokyōkai, 1928), 55. On the earthquake, see Hidemichi Kawanishi, *Tōhoku: Japan's Constructed Outland* (Leiden: Brill, 2016), 112–113.

155. Arano, *Naniwa Kirisutokyōkai ryakushi,* 80–82, 87, 95.

Epilogue

1. J. Charles Schencking, *The Great Kantō Earthquake and the Chimera of National Reconstruction in Japan* (New York: Columbia University Press, 2013), 2.

2. Ibid., 38, 31.

3. "Airplane Reveals Destruction," *New York Times*, 10 September 1923, 3.
4. Schencking, *The Great Kantō Earthquake*, 44.
5. Huffman, *Creating a Public*, 302.
6. Oleg Benesch and Ran Zwigenberg, *Japan's Castles: Citadels of Modernity in War and Peace* (Cambridge: Cambridge University Press, 2019), 106. See also Andrew Gordon, "Social Protest in Imperial Japan: The Hibiya Riot of 1905," *Japan Focus: The Asia-Pacific Journal* 12, no. 29 (20 July 2014): article 3, https://apjjf.org/2014/12/29/Andrew-Gordon/4150/article.html.
7. Ion, "The Cross under an Imperial Sun," 73. See also Prang, *A Heart at Leisure from Itself*, 79.
8. Prang, *A Heart at Leisure from Itself*, 151.
9. Morinaga, *"Rokutei" Ōiishi Seinosuke*, 329.
10. See Elise K. Tipton, *The Japanese Police State: The Tokkō in Interwar Japan* (Honolulu: University of Hawai'i Press, 1990).
11. Uchikawa Yoshimi and Matsushima Eiichi, eds., *Taishō nyūsu jiten* [Encyclopedia of Taishō news), vol. 7 (Tokyo: Mainichi Komiyunkēshiyon Shuppanbu, 1989), 405, citing *Tokyo Asahi shimbun* (13 February 1925).
12. Gluck, *Japan's Modern Myths*, 135.
13. Thomas T. Mackie and Richard Rose, eds., *The International Almanac of Electoral History* (New York: Macmillan, 1991), 276.
14. Carl G. Seaburg, "Bring Them Hope, Not Hell: A Short History of Universalist and Unitarian Evangelism," in *Salted with Fire: Unitarian Universalist Strategies for Sharing Faith and Growing Congregations*, ed. Scott Alexander (Boston: Skinner House Books of the Unitarian Universalist Association, 1994), 57.
15. This was with the exception of the Russian Orthodox Church, which failed to escape the widespread Japanese suspicions and mistrust stemming from the mission's explicit connections to Japan's enemy, the Russian state. Cary, *A History of Christianity in Japan*, 1:414–417.
16. Ibid., 366, 419.
17. Emily Anderson, *Christianity and Imperialism*, 64.
18. See J. Andrew Kirk, "'God Is on Our Side': The Anatomy of an Ideology," *Transformation* 27, no. 4 (2010): 239–247.
19. See Philip Jenkins, *The Great and Holy War: How World War I Became a Religious Crusade* (New York: HarperCollins, 2014), chap. 2.
20. George Heber Jones, "An Official Conference on Religion in Japan," *Journal of Race Development* 3, no. 2 (October 1912): 228.
21. Shields, *Against Harmony*, 163.
22. Jones, "An Official Conference on Religion," 226, 228.
23. Gluck, *Japan's Modern Myths*, 135.
24. Maxey, *The "Greatest Problem,"* 141.
25. Dohi, *Nihon Purotesutanto Kirisutokyō shi*, 133.
26. Ibid.
27. Inoue and Teeuwen, "Tracing Shintō in the History of Kami Worship," 406.
28. Garon, "Women's Groups and the Japanese State," 14–15.
29. Garon, *Molding Japanese Minds*, 7.
30. Josephson, *The Invention of Religion in Japan*, 133, 138.
31. Cary, *A History of Christianity in Japan*, 1:366.

32. Matsuo, "The Japanese Protestants in Korea, Part One," 406.

33. Emily Anderson, *Christianity and Imperialism,* 14.

34. Matsuo, "The Japanese Protestants in Korea, Part One," 404, citing "Sengo no Saizen-Keiei: Man-Kanjin no Nihonka" [Managing the front lines after the war: The Japanization of Manchurians and Koreans], *Shinjin* 5, no. 8 (August 1904): 1–5.

35. Matsuo, "The Japanese Protestants in Korea, Part One," 415.

36. Ibid., 413, citing the "Manual of the Japan Congregational Church" for years 1911–1920.

37. Matsuo, "The Japanese Protestants in Korea, Part Two," 593.

38. Hwansoo Kim, "'The Future of Buddhism Lies in Our Hands': Takeda Hanshi as a Sōtō Missionary," *Japanese Journal of Religious Studies* 37, no. 1 (2010): 99–135.

39. See Emily Anderson, *Christianity and Imperialism.* See also Howes, *Japan's Modern Prophet.*

40. On this document, see David Reid, "Secularization Theory and Japanese Christianity: The Case of the Nihon Kirisuto Kyōdan," *Japanese Journal of Religious Studies* 61, nos. 1–2 (March–June 1979): 347–378.

41. For the full text of this document, see Kyōdan Executive Committee of the United Church of Christ in Japan, "Confession of Wartime Responsibility during World War II, February 20, 1967," http://uccj-e.org/confession (accessed 26 May 2020).

42. Emily Anderson, *Christianity and Imperialism,* 10.

43. See Maxey, *The "Greatest Problem"*; Jaffe, "The Buddhist Cleric as Japanese Subject"; Hardacre, *Shintō and the State,* 120; and Mitsutoshi Horii, *The Category of Religion in Contemporary Japan: Shūkyō and Temple Buddhism* (New York: Palgrave Macmillan, 2018), chap. 2.

44. Shields, *Against Harmony,* chap. 2; Snodgrass, *Presenting Japan,* chaps. 5 and 9; Ōtani, "The Movement Called 'New Buddhism.'"

Bibliography

Archival Sources

Ebina Danjō shiryō [Ebina Danjō materials]: diaries, letters, memoranda, photos, and other documents. Dōshisha University Library Holdings.

Fujimichō Church Papers: Church Bulletin, Members directory, Service Programs, Photos, 1897–1931 Fujimichō Church Records Room; and Tokyo Women's University Holdings.

Records of the American Board of Commissioners for Foreign Missions Microfilms MS32, Unit 3: Missions to Asia: Reels 326–387, 1880–1919. Yale University Library Holdings.

Reinanzaka Church Papers: *Reinanzaka kyōhō* [church report], Reinanzaka Church Records Room.

Yuasa Jirō shiryō [Yuasa Jirō materials]: letters, memoranda, photos, and other documents. Dōshisha University Library Holdings.

Newspapers and Journals

Asahi shimbun [Morning Sun Newspaper], 1879–present

Christian Union, 1870–1893

Chūō kōron [Central Review], 1887–present; 1887–1931

Cigar Makers' Official Journal, 1875–1972

Fukuin shimpō [Gospel News], 1891–1901

Gakkyūkai [Student Association], 1920–

Herald of Gospel Liberty, 1808–1930

Japan Christian Year Book, 1903–1970

Jogaku zasshi [Women's Education Journal], 1885–1904

Johns Hopkins Circular, 1879–

Kirisutokyō shimbun [Christian Newspaper], 1880–1931

Kokumin no tomo [Nation's Friend], 1887–1898

Kokumin zasshi [People's Journal], 1910–1913

Kyūdō [Seeking the Way], 1904–1922

Meiroku zasshi [Meiji Six Journal], 1874–1875

Missionary Herald, 1880–1920

New York Times, 1851–present

Our Day: A Record and Review of Current Reform, 1888–1894
Reformed Church Review, 1849–1926
Rikugō zasshi [Cosmos Journal], 1880–1921
Shichi ichi zappō [71 General News]
Shinjin [New Man], 1900–1926
Shinjokai [New Women's World], 1909–1919
Taiyō [The Sun], 1895–1928
Tokyo Yūkan shimbun [Tokyo Evening News], 1910–1941

Books and Bound Volumes

Acts and Proceedings of the General Synod of the Reformed Church in America.

Alcock, Rutherford. *The Capital of the Tycoon.* Vol. 2. London: Longman, Green, Longman, Roberts, and Green, 1863.

Amherst College Alumni Address List. Amherst, MA, 1904.

Andō Rikinosuke. *Tokyo-shi zenzu* [Complete map of Tokyo City]. Tokyo: Andō Rikinosuke, 1905.

Annual Report of the American Board of Commissioners for Foreign Missions.

Annual Report of the Board of Foreign Missions of the Reformed Church in America.

Banno, Junji. *The Establishment of the Japanese Constitutional System.* Translated by J. A. A. Stockwin. London: Routledge, 1992.

Black, John R. *Young Japan: Yokohama and Yedo, a Narrative of the Settlement and the City from the Signing of the Treaties in 1858 to the Close of the Year 1879 with a Glance at the Progress of Japan during a Period of Twenty-One Years.* Vol. 1. London: Trubner and Co., 1880.

Burton, Margaret Ernestine. *The Education of Women in Japan.* London: Fleming H. Revell, 1914.

Cary, Otis. *A History of Christianity in Japan.* Vols. 1 and 2. New York: Fleming H. Revell, 1902.

Chamberlain, Basil H. *Things Japanese: Being Notes on Various Subjects Connected with Japan.* London: J. Murray, 1905.

Chikazumi Jōkan. *Shinkō mondai* [The faith problem]. Tokyo: Bunmeidō, 1904.

Clement, Ernest W. *A Short History of Japan.* Chicago: University of Chicago Press, 1915.

Colegrove, Kenneth. "The Japanese Privy Council." *American Political Science Review* 25, no. 4 (November 1931): 881–905.

Daidōji Yūzan. *Budō shoshinshū* [Initiation to the way of the warrior]. Edited by Tetsushi Furukawa. 1720. Repr., Tokyo: Iwanami shoten, 1943.

Dai Nihon Teikoku Naimusho tōkei hōkoku [Statistical report of the Home Ministry of the Great Empire of Japan], 1886–1945.

Davis, Jerome D. *A Maker of New Japan: Rev. Joseph Hardy Neeshima.* New York: Fleming H. Revell, 1894.

Davis, J. Merle. *Davis, Soldier, Missionary: A Biography of Rev. Jerome D. Davis, D.D., Lieutenant Colonel of Volunteers and for Thirty-Nine Years a Missionary of the*

American Board of Commissioners for Foreign Missions in Japan. Boston: Pilgrim Press, 1916.
Deforest, Charlotte B. *Evolution of a Missionary*. New York: Fleming H. Revell, 1914.
De Forest, J. F. *Yaso Kirisuto no tokusei* [Jesus Christ's special characteristics]. Translated by Tsunajima Kakichi. Tokyo: Beikoku seikyō shorui kaisha, 1888.
Directory of the Living Non-graduates of Yale University: Issue of 1914. New Haven, CT: Tuttle, Morehouse & Taylor, 1914.
Ebina Danjō. *Ebina Danjō*. Tokyo: Nihon Kirisutokyōdan shuppansha, 2003.
———. *Ebina Danjō no sekkyōshuū* [The collected sermons of Ebina Danjō]. Tokyo: Shinkyō shuppansha, 1973.
———. *Kirisutokyō gairon mikankō* [Unfinished draft of an introduction to Christianity]. Tokyo: Ebina Ichio, 1937.
Fukuzawa Yukichi. *Fukuzawa zenshū*. Tokyo: Jiji Shimpōsha, 1925–1926.
Gordon, M. L. *Thirty Eventful Years: The Story of the American Board Mission in Japan, 1869–1899*. Boston: American Board of Commissioners for Foreign Missions, 1901.
Griffis, William Elliot. *Guido Verbeck of Japan: A Citizen of No Country: A Life Story of Foundation Work Inaugurated by Guido Fridolin Verbeck*. London: Oliphant, Anderson and Ferrier, 1901.
Hani Motoko. *Hani Motoko: Hansei wo kataru* [Hani Motoko: Recounting half a life]. 1933. Repr., Tokyo: Nihon Tosho Senta-, 1997.
———. *Hansei wo kataru* [Telling half of my life]. 1933. Repr., Tokyo: Nihon Tosho Senta-, 1997.
Harada Tasuku. *Harada Tasuku ishū* [The collected works of Harada Tasuku]. Kyoto: Kawakita Insatsu, 1971.
Hearn, Lafcadio. *In Ghostly Japan*. Boston: Little, Brown, and Co., 1899.
Hiratsuka Raichō. *In the Beginning, When Woman Was the Sun: The Autobiography of a Japanese Feminist*. Translated by Teruko Craig. New York: Columbia University Press, 2006.
Hirooka Asa. *Isshū, isshin* [One round, one faith]. Tokyo: Fujin shūhōsha, 1919.
Historical Sketches of the Missions under the Care of the Board of Foreign Missions of the Presbyterian Church. Philadelphia: Woman's Foreign Missionary Society of the Presbyterian Church, 1891.
Hongō Kirisutokyō Kaidō (Takekawa-chō Kaidō) [Hongō Christian Church (The Takekawa-neighborhood Church)]. Tokyo: Shūeisha, 1891.
Hozumi Yatsuka. *Kokumin kyōiku: Aikokushin* [National education: Patriotism]. Tokyo: Yuhikaku, 1897.
Iglehart, Edwin Taylor, ed. *The Christian Movement in the Japanese Empire including Korea and Formosa: A Year Book for 1919*. 17th annual issue. Tokyo: Kyōbunkan, 1919.
Inoue Tetsujirō. *Bushidō sōsho* [Way of the warrior series]. 3 vols. Tokyo: Hakubunkan, 1906–1909.
———. *Kyōiku to shūkyō no shōtotsu* [The conflict of education and religion]. Tokyo: Tetsugaku Shoin, 1893.
Iseki, K. R., ed. *Who's Who Hakushi in Great Japan*. Vol. 3. Tokyo: Hattensha, 1926.

Ishikawa Sanshirō. *Ishikawa Sanshirō chosakushū*. Vol. 8, *Jijoden* [The collected writings of Ishikawa Sanshirō. Vol. 8, Autobiography]. Tokyo: Seishisha, 1977.

Ishikawa Takeyoshi. *Fuun kara kōun he* [From misfortune to fortune]. Tokyo: Shufu no Tomo sha, 1926.

———. *Shinkō zatsugo* [Some words on faith]. Tokyo: Shufu no Tomo sha, 1959.

Japan Yearbook. Tokyo: Japan Yearbook Office, 1911.

Kaigun Kyōiku Honbu. *Kaigun dokuhon* [Navy manual]. Tokyo: Kaigun Kyōiku Honbu, 1905.

Kanamori, Paul. *Kanamori's Life-story Told by Himself: How the Higher Criticism Wrecked a Japanese Christian—and How He Came Back*. Philadelphia: Sunday School Times Co., 1921.

Kanazawa Ryōta. *Shinsen Tokyo zenzu* [Newly compiled complete map of Tokyo]. Tokyo: Okura Yasugoro, 1892.

Katayama Sen. *Jiden* [Autobiography]. Tokyo: Kaizōsha, 1933.

———. *The Labor Movement in Japan*. Chicago: Charles H. Kerr and Co., 1918.

Katayama Tetsu. *Kaikō to tenbō* [Prospect and retrospect]. Tokyo: Fukumura shuppan kabushiki kaisha, 1967.

———. *Waga shi waga tomo* [Our teachers our friends]. Tokyo: Sōnessha, 1948.

Katō Naoshi. *Kobayashi Tomijirō den* [The biography of Kobayashi Tomijirō]. Tokyo: Keiseisha, 1911.

Kimura Kumaji. *Kimura Kumaji nikki* [The diary of Kimura Kumaji]. Tokyo: Tokyo Joshi Daigaku Hikaku Bunka Kenkyūsho, 2008.

Kinoshita Naoe. *Kinoshita Naoe zenshū* [The collected works of Kinoshita Naoe]. 20 vols. Edited by Yamagiwa Keishi. Tokyo: Kyōbunkan, 1990–2003.

Kiyozawa Manshi. *Kiyozawa Manshi zenshū* [The collected works of Kiyozawa Manshi]. Tokyo: Iwanami Shoten, 2002–2003.

Kozaki Hiromichi. *The Autobiography of a Japanese Pastor: Reminiscences of Seventy Years*. Translated by Kozaki Nariaki. Tokyo: Kyōbunkan, 1933.

———. *Kozaki Hiromichi zenshū* [The Collected Works of Kozaki Hiromichi], 6 vols. 1938. Repr., Tokyo: Nihon Tosho-senta, 2000.

———. *70-nen no kaikō* [Reminiscences of 70 years]. Tokyo: Keiseisha, 1927.

Kyōiku chokugo kanpatsu kankei shiryōshū [Collection of materials related to the promulgation of the imperial rescript on education]. Vol. 3. Tokyo: Kokumin seishin bunka kenkyūjo, 1939.

Leach, Henry. "The Heart of Things." *Chambers's Journal*, no. 6 (December 1906–November 1907): 193–196.

Madden, Maude Whitmore. *Women of the Meiji Era*. New York: Fleming H. Revell, 1919.

Maekawa Shinjirō. *Zetsudai naru jinkaku* [Tremendous character]. Tokyo: Seikōkai Shuppansha, 1929.

Mill, John Stuart. *Fujin no fukujū* [The subjection of women]. Translated by Kataguchi Tairirō. Tokyo: Shūeikaku, 1923.

———. *The Subjection of Women*. New York: D. Appleton and Co., 1869.

Miller, E. Rothesay. *Sketch of the North Japan Mission*. New York: Board of Foreign Missions, Reformed Church of America, 1901.

Miller, Henry K. *History of the Japan Mission of the Reformed Church in the United States, 1879–1904*. Philadelphia: Board of Foreign Missions, Reformed Church of the United States, 1904.

Mimatsu Shunpei. *Uemura sensei no omoide* [Memories of Dr. Uemura]. Tokyo: Arupasha, 1935.

Mita Shōgyō Kenkyūkai, ed. *Keiō Gijūku shūshin meiryū retsuden* [Series of biographies of famous alumni of Keiō Private Academy] Tokyo: Jigyō no Sekai sha, 1909.

Moore, Jairus P. *Forty Years in Japan, 1883–1923*. Philadelphia: Board of Foreign Missions, Reformed Church in the United States, 1925.

Mossman, Samuel. *New Japan, the Land of the Rising Sun: Its Annals during the Past Twenty Years, Recording the Remarkable Progress of the Japanese in Western Civilization*. London: John Murray, 1873.

Nihon Kirisutokyōdan, ed. *Gojin no senseitachi* [Five teachers]. Tokyo: Nihon Kirisutokyōdan Shuppanbu, 1960.

Nihon Kirisuto Shin Sakae Kyōkai 60-nen shi Iinkai, ed. *Nippon Kirisuto Shin Sakae Kyokai 60-nen shi* [Sixty-year history of the Shin Sakae Church]. Tokyo: Nihon Kirisuto Shin Sakae Kyōkai, 1933.

Nihon Kumiai Hongō Kirisutokyōkai. *Hongō Kirisutokyōkai sōritsu 50-nen shi* [The fifty-year history of the establishment of Hongō Church]. Tokyo: Nihon Kumiai Hongō Kirisutokyōkai, 1936.

Nishii Toyosaku. *Shishaku Tanaka Fujimaro Den* [Biography of Viscount Fujimaro Tanaka]. Tokyo: Kōsaijuku, 1934.

Nitobe Inazō. *Bushido: The Soul of Japan*. Philadelphia: Leeds and Biddle Co., 1900.

Ōsugi Sakae. *The Autobiography of Ōsugi Sakae*. Translated Byron K. Marshall. Berkeley: University of California Press, 1992.

Ozaki Yukio. *The Autobiography of Ozaki Yukio: The Struggle for Constitutional Government in Japan*. Translated by Hara Fujiko; edited by Marius Jansen. Princeton, NJ: Princeton University Press, 2001.

Pettee, James Horace. *A Chapter of Mission History in Modern Japan Being a Sketch for the Period since 1869 and a Report for the Years since 1893 of the American Board's Mission and the Kumiai Churches in Their Affiliated Work*. Tokyo: Seishibunsha, ca. 1895.

Presbyterian Board of Foreign Missions relating to Japan and Korea, 1900–1914. Cleveland: Presbyterian Board, 1917.

Prichard, Marianna Nugent, and Norman Young Prichard. *Ten against the Storm*. New York: Friendship Press, [1957].

Proceedings of the General Conference of Protestant Missionaries in Japan, Held in Osaka. Yokohama: R. Meiklejohn and Co., 1883.

Proceedings of the General Conference of Protestant Missionaries in Japan, Held in Tokyo, October 24–31, 1901. Tokyo: Methodist Publishing House, 1901.

Saiga Hiroyoshi. *Saigō nanshūoū: daijinkan no ikan* [Venerable man of the South, Saigō: Magnificent example of the great character]. Tokyo: Shizendō Shoten, 1919.

Saitō Takeshi. *Omoide no hitobito* [The people of my recollections]. Tokyo: Shinkyō shuppansha, 1965.

Scidmore, Eliza Ruhamah. *Jinrikisha Days in Japan.* New York: Harper and Brothers, 1904.

Seki Kōsaku. *Inoue hakase to kirisutokyōto.* [Dr. Inoue and Christianity]. Tokyo: Tetsugaku Shoin, 1893.

"Shiba kōen no zu [Shiba Park map]." In Shiyakusho shishi hensan kakari, ed., *Tokyo annai 2* [Tokyo guide 2]. Tokyo: Shōkadō, 1907.

Shigenaga Yoshihide, ed. *Meiji Jingū gozōei kinen shashinchō* [Commemorative photo album of the construction of Meiji Shrine]. Tokyo: Yoshida shoten, 1920.

Shimada Saburō. *Kinshū wa zeigen wo hiromu* [Prohibition expands tax revenues]. Tokyo: Ginza Kaikan, 1908.

Shimazaki Tōson. *Chikuma River Sketches.* Translated by William E. Naff. Honolulu: University of Hawai'i Press, 1991.

Shindler, Robert. *From the Usher's Desk to the Tabernacle Pulpit: The Life and Labors of Charles Haddon Spurgeon.* New York: A. C. Armstrong and Son, 1892.

Sutcliffe, Anthony, ed. *Metropolis 1890–1940.* London: Mansell, 1984.

Suzuki Bunji. *Rōdō undō nijūnen* [Twenty years of the labor movement]. Tokyo: Sōdōmei 50-nen shi Kankō Iinkai, 1966.

Tamura Naoomi. *Shinkō 50-nen* [Fifty years of faith]. Tokyo: Keiseisha, 1924.

Treaty of Amity and Commerce between the United States and Japan, 1858.

Tsunajima Kakichi. *Gyakkyō no fukuin* [The gospel of adversity]. Tokyo: Keiseisha, 1924.

———. *Hainichi Mondai to Kirisutokyō-tō* [The Anti-Japanese problem and Christians]. Tokyo: Keiseisha, 1931.

Uemura Masahisa. "Fujimichō kyōkai sōritsu 30 nen" [Fujimichō Church at 30 years]. N.p., 1917.

———. *Uemura Masahisa zenshū* [The collected works of Uemura]. 8 vols. Tokyo: Uemura Zenshū Kankōkai, 1932–1934.

Uemura Tamaki. *Fubo to warera* [Mother, father, and us]. Tokyo: Shinkyō Shuppansha, 1966.

Von Goethe, Johann Wolfgang. *Hermann and Dorothea.* Translated by Ellen Frothingham. New York: P. F. Collier & Son, 1909–1914.

Watase Tsunekichi. *Ebina Danjō sensei* [Dr. Ebina Danjō]. Tokyo: Ryūginsha, 1938.

Whitney, Clara A. *Clara's Diary: An American Girl in Japan.* Edited by William Steele and Tamiko Ichimata. Tokyo: Kodansha International, 1979.

Yamaji Aizan, Graham Squires, and A. Hamish Ion. *Essays on the Modern Japanese Church: Christianity in Meiji Japan.* Translated by Graham Squires. Ann Arbor: University of Michigan, Center for Japanese Studies, 1999.

Yamamoto Tadaoki. *Yamamoto Tadaoki den* [The autobiography of Yamamoto Tadaoki]. Tokyo: Yamamoto Tadaoki Hakushi Denki Kankōkai, 1953.

Yasuda Torao. *15-ku 6-gun Tokyo kubun zenzu* [Complete map of the 15 wards and 6 prefectures]. Tokyo: Tsunashima Kamekichi, 1878.

Yasukuni Jinja ichiran: Bekkaku kanpei [Yasukuni Shrine at a glance: Imperial shrine of distinction]. Tokyo: Yasukuni Jinja, 1911.

Yearbook of the Young Men's Christian Associations of North America.

Yokoi Tokio. *Hongō Kaidō gakujutsu kōen* [Hongō Church Science Lectures]. Tokyo: Keiseisha, 1892.

———. *Waga kuni no Kirisutokyō mondai* [The problems of Christianity in our country]. Tokyo: Keiseisha, 1894.

Yoshino Sakuzō. *Yoshino Sakuzō zenshū* [The collected works of Yoshino Sakuzō]. Tokyo: Iwanami Shoten, 1995–1996.

Yuasa Yozō. *Kozaki Hiromichi sensei no shōgai* [The life of Dr. Kozaki Hiromichi]. Kawasaki: Yuasa Yōzo, 1967.

———. *Nobiyuku kyōkai* [The growing church]. Tokyo: Kyōbunkan, 1941.

———. *Waga kuni ni okeru 3 dai kirisutokyō shisōka* [Three great Christian thinkers in our country]. Tokyo: Keiseisha, 1942.

Secondary Sources

Adas, Michael. *Machines as the Measure of Men: Science, Technology, and Ideologies of Western Dominance.* Ithaca, NY: Cornell University Press, 1989.

Addiss, Stephen, and Marilyn Stokstad, eds. *Tōkaidō, on the Road: Pilgrimage, Travel, and Culture.* Lawrence: University of Kansas Press, 1982.

Aiken, Katherine G. *Harnessing the Power of Motherhood: The National Florence Crittenton Mission, 1883–1925.* Knoxville: University of Tennessee Press, 1998.

Akiyama Shigeo. *Meiji jinbutsu shūi monogatari: Kirisutokyō no ichi keifu* [A collection of tales of Meiji figures: A genealogy of Christianity]. Tokyo: Kirisutokyō shuppan, 1982.

Aldrich, Megan. *Gothic Revival.* London: Phaidon, 1994.

Alexander, Scott, ed. *Salted with Fire: Unitarian Universalist Strategies for Sharing Faith and Growing Congregations.* Boston: Skinner House Books of the Unitarian Universalist Association, 1994.

Amamiya Eiichi. *Wakaki Uemura Masahisa* [Young Uemura Masahisa]. Tokyo: Shinkyō shuppan, 2007.

Ambaras, David. *Bad Youth: Juvenile Delinquency and the Politics of Everyday Life in Modern Japan.* Berkeley: University of California Press, 2006.

———. "Social Knowledge, Cultural Capital and the New Middle Class in Japan, 1895–1912." *Journal of Japanese Studies* 24, no. 1 (Winter 1998): 1–33.

Ambros, Barbara. *Women in Japanese Religions.* New York: New York University Press, 2015.

Anderson, Benedict. *Imagined Communities: Reflections on the Spread of Nationalism.* London: Verso, 1991.

Anderson, Emily. *Christianity and Imperialism in Modern Japan: Empire for God.* London: Bloomsbury, 2014.

———. "Containing Voices in the Wilderness: Censorship and Religious Dissent in the Japanese Countryside." *Church History* 83, no. 2 (June 2014): 398–421.

———. "Tamura Naoomi's *The Japanese Bride:* Christianity, Nationalism, and Family in Meiji Japan." *Japanese Journal of Religious Studies* 34, no. 1 (2007): 203–228.

Anderson, Gerald H., ed. *Biographical Dictionary of Christian Missions.* New York: Macmillan Reference, 1998.

Anderson, Marnie S. "Kishida Toshiko and the Rise of the Female Speaker in Meiji Japan." *U.S.-Japan Women's Journal,* nos. 30/31 (2006): 3–26.

——. *A Place in Public: Women's Rights in Meiji Japan*. Cambridge, MA: Harvard University Asia Center, 2010.

——. "Women and Political Life in Early Meiji Japan: The Case of the Okayama Joshi Konshinkai (Okayama Women's Friendship Society)." *U.S.-Japan Women's Journal*, no. 44 (2013): 43–66.

Andersson, Rene. "Burakumin and Shimazaki Tōson's Hakai: Images of Discrimination in Modern Japanese Literature." PhD diss., Lund University, 2000.

Anesaki Masaharu. *History of Japanese Religion, with Special Reference to the Social and Moral Life of the Nation*. London: Kegan Paul, Trench, Trubner and Co., 1930.

Antoni, Klaus. "Izumo as the 'Other Japan': Construction vs. Reality." *Japanese Religions* 30, nos. 1/2 (July 2005): 1–20.

Aoyama Nao. *Yasui Tetsu den* [The biography of Yasui Tetsu]. Tokyo: Ōzorasha, 1990.

Aoyoshi Katsuhisa. *Uemura Masahisa den* [The biography of Uemura Masahisa]. Tokyo: Kyōbunkan, 1935.

Arano Kōtarō, ed. *Naniwa Kirisutokyōkai ryakushi* [A brief history of Naniwa Church]. Osaka: Naniwa Kirisutokyōkai, 1928.

Arie, Daisuke. "Lost in Translation: How Japan's Intellectuals Translated *On Liberty* (1859) and Utilitarian Writings in the Meiji Era and After." *Yokohama Journal of Social Sciences* 14, no. 6 (February 2010): 667–683.

Auslin, Michael. *Negotiating with Imperialism: The Unequal Treaties and the Culture of Japanese Diplomacy*. Cambridge, MA: Harvard University Press, 2009.

Azama Hideki. *Tokyo-eki no kenchiku-ka Tatsuno Kingo den* [The biography of Tatsuno Kingo, architect of Tokyo Station]. Tokyo: Kōdansha, 2009.

Azama, Moriya. *Nihon Kirisutokyō Fujin Kyōfukai 50-nen shi* [The fifty-year history of the Japan Women's Christian Temperance Union]. Tokyo: Nihon Kirisutokyō Fujin Kyōfukai, 1936.

Baldwin, Gary. *Moser Glass: The Klabin Collection*. New York: Healing Wisdom, 2006.

Balla, Peter. *The Child-Parent Relationship in the New Testament and Its Environment*. Tübingen: Mohr Siebeck, 2003.

Baller, Paul F., Jr. "The American Board and the Dōshisha, 1875–1900." PhD diss., Yale University, 1947.

Ballhatchet, Helen. "Christianity and Gender Relationships in Japan: Case Studies of Marriage and Divorce in Early Meiji Protestant Circles." *Japanese Journal of Religious Studies* 34, no. 1 (2007): 177–201.

——. "Confucianism and Christianity in Meiji Japan: The Case of Kozaki Hiromichi." *Journal of the Royal Asiatic Society of Great Britain and Ireland*, no. 2 (1988): 349–369.

Bamba, Nobuya, and John F. Howes, eds. *Pacifism in Japan: The Christian and Socialist Tradition*. Vancouver: University of British Columbia Press, 1978.

Bardsley, Jan. *The Bluestockings of Japan: New Woman Essays and Fiction from Seitō, 1911–1916*. Ann Arbor: University of Michigan Press, 2007.

Baydar, Gülsüm. "The Cultural Burden of Architecture." *Journal of Architectural Education* 57, no. 4 (May 2004): 19–27.

Beasley, William G. *The Meiji Restoration*. Stanford, CA: Stanford University Press, 1972.

Beckmann, George M., and Genji Okubo. *The Japanese Communist Party, 1922–1945.* Stanford, CA: Stanford University Press, 1969.

Bencivenga, Ermanno. "Knowledge vs. Belief." *Philosophical Forum* 30, no. 1 (March 1999): 3–11.

Benesch, Oleg. *Inventing the Way of the Samurai: Nationalism, Internationalism, and Bushido in Modern Japan.* Oxford: Oxford University Press, 2014.

Benesch, Oleg, and Ran Zwigenberg. *Japan's Castles: Citadels of Modernity in War and Peace.* Cambridge: Cambridge University Press, 2019.

Berger, Peter. *The Desecularization of the World.* Grand Rapids, MI: Eerdmans, 1999.

———. *The Sacred Canopy: Elements of a Sociological Theory of Religion.* Garden City, NY: Doubleday, 1967.

Bernstein, Gail Lee. *Japanese Marxist: A Portrait of Kawakami Hajime, 1879–1946.* Cambridge, MA: Harvard University Press, 1976.

———, ed. *Recreating Japanese Women, 1600–1945.* Berkeley: University of California Press, 1991.

Bernstein, Gail Lee, Andrew Gordon, and Kate Wildman Nakai, eds. *Public Spheres and Private Lives in Modern Japan, 1600–1950.* Cambridge, MA: Harvard University Press, 2005.

Berry, Mary Elizabeth. *Hideyoshi.* Cambridge, MA: Harvard University Press, 1982.

Best, Ernest E. "Christian Faith and Cultural Crisis: The Japanese Case." *Journal of Religion* 41, no. 1 (January 1961): 17–27.

———. *Christian Faith and Cultural Crisis: The Japanese Case.* Leiden: Brill, 1966.

Bettinghaus, E. P., and M. J. Cody. *Persuasive Communication.* New York: Holt, Rinehart & Winston, 1987.

Bhabha, Homi. *The Location of Culture.* London: Routledge, 1994.

Blum, Mark L. *Cultivating Spirituality: A Shin Buddhist Anthology.* Albany: State University of New York Press, 2011.

Bognar, Botond. *Contemporary Japanese Architecture.* New York: Van Nostrand Reinhold, 1985.

Botsman, Daniel V. *Punishment and Power in the Making of Modern Japan.* Princeton, NJ: Princeton University Press, 2007.

Bowen, Roger M. *Rebellion and Democracy in Meiji Japan.* Berkeley: University of California Press, 1980.

Boxer, Charles R. *The Christian Century in Japan, 1559–1650.* Berkeley: University of California Press, 1951.

Braisted, William, trans. *Meiroku Zasshi: Journal of the Japanese Enlightenment.* Cambridge, MA: Harvard University Press, 1976.

Breen, John. "'Earnest Desires': The Iwakura Embassy and Meiji Religious Policy." *Japan Forum* 10, no. 2 (1998): 151–165.

Breen, John, and Mark Teeuwen. *Shinto in History: Ways of the Kami.* Honolulu: University of Hawai'i Press, 2000.

Breen, John, and Mark Williams, eds. *Japan and Christianity: Impacts and Responses.* Houndsmill, UK: Macmillan, 1996.

Brock, Peter, and Thomas Paul Socknat, eds. *Challenge to Mars: Essays on Pacifism from 1918 to 1945*. Toronto: University of Toronto Press, 1999.

Brook, Timothy, and Andre Schmid, eds. *Nation Work: Asian Elites and National Identities*. Ann Arbor: University of Michigan Press, 2000.

Brownstein, Michael C. "*Jogaku Zasshi* and the Founding of Bungakukai." *Monumenta Nipponica* 35, no. 3 (Autumn 1980): 319–336.

Bruce, Steve. *Politics and Religion*. Malden, MA: Blackwell, 2003.

Buchanan, Daniel C. *Japanese Proverbs and Sayings*. Norman: University of Oklahoma Press, 1965.

Bunkachō. "Bunka isan on-rain Cultural Heritage online." http://bunka.nii.ac.jp/heritages/detail/224516. Accessed 26 May 2020.

Burkman, Thomas. "The Urakami Incidents and the Struggle for Religious Toleration." *Japanese Journal of Religious Studies* 1, nos. 2–3 (June–September 1974): 143–216.

Burns, Susan. "Bodies and Borders: Syphilis, Prostitution, and the Nation in Japan, 1860–1890." *US-Japan Women's Journal English Supplement 15* (1998): 3–30.

Burns, Susan L. *Before the Nation: Kokugaku and the Imagining of Continuity in Early Modern Japan*. Durham, NC: Duke University Press, 2003.

Büttner, Clemens, and Stefan Weinzierl. "The Acoustics of Early Concert Venues in Japan." *Deutsche Gesellschaft für Akustik* (2010): 629–630.

Caldarola, Carlo. *Christianity: The Japanese Way*. Leiden: Brill, 1979.

Campbell, Courtney J. "Space, Place and Scale: Human Geography and Spatial History in *Past and Present*." *Past and Present* 238, no. 1 (May 2018): 23–45.

Chen, Jerome. *Yuan Shih-k'ai, 1859–1916: Brutus Assumes the Purple*. Stanford, CA: Stanford University Press, 1961.

Ching, Leo T. S. *Becoming Japanese: Colonial Taiwan and the Politics of Identity Formation*. Berkeley: University of California Press, 2001.

Choi, Byong-il. *Kindai Nihon no kaikaku-ha Kirisutokyō: Uemura Masahisa to Takakura Tokutarō no shisōshi-teki kenkyū* [Reformed Christianity in modern Japan: Intellectual history study of Uemura Masahisa and Takakura Tokutarō]. Fukuoka: Hanashōin, 2007.

Chong, Kelly H. *Deliverance and Submission: Evangelical Women and the Negotiation of Patriarchy in South Korea*. Cambridge, MA: Harvard University Asia Center, 2008.

Chūō kōron sha 70-nen shi [Seventy-year history of the Central Review Company]. Tokyo: Chūō Kōron sha, 1955.

Claeys, George, ed. *Encyclopedia of Nineteenth-Century Thought*. New York: Routledge, 2005.

Cohen, Doron. *The Japanese Translations of the Hebrew Bible: History, Inventory and Analysis*. Leiden: Brill, 2013.

Cohen, Robin. "Creolization and Cultural Globalization: The Soft Sounds of Fugitive Power." *Globalizations* 4, no. 3 (2007): 369–384.

Comte, Auguste. *The Essential Comte: Selected from Cours de la Philosophie Positive*. Translated and edited by Stanislav Andreski. London: Croom Helm, 1974.

Conroy, Hilary, Sandra T. W. Davis, and Wayne Patterson, eds. *Japan in Transition: Thought and Action in the Meiji Era, 1868–1912*. Canbury, NJ: Associated University Presses, 1984.

Copeland, Rebecca. *Lost Leaves: Women Writers of Meiji Japan*. Honolulu: University of Hawai'i Press, 2000.
Cortazzi, Hugh, ed. *Britain and Japan: Biographical Portraits*. Vol. 8. Folkestone, UK: Global Oriental, 2013.
Cronin, Joseph. *The Life of Seinosuke: Dr. Ōishi and the High Treason Incident*. New York: White Tiger, 2007.
Daniels, Roger. *The Politics of Prejudice: The Anti-Japanese Movement in California and the Struggle for Japanese Exclusion*. Berkeley: University of California Press, 1999.
Davidann, Jon Thares. "The American YMCA in Meiji Japan: God's World Gone Awry." *Journal of World History* 6, no. 1 (Spring 1995): 107–125.
———. *A World of Crisis and Progress: The American YMCA in Japan 1890–1930*. Bethlehem, PA: Lehigh University Press, 1998.
Davis, Winston. "Buddhism and the Modernization of Japan." *History of Religions* 28, no. 4 (May 1989): 304–339.
———. *Japanese Religion and Society: Paradigms of Structure and Change*. Albany: State University of New York Press, 1992.
Deal, William E. *Handbook to Life in Medieval and Early Modern Japan*. New York: Oxford University Press, 2006.
De Bary, William Theodore, Carol Gluck, and Arthur Tiedemann, eds. *Sources of Japanese Tradition*. Vol. 2, *1600 to 2000*. New York: Columbia University Press, 2005.
De Certeau, Michel. *The Practice of Everyday Life*. Translated by Steven Rendall. Berkeley: University of California Press, 1984.
Dening, Walter. "Confucian Philosophy in Japan: Reviews of Dr. Inoue Tetsujirō's Three Volumes on This Philosophy." *Transactions of the Asiatic Society of Japan* 36 (1908): 120–122.
De Vos, George, and Hiroshi Wagatsuma, eds. *Japan's Invisible Race: Caste in Culture and Personality*. Berkeley: University of California Press, 1966.
Ditmore, Melissa Hope, ed. *Encyclopedia of Prostitution and Sex Work*. Vol. 2. Westport, CT: Greenwood, 2006.
Doak, Kevin, ed. *Xavier's Legacies: Catholicism in Modern Japanese Culture*. Vancouver: University of British Columbia Press, 2012.
Dohi Akio. "1930 nendai ni okeru Nihon Kirusutokyōkai no seikatsu" [The Japanese Christian Church's activities during the 1930s]. *Kirisutokyō shakai mondai kenkyū* [The study of Christianity and social problems] 22 (March 1974): 140–160.
———. "Christianity and Politics in the Period of Taishō Democracy, Part 1." *Journal of Japanese Religions* 5, no. 4 (April 1969): 1–25.
———. "Christianity and Politics in the Period of Taishō Democracy, Part 2." *Journal of Japanese Religions* 7, no. 3 (July 1972): 42–68.
———. *Kindai tennōsei to kirisutokyō* [The modern emperor system and Christianity]. Kyoto: Dōshisha Daigaku Jinbun Kagaku Kenkyūjō Kenkyū Sōsho, 1996.
———. "Kozaki Hiromichi shisō to undō" [Kozaki Hiromichi: Thought and actions]. *Kirisutokyō shakai mondai kenkyū* [The study of Christianity and social problems] 16/17 (March 1970): 1–37.

———. *Nihon Purotesutanto kyōkai no seiritsu to tenkai* [The establishment and development of Japanese Protestant Christianity]. Tokyo: Nihon Kirisuto Kyōdan Shuppan kyoku, 1975.

———. *Nihon Purotesutanto Kirisutokyō shi* [A history of Japanese Protestantism]. Tokyo: Shinkyō Shuppansha, 1980.

———. "Sankyōkaidō: Seiji, kyōiku, shūkyō to no kanren ni oite 1" [The Conference of the Three Religions: In reference to politics, education, and religion 1]. *Kirisutokyō shakai mondai kenkyū* [The study of Christianity and social problems], no. 11 (March 1967): 90–115.

———. "Sankyōkaidō: Seiji, kyōiku, shūkyō to no kanren ni oite 2" [The Conference of the Three Religions: In reference to politics, education, and religion 2]. *Kirisutokyō shakai mondai kenkyū* [The study of Christianity and social problems] 14/15 (April 1969): 72–93.

Dorn, Elizabeth A. "Crusading against Prostitution: The Woman's Christian Temperance Union in Meiji Japan." *Japanese Religions* 29, nos. 1/2 (January 2004): 29–43.

———. "'For God, Home, and Country': The Women's Christian Temperance Union and Reform Efforts in Meiji Japan." PhD diss., University of Hawai'i, 2003.

Dōshisha Daigaku Jinbunkagaku Kenkyūsho, eds. *Kumamoto Bando kenkyū: Nihon Protestantism no ichi genryu to tenkai* [A study of the Kumamoto Band: The development of the first generation of Japanese Protestants]. Tokyo: Misuzu shobō, 1966.

Dōshisha Daigaku Jinbunken kenkyūjo and Kirisutokyō shakai mondai kenkyūkai, eds. *Nihon no kindaika to Kirisutokyō* [Japanese modernization and Christianity]. Kyoto: Doshisha Daigaku Jinbunken, 1973.

———. *Rikugō zasshi no kenkyū* [A study of *Cosmos Journal*]. Tokyo: Kyōbunkan, 1984.

———. *Shinjin, Shinjokai no kenkyū: Nijū seiki shodai Kirisutokyō ja-narisumu* [A study of *New Man* and *New Woman's World:* Early twentieth-century Christian journalism]. Kyoto: Jinbun Shoin, 1999.

Dōshisha Sōritsu 100-shūnen Kinen Shashinshū Henshū Iinkai, ed. *Dōshisha: Sono 100 nen no ayumi* [Doshisha: Its 100 years]. Kyoto: Dōshisha, 1975.

Dōyōkai rekishibukai. "Nihon Sekijūjisha kangofuyōseijo, sono 3: Nissei sensō to Nichiseki kangofu" [The history of nursing in Japan, vol. 3: Chinese-Japanese War and the Red Cross nurses]. *Kangofu zasshi* 36, no. 1 (January 1972): 74–80.

Drummond, Richard. *A History of Christianity in Japan.* Grand Rapids, MI: Eerdmans, 1971.

Duara, Prasenjit. *Rescuing History from the Nation: Questioning Narratives of Modern China.* Chicago: University of Chicago Press, 1995.

Duke, Benjamin. *The History of Modern Japanese Education: Constructing the National School: Constructing the National School System, 1872–1890.* New Brunswick, NJ: Rutgers University Press, 1999.

Dupré, Louis. *The Enlightenment and the Intellectual Foundations of Modern Culture.* New Haven, CT: Yale University Press, 2004.

Durkheim, Émile. *Elementary Forms of Religious Life.* Translated by Joseph Ward Swain. London: Allen & Unwin, 1916.

Duus, Peter. "Nagai Ryūtarō and the 'White Peril,' 1905–1944." *Journal of Asian Studies* 31, no. 1 (November 1971): 41–48.

———. *Party Rivalry and Political Change in Taishō Japan*. Cambridge, MA: Harvard University Press, 1968.

———. "Yoshino Sakuzō: The Christian as Political Critic." *Journal of Japanese Studies* 4, no. 2 (Summer 1978): 301–326.

Duus, Peter, and John Whitney Hall, eds. *Cambridge History of Japan*. Vol. 6. Cambridge: Cambridge University Press, 1988.

Eagle, David E. "Historicizing the Megachurch." *Journal of Social History* 48, no. 3 (1 March 2015): 589–604.

Earns, Lane. "The Foreign Settlement in Nagasaki, 1859–1869." *The Historian* 56, no. 3 (1994): 483–500.

Ebisawa Arimichi and Ōuchi Saburō. *Nihon Kirisutokyō shi* [The history of Japanese Christianity]. Tokyo: Nihon Kirisuto Kyōdan Shuppan kyoku, 1970.

Eder, Elizabeth. *Constructing Opportunity: American Women Educators in Early Meiji Japan*. London: Lexington Books, 2003.

Elison, George. "Kōtoku Shūsui: The Change in Thought." *Monumenta Nipponica* 22, nos. 3/4 (1967): 437–467.

Ellwood, R. *Tenrikyō: A Pilgrimage Faith*. Tenri: Tenrikyō University, 1982.

Endō Kōichi. "Tagawa Daikichirō no seiji shisō" [The political thought of Tagawa Daikichiro]. *Meiji Gakuin Daigaku shakai gaku—shakai fukushi gaku kenkyū*, no. 138 (16 March 2012): 1–62.

Engel, Heino. *Measure and Construction of the Japanese House*. Tokyo: Charles Tuttle, 1985.

Enns, Robert. "'Slander against Our People': Tamura Naomi and the Japanese Bride Incident [on the History of Protestant Christianity in Japan]." *Japanese Religions* 18, no. 1 (January 1993): 15–46.

Faison, Elyssa. *Managing Women: Disciplining Labor in Japan*. Berkeley: University of California Press, 2007.

Finn, Dallas. *Meiji Revisited: The Sites of Victorian Japan*. New York: Weatherhill, 1995.

Forbes, Roy Tetsuo. "Schism, Orthodoxy and Heresy in the History of Tenrikyo: Three Case Studies." MA thesis, University of Hawai'i, Manoa, May 2005.

Foucault, Michel. *Discipline and Punish: The Birth of the Prison*. Translated Alan Sheridan. New York: Vintage Books, 1995.

Fox, Grace Estelle. *Britain and Japan, 1858–1883*. Oxford: Clarendon, 1969.

Fraser, Nancy. "Rethinking the Public Sphere: A Contribution to the Critique of Actually Existing Democracy." *Social Text*, nos. 25–26 (1990): 56–80.

Frédéric, Louis, and Käthe Roth. *Japan Encyclopedia*. Cambridge, MA: Harvard University Press, 2002.

Frederick, Sarah. *Turning Pages: Reading and Writing Women's Magazines in Interwar Japan*. Honolulu: University of Hawai'i Press, 2006.

Freedman, Alisa, Laura Miller, and Christine R. Yano, eds. *Modern Girls on the Go: Gender, Mobility, and Labor in Japan*. Stanford, CA: Stanford University Press, 2013.

Fridell, Wilbur M. "A Fresh Look at State Shinto." *Journal of the American Academy of Religion* 44, no. 3 (1976): 547–561.

———. "Government Ethics Textbooks in Late Meiji Japan." *Journal of Asian Studies* 29, no. 4 (August 1970): 823–833.

———. *Japanese Shrine Mergers, 1906–1912.* Tokyo: Sophia University Press, 1973.

Fuess, Harald. *Divorce in Japan: Family, Gender, and the State, 1600–2000.* Stanford, CA: Stanford University Press, 2004.

Fujimichō Kyōkai 100-nen Shiryō Iinkai, ed. *Fujimichō Kyōkai 100-nen shi: Bunshū, nenpyō* [The 100-year history of Fujimichō Church: Anthology, chronology]. Tokyo: Nihon Kirisutokyōdan, 1987.

Fujimori Terunobu. *Kindai Nihon no yōfū kenchiku: Kaika hen* [Western architecture of modern Japan: Civilization volume]. Tokyo: Chikuma shobō, 2017.

Fujio Ikado and James R. McGovern, comps. *A Bibliography of Christianity in Japan: Protestantism in English Sources, 1859–1959.* Tokyo: Committee on Asian Studies, International Christian University, 1966.

Fujio Yoshinori. *Iwamoto Yoshiharu: Seigi to ai ni ikite* [Iwamoto Yoshiharu: Living by righteousness and love]. Tokyo: Asahi Shuppansha, 2005.

Fujitani, Takashi. *Splendid Monarchy: Power and Pageantry in Modern Japan.* Berkeley: University of California Press, 1993.

Fujita Yoshimi. *Meiji Jogakkō no sekai* [The world of Meiji Girls' School]. Tokyo: Shōeisha, 1984.

———. "'Meiji jogakkō wo oboegaki: Meiji-ki Roman-shugi to Kirisutokyō" [Remembering Meiji Girls' School: Romanticism and Christianity]. *Risshō Daigaku bungakubu ronsō* 71 (1981): 27–51.

Fukada Mikio. "Shisō to shinkō no setten: Hani Motoko no kyōikuron" [The connection of thought and faith: Educational philosophy of Motoko Hani]. *Kirisutokyō kenkyū* 38, nos. 1–2 (February 1974): 180–198.

Fullerton, W. Y. *Charles Haddon Spurgeon: A Biography.* New York: Hodder and Stoughton, 1919.

Furukawa Eishi. *Miyagi Michio den* [The biography of Miyagi Michio]. Tokyo: Shinchōsha, 1962.

Furuya, Yasuo, ed. and trans. *A History of Theology in Japan.* Grand Rapids, MI: Eerdmans, 1997.

Futaba Nursery School, a Social Welfare Corporation. "100 nen no ayumi" [Our century-long history]. http://www.futaba-yuka.or.jp/main_site/history.html. Accessed 7 November 2019.

Garner, Mark. "Preaching as a Communicative Event: A Discourse Analysis of Sermons by Robert Rollock (1555–1599)." *Renaissance and Reformation Review* 9, no. 1 (2007): 45–70.

Garon, Sheldon. *Molding Japanese Minds: The State in Everyday Life.* Princeton, NJ: Princeton University Press, 1997.

———. *The State and Labor in Modern Japan.* Berkeley: University of California Press, 1987.

———. "State and Religion in Imperial Japan, 1912–1945." *Journal of Japanese Studies* 12, no. 2 (1986): 273–302.

———. "Women's Groups and the Japanese State: Contending Approaches to Political Integration, 1890–1945." *Journal of Japanese Studies* 19, no. 1 (1993): 5–41.

———. "The World's Oldest Debate? Prostitution and the State in Imperial Japan, 1900–1945." *American Historical Review* 98, no. 3 (June 1993): 710–733.

Garon, Sheldon, Barbara Molony, Werner Pascha, and Ben-Ami Shillony, eds. *Japan: State and People in the Twentieth Century: Papers Presented at the STICERD 20th Anniversary Symposium.* London: London: Suntory Centre, Suntory and Toyota International Centres for Economics and Related Disciplines, London School of Economics and Political Science, 1999.

Geertz, Clifford. *The Interpretation of Cultures: Selected Essays.* London: Hutchinson, 1975.

George, P. A. *Enlightenment of Women and Social Change.* New Delhi: Northern Book Center, 2006.

Germany, Charles. *Protestant Theologies in Modern Japan.* Tokyo: International Institute for the Study of Religions Press, 1965.

Giddens, Anthony. *Modernity and Self-Identity: Self and Society in the Late Modern Age.* Stanford, CA: Stanford University Press, 1991.

Gierlyn, Thomas F. "A Space for Place in Sociology." *Annual Review of Sociology* 26 (2000): 463–496.

Gluck, Carol. *Japan's Modern Myths: Ideology in the Late Meiji Period.* Princeton, NJ: Princeton University Press, 1985.

Goodman, David G., and Masanori Miyazawa. *Jews in the Japanese Mind: The History and Uses of a Cultural Stereotype.* Cambridge, MA: Harvard University Press, 2000.

Gordon, Andrew. *A Modern History of Japan from Tokugawa Times to the Present.* New York: Oxford University Press, 2014.

Grapard, Allan G. "Japan's Ignored Cultural Revolution: The Separation of Shinto and Buddhist Divinities in Meiji (shinbutsu bunri) and a Case Study: Tonomine." *History of Religions* 23, no. 3 (February 1984): 240–265.

———. *The Protocol of the Gods: A Study of the Kasuga Cult in Japanese History.* Berkeley: University of California Press, 1992.

Grunow, Tristan R. "Paving Power: Western Urban Planning and Imperial Space from the Streets of Meiji Tokyo to Colonial Seoul." *Journal of Urban History* 42, no. 3 (May 2016): 506–556.

Habermas, Jürgen. *The Structural Transformation of the Public Sphere: An Inquiry into a Category of Bourgeois Society.* Translated by Thomas Burger. 1978. Repr., Cambridge, MA: MIT Press, 1989.

Habermas, Jürgen, Sara Lennox, and Frank Lennox. "The Public Sphere: An Encyclopedia Article." *New German Critique* 1, no. 3 (1974): 49–55.

Halkias, Georgia T., and Richard K. Payne, eds. *Pure Lands in Asian Texts and Contexts: An Anthology.* Honolulu: University of Hawaiʻi Press, 2019.

Han, Jung-Sun N. *An Imperial Path to Modernity: Yoshino Sakuzō and a New Liberal Order in East Asia, 1905–1937.* Cambridge, MA: Harvard Asia Center, 2012.

Harada Tomohiko and Uesugi Satoru, eds. *"Kaihōrei" no seiritsu* [The establishment of "The Liberation Law"]. Tokyo: San'ichi Shobo, 1984.

Hara Makoto. *Reinanzaka Kyōkai no shinkō no ishizue* [The cornerstone of Reinanzaka Church's faith]. Tokyo: Nihon Kirisutokyōdan Reinanzaka Kyōkai, 2015.

Hardacre, Helen. "Creating State Shinto: The Great Promulgation Campaign and the New Religions." *Journal of Japanese Studies* 12, no. 1 (1986): 29–63.

———. *Shinto: A History.* New York: Oxford University Press, 2017.

———. *Shintō and the State, 1868–1988.* Princeton, NJ: Princeton University Press, 1991.

Hardacre, Helen, and Adam L. Kern, eds. *New Directions in the Study of Meiji Japan.* Leiden: Brill, 1997.

Harootunian, Harry D. *Toward Restoration: The Growth of Political Consciousness in Tokugawa, Japan.* Berkeley: University of California Press, 1970.

Harrington, Ann. *Japan's Hidden Christians.* Chicago: Loyola University Press, 1993.

———. "Women and Higher Education in the Japanese Empire (1895–1945)." *Journal of Asian History* 21, no. 2 (1987): 169–186.

Hastings, Sally A. "A Dinner Party Is Not a Revolution: Space, Gender, and Hierarchy in Meiji Japan." *U.S.-Japan Women's Journal (English Supplement),* no. 18 (2000): 107–132.

———. *Neighborhood and Nation in Tokyo, 1905–1937.* Pittsburgh: University of Pittsburgh Press, 1995.

———. "Women Educators of the Meiji Era and the Making of Modern Japan." *International Journal of Social Education* 6, no. 1 (1991): 83–94.

Hastings, Thomas John. *Practical Theology and the One Body of Christ: Toward a Mission-Ecumenical Model.* Grand Rapids, MI: Eerdmans, 2007.

Havens, Thomas R. H. *Nishi Amane and Modern Japanese Thought.* Princeton, NJ: Princeton University Press, 1970.

Hayashida Kazuhiro. "Development of Election Law in Japan." *Journal of Law and Politics* [Kyūshū University Law Society] 34, no. 1 (1967): 104–151.

Hayashi Makoto, Ōtani Eiichi, and Paul L. Swanson, eds. *Modern Buddhism in Japan.* Nagoya: Nanzan, 2014.

"The Heart of Lion's Sustainability." Accessed 27 April 2020. https://www.lion.co.jp/en/csr/story/about/.

Henning, Joseph M. *Outposts of Civilization: Race, Religion, and the Formative Years of American-Japanese Relations.* New York: New York University Press, 2000.

Herbermann, Charles G., Edward A. Pace, Conde B. Pallen, Thomas J. Shahan, and John J. Wynne, eds. *The Catholic Encyclopedia: An International Work of Reference on the Constitution, Doctrine, Discipline, and History of the Catholic Church.* Vol. 10. New York: Encyclopedia Press, 1911.

Hirai Yuka. "Shōgai 'atarashii kenchiku' wo tsukuri tsutzuketa kenchiku-ka Sone Tatsuzō" [Life: The architect who continued building "new architecture," Sone Tatsuzō]. *Inax Report,* no. 167 (July 2006): 5–14.

Hirata Yumi. *Josei hyōgen no Meiji shi* [The Meiji-era history of women's expression]. Tokyo: Iwanami Shoten, 1999.

Hirayama Yō. *Ōnishi Hajime to sono jidai* [Ōnishi Hajime and his times]. Tokyo: Tosho Senta, 1989.

Hiroshi, Shibuya, and Chiba Shin. *Living for Jesus: The Social and Theological Thought of Uchimura Kanzō.* Grand Rapids, MI: Eerdmans, 2013.

Hiyane Antei. *Nihon Kirisutokyō shi* [The history of Christianity in Japan]. 5 vols. Tokyo: Kyōbunkan, 1940.

———. *Nihon shūkyōshi* [The history of Japanese religion]. Tokyo: Sankyō shuppansha, 1925.

Hoare, James E. *Japan's Treaty Ports and Foreign Settlements: The Uninvited Guests, 1858–1899.* Folkestone, UK: Japan Library, 1994.

Hobsbawm, Eric, and Terrence Ranger, eds. *The Invention of Tradition.* Cambridge: Cambridge University Press, 1983.

Holtom, Daniel Clarence. "The Political Philosophy of Modern Shintō." DD diss., University of Chicago, 1922.

Horii, Mitsutoshi. *The Category of Religion in Contemporary Japan: Shūkyō and Temple Buddhism.* New York: Palgrave Macmillan, 2018.

Hori Madoka. *"Nijū kokuseki shijin" Noguchi Yonejirō* ["Dual citizen poet" Noguchi Yonejirō]. Nagoya: Daigaku shuppankai, 2012.

Howell, David L. *Geographies of Identity in Nineteenth-Century Japan.* Berkeley: University of California Press, 2005.

Howes, John F. *Japan's Modern Prophet: Uchimura Kanzō, 1861–1930.* Vancouver: University of British Columbia Press, 2006.

———, ed. *Nitobe Inazō: Japan's Bridge across the Pacific.* Boulder, CO: Westview, 1995.

Howland, Douglas. "Society Reified: Herbert Spencer and Political Theory in Early Meiji Japan." *Comparative Studies in Society and History* 42, no. 1 (January 2000): 67–86.

Huffman, James. *Creating a Public: People and Press in Meiji Japan.* Honolulu: University of Hawai'i Press, 1997.

Hunter, Janet, ed. *Japanese Women at Work.* New York: Routledge, 1993.

Hur, Nam-lin. *Death and Social Order in Tokugawa Japan: Buddhism, Anti-Christianity, and the Danka System.* Cambridge, MA: Harvard University Asia Center, 2007.

———. *Prayer and Play in Late Tokugawa Japan: Asakusa Sensōji and Edo Society.* Cambridge, MA: Harvard University Asia Center, 2000.

Hurst, G. Cameron, III. "Honor, and Loyality: The Bushidō Ideal." *Philosophy East and West* 40, no. 4 (October 1990): 511–527.

Ichikawa Fusae, Maruoka Hideo, Akamatsu Ryōko, Mitsui Tametomo, Yuzawa Yasuhiko, Ichibangase Yasuko, and Yamaguchi Miyoko, eds. *Nihon fujin mondai shiryō shūsei* [Compilation of materials on the Japanese woman question]. 10 vols. Tokyo: Domesu Shuppan, 1977–1981.

Ide Busaburō. *Yoshino Sakuzō to sono jidai* [Yoshino Sakuzō and his times]. Tokyo: Nihon Hyōron sha, 1988.

Ienaga Saburō. "Japan's Modernization and Buddhism." *Contemporary Religions in Japanese Religions* 6, no. 1 (1965): 1–41.

Iglehart, Charles W. *A Century of Protestant Christianity in Japan.* Tokyo: Charles E. Tuttle, 1959.

Ii Kiyoshi and Fugami Seizō, eds. *Reinanzaka Kyōkai 100-nen shi* [The one-hundred-year history of Reinanzaka Church]. Tokyo: Kirisutokyōdan Reinanzaka Kyōkai, 1979.

Ikeda bunsho kenkyūkai, ed. *Tōdai igakubu shodai sōri Ikeda Kensai: Ikeda bunsho no kenkyū* [First president of Tokyo University Medical Department: A study of Ikeda's writings]. Tokyo: Shibunkaku shuppan, 2006.

Ikeda Eishun. "Teaching Assemblies and Lay Societies in the Formation of Modern Sectarian Buddhism." *Japanese Journal of Religious Studies* 25, nos. 1/2 (Spring 1998): 11–44.

Imanaka Kanshi. "Ebina Danjō to sono shisō" [Ebina Danjō and his thought]. *Kirisutokyō shakai mondai kenkyū* [The study of Christianity and social problems] 23 (March 1975): 1–27.

———. "Kozaki Hiromichi no *Seikyō shinron* ni tsuite" [On Kozaki Hiromichi's *New essay on the relationship of politics and religion*]. *Kirisutokyō Shakai Mondai Kenkyū* 30 (1982): 1–18.

———. "Yokoi Shonan no Jitsugaku to Yōgaku" [Yokoi Shonan's Jitsugaku and Western studies]. *Kirisutokyo Shakai Mondai Kenkyu*, no. 4 (March 1961): 8–23.

Inoue, Nobutaka, and Mark Teeuwen. "Tracing Shintō in the History of Kami Worship." *Japanese Journal of Religious Studies* 29, nos. 3/4 (Fall 2002): 195–207.

Ion, A. Hamish. *American Missionaries, Christian Oyatoi, and Japan, 1859–73.* Vancouver: University of British Columbia Press, 2009.

———. *The Cross and the Rising Sun.* Vol. 1, *The Canadian Missionary Movement in the Japanese Empire, 1872–1931.* Toronto: Wilfrid Laurier University Press, 1990.

———. *The Cross and the Rising Sun.* Vol. 2, *The British Protestant Missionary Movement in Japan, Korea, and Taiwan, 1865–1945.* Toronto: Wilfrid Laurier University Press, 1993.

———. "Edward Warren Clark and Early Meiji Japan: A Case Study of Cultural Contact." *Modern Asian Studies* 11, no. 4 (1977): 557–572.

Irish, Ann B. *Hokkaidō: A History of Ethnic Transition and Development on Japan's Northern Island.* Jefferson, NC: McFarland and Co., 2009.

Irokawa Daikichi. *The Culture of the Meiji Period.* Edited by Marius B. Jansen. Princeton, NJ: Princeton University Press, 1985.

Isaka Michiko. *Zōjōji kyūkeidai chiku rekishi-teki kenzōbutsu nado chōsa hōkokusho* [A historical survey and report on the structure of Zōjō Temple's old precincts]. Tokyo: Keidai Kenkyū Jimu kyoku, 2003.

Isao Tsujino. "Ishikawa Sanshirō." *Kirisutokyō shakai mondai kenkyū* [The study of Christianity and social problems] 23 (March 1975): 83–115.

Ishii, Noriko Kawamura. *American Women Missionaries at Kobe College, 1873–1909: New Dimensions in Gender.* London: Routledge, 2004.

Isshiki Yoshiko. "Kawai Michiko ni okeru kokusaisei to sono shinkō" [Kawai Michiko's international character and her faith]. *Keisen Jogakuen Daigaku Jinbun Gakubu Kiyō* [Keisen Girls' College Faculty of Humanities bulletin] 3 (1991): 76–90.

Itō Katsuhiro. "Senkyōshi Sara Kurara Sumisu to Hokusei Gakuen" [Missionary Sara Clara Smith and Hokusei Gakuen]. *Aoyama Gakuin Joshi Tanki Daigaku sōgō bunka kenkyū nenpō* [Aoyama Gakuin Women's Junior College Comprehensive Cultural Studies Yearly Report] 8 (2000): 105–114.

Itō Kiyoshi. *Banchō Kyōkai 100-nen shi* [The one-hundred-year history of Banchō Church]. Tokyo: Nihon Kirisutokyōdan Banchō Kyōkai, 1986.

Itō Midori. "Hani Motoko and the Spread of Time Discipline into the Household." *Japan Review* 14 (2002): 135–147.

Ito, Yushi. *Yamaji Aizan and His Time: Nationalism and Debating Japanese History.* Folkestone, UK: Global Oriental, 2007.

Ives, Christopher. *Imperial Way Zen: Ichikawa Hakugen's Critique and Lingering Questions for Buddhist Ethics.* Honolulu: University of Hawai'i Press, 2009.

Iwai Fumio. *Ebina Danjō.* Tokyo: Nihon Kirisuto Kyōdan Shuppan kyoku, 1973.

Iwai, Shuma. "Japanese Christianity in the Meiji Era: An Analysis of Ebina Danjo's Perspective on Shintoistic Christianity." *Transformation: An International Journal of Holistic Mission Studies* 25, no. 4 (October 2008): 195–204.

Iwata Fumiaki. *Kindai Bukkyō to seinen: Chikazumi Jōkan to sono jidai* [Modern Buddhism and youth: Chikazumi Jōkan and his times]. Tokyo: Iwanami Shoten, 2014.

James, Edward T., Janet Wilson James, and Paul S. Boyer, eds. *Notable American Women, 1607–1950: A Biographical Dictionary.* Vol. 2. Cambridge, MA: Radcliffe College, 1971.

Jansen, Marius B., ed. *Changing Japanese Attitudes toward Modernization.* Princeton, NJ: Princeton University Press, 1965.

Jansen, Marius B., and Gilbert Rozman, eds. *Japan in Transition from Tokugawa to Meiji.* Princeton, NJ: Princeton University Press, 1986.

Jenkins, Philip. *The Great and Holy War: How World War I Became a Religious Crusade.* New York: HarperCollins, 2014.

Jennings, J. Nelson. *Theology in Japan: Takakura Tokutaro, 1885–1934.* New York: University Press of America, 2005.

Jinnai Hibenobu. *Tokyo: A Spatial Anthropology.* Translated by Kimiko Nishimura. Berkeley: University of California Press, 1995.

Jones, George Heber. "An Official Conference on Religion in Japan." *Journal of Race Development* 3, no. 2 (October 1912): 224–231.

Josephson, Jason Ananda. *The Invention of Religion in Japan.* Chicago: University of Chicago Press, 2012.

Joshi Gakuin. https://www.joshigakuin.ed.jp/school/deveropment/. Accessed 26 May 2020.

Joshi Gakuin Hensan Iinkai. *Joshi Gakuin no Rekishi* [The history of Joshi Gakuin]. Tokyo: Joshi Gakuin, 1985.

Kaide Sumiko. *Fujii Koto to sono shiyū: Josei shōnen hogoshi dai ichi-gō no ayumi* [Fuji Koto and her teachers and friends: The path of the first women's probation officer]. Tokyo: Kirisuto Shinbun sha, 1986.

———. *Noguchi Yuka no shōgai* [The life of Noguchi Yuka]. Tokyo: Kirisuto Shimbun sha, 1974.

Kamemiya Michiko. *Nihon Sekijūjisha to kangofu* [The Japanese Red Cross Society and nursing]. Tokyo: Domesu shuppan, 1983.

Kanda Myōjin shikō kankōkai. *Kanda Myōjin shikō* [Historical consideration of Kanda Myōjin]. Tokyo: Kanda Myōjin Shikō Kankō Kai, 1992.

Kanda Tetsuo. *Ai no Ijin: Niijima Jō* [Great man of love: Niijima Jō]. Maebashi, Japan: Gunma Bunka Kyōkai, 1948.

Kan Shina. *Naruse Jinzō sensei no joshi kyōiku* [The women's education of Dr. Naruse Jinzō]. Tokyo: Naruse Jinzō Sensei no Joshi Kyōiku Kankō Kai, 1981.

Kanzaki Kiyoshi. *Gendai Nihon no fujin* [Modern Japanese women]. Tokyo: Sangaku Shōbo, 1940.

Karasawa Buyasu. "Saisei gakusha haikō no rekishi" [History of the closing of the Saisei Gakusha]. *Nihon Ishigaku zasshi* 40, no. 3 (September 1994): 293–303.

Kasahara Yoshimitsu. "'Nihon Kirisutokyō' Hihan" [Critiquing Japanese Christianity]. *Kirisutokyō shakai mondai kenkyū* [The study of Christianity and social problems] 22 (March 1974): 114–139.

Kassel, Marleen. *Tokugawa Confucian Education: The Kangien Academy of Hirose Tanso: 1782–1856.* Albany: State University of New York Press, 1996.

Kawanishi Hidemichi. *Tōhoku: Japan's Constructed Outland.* Leiden: Brill, 2016.

Kawasaki Tsukasa. *Takagi Mizutarō: Sono heibon no shōgai wo tadotte* [Takagi Mizutarō: Following his ordinary life]. Tokyo: Kindai Bungeisha, 2010.

Keene, Donald. *Emperor Meiji and His World, 1852–1912.* New York: Columbia University Press, 2002.

Ketelaar, James. *Of Heretics and Martyrs in Meiji Japan: Buddhism and Its Persecution.* Princeton, NJ: Princeton University Press, 1990.

Kilde, Jeanne Halgren. *When Church Became Theatre: The Transformation of Evangelical Architecture and Worship in Nineteenth-Century America.* Oxford: Oxford University Press, 2002.

Kim, Hwansoo. "'The Future of Buddhism Lies in Our Hands': Takeda Hanshi as a Sōtō Missionary." *Japanese Journal of Religious Studies* 37, no. 1 (2010): 99–135.

Kimu Mungiru. *Kindai Nihon Kirisutokyō to Chōsen: Ebina Danjō no shisō to kōdō* [Modern Japanese Christianity and Korea: Ebina Danjō's thought and actions]. Tokyo: Akashi Shoten, 1998.

Kimura Keiko. *Kawai Michi no shōgai: Hikari ni ayunda hito* [Kawaii Michi's life: A person walking in the light]. Tokyo: Iwanami Shoten, 2002.

Kinya Katsuo. *Iwaya Sazanami: Otogi sakka he no michi* [The path to becoming a fairytale author]. Tokyo: Keiō Gijuku Daigaku Shuppansha, 2000.

Kirisutokyō Bunka Gakkai, ed. *Purotesutanto Jinbutsushi—Kindai Nihon no Bunka Keisei* [History of Protestant figures: The formation of modern Japanese culture]. Tokyo: Yorudansha, 1990.

Kirisutokyō gakkō kyōiku dōmei, ed. *Nihon ni okeru Kirisutokyō gakkō kyōiku genjō* [The existing condition of Christian school education in Japan]. Tokyo: Kirisutokyō Gakkō Kyōiku Dōmei, 1961.

Kirisutokyō shigakkai, eds. *Kindai Nihon no Kirisutokyō to joshi kyōiku* [Modern Christianity and women's education]. Tokyo: Kyōbunkan, 2016.

Kirk, J. Andrew. "'God Is on Our Side': The Anatomy of an Ideology." *Transformation* 27, no. 4 (2010): 239–247.

Kiryū-shi kyōiku iinkai. *Kiryū Meijikan jūyōbunkazai kyū-Gunma-ken eiseijo* [Kiryū Meijikan: Important cultural property, the Old Gunma Prefecture Public Health Bureau]. Kiryū: Kiryū-shi kyōiku iinkai, 1986.

Kishimoto Hideo, ed. *Japanese Religion in the Meiji Era.* Translated by John F. Howes. Tokyo: Ōbunsha, 1956.

Kitamura Shingo. *Ōishi Seinosuke monogatari: Taigyaku jikken no giseisha* [The story of Ōishi Seinosuke: Victim of the Great Treason Incident]. Suzuka, Japan: Kitamura Shōnika Iin, 2001.

Kita Shiminkan kinen shihenshū iinkai. *61 nen wo kaerimite: Osaka Shiritsu Kita Shiminkan* [Looking back on sixty-one years: The Osaka Municipal Northern People's House]. Osaka: Osaka Shiminsei kyoku, 1983.

Kobayashi Yasushige. *Ueno Kōen* [Ueno Park]. Tokyo: Tokyo Kyōgakusha, 1980.

Kōbe shimbun bunka seikatsu bu, ed. *Hito moyuru shirarezaru kindai Hyōgo no senkakushatachi* [A single sprout: The unknown pioneers of modern Hyōgo]. Kobe: Kōbe shimbun sōgō shuppan sentā, 2001.

Konishi, Sho. "The Emergence of an International Humanitarian Organization in Japan: The Tokugawa Origins of the Japanese Red Cross." *American Historical Review* 119, no. 4 (October 2014): 1129–1153.

Kōsaka Morihiko. *Aru Meiji riberarisuto no kiroku: Kokō no sentōsha Takekoshi Yosaburō Den* [Some Meiji liberalist documents: The biography of Takekoshi Yosaburō, fighter for isolation]. Tokyo: Chūō Kōron Shimbun sha, 2002.

Koschmann, J. Victor, ed. *Authority and the Individual in Japan: Citizen Protest in Historical Perspective.* Tokyo: University of Tokyo Press, 1978.

Kowsky, Francis R. "The Architecture of Frederick C. Withers (1828–1901)." *Journal of the Society of Architectural Historians* 35, no. 2 (May 1976): 83–107.

Krämer, Hans Martin. *Shimaji Mokurai and the Reconception of Religion and the Secular in Modern Japan.* Honolulu: University of Hawai'i Press, 2015.

Kublin, Hyman. *Asian Revolutionary: The Life of Katayama Sen.* Princeton, NJ: Princeton: University Press, 1964.

———. "The Japanese Socialists and the Russo-Japanese War." *Journal of Modern History* 22, no. 4 (December 1950): 322–339.

———. "The Origins of Japanese Socialist Tradition." *Journal of Politics* 14, no. 2 (May 1952): 257–280.

Kudō Eiichi. "Ashio kōdoku jiken ni okeru Ushioda Chiseko: Kirisutokyō no mondai wo chūshin to shite" [Chiseko Ushioda and her Christian faith in the Ashio mine pollution case]. *Mita gakkai zasshi* 75, no. 3 (June 1982): 3–16.

———. *Meiji-ki no Kirisutokyō: Nihon Purotesutanto shiwa* [Meiji-era Christianity: A discussion of Japanese Protestant history]. Tokyo: Kyōbunkan, 1979.

———. *Nihon shakai to Purotesutanto dendo* [Japanese society and Protestant evangelism]. Tokyo: Nihon Kirisuto Kyōdan Shuppansha, 1959.

Kuniyasu Take. "Ebina Danjō no sensō ron" [Ebina Danjō's arguments on war]. *Kirisutokyō shakai mondai kenkyū* [The study of Christianity and social problems] 23 (March 1975): 44–82.

———. "*Rikugō Zasshi* ni arawareta Harada Tasuku: Sono kindaika ronri ni fureru" [Harada Tasuku as he appeared in *Cosmos:* Touching on his modernist principles]. *Kirisutokyō shakai mondai kenkyū* [The study of Christianity and social problems] 30 (March 1982): 147–165.

Kuno, Akiko. *Unexpected Destinations: The Poignant Story of Japan's First Vassar Graduate.* New York: Kodansha International, 1993.

Kuwabara Saburō, ed. *Iwaya Sazanami nikki honkoku to kenkyū: Ji Meiji nijūnen shi Meiji nijū nana nen* [Reprint of Iwaya Sazanami's diary: From Meiji 20 to Meiji 27]. Tokyo: Keiō Gijuku Daigaku Shuppansha, 1998.

Kuyama Yasushi, ed. *Kindai Nihon to Kirisutokyō* [Modern Japan and Christianity]. Nishinomiya, Japan: Kirisutokyō Gakuto Kyōdaidan, 1956.

Kyōdan Executive Committee of the United Church of Christ in Japan. "Confession of Wartime Responsibility during World War II, February 20, 1967." Translated and edited by Suzuki Masahisa. http://uccj-e.org/confession. Accessed 6 March 2019.

Kyōgoku Junichirō. *Uemura Masahisa: Sono hito to shisō* [Uemura Masahisa: The man and his thought]. Tokyo: Shinkyō shuppan, 1966.

Kyūdō Kaikan. http://www.kyudo-kaikan.org/top.html. Accessed 6 March 2019.

Lande, Aasulv. *Meiji Protestantism in History and Historiography: A Comparative Study of Japanese and Western Interpretation of Early Protestantism in Japan.* New York: Peter Lang, 1989.

Large, Stephen S. "Buddhism and Political Renovation in Prewar Japan: The Case of Akamatsu Katsumaro." *Journal of Japanese Studies* 9, no. 1 (Winter 1983): 33–66.

———. "Buddhism, Socialism, and Protest in Prewar Japan: The Career of Seno'o Girō." *Modern Asian Studies* 21, no. 1 (1987): 153–171.

———. "Nishio Suehiro and the Japanese Social Democratic Movement, 1920–1940." *Journal of Asian Studies* 36, no. 1 (November 1976): 37–56.

———. *The Rise of Labor in Japan: The Yūaikai, 1912–19.* Tokyo: Sophia University Press, 1972.

———, ed. *Shōwa Japan: Political, Economic, and Social History, 1926–1989.* New York: Routledge, 1998.

Lee, Edwin. "Nichiren and Nationalism: The Religious Patriotism of Tanaka Chigaku." *Monumenta Nipponica* 30, no. 1 (1975): 19–35.

Lefebvre, Henri. *The Production of Space.* Translated by Donald Nicholson-Smith. Malden, MA: Blackwell, 1991.

Levin, Miriam, Sophie Forgan, Martina Hessler, Robert H. Kargon, and Morris Low, eds. *Urban Modernity: Cultural Innovation in the Second Industrial Revolution.* Cambridge, MA: MIT Press, 2010.

Lewis, Michael. *Rioters and Citizens: Mass Protest in Imperial Japan.* Berkeley: University of California Press, 1990.

Li, Yuk-Heung. "Women's Education in Meiji Japan and the Development of Christian Girls' Schools." PhD diss., University of Hong Kong, 1993.

Lopez, Donald S., Jr., ed. *Curators of the Buddha: The Study of Buddhism under Colonialism.* Chicago: University of Chicago Press, 1995.

Lowy, Dina. *The Japanese "New Woman": Images of Gender and Modernity.* New Brunswick, NJ: Rutgers University Press, 2007.

———. "Nora and the 'New Woman': Visions of Gender and Modernity in Early Twentieth-Century Japan." *U.S.-Japan Women's Journal,* no. 26 (2004): 75–97.

Lublin, Elizabeth Dorn. *Reforming Japan: The Women's Christian Temperance Union in the Meiji Period.* Vancouver: University of British Columbia Press, 2010.

Lucas, Paul R. "The Church and the City: Congregationalism in Minneapolis, 1850–1890." *Minnesota History* 44, no. 2 (Summer 1974): 55–69.

Mackie, Thomas T., and Richard Rose, eds. *The International Almanac of Electoral History*. New York: Macmillan, 1991.

Mackie, Vera. *Creating Socialist Women in Japan: Gender, Labour, and Activism, 1900–1937*. Cambridge: Cambridge University Press, 1997.

———. *Feminism in Modern Japan: Citizenship, Embodiment and Sexuality*. Cambridge: Cambridge University Press, 2002.

Maki Fumihiko. *Miegakure suru no toshi: Edo kara Tokyo e* [The seen and unseen city: From Edo to Tokyo]. Tokyo: Kagoshima Shuppankai, 1980.

Maki, John M. *A Yankee in Hokkaido: The Life of William Smith Clark*. Sapporo: Hokkaido University Press, 1996.

Marshall, Byron K. *Academic Freedom and the Japanese Imperial University, 1868–1939*. Berkeley: University of California, 1992.

Marx, Edward. *Leonie Gilmour: When East Weds West*. Lexington, KY: Botchan Books, 2013.

Masao Ōta. "Ishikawa Sanshirō, Hongō kyōkai to heimeinsha" [Ishikawa Sanshirō, Hongō Church and the *Heiminsha*]. *Shoki shakaishugi kenkyū* 18 (2005): 58–75.

———. "Yoshino Sakuzō nenbu" [A chronology of Yoshino Sakuzō]. *Kirisutokyō shakai mondai kenkyū* [The study of Christianity and social problems] 16/17 (March 1970): 216–230.

Matsuda Shigeo, ed. *Abe Isoo nenpyō, chosaku mokuroku* [Abe Isoo chronology, works index]. Kurashiki: Matsuda Shigeo, 2002.

Matsuoka Hachirō. "Yoshino Sakuzō to Kirisutokyō no eikyō 4" [Yoshino Sakuzō and the influence of Christianity, 4]. *Tōyō hōgaku* 37, no. 2 (January 1994): 41–65.

Matsuo Takayoshi. "The Development of Democracy in Japan—Taishō Democracy: Its Flowering and Breakdown." *Developing Economies* 4, no. 4 (December 1966): 612–637.

———. "The Japanese Protestants in Korea, Part One: The Missionary Activities of the Japanese Congregational Church in Korea." Translated by S. Takiguchi. *Modern Asian Studies* 13, no. 4 (1979): 401–429.

———. "The Japanese Protestants in Korea, Part Two: The 1st March Movement and the Japanese Protestants." Translated by S. Takiguchi. *Modern Asian Studies* 13, no. 4 (1979): 581–615.

———. "Profile of Asian Minded Man VII: Yoshino Sakuzō." *Developing Economies* 5, no. 2 (June 1967): 388–404.

———. *Taishō demokurashi no kenkyū* [A study of Taishō democracy]. Tokyo: Aoki Shoten, 1966.

Maus, Tanya. "Ishii Juji, the Okayama Orphanage, and the Chausubaru Settlement: A Vision of Child Relief through Communal Labor and a Sustainable Local Economy, 1887–1926." PhD diss., University of Chicago, 2007.

Maxey, Trent. *The "Greatest Problem": Religion and State Formation in Meiji Japan*. Cambridge, MA: Harvard University Asia Center, 2014.

McCollough, Helen Craig. *The Tale of the Heike*. Stanford, CA: Stanford University Press, 1988.

McConnell, Andy. *Miller's 20th-Century Glass*. London: Miller's Buying Guides, 2006.

Mehl, Margaret. *Private Academies of Chinese Learning in Meiji Japan: The Decline and Transformation of the Kangaku juku*. Copenhagen: Nordic Institute of Asian Studies, 2003.

———. "Women Educators and the Confucian Tradition in Meiji Japan (1868–1912): Miwada Masako and Atomi Kakei." *Women's History Review* 10, no. 4 (2001): 579–602.

Millard, Thomas F. "Japanese Immigration into Korea." *Annals of the American Academy of Political and Social Science* 34, no. 2 (September 1909): 183–189.

Minear, Richard H. *Japanese Tradition and Western Law: Emperor, State, and Law in the Thought of Hozumi Yatsuka*. Cambridge, MA: Harvard University Press, 1970.

Minegishi Hideo. "Kindai Nihon Kirisutokyō shakai kōken ron: Kobayashi Tomijiro, Kurosawa Torizō, Morinagawa Taichirō" [Modern Japan Christian social contributions: Kobayashi Tomijiro, Kurosawa Torizō, Morinagawa Taichirō]. *Ōkurayama ronshū* (25 March 2017): 133–151.

Misawa Hiroaki. *Ooinaru isan: Nagasaki no kyōkai* [A great heritage: The churches of Nagasaki]. Tokyo: Chi Shobō, 2000.

"Mitani Tamiko" hensan iinkai, ed. *Mitani Tamiko*. Tokyo: Joshi Gakuin, 1991.

Miyakoda Toyosaburō. *Tsuda Sen: Meiji no Kirisutosha* [Tsuda Sen: A Meiji Christian]. Tokyo: Miyakoda Toyosaburō, 1972.

Mizuno Hirota. "Meiji-ki yōmeigaku kenkyū no bokkō: Inoue Tetsujirō *Nihon Yōmeigaku-ha no tetsugaku*" [The sudden rise of Yōmei studies in the Meiji period: Inoue Tetsujiro *The Philosophy of the Japan Yōmei Studies School*]. *Shisōshi kenkyū* 24 (December 2017): 68–85.

Mohan, Braj. "A Demonstration of the Discourse Dissection Model (DDM) with an Analysis of FD Roosevelt's 'Pearl Harbour' Address to the Nation." *SKASE Journal of Theoretical Linguistics* 3 (2016): 62–86.

Mohr, Michael. *Buddhism, Unitarianism, and the Meiji Competition for Universality*. Cambridge, MA: Harvard University Press, 2014.

Morinaga Eisaburō. *Rokutei Ōishi Seinosuke* [The particular Ōishi Seinosuke]. Tokyo: Iwanami Shoten, 1977.

Morioka Kiyomi. *Chihō no shōtoshi ni okeru Kirisutokyō kyōkai no keisei: Kōzuke Annaka Kyōkai no kōzō bunseki* [The formation of a Christian church in a countryside village: A structural analysis of Kōzuke Annaka Church]. Tokyo: Nihon Kirisuto Kyōdan Senkyō Kenkyūsho, 1959.

———. *Meiji Kirisutokyokai keisei no shakaishi* [The social history of the formation of the Meiji Christian Church]. Tokyo: University of Tokyo Press, 2005.

———. "Meiji zen-ki ni okeru shizoku to Kirisutokyō" [The warrior class and Christianity in the early Meiji era]. *Shukutoku Daigaku shakai gakubu kenkyū kiyō* 38 (2004): 125–129.

Motohisa Yamakage. *The Essence of Shinto: Japan's Spiritual Heart*. Translated by Mineko Gillespie, Gerald Gillespie, and Yoshitsugu Komuro. Tokyo: Kōdansha, 2006.

Motoi Yasuhiro. "Doshisha Shingakkan no hensen: 30-ban kyōshitsu kara Kura-ku shingakkan he" [Changes of the Doshisha Theology Hall: From Room 30 to Clark Hall of Theology]. *Kirisutokyō kenkyū* 70, no. 1 (June 2008): 1–22.

Mulhern, Chieko Irie. *Heroic with Grace: Legendary Women of Japan*. New York: M. E. Sharpe, 1991.

Mullins, Mark. *Christianity Made in Japan: A Study of Indigenous Movements*. Honolulu: University of Hawai'i Press, 1998.

———, ed. *Handbook of Christianity in Japan*. Leiden: Brill, 2003.

Muramatsu Teijirō. *Nihon kindai kenchiku shi no-to: saiyō kan wo tateta hitobito* [Modern Japanese architecture history notebook: The people who built Western buildings]. Tokyo: Sekai Shoin, 1965.

Murata Yukio. "Tamura Naoomi no kodomo no kenri shisō: Sono keiseikatei to kodomo no ken wo chūshin ni" [Consideration of the rights of children—focusing on Naoomi Tamura's life and his views on the rights of children]. *Kokusai bunka kenkyū henshū* 8 (2010): 17–31.

Myers, Ramon H., and Mark R. Peattie, eds. *The Japanese Colonial Empire, 1895–1945*. Princeton, NJ: Princeton University Press, 1984.

Nagasaki Bunkensha, eds. *Nagasaki Yūgaku 2: Nagasaki/Amakusa no kyōkai to junreichi kanzen gaido* [Nagasaki study-travel 2: Complete guide to the churches and pilgrimage sites of Nagasaki-Amakusa]. Nagasaki: Nagasaki Bunkensha, 2005.

Najita, Tetsuo, and J. Victor Koschmann, eds. *Conflict in Modern Japanese History*. Princeton, NJ: Princeton University Press, 1982.

Nakajima Kuni. *Naruse Jinzō*. Tokyo: Yoshikawa Kyōbunkan, 2002.

Nakamoto Kahoru. "1930 nendai Tokyo YWCA *Watashidomo no ie* ni okeru shakai jigyō to kyōiku katsudō no tenkai" [The development of social work and educational activities in the 1930s Tokyo YWCA *Our House*]. *Tōyō Daigaku daigakuin kiyō*, no. 47 (2010): 405–426.

Nakamura, Ellen. "Working the Siebold Network: Kusumoto Ine and Western Learning in Nineteenth-Century Japan." *Japanese Studies* 28, no. 2 (September 2008): 197–211.

Nakamura Hajime, Asahara Kazuo, and Kanaoka Shūyū, eds. *Ajia Bukkyōshi Nihonhen*. Vol. 8, *Gendai Bukkyo* [Asia Buddhist history, Japan. Vol. 8: Modern Buddhism]. Tokyo: Kōsei Shuppansha, 1973–1976.

Nakamura, James I. "Meiji Land Reform, Redistribution of Income, and Saving from Agriculture." *Economic Development and Cultural Change* 14, no. 4 (July 1966): 428–439.

Nakamura Kennosuke. *Senkyōshi Nikolai to Meiji Nihon* [Missionary Nikolai and Meiji Japan]. Tokyo: Iwanami Shoten, 1996.

Nakanishi Kazuko. "Futaba Yōchien kara Futaba ikuen he no ayumi ni kansuru—kōsatsu: Yōgo to kyōiku wo awasemotsu boiku to netowa-ku tsukuri no mosaku [Searching to construct a network for infant care and education: A study of the process of construction from Futaba Kindergarten to Futaba Nursery School]." *Japanese*

Journal of the Historical Studies of Early Childhood Education and Care 4 (2009): 29–46.

Narahara Shunsaku. *Ogino Ginko, jitsuroku: Nihon no joi dai ichi gō* [The true story of Ogino Ginko, Japan's first woman physician]. Tokyo: Kokusho Kankōkai, 1984.

Natsume Sōseki. *Sanshirō: A Novel.* Translated by Jay Rubin. Seattle: University of Washington Press, 1977.

Nelson, John K. "Social Memory as Ritual Practice: Commemorating Spirits of the Military Dead at Yasukuni Shinto Shrine." *Journal of Asian Studies* 62, no. 2 (May 2003): 443–467.

———. *A Year in the Life of a Shinto Shrine.* Seattle: University of Washington Press, 1996.

Neu, Charles E. *An Uncertain Friendship: Theodore Roosevelt and Japan, 1906–1909.* Cambridge, MA: Harvard University Press, 1967.

Neuhaus, Dolf-Alexander. "Assimilating Korea: Japanese Protestants, 'East Asian Christianity' and the Education of Koreans in Japan, 1905–1920." *Paedagogica Historica* 52, no. 6 (2016): 614–628.

Nichigai asoshie-tsu, eds. *20 seiki nihon jinmei jiten.* Tokyo: Nichigai asoshie-tsu, 2004.

Nihon Kirisutokyōdan Ginza Kyōkai. *Ginza Kyōkai 90-nen shi* [The 90-year history of Ginza Church]. Tokyo: Nihon Kirisutokyōdan Ginza Kyōkai, 1981.

Nihon Kirisutokyō Rekishi Daijiten Henshū Iinkai, ed. *Nihon Kirisutokyō Daijiten* [Dictionary of the history of Christianity in Japan]. Tokyo: Kyōbunkan, 1988.

———. *Nihon Kirisutokyō shi nenpyō: Purotesutanto no bubun* [Japan Christian historical chronology: Protestant section]. Tokyo: Kyōbunkan, 1988.

Nihon Purotesutanto shi kenkyūkai. *Nihon Purotesutanto shi no sho mondai.* Tokyo: Yuzankaku, 1983.

Nihon rekishi daijiten [Japanese historical encyclopedia]. 10 vols. Tokyo: Shogakukan, 2000.

Nihon rekishi gakkai, ed. *Meiji isshin shinjinmei jiten* [Meiji Restoration new biographical dictionary]. Tokyo: Yoshikawa kyōbunkan, 1981.

Nimura Kazuo. *The Ashio Riot of 1907: A Social History of Mining in Japan.* Durham, NC: Duke University Press, 2000.

Nirei Yosuke. "The Ethics of Empire: Protestant Thought, Moral Culture, and Imperialism in Meiji Japan." PhD diss., University of California, Berkeley, 2004.

———. "Globalism and Liberal Expansionism in Meiji Protestant Discourse." *Social Science Japan Journal* 15, no. 1 (2012): 75–92.

———. "Toward a Modern Belief: Modernist Protestantism and Problems of National Religion in Meiji Japan." *Japanese Journal of Religious Studies* 34, no. 1 (2007): 151–175.

Nishiyama Matsunosuke, ed. *Edogaku jiten* [Encyclopedia of Edo studies]. Tokyo: Kōbundō, 1984.

Nolte, Sharon H. *Liberalism in Modern Japan: Ishibashi Tanzan and His Teachers, 1905–1960.* Berkeley: University of California Press, 1987.

Nolte, Sharon H., and Sally Ann Hastings. "The Meiji State's Policy toward Women." In *Recreating Japanese Women, 1600–1945,* ed. Gail Lee Bernstein, 151–174. Berkeley: University of California Press, 1991.

Nosco, Peter. "The Experiences of Christians during the Underground Years and Thereafter." *Japanese Journal of Religious Studies* 34, no. 1 (2007): 85–97.

Notehelfer, F. G. *American Samurai: Captain L. L. Janes and Japan.* Princeton, NJ: Princeton University Press, 1985.

———. "Between Tradition and Modernity: Labor and the Ashio Copper Mine." *Monumenta Nipponica* 39, no. 1 (Spring 1984): 11–24.

———. *Japan through American Eyes: The Journal of Francis Hall, 1859–1866.* Princeton, NJ: Princeton University Press, 1993.

———. *Kōtoku Shūsui: Portrait of a Japanese Radical.* London: Cambridge University Press, 1971.

Oda Masayasu. "Senzen-ki ni okeru Nihon no Kirisutokyō bunpo to chiikikubun" [Distribution of Christianity and the Division of the Region in Prewar Japan]. *Komazawa chiri,* no. 53 (2017): 23–34.

Offner, Clark B., and H. Van Straelen. *Modern Japanese Religions, with Special Emphasis on Their Doctrines of Healing.* Leiden: Brill, 1963.

Ōgawa Manako. "'Hull-House' in Downtown Tokyo: The Transplantation of a Settlement House from the United States into Japan and the North American Missionary Women, 1919–1945." *Journal of World History* 15, no. 3 (September 2004): 359–387.

Ogino Ginko Joshi Kenshō Hi Kensetsu Kiseikai. *Ogino Ginko.* Setanamachi: Seitanamachi and Ogino Ginko Joshi Kenshō Hi Kensetsu Kisei Kai, 1967.

Ōhama Tetsuya. *Kindai minshū no kiroku* [Record of the modern people]. Vol. 8. Tokyo Shinjinbutsu, 1978.

———. *Meiji Kirisutokyōkai shi no kenkyū* [A historical study of the Meiji Christian Church]. Tokyo: Yoshikawakō Bunkan, 1979.

———. *Ōe Sumi sensei* [Professor Ōe Sumi]. Tokyo: Tokyo Kaseigakuin Kōinkai, 1978.

Ōkubo Toshiaki. *Meirokusha* [The Meiji Six Society]. Tokyo: Kōdansha, 2007.

Ōkura zaibatsu kenkyū, ed. *Ōkura zaibatsu no kenkyū* [Study of Ōkura Industrial Group]. Tokyo: Chikafuji shuppansha, 1982.

Ōmori Toshio. *Tokyo Teikoku Daigaku Setsurumento jūni nen shi* [Twelve-year history of Tokyo Imperial University Settlement]. Tokyo: Hisayama sha, 1998.

Oshio Tsutomu. "Takakura sensei no deatta hitobito" [People who met Dr. Takakura]. *Fukuin to sekai* [The gospel and the world] 3, no. 2 (1954): 37–46.

Ōta Masao. "Ishikawa Sanshirō, Hongō kyōkai to heiminsha" [Ishikawa Sanshirō, Hongō Church, and the *Heiminsha*]. *Shoki shakai shugi kenkyū* 18 (2005): 58–75.

Ōuchi Saburō. *Nihon Kirisutokyō shi* [History of Japanese Christianity]. Tokyo: Nihon Kirisuto Kyōdan Shuppan kyoku, 1970.

Ōzawa Saburō. *Nihon Purotesutanto shi kenkyū* [A historical study of Japanese Protestantism]. Tokyo: Tōkai Daigaku Shuppansha, 1964.

———. *Purotesutanto 100-nen shi kenkyū* [One-hundred-year history of Protestantism]. Tokyo: Nihon Kirisutokyōdan Shuppan bu, 1961.

———. *Uchimura Kanzō fukei jiken* [The Uchimura Kanzō Lèse-Majesté incident]. Tokyo: Shinkyō Shuppansha, 1961.

Ōzawa Takeshi. *Shashin de miru Bakumatsu, Meiji: Wa-zu-wikku Korekusshon hizō no-koshashin ni-sen mai no naka kara, mihatsuhyō 100 mai wo fukumu 430 mai wo gensen* [Seeing Bakumatsu and Meiji through photo: Comprising 100 unpublished photos and 430 carefully selected photos from among the treasured Wazuik Collection Prize of 2,000 old photographs]. Tokyo: Sekai Bunkasha, 1990.

Paramore, Kiri. *Ideology and Christianity in Japan.* London: Routledge, 2009.

Patessio, Mara. "The Creation of Public Spaces by Women in the Early Meiji Period and the Tokyo Fujin Kyōfūkai." *International Journal of Asian Studies* 3, no. 2 (2006): 155–182.

———. "*Iratsume* and Journals for Women in the Early Meiji Period." *Kenkyū: Proceedings of the Post-graduate Network in Japanese Studies Research Seminar in Japanese Studies* (28 July 2002): 19–28.

———. *Women and Public Life in Early Meiji Japan: The Development of the Feminist Movement.* Ann Arbor: University of Michigan Press, 2011.

Patrick, Hugh T., ed. *Japanese Industrialization and Its Social Consequences.* Berkeley: University of California Press, 1976.

Pierson, John. *Tokutomi Sohō, 1863–1957: A Journalist for Modern Japan.* Princeton, NJ: Princeton University Press, 1980.

Powles, Cyril. "Yasukuni Jinja Hōan: Religion and Politics in Contemporary Japan." *Pacific Affairs* 49, no. 3 (Autumn 1976): 491–505.

Prang, Margaret. *A Heart at Leisure from Itself: Caroline MacDonald of Japan.* Vancouver: University of British Columbia Press, 1995.

Pratt, Mary Louise. *Imperial Eyes: Travel Writing and Transculturation.* New York: Routledge, 1992.

Psarra, Sophia. *Architecture and Narrative: The Formation of Space and Cultural Meaning.* New York: Routledge, 2009.

Pyle, Kenneth. *The New Generation in Meiji Japan: Problems of Cultural Identity, 1885–1895.* Stanford, CA: Stanford University Press, 1969.

Reid, David. *New Wine: The Cultural Shaping of Japanese Christianity.* Berkeley: Asian Humanities Press, Nanzan Institute for Religion and Culture, 1991.

———. "Secularization Theory and Japanese Christianity: The Case of the Nihon Kirisuto Kyōdan." *Japanese Journal of Religious Studies* 61, nos. 1/2 (March–June 1979): 347–378.

Reinanzaka bunshū mokusen [Catalog of collected documents on Reinanzaka Church]. Kyoto: Dōshisha Daigaku Bunrigaku Kenkyūsho, 1998.

Reynolds, E. Bruce. *Japan in the Fascist Era.* New York: Palgrave Macmillan, 2004.

Reynolds, Jonathan. "Teaching Architectural History in Japan: Building a Context for Contemporary Practice." *Journal of the Society of Architectural Historians* 61, no. 4 (December 2002): 530–536.

Ritchie, Donald. *Tokyo: A View of the City.* London: Reaktion Books, 1999.

Roden, Donald. *Schooldays in Imperial Japan: A Study in the Culture of a Student Elite.* Berkeley: University of California Press, 1980.

Rogers, Minor L., and Ann T. Rogers. "The Honganji: Guardian of the State (1868–1945)." *Japanese Journal of Religious Studies* 17, no. 1 (March 1990): 3–28.

Roggendorf, Joseph. "Shimazaki Tōson: A Maker of the Modern Japanese Novel." *Monumenta Nipponica* 7, nos. 1/2 (1951): 40–66.

Rose, Barbara. *Tsuda Umeko and Women's Education in Japan*. New Haven, CT: Yale University Press, 1992.

Rosenstone, Robert A. *Mirror in the Shrine: American Encounters with Meiji Japan*. Cambridge, MA: Harvard University Press, 1988.

Rozman, Gilbert. "Edo's Importance in the Changing Tokugawa Society." *Journal of Japanese Studies* 1, no. 1 (Autumn 1974): 91–112.

Rudolph, Susanne Hoeber, and James Piscatori, eds. *Transnational Religion and Fading States*. Boulder, CO: Westview, 1997.

Rutschman-Byler, Jiryū Mark. "Soto Zen in Meiji Japan: Life and Times of Nishiari Bokusan." PhD diss, University of California, Berkeley, 2014.

Saba Wataru. *Uemura Masahisa to sono jidai* [Uemura Masahisa and his times]. 5 vols. 1937–1944. Repr., Tokyo: Kyōbunkan, 2000.

Sachs, William L. "'Self-Support': The Episcopal Mission and Nationalism in Japan." *Church History* 58, no. 4 (December 1989): 489–501.

Sakai, Shizu. "History of Medical Care at Inpatient Facilities in Japan." *Journal of the Medical Association of Japan* 54, no. 6 (November/December 2011): 351–356.

Samuels, Richard J. *Rich Country, Strong Army: National Security and the Technological Transformation of Japan*. Ithaca, NY: Cornell University Press, 1994.

Sand, Jordan. *House and Home in Modern Japan: Architecture, Domestic Space and Bourgeois Culture*. Cambridge, MA: Harvard University Asia Center, 2004.

Sawada, Janine Tasca. *Practical Pursuits, Religion, Politics and Personal Cultivation in Nineteenth Century Japan*. Honolulu: University of Hawai'i Press, 2004.

Scalapino, Robert. *Democracy and the Party Movement in Pre-war Japan: The Failure of the First Attempt*. Berkeley: University of California Press, 1953.

Scheiner, Irwin. *Christian Converts and Social Protest in Meiji Japan*. Berkeley: University of California, 1970.

———, ed. *Modern Japan: An Interpretive Anthology*. New York: Macmillan, 1974.

Schenking, J. Charles. "Catastrophe, Opportunism, Contestation: The Fractured Politics of Reconstructing Tokyo following the Great Kantō Earthquake of 1923." *Modern Asian Studies* 40, no. 4 (October 2006): 833–873.

———. *The Great Kantō Earthquake and the Chimera of National Reconstruction in Japan*. New York: Columbia University Press, 2013.

Schroeder, Jeff. "After Kiyozawa: A Study of Shin Buddhist Modernization, 1890–1956." PhD diss., Duke University, 2015.

Schwantes, Robert S. "Christianity versus Science: A Conflict of Ideas in Meiji Japan." *Far Eastern Quarterly* 12, no. 2 (February 1953): 123–132.

Seidensticker, Edward. *Low City, High City: Tokyo from Edo to the Earthquake*. New York: Knopf, 1983.

———. *Tokyo from Edo to Showa 1867–1989: The Emergence of the World's Greatest City*. Clarendon, VT: Tuttle, 2010.

Sekioka Kazushige. "Ebina Danjō ni okeru sekaishugi to Nihonshugi" [Universalism and Japan-ism in Ebina Danjō]. *Kirisutokyō shakai mondai kenkyū* [The study of Christianity and social problems] 44 (December 1995): 26–48.

Seton-Watson, Hugh. *Nations and States: An Inquiry into the Origins of Nations and the Politics of Nationalism.* Boulder, CO: Westview, 1977.

Shapiro, Michael Isaac. "Christian Culture and Military Rule: Assimilation and Its Limits during the First Decade of Japan's Colonial Rule in Korea, 1910–19." PhD diss., University of California, Berkeley, 2010.

Shenk, Wilbert R. "Rufus Anderson and Henry Venn: A Special Relationship?" *International Bulletin of Missionary Research* 5, no. 4 (October 1981): 168–172.

Sherif, Ann. *Mirror: The Fiction and Essays of Kōda Aya.* Honolulu: University of Hawai'i Press, 1999.

Shiba Ryōtarō. *Hongō kaiwai* [The Hongō neighborhood]. Tokyo: Asahi Shimbun sha, 2005.

Shields, James Mark. *Against Harmony: Progressive and Radical Buddhism in Modern Japan.* New York: Oxford University Press, 2017.

Shigeru Yoshiki. *Meiji shoki Kōbe dendō to D. C. Greene* [Early Meiji Kōbe evangelism and D. C. Greene]. Tokyo: Shinkyō Shuppansha, 1986.

Shilloy, Ben-Ami, ed. *The Emperors of Modern Japan.* Leiden: Brill, 2008.

Shimazono Susumu. "State Shinto in the Lives of the People: The Establishment of Emperor Worship, Modern Nationalism, and Shrine Shinto in Late Meiji." *Japanese Journal of Religious Studies* 36, no. 1 (2009): 93–124.

Shimazu, Naoko. *Japanese Society at War: Death, Memory and the Russo-Japanese War.* Cambridge: Cambridge University Press, 2009.

"Shinshitei no bunkazai" [Newly designated cultural assets]. *Gekkan Bunkazai* [Cultural assets monthly], no. 538 (July 2008): 12–41.

Shiono Kazuo. *Nihon Kumiai Kirisuto kyōkai shi kenkyū josetu* [Introduction to the historical study of the Japanese Congregational Church]. Tokyo: Shinkyō Shuppansha, 1995.

Sievers, Sharon L. *Flowers in Salt: The Beginning of Feminist Consciousness in Modern Japan.* Stanford, CA: Stanford University Press, 1983.

Silberman, Bernard S. "The Political Theory and Program of Yoshino Sakuzō." *Journal of Modern History* 31, no. 4 (December 1959): 310–324.

Simmel, Georg. *The Sociology of Georg Simmel.* Translated and edited by Kurt Wolff. New York: Free Press, 1950.

Skya, Walter A. *Japan's Holy War: The Ideology of Radical Shinto Ultranationalism.* Durham, NC: Duke University Press, 2009.

Smethurst, Richard. *From Foot Soldier to Finance Minister: Takahashi Korekiyo, Japan's Keynes.* Cambridge, MA: Harvard University Asia Center, 2007.

Smith, Henry D., II. *Japan's First Student Radicals.* Cambridge, MA: Harvard University Press, 1972.

———. "Tokyo as an Idea: An Exploration of Japanese Urban Thought until 1945." *Journal of Japanese Studies* 4, no. 1 (Winter 1978): 45–80.

Smith, Ryan K. "The Cross: Church Symbol and Contest in Nineteenth-Century America." *Church History* 70, no. 4 (December 2001): 705–734.

Snodgrass, Judith. *Presenting Japan to the West: Orientalism, Occidentalism, and the Columbian Exposition.* Chapel Hill: University of North Carolina Press, 2003.

Sōda, Iichirō. "Tokyo no Tenrikyō" [Tokyo's Tenrikyō]. *Glocal Tenri* (March 2015): 3.

Soltau, Addison. "Uemura Masahisa (1857–1925): First Generation Pastor, Christian Leader and Instinctive Proponent of Indigenized Christianity in Japan 1982." DD diss., Concordia Seminary, 1982.

Spence, Jonathan. *The Search for Modern China*. New York: Norton, 1990.

Sprunger, Keith L. "Church Architecture and Worship in a Dutch Context." *Church History* 66, no. 1 (March 1997): 36–53.

Stanley, Thomas A. *Ōsugi Sakae, Anarchist in Taisho Japan: The Creativity of the Ego*. Cambridge, MA: Harvard University Press, 1982.

Stanton, Phoebe B. *The Gothic Revival and American Church Architecture: An Episode in Taste, 1840–1856*. Baltimore: Johns Hopkins University Press, 1968.

Starling, Jessica. "Neither Nun nor Laywoman: The Good Wives and Wise Mothers of Jōdo Shinshū Temples." *Japanese Journal of Religious Studies* 40, no. 2 (Summer 2013): 277–301.

Steege, Gwen W. "The 'Book of Plans' and the Early Romanesque Revival in the United States: A Study in Architectural Patronage." *Journal of the Society of Architectural Historians* 46, no. 3 (September 1987): 215–227.

Steele, M. William. "The Great Northern Famine of 1905–1906: Two Sides of International Aid." *Asian Cultural Studies* 39 (March 2013): 1–15.

Sugii, Mutsurō. "Ie-ru no Nihonjin" [Japanese at Yale]. *Dōshisha Amerika kenkyū*, no. 13 (1977): 69–93.

———."Keiseisha ni tsuite" [On the Keiseisha]. *Kirisutokyō shakai mondai kenkyū* [The study of Christianity and social problems] 30 (March 1982): 62–87.

———. *Kumamoto bando kenkyū* [Study of the Kumamoto band]. Kyoto: Doshisha Daigaku Jinbun kagaku kenkyūjo, 1965.

———. *Meiji-ki Kirisutokyō no kenkyū* [A study on Meiji-period Christianity]. Kyoto: Dōbōsha Shuppan, 1984.

———. "Nisshin Sensō to Kirisutokyō (1): *Kirisutokyō shinbun* to *Fukuin shimpō* wo chūshin to shite" [The Sino-Japanese War and Christianity (1): Concentrating on *The Christian News* and *The Evangelist*]. *Kirisutokyō shakai mondai kenkyū* [The study of Christianity and social problems] 31 (March 1983): 236–353.

———. "Nisshin Sensō to Kirisutokyō (2): *Kirisutokyō shinbun* to *Fukuin shimpō* wo chūshin to shite" [The Sino-Japanese War and Christianity (2): Concentrating on *The Christian News* and *The Evangelist*]. *Kirisutokyō shakai mondai kenkyū* [The study of Christianity and social problems] 32 (March 1984): 173–214.

Sumiya Etsuji. "Meiji Kirisutokyō-to no shakaishugi shisō 1: Matsui Chito no 'Shakaishugi' ni tsuite" [Meiji Christians' socialist thought (1): On Matsui Chito's "socialism"]. *Kirisutokyō shakai mondai kenkyū* [The study of Christianity and social problems] 6 (April 1962): 1–20.

Sumiya Mikio. "Chūsan kaikyū no seiritsu to Kirisutokyō" [The establishment of the middle class and Christianity]. *Fukuin to seikai* [The gospel and the world] 6 (1954): 23–28.

———. *Gendai Nihon no keisei to Kirisutokyō* [Christianity and the formation of modern Japan]. Tokyo: Shinkyō Shuppansha, 1962.

———. *Kindai Nihon no keisei to kirisutokyō* [Christianity and the development of modern Japan]. Tokyo: Shinkyō Shuppansha, 1950.

———. *Nihon Purotesutanto shiron* [A history of Japanese Protestantism]. Tokyo: Shinkyō Shuppansha, 1983.

———. *Nihon shakai to Kirisutokyō* [Japanese society and Christianity]. Tokyo: University of Tokyo Press, 1954.

Suzuki Norihisa. *Meiji shūkyō shichō no kenkyū* [A study on trends in Meiji religious thought]. Tokyo: Tokyo Daigaku Shuppankai, 1979.

———. *Uchimura Kanzō to sono jidai: Shiga Shigetaka to no hikaku* [Uchimura Kanzō and his times: A comparison with Shiga Shigetaka]. Tokyo: Nihon Kirisuto Kyōdan Shuppan kyoku, 1975.

Tabata Shinobu. "Yoshino Sakuzō no heiwa ron" [Yoshino Sakuzō's arguments on peace]. *Kirisutokyō shakai mondai kenkyū* [The study of Christianity and social problems] 6 (April 1962): 21–33.

Taguchi Takeshi. *Taguchi Ukichi.* Tokyo: Furukawa Hirobumi Kan, 2000.

Takahashi Masao. *Meiji no Kirisutokyō* [Meiji Christianity]. Tokyo: Yoshikawa Kyōbunkan, 2003.

———, ed. *Nihon Purotesutanto shi no shosō* [Various aspects of Japanese Protestant history]. Saitama: Seigakuin Daigaku Shuppankai, 1995.

———. *Shimada Saburō den* [The biography of Shimada Saburō]. Tokyo: Mahoroba shobō, 1988.

Takahashi Mikio. *Hongōkan no hanseiki* [The half-century of the Hongōkan]. Tokyo: Takahashi Mikio, 2007.

Takasaki Sōji. *Tsuda Sen Hyōden: Mō Hitotsu no kindaika wo mezashita hito* [A critical biography of Tsuda Sen: Another person aiming for modernization]. Urayasu, Japan: Sōfūkan, 2008.

Takeda Kiyoko. *Higher Education for Tomorrow: International Christian University and Postwar Japan.* Tokyo: International Christian University Press, 2003.

———. *Nihon Purotesutanto ningen keisei ron* [The formation of Japanese Protestant humanity]. Tokyo: Meiji Tosho Shuppan, 1963.

———. "Rikugō zasshi" [Cosmos magazine]. *Shisō* 462 (December 1962): 109–120.

———. *Uemura Masahisa: Sono shisō-teki kōsatsu* [Uemura Masahisa: An ideological inquiry]. Tokyo: Kyōbunkan, 2001.

Takenaka Masao. "Ningen to bunka: *Rikugō zasshi* ni okeru Uchigasaki Sakusaburō" [Humanity and culture: Uchigasaki Sakusaburō in *Cosmos*]. *Kirisutokyō shakai mondai kenkyū* [The study of Christianity and social problems] 31 (March 1983): 1–28.

———. *Reconciliation and Renewal in Japan.* New York: Student Volunteer Movement for Christian Missions and Friendship Press, 1957.

Tanaka, Kei. "Japanese Picture Marriage and the Image of Immigrant Women in Early Twentieth Century California." *Japanese Journal of American Studies,* no. 15 (2004): 115–138.

Tanaka Masato. "Nihon Hantei Dōmei no kenkyū: Kyōsanshugi undō to heiwa undō" [A study on the Japanese Anti-Imperialist League: The communist movement and the peace movement]. *Kirisutokyō shakai mondai kenkyū* [The study of Christianity and social problems] 35 (March 1987): 175–217.

Tanaka Tomoko. *Kindai Nihon kōtō kyōiku taisei no reimei: Kosakusuru chiki to kuni to Kirisutokyōkai* [The dawn of the modern Japanese high school education system: The intersection of region, country, and the Christian world]. Kyoto: Shibunkaku shuppan, 2012.

———. "Meiji shoki no Kōbe to senkyō i Beri: Iiryō wo meguru chiiki no rikigaku" [The missionary medical doctor Berry in Kobe: The regional dynamics of medical work in the early Meiji era]. *KSMK* 52 (December 2003): 58–81.

Tansman, Alan, ed. *The Culture of Japanese Fascism*. Durham, NC: Duke University Press, 2009.

Tenrikyo Overseas Mission Department. *A Historical Sketch of Tenrikyo*. Translation of *Oyasama Nensai to tomoni* [To accompany Oyasama's anniversary]. Tenri: Tenri Doyusha, 1990.

Terazono Tsukasa. "Uemura Masahisa to Kunikida Doppo" [Uemura Masahisa and Kunikida Doppo]. *Kokugo to Kokubungaku*, no. 351 (July 1953): 37–44.

Thal, Sarah. *Rearranging the Landscape of the Gods: The Politics of a Pilgrimage Site in Japan, 1573–1912*. Chicago: University of Chicago Press, 2005.

Thelle, Notto. *Buddhism and Christianity in Japan: From Conflict to Dialogue, 1854–1899*. Honolulu: University of Hawai'i Press, 1987.

Thomas, Winburn. *Protestant Beginnings in Japan: The First Three Decades, 1859–1889*. Tokyo: Charles E. Tuttle, 1959.

Tipton, Elise K., ed. *The Japanese Police State: The Tokkō in Interwar Japan*. Honolulu: University of Hawai'i Press, 1990.

———. *Society and the State in Interwar Japan*. London: Routledge, 1997.

Tipton, Elise K., and John Clark, eds. *Being Modern in Japan: Culture and Society from the 1910s to the 1930s*. Honolulu: University of Hawai'i Press, 2000.

Tokyo joshi kōtō shihan gakkō [Tokyo women's higher normal school]. Tokyo: Daiichi Shobō, 1981.

Tokyo no shōbō 100 nen no ayumi—Meiji gōki [One hundred years of Tokyo firefighting—the late Meiji period]. Tokyo: Tokyo Shōbōchō, 1980.

Tomasi, Massimiliano. "Oratory in Meiji and Taishō Japan: Public Speaking and the Formation of a New Written Language." *Monumenta Nipponica* 71, no. 1 (Spring 2002): 43–71.

Tomida, Hiroko. *Hiratsuka Raichō and Early Japanese Feminism*. Leiden, Netherlands: Brill, 2004.

Tomita Hiroyuki and Kami Shōichirō, eds. *Nihon Kirisuto kyōjidō bungaku zenshū* [Complete works of Christian juvenile literature]. Tokyo: Kyōbunkan, 1984.

Tonkiss, Fran. *Space, the City and Social Theory: Social Relations and Urban Forms*. Cambridge, UK: Polity, 2005.

Tōya Tetsushi, ed. *Fujimichō 80-nen shi* [The eighty-year history of Fujimichō Church]. Tokyo: Kirisutokyōdan Fujimichō Kyōkai, 1978.

Tseng, Alice Y. "Styling Japan: The Case of Josiah Condor and the Museum at Ueno, Tokyo." *Journal of the Society of Architectural Historians* 63, no. 4 (December 2004): 472–497.

Tsubouchi Yuzō. *Yasukuni*. Tokyo: Shinchōsha, 1999.

Tsukada Osamu. *Tennōseika no Kirisutokyō: Nihon no Seikōkokai no tatakai to kunan* [Emperor-system Christianity: The battle and hardship of the Japan Episcopal Church]. Tokyo: Shinkyō Shuppansha, 1981.

Tsuzuki Chushichi. "Kōtoku, Ōsugi, and Japanese Anarchism." *Hitotsubashi Journal of Social Studies* 3, no. 1 (March 1966): 30–42.

———. *The Pursuit of Power in Modern Japan 1825–1995*. Oxford: Oxford University Press, 2000.

Tucker, John. "Tokugawa Intellectual History and Prewar Ideology: The Case of Inoue Tetsujirō, Yamaga Sokō, and the Forty-Seven Rōnin." *Sino-Japanese Studies* 14 (2002): 35–70.

Turnbull, Stephen. *Japan's Hidden Christians, 1549–1999*. Vol. 2, *Secret Christianity in Japan*. Richmond, UK: Curzon, 2000.

Uchifuji Masa. *Reinanzaka to watashi: Sōritsu 100 nen kinen bunshū* [Reinanzaka and I: Anthology commemorating one hundred years since foundation]. Tokyo: Nihon Kirisutokyōdan Reinanzaka Kyōkai Sōritsu 100 nen Kinen Jigyō Jikkō Iinkai, 1979.

Uchikawa Yoshimi and Matsushima Eiichi, eds. *Taishō nyūsu jiten* [Encyclopedia of Taishō news]. Vol. 7. Tokyo: Mainichi Komiyunkēshiyon Shuppanbu, 1989.

Umemoto Jusō. *Tatakau bokushi Tamura Naoomi no chōsen* [The fighting pastor Tamura Naoomi's Korea]. Tokyo: Ōzōsha, 2010.

Uniya Michiyo. "Hani Motoko: Sono oitachi to shisō keisei" [Hani Motoko: Her development and intellectual formation]. *Seikatsu Gakuin Tanki Daigako kiyō* 3 (25 March 1980): 93–109.

Uno, Kathleen S. *Passages to Modernity: Motherhood, Childhood, and Social Reform in Early Twentieth-Century Japan*. Honololu: University of Hawai'i Press, 1999.

Unuma Hiroko. *Kindai Nihon no kirisutokyō shisōkatachi* [Modern Japan's Christian intellectuals]. Tokyo: Nihon Kirisuto Kyōdan, 1989.

———. *Shika ni yori Nihon Kirisutokyōshi* [Japanese Christian history according to historians]. Ageo, Japan: Seigakuin Daigaku Shuppankai, 1992.

Van Compernolle, Timothy J. *The Uses of Memory: The Critique of Modernity in the Fiction of Higuchi Ichiyō*. Cambridge, MA: Harvard University Asia Center, 2006.

Van Hecken, Joseph Leonard. *The Catholic Church in Japan since 1859*. Tokyo: Herder Agency, 1963.

Victoria, Brian Daizen. *Zen at War*. Lanham, MD: Rowman & Littlefield, 2006.

Visita, Christine Manzano. "Japanese Cultural Transition: Meiji Architecture and the Effect of Cross-Cultural Exchange with the West." *The Forum: Cal Poly's Journal of History* 1, no. 1 (2009): 33–53.

Wada Yōichi. *Dōshisha no shisōkatachi* [The intellectuals of Dōshisha]. Kyoto: Dōshisha Daigakusei Kyō Shuppan bu, 1965–1973.

———. "Kirisuto-sha no junan to teikō" [Passive resistance among Christians]. *Kirisutokyō shakai mondai kenkyū* [The study of Christianity and social problems] 10 (April 1966): 1–13.

———. "Uemura Masahisa to Nihon kokka kenryoku: Kirisutokyōto no sensō kyōryoku wo rikai suru tame ni" [Uemura Masahisa and Japan's state authority: In order to understand Christians' war collaboration]." *Kirisutokyō shakai mondai kenkyū* [The study of Christianity and social problems] 9 (April 1965): 3–15.

Wakita Haruko, Anne Bouchy, and Ueno Chizuko, eds. *Gender in Japanese History.* Vol. 2. Osaka: Osaka University Press, 1999.

Wakuda Tetsuji. "Kindai Nihon ni okeru massaaji iryō no dōnyū" [First introduction of massage treatment in modern Japan]. *Nihon ishigaku zasshi* 49, no. 2 (July 2003): 263–276.

Walthall, Anne, ed. *The Human Tradition in Modern Japan.* Wilmington, DE: Scholarly Resources, 2002.

Wasaki Kotarō. "Kindai Nihon ni Okeru 'hanmon seinen' no saikentō: 1900 nendai ni okeru seinen no henyō katei" [Reexamining "Anguished Youth" in modern Japan: The transformative process of youth in the 1900s]. *Nihon no kyōiku shigaku: Kyōiku shigakkai kiyō* 55 (2012): 19–31.

Washington, Garrett L., ed. *Christianity and the Modern Woman in East Asia Christianity and the Modern Woman in East Asia.* Leiden: Brill, 2018.

———. "Fighting Brick with Brick: Chikazumi Jōkan and Buddhism's Response to the Christian Spatial Menace in Japan." *Cross-Currents: East Asian History and Culture Review E-Journal,* no. 6 (March 2013): 95–120.

———. "St. Luke's Hospital and the Modernisation of Japan, 1874–1928." *Health and History* 15, no. 2 (December 2013): 5–28.

Watanabe, Hiroshi. *The Architecture of Tokyo: An Architectural History in 571 Individual Presentations.* Stuttgart: Edition Axel Menges, 2001.

Watanabe Toshio. "Josiah Conder's Rokumeikan: Architecture and National Representation in Meiji Japan." *Art Journal* 55, no. 3 (Fall 1996): 21–27.

Wendelken, Cherie. "The Tectonics of Japanese Style: Architect and Carpenter in the Late Meiji Period." *Art Journal* 55, no. 3 (Fall 1996): 30–34.

Whiffen, Marcus. *American Architecture since 1780: A Guide to the Styles.* Cambridge, MA: MIT Press, 1992.

White, L. Michael. *Building God's House in the Roman World.* Baltimore: Johns Hopkins University Press, 1990.

Wilson, Sandra, ed. *Nation and Nationalism in Japan.* London: Routledge Curzon, 2002.

Wolniewiscz, Richard. "Ethnic Church Architecture." *Polish American Studies* 54, no. 1 (Spring 1997): 53–73.

Wright, Gwendolyn. "Cultural History: Europeans, Americans, and the Meanings of Space." *Journal of the Society of Architectural Historians* 64, no. 4 (2005): 436–440.

Yamaguchi Teruomi. *Meiji kokka to shūkyō* [The Meiji state and religion]. Tokyo: Tokyo Daigaku Shuppankai, 1999.

Yamanashi Atsushi. "20-seki shodai ni okeru tenkanki no Nihon Katorikku kyōkai: Nihonjin Katorikkusha to Furansujin senkyōshi to no kankei wo chūshin ni." *Aruzasu Nichi-Ō chiteki kōtsūryū jigyō Nihon kenkyū semina—"Meiji" hōkokusho* (2010): 1–12.

Yamauchi Haruko. *Asakawa Kan'ichi ron: Sono gakumon keisei to jissen* [Kan'ichi Asakawa: His development as an academic practitioner]. Tokyo: Waseda Daigaku shuppanbu, 2009.

Yasukuni Jinja shamusho. *Yasukuni jinja* [Yasukuni shrine]. Tokyo: Yasukuni Jinja Shamusho, 1976.

Yasutake, Rumi. "Men, Women, and Temperance in Meiji Japan: Engendering WCTU Activism from a Transnational Perspective." *Japanese Journal of American Studies*, no. 17 (2006): 91–111.

———. *Transnational Women's Activism: The United States, Japan, and Japanese Immigrant Communities in California, 1859–1920.* New York: New York University Press, 2004.

———. "Transnational Women's Activism: The Women's Christian Temperance Union in Japan and Beyond, 1858–1920." PhD diss., University of California, Los Angeles, 1998.

Yates, Charles S. "Saigō Takamori in the Emergence of Meiji Japan." *Modern Asian Studies* 28, no. 3 (July 1994): 449–474.

Yohn, Susan M. "Crippled Capitalists: The Inscription of Economic Dependence and the Challenge of Female Entrepreneurship in Nineteenth-Century America." *Feminist Economics* 12, nos. 1–2 (January 2006): 85–109.

Yoshida Chiyo. *Hyōden Suzuki Bunji: Minshu-teki rōdō shi kankei wo mezashite* [A critical biography of Suzuki Bunji: Working for democratic labor and management relations]. Tokyo: Nihon Hyōron sha, 1988.

Yoshimi Shun'ya. "Undōkai no shisō: Meiji Nihon to shukusai bunka" [The ideology of the field day: Meiji Japan and national holiday culture]. *Shisō* 845 (1994): 137–162.

Yoshinaga Shin'ichi. "Theosophy and Buddhist Reformers in the Middle of the Meiji Period: An Introduction." *Japanese Religions* 34, no. 2 (2009): 119–131.

Yoshinare Akiko. *Ebina Danjō no seiji shisō* [The political thought of Ebina Danjō]. Tokyo: Tokyo Daigaku Shuppankai, 1982.

———. "Uemura Masahisa no 'Meiji Bushidō' kara no bunri" [Uemura Masahisa's separation from "Meiji Bushidō"]. *Meiji gakuin daigaku Kirisutokyō kenkyū kiyō* 50 (January 2018): 249–268.

Yumichō Hongō Kyōkai. *Yumichō Hongō Kyōkai 100-nen shi* [The one-hundred-year history of Yumichō Hongō Church]. Tokyo: Nihon Kirisutokyōdan Yumichō Hongō Kyōkai, 1986.

Index

Page references in **boldface** type refer to illustrations.

About the Author

Garrett L. Washington is associate professor of history at the University of Massachusetts, Amherst, where he teaches courses on Japanese history, US-Japan relations, and the intersection of race, religion, and nation in East Asia. He has published articles on Japanese Protestant churches in Tokyo, Buddhism's response to Protestant church space in Tokyo, and the role of St. Luke's Hospital in the rise of public health in *Japanese Studies*, *Crosscurrents: East Asian History and Culture Review E-Journal*, and history in *Health and History*. He is also editor and contributing author of *Christianity and the Modern Woman in East Asia* (2018).